NATIONAL GEOGRAPHIC

GUIDE TO

State Parks

OF THE

United States

NATIONAL GEOGRAPHIC
WASHINGTON, D.C.

CREDITS

**Published by the
National Geographic Society**
John M. Fahey, Jr., *Chairman of the
Board and Chief Executive Officer*
Timothy T. Kelly, *President*
Declan Moore, *Executive Vice President;
President, Publishing*
Melina Gerosa Bellows, *Executive Vice
President; Chief Creative Officer,
Books, Kids, and Family*

Prepared by the Book Division
Barbara Brownell Grogan, *Vice
President and Editor in Chief*
Jonathan Halling, *Design Director,
Books and Children's Publishing*
Marianne R. Koszorus, *Director of
Design*
Barbara Noe, *Senior Editor*
Carl Mehler, *Director of Maps*
R. Gary Colbert, *Production Director*
Jennifer A. Thornton, *Managing Editor*
Meredith C. Wilcox, *Administrative
Director, Illustrations*

Staff for First Edition
Barbara A. Noe
    Project Editor
Suez Kehl
    Art Director
Caroline Hickey
    Senior Researcher
Mary Jenkins
    Illustrations Editor

Bob Devine, Jerry Camarillo
Dunn, Jr., Sean M. Groom,
K. M. Kostyal, Mark Miller,
Barbara A. Noe, Geoffrey O'Gara,
Jeremy Schmidt, Thomas Schmidt,
John M. Thompson, Dan Whipple,
Mel White, Susan Young
    Writers

2011 Edition
Caroline Hickey
    Project Editor
Sanaa Akkach,
    Art Director
Mary Stephanos
    Text Editor
Linda Makarov
    Designer
Kay Hankins
    Illustrations Editor
Nicholas P. Rosenbach
    Researcher
Steven Gardner, Michael McNey
    Map Research and Production
Judith Klein
    Production Editor
Lisa A. Walker
    Production Project Manager
Marshall Kiker
    Illustrations Specialist
Nicola Payne
    Contributor

Fly-fishing at Housatonic Meadows State Park, Connecticut

COVER ILLUSTRATION: Glade Creek Grist
Mill, Babcock State Park, WV
PAGE ONE: Moose, Baxter State Park, ME
PREVIOUS PAGES: Eklutna Lake, Chugach
State Park, AK
FACING PAGE: Anza-Borrego Desert State
Park, California

CONTENTS

6

7

Yucca trees, Red Rock State Park, NV

Eldorado Canyon State Park, CO

THE UNITED STATES has more than 5,800 state parks, occupying 12 million plus acres. Their annual visitation numbers are staggering—three-quarters of a billion people, three times the number of visits made to national parks. State parks comprise a multitude of scenic wonders—mountains, lakes, rivers, deserts, and seacoasts; abundant and diverse wildlife; and profusions of wildflowers. They display the ancient imprints of glaciers, volcanoes, and floods. Yet few are known beyond their immediate areas. This book introduces you to more than 200 of the wildest and most scenic of the parks, as well as ones that stand out for their cultural or historical significance.

As you set out to explore these public treasures, it's worth reflecting on the role of the Civilian Conservation Corps in their evolution. Back in the 1930s, fewer than half the states had any kind of state parks program. In those Great Depression years, President Franklin D. Roosevelt created the CCC to put unemployed but able-bodied young men to work. Their job was to improve the public lands that had been ravaged by logging and by the Revolutionary and Civil Wars. It was also hoped that such a program would preserve the rapidly diminishing recreational acreage.

In Armylike settings throughout the country, these men rose at dawn to operate stone quarries, dig drainage ditches, cut trails, reintroduce wildlife, and fight forest fires—for as little as a dollar a day. They cleared ridges to reveal spectacular vistas, planted thousands of tree seedlings, and from native materials built handsome lodges and cabins, many still in use today. The coming of World War II effectively disbanded the CCC, but in its nine years more than three million youths had laid the foundation for many of our state parks. And their rich legacy is still ours to cherish and enjoy.

Our staff selected the parks to include in this guide with the generous help of the state park directors, who made recommendations for their states. Our regional travel writers explored every park to report on their findings; they were helped immeasurably by the individual park staffs. Ney Landrum, formerly Executive Director of the National Association of State Park Directors, was most generous with his support and advice throughout the project.

Many small tips have been included in this volume. The suggestions come directly from the staffs of the individual parks. They might send you to the best place to drop a fishing line or a knockout spot to see the sunset.

Most parks are open daily year-round. Campgrounds are common in state parks. We have listed the number of tent and RV sites; call the park for specific hook-up information. Most campgrounds admit visitors on a first-come, first-served basis, but often accept reservations. Each park's camping section tells you when these are advised. Be sure to visit the parks' websites for more information on camping in and near the parks.

Information about every park has been checked and, to the best of our knowledge, is correct as of press date. However, call ahead when possible, as visitor information often changes.

MAP KEY

■ State Park Site	State Park Boundary
■ Point of Interest	State or International Boundary
⚲ Ranger Station, Visitor Center, Park Headquarters	U.S. Interstate, U.S. Federal, or Trans-Canada Highway — 294 12 17
△ Campground, Campsite	State or Local Road — 36 29 11
⌂ Park Cabin	Unpaved Road
⊏ Picnic Shelter	Jeep Trail
⼤ Picnic Area	Bike Trail
⛳ Golf Course	Major Trail
◇ Downhill Ski Area	Local Trail
⬳ Boat Launch or Dock	Ferry
— Canoe Launch or Take-Out	Aerial Tram
➤ Airboat Tours	
Å Observation Tower	ABBREVIATIONS
•—• Gate	Cr. .... Creek
)(Tunnel	Fk. .... Fork
☆ Vista, Overlook	HWY. .... Highway
	I. .... Island
✕ Rapid	Mt.-s. .... Mount-ain-s
✳ Waterfall	PKWY. .... Parkway
	P.P. .... Provincial Park
○ Spring	Pt. .... Point
• Well	R. .... River
⌖ Palm Springs	
• Town, Village	National Park State Park Wildlife Area
ǀ Dam	Forest Swamp

NEW ENGLAND

MAINE

Baxter
Cobscook Bay
Lily Bay
Grafton Notch
Rangeley Lake

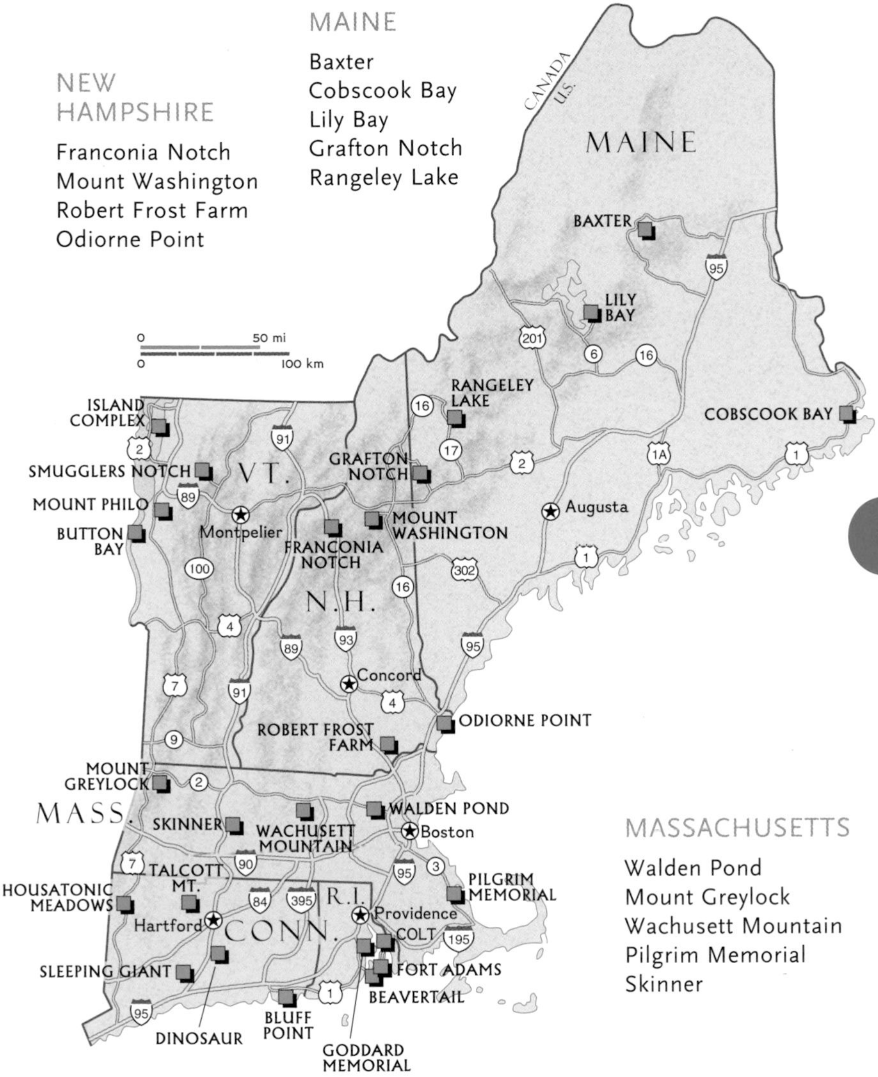

NEW HAMPSHIRE

Franconia Notch
Mount Washington
Robert Frost Farm
Odiorne Point

MASSACHUSETTS

Walden Pond
Mount Greylock
Wachusett Mountain
Pilgrim Memorial
Skinner

VERMONT

Island Complex
Smugglers Notch
Button Bay
Mount Philo

CONNECTICUT

Housatonic Meadows
Talcott Mountain
Dinosaur
Sleeping Giant
Bluff Point

RHODE ISLAND

Fort Adams
Beavertail
Colt
Goddard Memorial

Franconia Notch State Park, New Hampshire

Baxter

18 miles from Millinocket on park access road

■ 209,501 acres ■ Mid-May to mid-Oct., Dec. through March ■ Nonresident vehicle fee ■ No pets, RVs, or motorcycles ■ New England's largest state park ■ Maine's highest mountain ■ Wildlife viewing ■ Hiking, boating, fishing (license required)

In the early 1900s, when paper companies and developers started gobbling up the vast Maine woods, Gov. Percival Baxter argued that a portion of the state should be set aside as a wilderness area. In 1930, using his own money, he began buying plots at the edge of the North Woods and giving them to the state. Thirty-two years and 28 purchases later, the governor had built up the empire of mountains, lakes, and wildlife that would bear his name. Today, a special Baxter State Park Authority administers the park in strict adherence to Baxter's will. He stipulated that preservation of the park's wild character be the top priority, with recreational use a secondary concern.

The park's skyline is dominated by Katahdin, actually a cluster of mountains whose highest point, Baxter Peak, is named in honor of the governor. "Man is born to die. His works are short-lived. Buildings crumble, monuments decay, wealth vanishes but Katahdin in all its glory forever shall remain the mountain of the people of Maine," Governor Baxter wrote of the state's highest peak.

He was not the first person to be impressed by the great gray mountain, which rises abruptly from the wooded plain. America's

Sunset on the prairie

early environmental writer, Henry David Thoreau, traveled by foot, train, boat, and horse and buggy to reach Katahdin in 1846. He was among the first white men known to have scaled the mountain's steep rocky slope, which he immortalized as "vast, titanic, inhumane" in his 1864 book, *The Maine Woods.*

Baxter State Park is still best seen by walking. Short, flat trails follow rivers or lead to ponds frequented by moose. Longer trails will take you to waterfalls and lakes, and strenuous trails climb to the tops of the park's many mountains, including Katahdin, the northern terminus of the Appalachian Trail. Call the hiker information line at 207-723-4636 for daily trail updates.

What to See and Do

If you have only a day to spend at Baxter, a drive along the **tote road**—old logging roads in Maine that are unimproved—with stops for short walks and wildlife viewing, will give you a good flavor of the rugged region. With a little advance planning, you can stretch this trip and stay overnight at one of the campgrounds or in cabins along the way. Before journeying into the park, fill your gas tank and stock up on food and water; there are no stores, gas stations, or drinking water sources in the park. At the **Visitor Center** south of Baxter's entrance gate, obtain a map of the park. Here staff can also tell you if certain popular parking lots are full. If this is the case, alternatives will be suggested.

Just beyond the gate where you register you'll reach a fork; to the right is **Roaring**

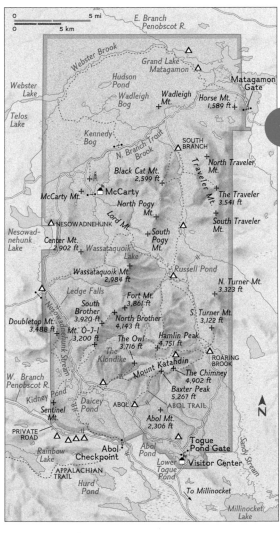

Brook, a popular starting point for treks up Mount Katahdin. Even if you don't want to go all the way to the top, try to take the steep, 3.3-mile trail to **Chimney Pond,** a picturesque moose watering hole in the shadow of Baxter Peak. Many hikers stay at the campsites or in the bunkhouse at the pond before making the final ascent of Mount Katahdin.

Backtrack to the main park loop road and head in the direction of Abol Campground. Your first stop is **Abol Pond,** a popular feeding ground for moose, with a small sandy beach and picnic area. About 2 miles up the road, you'll find the wooded campground. From here, the steep, rocky **Abol Trail** climbs up the south face of Katahdin. This rugged, 7.6-mile round-trip trail—visible as a wide slash on the mountainside—is the shortest route to Baxter Peak. It closely parallels the route Thoreau took.

About 4.5 miles farther up the road, turn left on Daicey Pond Road to popular **Daicey Pond.** A loop trail edges the water, offering excellent views of Katahdin. Several small cabins also offer great mountain and lake views. You can rent canoes at Daicey and more than a dozen other ponds.

Nearby **Kidney Pond,** reachable by trail or park road, is well worth a stop. The cabins here face the water, where loons nest and moose visit frequently. At sunrise or sunset, or on a moonlit night, enjoy the quiet beauty by canoe.

Bull moose in Russell Pond

From Kidney Pond, several trails lead to more remote ponds, including **Celia** and **Jackson,** where canoes are available for a leisurely paddle. Both are home to brook trout, which can be caught by fly-fishing only. A popular 2.5-mile trail wends from Kidney Pond to the top of **Sentinel Mountain.** Four miles up the road beyond Kidney Pond, swimmers enjoy sliding down the slippery rocks of **Ledge Falls.**

PARK TIP: *Be on the lookout for moose and other wildlife at Dwelley Pond.*

Drive 5.7 miles north of Nesowadnehunk Campground to the sign for **Dwelley Pond Trail** on the right-hand side. From here, it's a leisurely, level 1.4-mile walk to the pond, a favorite for moose watchers. Your chances for a sighting are good in this quiet, tranquil spot, and you may glimpse a black bear, deer, or other Maine wildlife along the trail. Remember keep at least 200 feet between you and a moose, and never get near a bull in rut or in between a cow moose and her calf. If you think you might be interested in paddling on this small pond, you need to get a key for the canoe padlocks at Nesowadnehunk Campground. (Fees for canoe rental are $1/hr. including life vests and paddles.)

Further Adventures

Most one-day visitors to Baxter get only as far as Nesowadnehunk, about 17 miles into the park. But if you have more time and want to get away from the crowds, a journey to the park's remote northern end is worth the effort. It is about 17 miles from Nesowadnehunk to the turnoff for the **Upper** and **Lower South Branch Ponds.** Here you'll find tent sites and a bunkhouse, as well as canoes for rent and a variety of hiking trails. A short path leads to **South Branch Falls,** while **South Branch Mountain Trail** (Black Cat) and **Traveler Mountains** are more strenuous climbs. **Grand Lake Matagamon,** home to eight types of fish including salmon and yellow perch, is a few miles up the road. For a good view of the 4,000-acre lake, climb the mile and a half to the summit of **Horse Mountain.** From the park's north entrance, you can follow the paved road to Patten and back to I-95.

In winter, the park is open for snowshoeing, cross-country skiing, and snowmobiling. To camp or climb above timberline, you must register two weeks in advance, have proof of winter mountaineering experience, and travel in groups of four or more.

Camping and Lodging

Baxter has 10 campgrounds, with a range of accommodations—tent sites as well as wooden lean-tos. Reservations are necessary, especially for July and August. The park has a rolling-reservation system; visit the park's website or phone for instructions on how to make a reservation. Limited sites are available on a first-come, first-served basis. Other park lodging can be found at the Katahdin Lake Wilderness Camp; see www.katahdinlakewildernesscamps.com.

Baxter State Park, 64 Balsam Dr., Millinocket, ME 04462; 207-723-5140; www.baxterstateparkauthority.com

15

Cobscook Bay

5 miles south of Dennysville on US 1

- 871 acres ■ Mid-May to mid-Oct., trails open year-round
- Day-use fee in summer ■ Walking trails ■ Clamming

Cobscook Bay State Park has the look of the Maine coast before the birth of ubiquitous outlet malls and restaurants. Far from the hub-bub of the southern part of the state, you'll discover a quiet seaside retreat dominated by towering spruce trees. Whether just stopping for a picnic lunch or pitching your tent for the night, Cobscook is a good jumping-off point for further exploration of Down East Maine.

What to See and Do

You've set up camp at a site with sweeping views of **Whiting Bay** and realize you've forgotten to pack dinner. No problem. Cobscook Bay is Maine's only state park with a clamming area where visitors are allowed to dig. Bring a big pot and plan to get dirty as you try your hand (at low tide) at this popular Maine activity. After tending to your scraped knuckles, watch the setting sun cast a pink glow over the shimmering waters as you dine on your handpicked steamers.

If you're an early bird, scramble up **Cunningham Mountain** for views of the sun rising over secluded Whiting Bay, part of the larger Cobscook Bay. Leaving from Broad Cove Road, the 0.2-mile trail climbs up the granite hill. From this vantage, you may be one of the first people in the lower 48 states to see the sunrise. If you hike up in the pre-dawn darkness, don't forget a flashlight since the path is rocky. This walk connects to a nature trail that follows the park's western edge through the woods.

REVERSING FALLS: The local Maliseet and Passamaquoddy Indians called the area Cobscook, or "waterfall," for the reversing falls that are a short distance from the park. The flow of water in the bay reverses direction every 6 hours, and at high tide, the water is 24 feet higher than at low tide. The best time to see the falls is a couple of hours before high tide, when the incoming water is at its most turbulent. Ask the park ranger for directions and a tide chart.

Another path, the 0.75-mile **Anthony's Beach Trail,** meanders through the woods and along the rocky shore to a large wharf. Be sure to follow the trail blazes; it's easy to get lost.

The park's jagged shoreline and many coves lend themselves to sea kayaking. Numerous islands and small bays may be easily reached by small motorboat or canoe. Boat launch facilities are found near the park's middle and northwest corners. There are no boats for rent.

More than 200 species of birds have been sighted at Cobscook Bay, including bald eagles. The park office has bird lists, as well as a collection of field guides available for visitor reference.

Camping

Cobscook Bay offers 106 tent and RV sites, with nearby shower facilities. Four secluded spots are accessible only by short trail. A couple

Cobscook Bay

dozen sites are available on a first-come, first-served basis. A few sites have wooden Adirondack shelters. Reservations advised in season; call 207-624-9950 or 800-332-1501 (Maine only) or visit www.camp withme.com. Camping fee.

Nearby Sights

The picturesque fishing village of **Lubec,** located about 10 miles from Cobscook Bay, is the easternmost town in the United States. Follow the signs to **Quoddy Head State Park,** the easternmost point of land in the contiguous U.S., guarded by a candycane-striped lighthouse *(now closed).*

From Lubec, cross Franklin D. Roosevelt Memorial Bridge to Campobello Island and **Roosevelt Campobello International Park** *(506-752-2922. Mem. Day–early Oct.),* the New Brunswick, Canada, vacation home of President Franklin D. Roosevelt's family. Sitting amid a 2,800-acre memorial park, the large wooden cottage has 34 rooms furnished much as they were when FDR spent his boyhood summers here in the early 1900s.

Cobscook Bay State Park, 40 S. Edmunds Rd., Edmunds Township, ME 04628; 207-726-4412; www.maine.gov/doc/parks

Lily Bay

9 miles north of Greenville, along eastern shore of Moosehead Lake

■ 925 acres ■ Mid-May to mid-Oct., trails open year-round ■ Day-use fee ■ New England's largest lake ■ Fishing (license required), boating, wildlife viewing

At the southern end of the undeveloped expanse known as the North Woods, the **Moosehead Lake** area offers wilderness adventure coupled with nearby creature comforts. Within the confines of Lily Bay, a 2-mile one-way trail snakes along the lakeshore, a swimming beach, and boat docking facilities (for campers only).

One way to see the largest lake in New England—measuring 74,890 acres—is to take a floatplane ride. There are flying services in Greenville *(Moosehead Lake Chamber of Commerce, 207-695-2702)*, which can also arrange a stay at one of the lake's remote camps. For a more down-to-earth adventure, troll the lake in a motorboat for trout or landlocked salmon. Boats are available for rent near the park. Also in town, you can book a lake tour on the **Katahdin** *(Waterfront. 207-695-2716. July–Aug. daily, May–June & Sept. Sat.–Sun.; fare)*, a refurbished steamboat. As the lake's name suggests, many moose inhabit the area. For the best moose-watching, drive slowly on the back roads, especially along boggy areas.

Rising sharply from the lake's floor, **Mount Kineo**'s 800-foot cliff towers over the clear water. Technically a peninsula, Kineo is accessible to visitors only by water; rent a canoe or catch a water taxi *(Mount Kineo Golf Course. 207-534-9012. Fare)* from Rockwood on the lake's western shore for the 1-mile journey. Steep paths lead to a lookout tower, and a shore path rings the rocky formation.

Camping

Lily Bay has 90 primitive tent and RV sites with showers, no hook-ups. Reservations advised in season; call 207-624-9950 (Mon.–Fri., 9 a.m.–4 p.m.) or 800-332-1501 (Maine only) or at www.camp withme.com. Camping fee.

Lily Bay State Park, 13 Myrle's Way, Greenville, ME 04441; 207-695-2700; www.maine.gov/doc/parks

Grafton Notch

8 miles north of Newry on Maine 26

■ 3,192 acres ■ Mid-May to mid-Oct., trails open year-round ■ Day-use fee ■ No camping ■ Waterfalls ■ Hiking

The Bear River carved this narrow passageway through the mountains of far western Maine. In late spring, with the help of melting snow, the river rages through the gorge, forming several waterfalls only a short walk from the road. The largest cascade is **Screw Auger**

Falls, at the park's southern end. Over the years, the falling water has gouged rounded potholes in the boulders that stand in the river's path. To the north, a 0.25-mile trail leads to **Moose Cave,** where water flowing under huge slabs of granite gurgles eerily.

Elsewhere, the Appalachian Trail and many other paths scale the peaks surrounding the notch. For spectacular views of the valley, try the 2-mile **Eyebrow Loop Trail** or the newly rebuilt **Table Rock Trail.** A strenuous day hike ascends Old Speck Mountain, offering views of the Mahoosuc Range and the White Mountains.

Grafton Notch State Park, 1941 Bear River Rd., Newry, ME 04261; 207-824-2912; www.maine.gov/doc/parks

19

Screw Auger Falls

Rangeley Lake

Southern shore of Rangeley Lake between Maine 4 and Maine 17, on South Shore Rd.

- 869 acres ▪ Mid-May through Sept., trails open year-round
- Day-use fee ▪ Boating, swimming, fishing (license required)

Nestled in the heart of western Maine's mountains, this park is popular with fishermen of trout and landlocked salmon. Listen carefully at night and you'll hear the haunting call of loons. At dusk, drive slowly on the roads along the lake and you're apt to see a moose out for a stroll.

Whether from shore or aboard a boat, you'll enjoy views of the surrounding mountains. Boat tours and rentals are available in the town of Rangeley *(Chamber of Commerce, 207-864-5364),* on the northern shore. Trails lead up nearby **Bald** and **Saddleback Mountains,** both offering excellent area vistas. Winter sports enthusiasts flock to the **Saddleback ski area** *(207-864-5671).*

Camping

The park has 50 tent sites, with showers, including three group sites for parties of ten or more. Reservations 207-624-9950 or 800-332-1501 (Maine only) or at www.campwithme.com. Camping fee.

Rangeley Lake State Park, HC 32 Box 5000, Rangeley, ME 04970; .207-864-3858; www.maine.gov/doc/parks

Franconia Notch

I-93 between Lincoln and Franconia

- 6,440 acres ▪ Year-round ▪ Covered bridges ▪ Waterfalls
▪ Aerial tramway ▪ Hiking, biking, skiing, snowmobiling,
fishing (license required)

In a narrow valley in the White Mountains, Franconia Notch was formed by glaciers thousands of years ago. The slow-moving snow and ice also sculpted the famed Old Man of the Mountain. Sometime during the night of May 3, 2003, the symbol of New Hampshire gave into nature's continuing forces and collapsed. Immortalized by Nathaniel Hawthorne in an 1850 tale, the stone face began drawing visitors to the park in the late 19th century. Stagecoaches and the railroad brought people from all over to stay at the luxurious Profile House.

When the inn burned down in 1923, efforts to rebuild failed, and timber on the 6,000-acre parcel owned by the hotel was put up

20

Flume Bridge

for sale. The Society for the Protection of New Hampshire Forests began a nationwide campaign to save Franconia Notch. The group raised 200,000 dollars, which was matched by the state legislature, and in 1928 the notch became a state park and forest reservation. Now a scenic parkway (I-93) edged with hiking trails and other natural attractions runs through the long, skinny park, showcasing the timbered notch to perfection.

The park is best seen in the fall, when the brightly colored trees offset the notch's gray granite walls. Beware, however, of hordes of leaf peepers and their accompanying tour buses. Plan to start your day early to stay ahead of the crowd.

What to See and Do

Begin at the parkway's southern end at **The Flume Gorge** (*mid-May–Oct.; adm. fee*). During an 1808 fishing trip, 93-year-old Aunt Jess Guernsey discovered this narrow, rocky canyon, threaded by rushing Flume Brook. Stop first at the large **Visitor Center,** where a video presentation, photographs, and other memorabilia recount the notch's history.

Then ride the shuttle bus or walk along the well-groomed trail to Boulder Cabin, where a scenic hike into Flume Gorge begins. Stroll along the boardwalks that cling to 90-foot granite walls, then climb numerous steps out of the chasm. Farther along, the trail wends downhill through the woods, and crosses the Pemigewasset River at Sentinel Pine Bridge, built in 1939 from a huge pine tree that was felled by a hurricane from a nearby cliff. The covered bridge overlooks a large stone pool created by glaciers at the end of the Ice Age. Edged with numerous rain shelters, the trail circles back to the Visitor Center.

The next stop on the northbound park road is **The Basin.** A short paved trail leads to a large, rounded rock basin carved by the Pemigewasset River. Here, naturalist and writer Henry David Thoreau watched the gently cascading water and proclaimed, "This pothole is perhaps the most remarkable curiosity of its kind in New England." Among several hiking trails that explore nearby **Lonesome Lake** and the surrounding mountains is a popular 6-mile

21

loop that follows the Cascade and Cascade Brook Trails to the tree-fringed lake. From here, head downhill on the Lonesome Lake Trail to Lafayette Campground and then along the Pemi Trail back to The Basin. The loop can also be done from the campground.

Many have stopped at the roadside overlook to get a glimpse of the famed Old Man. Today, visitors stop to remember. Even without the Great Stone Face, **Profile Lake** is still as popular a spot for summer visitors as it was during the 19th century. The lake is well known for its brook trout and is open to fly-fishing only. Overlooking the lake, a museum details the history of the Old Man of the Mountain.

PARK TIP: *Climb the high-arched Gov. Gallen Memorial Bridge for an amazing view of the Franconia Region and Sugar Hill.*

At the park's north end lies the **Cannon Mountain ski area** *(603-823-8800)*. In summer and winter, an aerial tram *(fare)* whisks visitors up the mountain, where trails lead to a summit observation tower. There are more than 25 miles of trails for skiers and snowboarders. The area, site of North America's first aerial tramway, began operation in 1938. Nestled at the mountain's base, the **New England Ski Museum** *(603-823-7177. Mem. Day–Columbus Day, Dec.–March)* displays skis dating from the 1890s, the ski parka of Minnie Dole (founder of the National Ski Patrol), and more.

Across from the ski area, a steep, rocky trail leads to **Bald Mountain** summit, a spot to watch the sun set over the White Mountains. The loop trail winds to **Artists Bluff,** which overlooks Echo Lake before heading back to the parking lot.

Extending the length of the park, a paved recreation trail runs 9 miles between The Flume Gorge and Cannon Mountain. Many bikers take their time, visiting sights on the northbound, slightly uphill journey, then whiz back southward for a full day's ride. Snowmobilers and cross-country skiers use the trail in winter.

If you have a boat or canoe, enjoy the placid waters of **Profile** or **Echo Lake.** Both lakes offer fishing, and Echo Lake has a small swimming area.

The Governor Gallen Memorial Bridge affords an excellent spot for snapping photos of the classic New England foliage on a crisp fall day. To locate the bridge, leave I-93 on the north end of the park at exit 34-C on the old park road. The bridge is accessible to all, with plenty of parking.

Camping

The park has 97 tent sites (mid-May–early Oct.), with shower facilities (fee). Primitive camping, with no water or facilities, available in winter. No pets. Reservations advised in season; call 877-647-2757. Camping fee. Nearby Cannon Mountain RV Park has 7 year-round RV sites. Reservations advised; call 603-271-3628. Camping fee.

Franconia Notch State Park, Rte. 3, Franconia, NH 03580; 603-823-8800; www.nhstateparks.org; www.cannonmt.com

Mount Washington

Via Mount Washington Auto Road, on N.H. 16 in Gorham; or Mount Washington Cog Railway, off US 302 near Bretton Woods

■ 59 acres ■ Mid-May to mid-Oct. ■ No camping ■ Highest mountain in New England ■ Weather observatory ■ Historic hotel

Ammonoosuc River and Mount Washington

The 6,288-foot summit of Mount Washington is lashed with weather reputed to be the worst in the world. In 1934, meteorologists recorded on its summit one of the highest wind velocities ever measured on Earth—231 mph. Winds in excess of hurricane force (75 mph) sweep across the mountain more than 100 days per year. So why venture to the top? Simple, the views. On a clear day (fewer than 180 days a year), you can see more than 90 miles to Vermont, Massachusetts, Maine, Quebec, and the Atlantic Ocean.

What to See and Do

Getting to the top of New England's highest mountain is half the fun. Whatever route you choose, remember that the weather can change quickly and the top of the mountain is always cooler than the base, so bring warm clothing. You can drive up the 8-mile **Mount Washington Auto Road** *(fee),* which opened in 1861 as a carriage road. Beginning on N.H. 16 in Gorham, putter up the steep, winding road to the summit in your own car, or catch a ride in a van *(fee)* with a guide. For a more interesting experience, take the **Mount Washington Cog Railway** *(603-278-5404 or 800-922-8825. Sat.–Sun. in May, daily Mem. Day–Oct.; fare).* The 3-mile railway, one of the world's steepest, made its first run in 1869. A unique rack-and-pinion system and coal-fired steam engines push wood-and-aluminum railway cars up the mountain. The railway base station is located off US 302, near Bretton Woods.

> **WHY IS THE WEATHER SO BAD?**
> Imagine water rushing over a small boulder in a raging stream. That is the same effect the wind has on Mount Washington. Not only is the mountain the tallest mass of rock around, it also happens to lie in the path of the three major storm tracks that affect the Northeast. This turbulent air—pushed over the lofty peak—gains speed as it rises from the valley below, just as a river gains velocity as it passes over a rapid.

The mountain's first recorded climb was made in 1642 by Darby Field, of Exeter, New Hampshire. Today several hiking trails, including the **Appalachian Trail,** lead up the steep slopes. *(Only experienced hikers should attempt an ascent.)*

PARK TIP: *Mount Washington's unique alpine flowers and plants thrive along the Alpine Garden Trail.*

At the summit, visit the Mount Washington Observatory's **museum** *(603-356-2137. Mid-May–mid-Oct.; adm. fee),* which features exhibits about the peak's natural and human history. At the **observatory** *(tours, fee for non-members),* staff monitor the harsh weather. By the mid-1800s two hotels competed to accommodate visitors. A fire in 1908 virtually destroyed the "City Among the Clouds," sparing only the stone **Tip-Top House** *(open for tours, weather permitting),* believed to be the world's oldest mountaintop hostelry. The hotel was built in 1853 using only native stones and wood.

Nearby Sights

The famed **Bretton Woods** area is located at the mountain's western base, on US 302. The picturesque **Mount Washington Hotel** *(603-278-1000 or 800-258-0330. Guided tours)* opened in 1902 as a European-style spa, attracting trainloads of wealthy visitors during its heyday. In 1944, representatives from 44 countries met here to sign the Bretton Woods Accord, a post-World War II trade and financial assistance plan that established the World Bank and International Monetary Fund. The hotel's elegant rooms are still open to guests.

Mount Washington State Park, P.O. Box D, Gorham, NH 03581; 603-466-3347; www.nhstateparks.org

Robert Frost Farm

2 miles south of the Derry Circle on N.H. 28

■ 64 acres ■ Call for hours ■ User fee ■ No camping ■ National Historic Landmark ■ Nature-poetry trail

Derry Farm in autumn

At Derry Farm, poet Robert Frost tried his hand at poultry farming in the early 1900s. Inspired by the plants, animals, and landscapes that surrounded him, his writing flourished—later bringing him critical acclaim and four Pulitzer Prizes.

In a 1952 letter, Frost commented, "I might say the core of all my writing was probably the five free years I had there on the farm down the road from Derry Village … The only thing we had plenty of was time and seclusion."

The family sold the farm in 1911. It passed through many hands before becoming a garage and auto junkyard in the 1940s. The state acquired the land in 1964 and began restoring the two-story white clapboard New England farmhouse and farmland to its turn-of-the-20th-century condition. The house was refurbished with the guidance of Frost's eldest daughter, Lesley Frost Ballantine, who selected furnishings representative of ones the family had owned. Guided tours of the house are available. Check with park on days and times.

Retrace Frost's steps on the farm's footpaths, which he shoveled himself in winter, by taking a stroll along the **Hyla Brook poetry and nature trail.** You will pass many of the man-made and natural features that appear in Frost's poems. "Mending Wall," for example, lyrically recalls how each spring Frost and his neighbor Napoleon Guay replaced the stones that had fallen off the rock wall separating their properties. In the poem "Hyla Brook," Frost describes the seasonal creek he named for its peepers, tiny tree frogs of the genus Hyla. Check with the site for information on summertime lectures and readings.

Robert Frost Farm State Historic Park, P.O. Box 1075, Derry, NH 03038; 603-432-3091; www.nhstateparks.org

25

Odiorne Point

3 miles south of Portsmouth, on US 1A in Rye

- 334 acres ▪ Year-round ▪ Adm. fee daily May to late Oct. and weekends year-round ▪ No camping ▪ Seacoast Science Center ▪ Remnants of Army fort ▪ Walking and biking trails

Sunrise over Odiorne Point

In 1623, British settlers landed on this windy point of land and built a small fishing and trading community—the first European settlement in New Hampshire. They dubbed it Pannaway Plantation. In 1660, John Odiorne and his family joined the settlement, which by that time had become a thriving farm center for the nearby town of Portsmouth.

Two hundred years later, the point had grown into a popular seaside retreat. Among the posh hotels and summer cottages that cropped up along the shore was a 1920 residence built by the Sugden family.

At the outbreak of World War II, the U.S. Army requisitioned the strip of land to protect the nearby Portsmouth Naval Shipyard. The point was turned into Fort Dearborn, the Sugdens' stone farmhouse became officers' quarters, and many of the area's seaside estates were demolished. After the war, a legal technicality prevented the families from returning to their land. The Army declared the land surplus property in the late 1950s and sold it to the state of New Hampshire in 1961, whereby it became a state park. Existing remnants of the fort, including bunkers and machine-gun emplacements, can be found in the hills overlooking the Atlantic Ocean.

PARK TIP: *A great place for ocean fishing is the jetty—protecting Little Harbor—at the end of Frost Point.*

What to See and Do

Kids of all ages will enjoy learning about marine life at the **Seacoast Science Center** *(603-436-8043. Adm. fee),* located at the park's south end. Daily programs teach children and their parents about lobsters and other sea dwellers, as well as about the plants and animals that live in the marshes and woodlands of Odiorne Point—the largest undeveloped seashore on New Hampshire's 18-mile coastline. Kids can peer into a thousand-gallon tank swarming with sea creatures, then feel and study a plethora of specimens in a touch-tank. The science center is built around the Sugden House, where the family lived until 1942. Displays describe the point's history from the early settlers to its use as a World War II fort and its current educational mission. Large picture windows overlook the Gulf of Maine and Portsmouth Harbor.

After learning about the point's landscapes and habitats in the science center, go out and see them firsthand. Walk along the rocky shore and examine tide pools for sea urchins, crabs, and other animals temporarily trapped in the shallow waters by the receding tide. In the center of the park, a man-made freshwater pond offers a good place for birdwatching, and along the ocean, the rocky shore gives way to a pebble beach and a freshwater marsh. A saltwater marsh lies at the park's northern border.

FRUITFUL SHORES: Shortly after New Hampshire's first European settlers landed at Odiorne Point, another group of travelers came ashore in 1630 a few miles north along the Piscataqua River. Since the riverbanks were covered with strawberry plants, they called their fledgling settlement Strawbery Banke. With a ready supply of timber, the town—renamed Portsmouth in 1653 —soon became known for shipbuilding. Today, Strawbery Banke Museum *(Marcy St. 603-433-1100. Late April–early Nov.; adm. fee)* comprises many restored buildings from the town's long history.

A paved hike-and-bike trail runs the length of the park, while dirt trails pass by batteries, bunkers, and other remnants of Fort Dearborn. You can also see the remains of formal gardens dating from the point's heyday as a resort community.

At the park's northern entrance, a short trail leads to **Frost Point.** One of the area's early settlers, George Frost owned a house on this spit of land that juts into the sea and offers commanding views of the length of the park.

Odiorne Point State Park, P.O. Box 606, Rye Beach, NH 03871; 603-436-7406; www.nhstateparks.org

27

Island Complex

7 miles west of St. Albans off Vt. 36, via ferry from Kamp Kill Kare

- 563 acres (Burton Island) ▪ Mid-May to Labor Day ▪ Day-use fee ▪ No cars ▪ Remote islands ▪ Hiking and nature trails ▪ Fishing (license required)

A string of bucolic islands in Lake Champlain, Vermont's Island Complex comprises three unusual state parks. Accessible only by state-run ferry or private boat, these three isles provide different levels of escape for day and overnight visitors.

Burton is the string's largest and most developed island, where most visitors head. If you're searching for a more remote experience, try Knight Island, dotted with small ponds and primitive camping sites, or undeveloped Woods Island—reachable only by private boat.

All three islands were farmed extensively from the early 1800s to the early 1960s when the state acquired the land. Original plans called for building a causeway, but plans were scrapped and the islands have remained vehicle-free. Today the former farm fields contain trails that pass by remnants of stone fences, evidence of abandoned corn and bean fields, and even old foundations and farm implements.

What to See and Do

Much of what you do on these islands depends on your mode of transportation and how long you stay. If you plan to camp, 253-acre

Peaceful Knight Island, Lake Champlain

Burton Island, which has potable water, hot showers, and a small store and restaurant that sells basic supplies, is a good base of operations. To get here, take the state-run *Island Runner* ferry *(contact park for information; fare)* from Kamp Kill Kare, a former boys camp on the Lake Champlain shore. Or slide your own boat up to one of the marina's 100 boat slips or 15 moorings—often full during peak summer weekends. You can rent a canoe, kayak, or rowboat at the marina and explore the island's wooded, rocky coves. Remember that once you get to Burton Island, you'll travel by foot, so pack lightly. Park staff will cart gear to campsites for a small fee or lend you a pushcart.

PARK TIP: *Enjoy commanding views of the forest-covered Adirondacks from Burton Island's southern tip.*

Away from the marina's hubbub, the island is mostly quiet and undeveloped. A short distance away, a small wooden building houses the island's **Nature Center,** where a resident naturalist conducts programs. In the 1800s, turkeys, sheep, and milk cows roamed the pastoral landscape. Farmwork was done by horses or tenant farmers, many of whom were Abenaki Indians. You can see rusted implements and other artifacts from the farming days in the Nature Center. A short **nature trail** that begins nearby passes through abandoned fields, offering good views of the town of St. Albans Bay, a thriving shipping community in the late 18th century.

To access the southern point of the island, walk down the very easy 1.3-mile southern tip trail surrounded by purple flowering raspberries, Jerusalem artichoke, and staghorn sumac. It's an amateur naturalist's delight, where you can watch resident goldfinches, warblers, ospreys feeding on fish, and great blue herons.

Short walking trails leave from the camping area. The 0.8-mile **North Shore Trail** parallels rocky shoreline. A brochure recounts the island's geological history and describes the plants and animals along it. Take the **Eagle Bay Birding Trail** back to the campground.

The 185-acre **Knight Island** was also heavily farmed before becoming a private campground in the 1980s. All but 10 acres on the island's southern tip were acquired by the state in 1990. Arrangements must be made on Burton Island for a ferry ride *(fare)* to and from Knight Island, or you can take a private boat. Strong paddlers can reach the island by canoe or sea kayak from North Hero and Knight Point State Parks, both located west of the island and accessible by car on US 2; overnight parking is permitted at these parks. A **hiking trail** rings Knight Island, passing small ponds and rocky outcroppings with views of Lake Champlain and northwestern Vermont.

Further Adventures

To truly get away from the crowds, head to 125-acre **Woods Island,** a short motorboat ride or an invigorating paddle by canoe or kayak from Burton Island. Many had grand visions for this small island, which was also a tenant's farm in the 1800s. An abandoned, uncompleted airstrip runs down the island's center, a remnant of a developer's dream to build a secluded business retreat.

Today, only foundations of a farmhouse and a few weatherworn pieces of farm equipment recall past development. One hiking trail follows the shoreline around the island; another cuts across the island and the abandoned airstrip.

Camping

Burton Island: 17 tent sites, 4 primitive paddler sites, and 26 wooden lean-tos, with shower facilities. Reservations needed on weekends July and August. Knight Island: 6 lean-tos and 1 tent site, with no potable water and limited facilities. A camping permit must be obtained from Burton Island. During the week, boat service is available by reservation only. Woods Island: 5 primitive tent sites, with no potable water or facilities. A camping permit must be obtained from Burton Island.

Campsite reservations for all islands are necessary and can be made up to 11 months in advance. Call 888-409-7579 or check the website for reservation information. Camping fee.

Burton Island State Park, P.O. Box 123, St. Albans Bay, VT 05481; 802-524-6353; www.vtstateparks.com/htm/burton.htm

Smugglers Notch

Between Stowe and Jeffersonville off Vt. 108

- 43 acres (state park), 44,000 acres (Mt. Mansfield State Forest)
- Mid-May to mid-Oct. • Mountain pass • Rock formations • Hiking

A giant slice between Mount Mansfield and Sterling Peak, Smugglers Notch runs north to south between the towns of Jeffersonville and Stowe. Some geologists believe that a glacial-melt river carved the notch about 12,000 years ago. In more recent years, it became a route for smugglers. An 1807 embargo forbidding trade with Great Britain and Canada prompted Vermonters to sneak cattle and other goods through the narrow passageway to their northern neighbors. Later, fugitive slaves are said to have used the notch as an escape route to Canada. During Prohibition, locals brought in whiskey over a makeshift road that had been built through the gap in 1922.

Smugglers Notch is the newest, old park in Vermont. In 2003, the 1930s campground built by the Civilian Conservation Corps (CCC) was dismantled rock by rock and moved one-half mile down the mountainside. The parks department took great precautions to maintain the integrity of the old buildings. They dismantled the old stone fireplaces, picked up the 14 lean-tos, the ranger's house, and even the original toilet, and relocated and reassembled them in an identical fashion. (The only facility that was replaced housed the showers and a second bathroom.) The new location, with better views and less noise, is one-half mile off narrow, two-lane Vt. 108 *(portions closed in winter),* which winds through the gap, visiting several interesting attractions along the way.

What to See and Do

From the south, begin your journey in the quaint town of **Stowe,** Vermont's oldest ski resort. A short distance away, on Vt. 108, you come to the **Mount Mansfield Toll Road** *(802-253-3000. Spring–first snowfall; toll),* a steep auto road that winds up to the southern

View through Smugglers Notch

summit, or "nose," of Vermont's highest mountain. There, spectacular views of much of the Green Mountain State, neighboring New York, New Hampshire, and Quebec await you. You can also ride the **Stowe Mountain Resort Gondola** *(802-253-3000. Mid-June–Oct. & ski season; fare)* to the 4,393-foot summit and its mountaintop eatery.

Heading north again on Vt. 108, you'll pass the **State Ski Dormitory,** which started by offering bunks and hearty meals to CCC workers in 1934. Those same workers were responsible for the trail cutting that led to the basis for today's ski trails. In 1940, the dorm opened as the first state-operated ski lodge.

Just south of the park information booth, stop at **Big Spring,** the site of a 1920s restaurant where customers were invited to catch a trout in the pool and have it fried up for dinner. Now returned to its natural state, the spring offers cool, fresh drinking water. From here, the road enters the shadows of Smugglers Notch, where 1,000-foot cliffs block out the sun. The rocky cliffs are the ideal home for the peregrine falcons that have recently returned to Vermont after a 30-year absence.

> **CHIN UP:** The summit of Mount Mansfield is often referred to as the chin. This is because the mountain's profile is said to resemble the outline of a reclining man's face. Following the mountain ridge, you will also see the forehead, nose, and Adam's apple.

A short distance above the notch's information booth, you will see the **Old Smugglers Face** in Mount Mansfield State Forest. Other odd rock formations, such as the Elephant's Head and the Hunter and His Dog, can also be found here. But don't just look up in this mountain passage; some of the more interesting features may be under your feet. Because of the often Arctic-like conditions on Mount Mansfield, many rare alpine species of plants thrive here, including the butterwort, a tiny yellow carnivorous flower.

Several hiking trails ascend from the notch to Mount Mansfield and Sterling Pond. One of the most popular routes climbs along a 2.2-mile section of the **Long Trail** to the **Lake of the Clouds.**

From the notch, Vt. 108 descends out of the mountains and passes the **Smugglers Notch Resort** *(800-451-8752),* a popular ski area, before reaching the small town of Jeffersonville.

Camping

Smugglers Notch has 20 tent sites, 6 of which accommodate RVs (no hook-ups), with showers; 14 lean-to sites. Reservations advised in season; call 888-409-7579. Camping fee.

Smugglers Notch State Park, 6443 Mountain Rd., Stowe, VT 05672; 802-253-4014; www.vtstateparks.com/htm/smugglers.htm

Button Bay

6 miles northwest of Vergennes, on Lake Champlain

■ 253 acres ■ Mid-May to Columbus Day ■ Day-use fee ■ Fossils
■ Nature Center ■ Swimming pool, boating, fishing (license required)

Nearly 500 million years ago, Button Bay was part of a continental shelf submerged in a warm shallow sea full of life. The park's limestones and limey shales preserve many fossils dating from that time; its fossilized coral is among the world's oldest. About 12,000 years ago, a chilly ocean called the Champlain Sea—predecessor of Lake Champlain—covered the region. A clam species living today in Button Bay has been traced back to a species that existed here in those times.

To explore the geological history of Button Bay, follow the nature trail to **Button Point,** where you can see large, fossilized sea snails, as well as the park's namesake buttonlike concretions, formed when calcium mixed with clay in the Champlain Sea. Fossil-collecting is prohibited, so visit the nearby **Nature Center,** which details the bay's geologic history. The park also offers boat rentals and a swimming pool.

Camping

The park has 59 tent or RV sites and 13 lean-tos, with shower facilities. Reservations advised in season; call 802-475-2377 or 888-409-7579. Camping fee.

Button Bay State Park., Rd. 3, Box 4075, Vergennes, VT 05491; 802-475-2377; www.vtstateparks.com/htm/buttonbay.htm

Mount Philo

2 miles north of North Ferrisburg, off US 7

▪ 237 acres ▪ Mid-May to mid-Oct. ▪ Day-use fee ▪ Mountain and lake views ▪ Hiking

Like Button Bay, the beehive-shaped Mount Philo was created by the former Champlain Sea. Several thousand years ago, chilly waters surrounded the mountain, creating an island; if you look, you'll see evidence of a wave-cut terrace halfway up the mountain slope.

A narrow, one-way loop road winds up the 968-foot mountain to a view that takes in the Adirondacks across Lake Champlain. Hiking trails also ascend the mountain. You can swim and boat on Lake Champlain at nearby **Button Bay State Park.**

Champlain Valley and Lake Champlain, from Mount Philo

Camping

The park has 7 tent sites and 3 lean-to sites. Reservations advised in season; call 888-409-7579. Camping fee.

Mount Philo State Park, Rd. 1, 5425 Mt. Philo Road, Charlotte, VT 05445; 802-425-2390; www.vtstateparks.com/htm/philo.htm

Walden Pond

On Mass. 126 in Concord

■ 411 acres ■ Parking fee (reservations required) ■ Year-round ■ No camping ■ National Historic Landmark ■ Walking, boating, fishing (license required)

Colorful fall foliage along Walden Pond

34

Henry David Thoreau began his two-year experiment in simple living in the woods beside Walden Pond in 1845. He spent $28.12—half on supplies—and built a tidy, one-room wooden house on land loaned to him by Ralph Waldo Emerson, a friend from his days at Harvard College. Thoreau spent his time in Walden Woods reading, studying nature, and gardening. Drawing on experiences during an 1839 trip with his late brother, he drafted his first book, *A Week on the Concord and Merrimack Rivers.* He also made the first accurate survey of the glacially formed pond, where he sometimes sat in a boat playing the flute. Far from being a hermit, Thoreau often entertained visitors at his rustic home and walked the short distance to Concord Center.

In September 1847, Thoreau completed his experiment and returned to his family's home, where he continued to study and write, as well as to lecture audiences throughout New England. *Walden,* the book that describes his life at the pond, was published in 1854. Thoreau died of tuberculosis in 1862, at the age of 44.

What to See and Do

"I went to the woods because I wished to live deliberately, to front only the essential facts of life, and see if I could not learn what it had to teach, and not, when I came to die, discover that I had not lived," Thoreau wrote in *Walden.* While he came to discover life, thousands of visitors now make the short trek from Boston to capture a bit of the aura of one of our first conservationists. Whether you are a Thoreau fan or not, it's hard not to be caught up in the contemplative nature of the park, but be warned that you won't be contemplating alone. For a more peaceful visit, come in the late fall, winter, or early spring, or early in the morning. *(To maintain the peaceful nature of the place, visitors are limited; call the park for reservations.)* At these times, you can sit on a rock with the crystal-clear water lapping at your feet as Thoreau must have done more than 150 years ago. The pond is a popular spot with families, who enjoy shoreside picnic dinners while watching the sun set over the tall, straight pine trees.

> **WRITERS' RESTING PLACE:** A short distance from Walden Pond, in the town of Concord, many of America's best known authors have come to rest at the Sleepy Hollow Cemetery *(Mass. 62)*. In addition to Henry David Thoreau and his family, Ralph Waldo Emerson, Louisa May Alcott, and Nathaniel Hawthorne are buried in the graveyard's Author's Ridge.

Begin your tour of the park with a walk around the pond. On the far side, follow the signs to the site of Thoreau's long-vanished house. A half century ago, an amateur archaeologist located the remnants of the fireplace that had provided the writer with both heat and companionship. A fieldstone marker and plaque mark the spot of one of the most visited former homesites in America.

> **PARK TIP:** *An excellent spot for quiet reflection is Emerson's Cliff, the highest point within the reservation.*

35

A re-creation of Thoreau's tiny house is located near the parking lot across Mass. 126 from the pond. Peer through the windows to see what a cozy little home 28 dollars would buy in 1845. Nearby, a small store sells books and trinkets that commemorate the writer.

For a different perspective, try paddling or fishing the pond. In Thoreau's day the pond didn't hold many fish, but now it's stocked with trout.

At 274 feet above sea level, Emerson's Cliff, located along a trail branching off Esker Trail, is a nice retreat for visitors. Nearby Heywood's Meadow furnishes a wetland habitat home to numerous species such as wood ducks, beavers, and turtles.

In winter, the trails that wind through woods and meadows are popular with cross-country skiers, and ice skaters glide atop the frozen pond.

Walden Pond State Res., Rte. 126, Concord, MA 01742; 978-369-3254; www.mass .gov/dcr

Re-creation of Thoreau's cabin, Walden Pond

Mount Greylock

Accessible via Mass. 2 in North Adams or US 7 in Lanesborough

- 12,500 acres ▪ Year-round, but no road access Nov. to mid-May
- Hiking, skiing, backpacking

Potter Mountain from base of Mount Greylock

"It was such a country as we might see in dreams, with all the delight of paradise," Henry David Thoreau proclaimed upon reaching Mount Greylock's summit in 1844. The 3,491-foot mountain, the highest in Massachusetts, also inspired awe in Ralph Waldo Emerson and Herman Melville. Some believe the snowcapped, rounded mountain was the inspiration for Melville's famed white whale in *Moby Dick.*

Later in the 19th century, concern over heavy logging prompted a group of local residents to purchase land on the summit for recreational purposes. When that venture failed, Mount Greylock was turned over to the Commonwealth. The park celebrated its centennial in 1998.

What to See and Do

Today's visitors normally have a much easier time reaching the summit of Mount Greylock than did Thoreau and his counterparts. In 1906 an auto road that ascended the mountain from the south was completed. Most visitors still begin their trip at the park's southern entrance, where the **Visitor Center** offers tourist information and nature programs.

From the Visitor Center, the road heads up the mountain, passing **Rounds Rock,** where a short trail leads through a field of blueberries to an overlook with views of Connecticut and New York. The road continues up through thick forest to the summit, crowned by an enormous granite tower. The **War Memorial** was erected in 1932 to commemorate those from the state who served in World War I. A dozen lights, together forming the most powerful beacon in Massachusetts, honor fallen heroes. The "perpetual light" was extinguished during World War II so as not to attract enemy aircraft. Today, lights still shine except during bird migrations. A tower observation deck *(mid-May–mid-Oct.)* offers views of five states. Some people think the mountain's name comes from the fact that it's often locked in dark clouds.

PARK TIP: *For a dramatic sunrise or sunset go to Stony Ledge.*

The Civilian Conservation Corps (CCC) completed construction in 1937 of the rustic stone **Bascom Lodge** on the summit. With stone fireplaces, hand-hewn spruce beams, and large porch, the lodge provides a welcome retreat for diners and overnight guests.

From the summit, the auto road snakes down the mountain's steeper north face, passing **The Hopper,** a large basin that resembles a grain hopper, and going into the town of North Adams.

Further Adventures

In addition to the stunning sunrises and sunsets from Stony Ledge, views extend north into Vermont. Take a moment to locate The Hopper, a unique geologic valley surrounded on three sides by steep slopes that support stands of old-growth red spruce forest.

Mount Greylock has 70 miles of hiking, mountain biking, snowmobiling and cross-country skiing trails, including 11.5 miles of the **Appalachian National Scenic Trail.** Departing from the Visitor Center, the easy 2-mile **Bradley Farm Interpretive Trail** cuts through an abandoned pasture. Popular with hikers and skiers, the relatively flat 1.5-mile **CCC Dynamite Trail** skirts Saddleball Mountain, where dynamite boxes discarded by CCC workers in the 1930s can be seen. The strenuous 3.7-mile **Bellows Pipe Trail** is the route Thoreau took to the summit in 1844.

Camping and Lodging

Mount Greylock has 15 primitive tent sites (late May–mid-Oct.) and 7 group sites. For reservations, call 877-422-6762. Camping fee. Bascom Lodge (mid-May–mid-Oct.) accommodates 36 guests; for reservations, call 413-743-1591.

QUICK DESCENT: Mount Greylock was a downhill skiing mecca in the 1930s and '40s, when the Civilian Conservation Corps built a steep run on the mountain's east face. Skiers came from Boston and New York to tackle the bone-rattling Thunderbolt Trail. In 1948, Norwegian Per Klippgen made the 1.6-mile run in a record speed of 2 minutes and 9 seconds. Today the trail is used mostly by hikers, but each year a few daring skiers schuss down the treacherous slope.

37

Mount Greylock State Reservation, P.O. Box 138, Rockwell Rd., Lanesborough, MA 01237; 413-499-4262; www.mass.gov/dcr

Wachusett Mountain

Between Princeton and Westminster, off Mass. 140

- 2,208 acres ■ Year-round, but road closes late Oct. to Mem. Day
- No camping ■ Scenic views ■ Hiking, skiing

Before white settlers arrived in the mid-1600s, the Nipmuc tribe lived "by the great hill," which in Algonquin, their native language, sounds like "wachusett." In 1675, King Philip's War broke out between European settlers and New England Indians, who used the

mountain as a staging area for an attack on the nearby town of Lancaster. Soon after the war ended, much of the Indian land, including Wachusett Mountain, became the property of the Massachusetts colony.

Throughout the 19th century, the mountain's sweeping views lured visitors to its summit, including Henry David Thoreau, who in 1843 walked here from Concord. Grand hotels crowned the summit by the turn of the 20th century, when the state purchased the land for public use. Wachusett became Massachusetts' second state natural reservation in 1900.

Today, a paved road winds to the 2,006-foot mountaintop, which is much less developed than it was a century ago. From here, the city of Boston is sometimes visible nearly 50 miles to the east. Sixty miles to the west,

Princeton nestled at base of Wachusett Mountain

the light atop Mount Greylock shines this far at night.

Nearly 20 miles of hiking trails crisscross the wooded mountain. Try the steep, 1-mile **Mountain House Trail,** which visits the remnants of one of the old summit hostelries. The gentle **Dickens Trail** connects the park with the adjacent Wachusett Meadows Wildlife Sanctuary.

On the mountain's northern slope, the **Wachusett Mountain Ski Area** *(978-464-2300)* has 20 trails, 16 lit for night skiing.

Wachusett Mountain State Reservation, P.O. Box 248, Princeton, MA 01541; 978-464-2987; www.mass.gov/dcr

38

Pilgrim Memorial

Water St., off US 44 in Plymouth

▪ 9 acres ▪ Year-round ▪ No camping ▪ Plymouth Rock

In 1620, English settlers known as the Pilgrims, in search of religious and political freedom, came ashore at Plymouth Harbor and established a small colony. The large granite rock on which they're supposed to have stepped rests along the waterfront beneath a canopy designed by McKim, Mead & White and dedicated in 1921. The *Mayflower II,* a full-size reproduction of the ship that brought the settlers to America, is anchored nearby. "Sailors" and "passengers" in period costumes discuss their journey from England.

    Plimoth Plantation *(Plimoth Plantation Hwy., S of Plymouth. 508-746-1622. April–Nov.; adm. fee),* a detailed re-creation of the Pilgrim settlement and Wompanoag village as it appeared in 1627, sits on a hill overlooking the ocean.

    Directly across Water Street from Plymouth Rock at the top of Cole's Hill stands a bronze statue of Massasoit, leader of the Wompanoag people, who inhabited the area at the time of the Pilgrims' arrival. Nearby you will find a granite sarcophagus containing remains of a number of settlers who died during the first winter and were originally interred in the side of the hill.

Pilgrim Memorial State Park, P.O. Box 66, S. Carver, MA 02366; 508-866-2580; www.mass.gov/dcr/parks/southeast/plgm.htm

39

Skinner

Off Mass. 47, in Hadley

▪ 390 acres ▪ Year-round, but road closes mid-Nov. to mid-April ▪ Adm. fee May through Oct. ▪ No camping ▪ Historic inn

Spectacular views of the Connecticut River Valley have lured visitors to **Mount Holyoke** since the 1800s. In the 1890s, Joseph Allen Skinner bought Summit House *(closed for renovations),* drawing diners and dancers to enjoy the views. When a powerful hurricane destroyed part of the hotel in 1938, Skinner donated it and 375 mountaintop acres to the state. Restored to its early 19th-century appearance, the Victorian inn is open for tours. Visitors can drive or hike up to the 942-foot summit *(mid-April–mid-Nov.).*

    Skinner is located within the nearly 4,000-acre **Holyoke Range State Park** *(413-586-0350),* which stretches the length of the mountain range and offers over 45 miles of hiking, cross-country skiing, and horseback riding trails. In April and September, you can watch migrating hawks as they ride the hot air thermals rising from the mountains.

Skinner State Park, P.O. Box 91, Hadley, MA 01035; 413-586-0350; www.mass.gov/dcr

Fort Adams

3 miles south of downtown Newport on Harrison Ave.

■ 105 acres ■ Year-round ■ No camping ■ Historic fort ■ Yachting museum ■ Sailing center ■ Accessible by water taxi

After the nation's capital was burned during the War of 1812, the military decided a fort was needed to protect the entrance to Narragansett Bay and Newport Harbor. Construction on a fort named after the second president, John Adams, began in 1824 under the direction of

Aerial view of Fort Adams

Lt. Col. Joseph Totten, the foremost military architect of the day. The huge fortification, which was intended to garrison 2,400 men and hold nearly 500 cannon, took 33 years to build. By the time it was completed, the threat of an ocean-borne attack had passed, so the fort was never used to defend the coast's thriving shipping ports.

One way that an invading force could have taken the fort was by tunneling to the base of its walls, then setting charges to take them down. To counter such an attack, a network of underground tunnels was built beneath the fort walls to listen for sounds of enemy digging.

What to See and Do

During the summer, you can tour the imposing structure, with its commanding view of the bay and the posh town of Newport. The fort is operated by the Fort Adams Trust and hosts many special events; see www.fortadams.org.

Newport, long a playground of the rich and a mecca for yachtsmen, is well known for its excellent sailing. In the shadow of the fort, the **Museum of Yachting** *(401-847-1018. Mid-May–Oct.; adm. fee)* houses all kinds of restored yachts and memorabilia that celebrate the sport of sailing. Each year the museum hosts several regattas. The largest, held over Labor Day, is the **Classic Yacht Regatta,** which attracts more than 100 vintage yachts.

If you want to hit the water in your own boat, head over to the state park's sailing center. **Sail Newport** *(401-846-1983. Mem. Day–Columbus Day),* a nonprofit community agency, offers sailboat and windsurfing rentals and instruction. Another community group, **Shake-A-Leg** *(401-849-8898),* provides sailing instruction and boats specially equipped for the physically handicapped.

Located on a hill overlooking the park, the fort's former commanding officer's quarters became the summer home of President Dwight Eisenhower. The two-story clapboard house, built in 1873, is now available for conferences and weddings. Each August, the park hosts the **Newport Jazz and Folk Festivals** *(401-848-5055).*

> PARK TIP: *Don't miss the popular "listening tunnel" tours (fee) under the fortification.*

Nearby Sights

Upon leaving the park, turn right and follow signs for **Ocean Drive,** a scenic roadway designed by Frederick Law Olmsted that follows the shoreline back into Newport. The childhood home of the late Jacqueline Kennedy Onassis, **Hammersmith Farm** *(private),* is located next to the park. The former working farm was the site of Jacqueline and John Kennedy's 1953 wedding reception and later became a summer White House. The drive then passes **Castle Hill Lighthouse** and **Brenton Point State Park** *(401-847-2400),* a popular kite-flying spot with stunning views of the Atlantic Ocean. Follow the Ocean Drive loop to Bellevue Avenue to see the best-known mansions, or "cottages." Built in 1895, Cornelius Vanderbilt's **The Breakers** *(401-847-1000. Call for hours; adm. fee)* is the most lavish estate in town and modeled on an Italian palace. **Rough Point** *(401-849-7300. Call for hours; adm. fee),* built in 1889, was the home of the heiress and philanthropist Doris Duke and contains many collections reflecting her eclectic style.

PINEAPPLE PORT: Travel around Newport and you're sure to notice pineapple motifs and flags decorating a lot of buildings. The tropical fruit became the town's symbol of hospitality in the 18th century. Sea captains brought pineapples home from the West Indies, where they also obtained molasses and sugar to make rum. A captain would place a pineapple on his front steps to indicate that he had returned from his voyage and that his home was welcoming visitors.

For exterior views of the lavish houses, stroll along the 7-mile round-trip **Cliff Walk** *(from Newport Beach to Bailey's Beach),* sandwiched between the estates' well-kept grounds and the pounding ocean surf.

Fort Adams State Park, Harrison Ave., Newport, RI 02840; 401-847-2400 or 401-841-0707; www.riparks.com/fortadams.htm

41

Beavertail

4 miles south of Newport Bridge, on southern tip of Conanicut Island

■ 153 acres ■ Year-round ■ No camping ■ Lighthouse museum
■ Scenic overlooks ■ Biking, fishing (license required for fresh water)

Jutting into Narragansett Bay, this rocky point of land was notorious among early sailors. More than 30 vessels were destroyed or ran aground on what became known as Shipwreck Rock. To aid wary sailors, a lighthouse was built on the rocks in 1749. Even with the aid of the light, however, ships still met with disaster. If you look closely among the jumble of rocks on the east side of the lighthouse, you can find some of the granite blocks that were being carried aboard the *H.F. Payton* when the vessel sank in 1859. The blocks, decorated with flowery designs, sat beneath the shallow water until a 1938 hurricane hurled some of them up on shore. The fierce hurricane also exposed the foundations of the original lighthouse, burned by the British in 1779. The foundations can still be seen across the road from the present-day lighthouse, which stands watch over the crashing waves. Built in 1856, it is now fully automated.

A **lighthouse museum** *(401-423-3270; mid-June–Labor Day)* in the assistant keeper's house recounts the treacherous early days of Beavertail and other Rhode Island lighthouses. It also details the technological changes that have made the seas safer for shipping.

In summer, park naturalists lead walks along the rocky shore. The paved loop road paralleling the shore is popular among cyclists.

Beavertail State Park, c/o Goddard Memorial S.P., 1905 Ives Rd., Warwick, RI 02818; 401-423-9941 (April–Oct.) or 401-884-2010; www.riparks.com/beaverta1.htm

Colt

On Hope Street in Bristol, off R.I. 114

■ 464 acres ■ Year-round ■ No camping ■ Historic farm ■ Open-air chapel and ornamental gardens ■ Biking and horseback-riding trails

Entering Colt Farm, you pass between bronze statues of Jersey bulls perched on marble pedestals—a fitting entrance to a farm that once was centered around cows. Samuel Colt, nephew of the Samuel Colt of revolver fame, began buying up old family farms in Bristol at the turn of the 20th century to create an estate overlooking Narragansett Bay.

A centerpiece of the farm was a heated stone barn with rubber and cork floors, built to house Colt's prized herd of Jersey cows. A grand champion bull, immortalized in the statue on the left side of the farm entrance, was one of Colt's favorites until it killed a farmworker and had to be shot. It is buried behind the stone barn, which still stands.

Colt believed his estate, including a lavish residence and two guest cottages, should be enjoyed by the public, even when he lived there. He had the words "Private Property, Samuel P. Colt, Public Welcome" inscribed in the marble gates.

Summer nature programs focus on the farm's history and its diverse plant and animal life. A 3-mile bike path circles the farm, and the 14.5-mile **East Bay Bike Path** passes through the park.

Colt State Park, Hope St., Bristol, RI 02809; 401-253-7482; www.riparks.com/colt.htm

Goddard Memorial

On Ives Road in Warwick, off US 1

- 489 acres ▪ Year-round ▪ No camping ▪ Hiking and horseback-riding trails ▪ Beach ▪ Performing arts center ▪ Golfing, boating

Once called the "finest example of private forestry in America," this former tree farm now offers spacious lawns, fields, and forested areas with tree varieties from around the world. In 1874, Henry Russell began planting acorns on the sand dunes along Greenwich Bay. After Russell's death, his cousin, Col. Robert Goddard, acquired the land and continued. Goddard built a mansion on the bayfront property. The lower floors housed the country's first insect zoo. Although fire destroyed The Oaks, as the house was known, in 1975, some outbuildings remain. Goddard's family donated the estate to Rhode Island for a park in 1927.

The stable now houses an equestrian center; a rebuilt bathhouse is on the beach. An octagonal building made to hold a carousel, which was moved to the park in 1931, serves as a performing arts center.

Today, 18 miles of horseback-riding and hiking trails wind through thick woods; the information station has trail maps.

Goddard Memorial State Park, 1095 Ives Rd., Warwick, RI 02818; 401-884-2010; www.ri parks.com/goddard.htm

43

Colt State Park along Narragansett Bay

Housatonic Meadows

1 mile north of Conn. 4 on US 7, in Sharon

- 451 acres ▪ Year-round ▪ Fly-fishing (license required)
- Hiking, canoeing

Located in the hilly northwest corner of the state, Housatonic Meadows State Park nestles in the curves of the Housatonic River. The park lies at the northern end of a stretch of US 7 designated as a scenic drive and is surrounded by the upland hills of Housatonic State Forest.

The Civilian Conservation Corps originally developed the park as a recreation site during the Depression. The centerpiece of the park, the Housatonic River, provides a host of aquatic activities. Along the riverbank, copses of evergreens and mixed hardwoods offer shade and solitude to campers and anglers, the swiftly running current invites canoeists, and the hills of the park and adjoining state forest beckon hikers.

What to See and Do

If you like fly-fishing, then Housatonic Meadows is your kind of park—head directly to the water. The **Housatonic River** runs shallow, cold, and swift, ideal for the trout lazing in the eddies of the boulder-strewn river bottom. The stretch of the river in the park is dedicated to catch-and-release fly-fishing. As the park awakens from winter and the spring runoff begins to recede, fly fishermen wade in from the park's shore, gracefully casting their lines in long, looping figure eights. Just as increasingly elongated arcs of fishing line begin to collapse, the angler's fly settles effortlessly on the water—an irresistible lure to trout scanning the passing flow for insects.

COVERED BRIDGES: Three traditional wooden, single-lane covered bridges along US 7 evoke the Yankee character of the towns near Housatonic Meadows. North of the park, the bridge at West Cornwall has spanned the Housatonic River and been in continuous use since 1864. At Kent Falls State Park (860-927-3238), you cross a second bridge on the short walk to a 250-foot-high series of cascades. Just south of the upscale village of Kent, at Bulls Bridge, a third covered bridge crosses the Housatonic, complete with a riverside parking area and short hiking trails. During the spring runoff, the roaring water under the bridge challenges some of New England's best kayakers.

Fly-fishing enthusiasts are not the only ones attracted to the valley's waters. The Housatonic's easy flowing and then roiling rapids with names such as **Pencil Sharpener** attract canoeists and kayakers of varying abilities. The stretch from West Cornwall (5 miles north of park) to the park's southern unit, known as the "covered bridge section," offers Class II to III waves and ledges. Several commercial outfits provide trips along this section of the river. Contact the park for information.

From the western edge of US 7, the park's meadows give way to the forested rise defining the Housatonic Valley. Inviting those who wish to stretch their legs and keep their feet dry, the trailhead of the

2.5-mile **Pine Knob Loop Trail** lies approximately half a mile south of the campground driveway. After fording **Hatch Brook,** follow the loop trail clockwise, climbing steeply uphill among pine trees. The thick underbrush and the running water of the brook seem to absorb all outside sounds as you wind to the trail's high point at **Pine Knob Summit** (1,120 feet).

Catch your breath at the rocky overlook and survey the expansive vista: The river lies at your feet, and beyond rises the stippled terrain of the Litchfield Hills—verdant in spring and summer and a palette of colors in autumn. Joining the Appalachian Trail for half a mile, you come to **Pine Knob** and another river valley before descending back toward the trailhead. After some initial scrambling down small crags, the descent eases and soon picks up the path of a creek, which has worn a flume several hundred feet long as it drops to river level at the meadows.

Camping

The park has 97 tent and RV sites (mid-April–Columbus Day), with showers. Reservations advised; call 877-668-2267. Camping fee.

Housatonic Meadows State Park, 159 Macedonia Brook Rd., Kent, CT 06757; 860-927-3238; www.ct.gov/dep

Daylilies along the Housatonic

Talcott Mountain

1.5 miles east of Conn. 10 on Conn. 185, near Simsbury

- 557 acres ▪ Year-round ▪ No camping ▪ Heublein Tower
- Hiking

Farmland and forest from atop Talcott Mountain

In northern Connecticut, the Farmington River meanders southward, seeking the path of least resistance through the tobacco fields and affluent towns around Hartford. The riverside meadows of the eastern floodplain quickly yield to talus piles below the exposed, greenish black, basaltic rock of Talcott Mountain, which rises dramatically to nearly 1,000 feet. A familiar landmark in the Farmington area interrupts the mountain's wooded ridgeline: Heublein Tower.

In 1914, food and beverage importer Gilbert Heublein constructed a summer home atop Talcott Mountain. Not 30 feet from the house's entrance, the exposed rock of the mountain drops away, providing a bird's-eye view of the valley. Built like a Bavarian alpine castle replete with a 165-foot tower, the house has unparalleled views of five states—an estimated 1,200 square miles. In 1965, the structure and surrounding 557 acres became Talcott Mountain State Park.

What to See and Do

Park along the access road or across Conn. 185 at Penwood State Park and look for the well-marked trailhead of the **Tower Trail.** The

1.25-mile trail delivers you, like Heublein's guests earlier in the 20th century, to the stone patio of Heublein Tower. Beginning with a steep climb, the trail levels off, closely following the mountain edge. Numerous outcrops overlook the river valley, a riot of reds and oranges in autumn. The stunted, gnarled trees along the ridge attest to the regular winds that buffet the rock face and carry the hang gliders you may spy soaring off to the west. Farther ahead, the trail gradually winds away from the cliffs, revealing an unusual pond in Talcott Mountain's upland forest. In sheltered, cooler pockets along the trail you will find stands of white birch among the chestnuts, oaks, ashes, and hemlocks.

A rock outcrop appears to your left as you approach the tower. Covered with lichen and home to Dutchman's-breeches, this damp crag allows close examination of the mountain's basalt cliffs. At **Heublein Tower** you can picnic or rest your legs. Then climb the stairs to the top and enjoy the panoramic view. On a clear day Hartford, Connecticut, and Springfield, Massachusetts, are visible, yet the noise and bustle remain far removed. Watch for turkey vultures and hawks and, in winter, the occasional bald eagle. The tower and house *(call park for tour schedule),* restored to its 1925 condition, showcase the eclectic Victorian and Art Nouveau furnishings and decor of the Heublein family.

Further Adventures

If you have some time and do not mind a more rugged, less traveled path, look for the blue blazes that cross the Tower Trail just north of the tower. Part of a large trail network that stretches throughout the state, the **Metacomet Trail** runs along the park's eastern border and allows a better opportunity to see white-tailed deer, wild turkeys, rabbits, and other wildlife than the more traveled Tower Trail. Listen for the loud, slow knocking of the shy pileated woodpecker. Large for a woodpecker, this variety is reclusive, so stop and look carefully if you hear one at work in the trees. The trail crosses Conn. 185 and continues into adjacent **Penwood State Park** *(860-242-1158).* In addition to the Metacomet Trail, five other hiking trails explore this 767-acre park, including a mile-long **nature trail** with a brochure *(available at park office)* describing the process of succession from meadow to forest.

> **KING PHILIP:** The rocky face of Talcott Mountain contains a shelter used by another, earlier, resident. A hollow in the cliff face north of Heublein Tower is known as King Philip's Cave. Sachem of the Wampanoag Indians and the leader of the Algonquian uprising bearing his name, King Philip is rumored to have watched Simsbury burn on March 26, 1676, from this cave. King Philip's War (1675–76) cost the colonies of southern New England dearly; approximately 2,500 colonists were killed, 13 settlements entirely destroyed, and New England's expansion was forestalled for nearly a century. The war also devastated the Algonquian and destroyed the national identities of Native Americans in the region.

Talcott Mountain State Park, c/o Penwood State Park, Gunn Mill Rd., Bloomfield, CT 06002; 860-242-1158; www.ct.gov/dep

Dinosaur

5 miles south of Hartford, in Rocky Hill

■ 60 acres ■ Year-round ■ No camping ■ North America's largest enclosed dinosaur trackway ■ Footprint casting ■ Nature trails

In 1966, a bulldozer disturbed an ancient lake bed beneath the soil of the Connecticut Valley. Excavations revealed nearly 2,000 dinosaur tracks from the early Jurassic period—200 million years ago. Most of these prints have been reburied to prevent erosion, but the Exhibit Center's geodesic dome protects about 600 tracks. Popular with children—be prepared for screams of "dinosaurs!" punctuated with "oohs" and "ahhs"—the park's exhibits begin at the parking lot. A 92-foot-long time line in the sidewalk leading to the Exhibit Center recounts the geological and paleontological history of the planet. (Man doesn't appear until the last few inches.)

At the **Exhibit Center** *(closed Mon.; adm. fee),* visitors circle a portion of the building's interior along a wide boardwalk just above the exposed bedrock containing the dinosaur tracks. Displays and interactive exhibits along the way explain the geological events that formed the lake and the sequence of events required to preserve the tracks. Other displays discuss how to interpret dinosaur travel behavior from footprint patterns. A 20-foot-long reconstruction of a dilophosaurus and several other period creatures are posed in a diorama depicting the shore of the long dried-up lake.

To make casts of dinosaur tracks in the **outdoor casting area** *(May–Oct.),* bring ten pounds of plaster of paris, a quarter-cup of vegetable oil, a mixing bucket, and cloth rags. Instructions are posted. **Nature trails** traverse swamps, woodlands, and meadows. Among the flora, look for ginkgo trees in fall. As if in fear of a lumbering, leaf-eating apatosaurus, these trees drop all their leaves in a single day.

Dinosaur State Park, 400 West St., Rocky Hill, CT 06067; 860-529-8423; www.dinosaurstatepark.org

Sleeping Giant

East of Conn. 10 on Mt. Carmel Ave., in Hamden

■ 1,500 acres ■ Year-round ■ Parking fee (weekends Mem. Day through Oct.) ■ No camping ■ Hiking, cross-country skiing

Reminiscent of the world in *Gulliver's Travels,* a range of hills north of New Haven creates the silhouette of a distinctly human figure lying on his back. The Sleeping Giant Park Association has labored since 1924 to protect the giant from quarrying and development by donating land to the park. With more than 30 miles of trails, the park provides a wooded retreat for urbanites. The popular 1.6-mile **Tower Path** climbs up the giant's arm and beneath the jutting chin before traversing the length of the torso to a stone tower planted on his left hip. Built during the 1930s, the tower offers views of New Haven County and a pleasant place to picnic.

The 1.5-mile **Nature Trail,** keyed to a pamphlet available at the trailhead, branches off from the Tower Trail. In winter, the park opens several trails for cross-country skiing and snowshoeing. The **Mill River,** a fine place to fish, slices through a grove of pine trees and a picnic area east of the resting giant.

Sleeping Giant State Park, Mt. Carmel Ave., Hamden, CT 06518; 203-789-7498; www.ct.gov/dep

Sleeping Giant's hip

Bluff Point

Depot Road in Groton, 0.5 mile south of US 1

■ 806 acres ■ Year-round ■ No camping ■ Bird-watching ■ Hiking ■ Wetlands and beach

Bluff Point protects a 1.5-mile-long peninsula, one of the last major parcels of undeveloped land on the Connecticut shoreline. Designated as a coastal reserve in 1975, Bluff Point can only be accessed by foot, horseback, or nonmotorized vehicle. A 3-mile **loop trail** allows for walks along rambling stone walls, through wooded stands, and past wetlands to the promontory of **Bluff Point.** Here the surf crashes 40 feet below against the boulders that trail into Long Island Sound. Look westward for the top of Bushy Point, a small island just beyond the peninsula. The erosional forces of the surf and wind now slowly eat away at the beach, a remnant of the Ice Age.

Birders seeking to add shorebirds to their list of sightings flock to Bluff Point. Ospreys nest beside the **Poquonnock River** on the western side of the park, sharing the habitat with smaller feathered friends, including loons and buffleheads that feed in the sea.

Returning you to your car, the trail's eastern leg skirts the stone foundation of the Governor Winthrop residence, built in the early 1700s for the state's first governor and located on a slight rise amid stone walls and an overgrown orchard.

Bluff Point State Park, c/o Fort Trumbull S.P., 90 Walbach St., New London, CT 06320; 860-444-7591; www.ct.gov/dep

MIDDLE ATLANTIC

CANADA
U.S.

N.Y.

Lake Ontario

Hudson River

0 — 100 mi
0 — 200 km

NIAGARA

LETCHWORTH

TAUGHANNOCK FALLS

Albany

PRESQUE ISLE

Lake Erie

ALLEGANY

Allegheny River

RINGWOOD

CONNETQUOT

RICKETTS GLEN

COOK FOREST

HIGH POINT

New York

Pittsburgh

P A .

Harrisburg

Trenton

N. J.

ALLAIRE

ISLAND BEACH

OHIOPYLE

WHITE CLAY CREEK

Philadelphia

GARDEN STATE PKWY.

FORT DELAWARE

GUNPOWDER FALLS

SWALLOW FALLS

PATAPSCO VALLEY

Annapolis

Dover

D E L .

BLACKWATER FALLS

CANAAN VALLEY

Washington, D.C.

M D .

CAPE HENLOPEN

TRAP POND

Charleston

W. VA.

ASSATEAGUE

WATOGA

WESTMORELAND

PIPESTEM

DOUTHAT

V A .

Richmond

BLUE RIDGE PKWY.

FIRST LANDING

FALSE CAPE

GRAYSON HIGHLANDS

PENNSYLVANIA

Ohiopyle
Presque Isle
Cook Forest
Ricketts Glen

NEW YORK

Niagara
Taughannock Falls
Letchworth
Allegany
Connetquot

NEW JERSEY

Island Beach
High Point
Ringwood
Allaire

DELAWARE

Cape Henlopen
Trap Pond
Fort Delaware
White Clay Creek

WEST VIRGINIA

Pipestem Resort
Blackwater Falls
Canaan Valley Resort
Watoga

MARYLAND

Assateague
Gunpowder Falls
Patapsco Valley
Swallow Falls

VIRGINIA

Grayson Highlands
Douthat
False Cape
First Landing
Westmoreland

51

Rhododendron bushes, Grayson Highlands State Park, Virginia

Niagara

20 miles north of Buffalo on Robert Moses Pkwy.

▪ 138 upland acres; 296 underwater acres ▪ Year-round ▪ Entrance fee for Prospect Point ▪ Entrance fee for Goat Island (Mem. Day to Labor Day) ▪ No camping ▪ Boat tour ▪ Discovery Center

Maid of the Mist beneath Horseshoe Falls

Visitors beware: the mist, thunder, breadth, and height of Niagara Falls may overwhelm you. Yet each year millions of people come to Niagara, the oldest state park in America, and one of the most popular. Few parks claim so many attractions in such a small area, but the essence remains the sound and fury of the Niagara River rushing downhill from Lake Erie toward Lake Ontario.

At the heart of this drama lies Goat Island, where the river splits to plunge more than 175 feet over the brinks of Horseshoe, Bridal Veil, and American Falls at a rate of 750,000 gallons per second. Wooded, with landscaped trails and bridges that follow the rapids to islets and all three falls, Goat Island is little more than half a mile long and half as wide. The river and shore west of here lie in Canada, while the Prospect Park section is on the eastern shore, or what is commonly called the "American side."

More than a century ago the park's land belonged to private entrepreneurs

PARK TIP: *To escape the crowds and explore Niagara's unique blend of natural wonders, take the trail through the Goat Island woods.*

who charged money to view the falls, sometimes through fence peepholes. After more than 15 years of lobbying by painter Frederick Church and landscape architect Frederick Law Olmsted, leaders of the "Free Niagara" movement, the state began to buy the land in 1885. Olmsted, who designed Central Park, let his love of trees and water direct his plan for the reservation.

What to See and Do

To avoid crowds, arrive at the falls before 8:30 a.m. or after 5 p.m., travel to the **Prospect Park** section for parking near the Visitor Center or take the American Rapids Bridge to **Goat Island** and park in one of the two lots. Once in the park take the Niagara Scenic Trolleys *(fee)*.

When visiting Goat Island, head to the northwest end, and follow the wooded trails along the rapids and across the footbridge to tiny **Luna Island,** where you can stand and see **Bridal Veil Falls** trailing into the void to your west, **American Falls** fuming to the east, and the *Maid of the Mist* tour boats chugging through the spray below. Next proceed uphill to the **Cave of the Winds** *(fee)* for an 175-foot elevator ride into the gorge and Bridal Veil Falls, where the Hurricane Deck allows you to experience the falls—translation, get wet. Continue counterclockwise around Goat Island to **Terrapin Point,** which juts to the edge of Canada's **Horseshoe Falls.**

You can also overlook the gorge and learn about the falls at the **Visitor Center** and **Discovery Center.** Climb up the **Observation Tower** *(fee),* or book passage on a *Maid of the Mist (fare)* for a journey to the center of Horseshoe Falls.

Niagara Falls State Park, P.O. Box 1132, Niagara Falls, NY 14303; 716-278-1796; www.nysparks.com/parks

Experiencing Bridal Veil Falls

Taughannock Falls

8 miles north of Ithaca on N.Y. 89

■ 783 acres ■ Year-round ■ Parking fee ■ Highest vertical single-drop falls east of the Rockies ■ Rim and gorge trails ■ Summer concerts ■ Swimming, boating, fishing (license required), cross-country skiing

Taughannock Falls in autumn

Viewed from the rim, the gorge—almost 400 feet deep and at least as wide—snakes through the forest plateau west of Cayuga Lake, a landscape ripe for legends about Indian massacres and leaping lovers. Near the head of the gorge, Taughannock Creek cascades in a silver ribbon into the cataract, falling 215 feet—30 feet farther than Niagara. From above you can hear the soft wash and warble of the falls and gaze on a fairyland set amid the hemlocks and white pines.

One legend claims the falls bear the name of a Delaware chieftain who, with 200 warriors, stood his ground along the gorge before a powerful Cayuga cornered and killed him and his men. The falls also tell a vivid tale of geological history. During the last million years, glaciers gouged the troughs that eventually became the Finger Lakes. Taughannock Creek and other streams that flow toward the lakes traveled over sandstone plate until reaching the steepened lake valley walls, which expose a thick layer of underlying shale. As this shale eroded faster than the sandstone, the result was the falls and the gorge, which is deepening to this day.

Modern history begins here after Native Americans vacated the area following the Revolutionary War. Mills grew up along the creek before the Civil War. Taughannock Falls first became a tourist attraction in the 1870s, when steamboats and a railroad started bringing visitors, and Victorian hotels sprouted up. After the hotels failed, the state began acquiring the land for a park in 1925.

What to See and Do

First, stop at the parking lot just off N.Y. 89 and obtain a park brochure and trail map. These will direct you up Park Road to the **Falls Overlook,** the only place you can drive to see the falls.

For a more dramatic perspective on the falls, take the interpretive **Gorge Trail,** an easy 1.5-mile round-trip hike leading to the base of the falls. This trail begins at the gorge parking lot and heads west along the creek bed. Walking along, note how the sky seems to shrink overhead as the canyon walls rise and the gorge fills with a mix of tall hemlocks, maples, birches, and locusts. The rush of the stream masks the sound of the falls almost until you break from the forest and cross a footbridge. Now the falls tower ahead, exhaling mist. At trail's end, you stand in what has been called a natural amphitheater, where the falls spew from a frowning lip and crash into a basin.

Adventurers with more time and plenty of stamina should tackle the **Rim Trail** (closed in winter), which loops about 2.6 miles around the gorge. This is a steep walk on undulating trails; be prepared with the proper footgear and a supply of water. After your workout, or if you just want to take it easy and catch a breeze off **Cayuga Lake,** head to the beach for a swim or some sunning.

Camping and Lodging

Taughannock has 76 tent and RV sites, with shower facilities; 16 cabins. Late March–mid-Oct. Reservations advised in season; call 800-456-2267. Camping fee.

Taughannock Falls State Park, P.O. Box 1055, Trumansburg, NY 14886; 607-387-6739; www.nysparks.com/parks

TAUGHANNOCK MONSTER: In 1879 workmen near the Taughannock House resort unearthed a "stone man" from under the driveway. Weighing 800 pounds, with a height of nearly 7 feet and a shoulder span of 18 inches, the "fossil" drew large crowds who paid 25 cents a look at what was dubbed the Taughannock Giant. Eventually, word got out that the hotel owner had made the giant from a mixture of ox blood, sugar, iron filings, sand, eggs, sulfur, salt, and phosphorous, baked in an oven.

Letchworth

40 miles south of Rochester off I-390, near Mount Morris

▪ 14,350 acres ▪ Year-round ▪ Entrance fee (Mem. Day through Oct., and weekends April, May, Nov., and late Dec. through Feb.) ▪ Bird conservation area ▪ Museum ▪ Historic inn ▪ White-water rafting ▪ Hot-air balloon rides ▪ Hiking, swimming, horseback riding, cross-country skiing ▪ Hunting, fishing (license required for both)

Late on any given sunny afternoon, from one of the many lookouts over the Big Bend on the Genesee River Gorge, you can watch the shadow of the western rim flood across the canyon floor, cross the river, and rise 600 feet up the eastern wall to announce dusk. In fall, the red, yellow, and orange leaves of maples, oaks, and beeches sway in the canyon drafts, painting the landscape with shifting colors. This is probably the East's most auto-accessible gorge park, as evidenced by the number of visitors on peak-color weekends. But on a weekday, the shadows, trees, and waterfalls seem to exist for you alone.

After millions of years of work, the swift and sometimes swollen Genesee River continues carving the 17-mile-long, 500-foot-deep gorge, which has been called the Grand Canyon of the East and stands at the heart of Letchworth State Park. The 1797 Treaty of Big Tree established reservations for the Seneca in this region that included areas now part of the park. Later, in 1859, nature lover and Native American admirer William Pryor Letchworth acquired the

October view from Inspiration Point

first parcel of what was to become the 1,000-acre centerpiece of this long, narrow park shouldering the gorge. He also renovated and expanded a building for his home. In 1907 he donated his property for the park.

PARK TIP: *The best spot to commune with nature and spot deer and other wildlife is along Trail 2 from Council Grounds to the High Bridge.*

What to See and Do

The most dramatic way to see Letchworth is to enter from the north; be sure to pick up a park map at the entrance. Your first stop is the **Mount Morris Dam Overlook,** where you can view the gorge twisting to the south. The steep, tall dam may look misplaced in the nearly dry gorge—unless you are here during winter thaws or spring runoff. From here, continue south along Park Road, stopping along the way at such overlooks as **Hogs Back,** where the river makes a horseshoe. If you want to feel your heart pound, check out the views of the **Big Bend** from the **Great Bend** and **Archery Field vistas.** On calm evenings, you are likely to see deer in the cornfields by Castile Entrance. The **William Pryor Letchworth Museum** *(mid-May–Oct.; donation)* houses Letchworth's collection of Native American and pioneer artifacts. Across the road his former home, now the **Glen Iris Inn,** offers fine dining. On a nearby hillside stands the **Seneca Council House,** the oldest known council house east of the Mississippi.

> **GENESEE WHITE WOMAN:** Mary Jemison was born at sea in 1743, as her family made its way to settle in the wilds of Pennsylvania. In 1758, during the French and Indian War, Delaware Indians killed her family and kidnapped her. She was adopted by the Seneca and chose to remain with them. When the 1797 Treaty of Big Tree established Seneca reservations, Mary was given 18,000 acres of her own land, near the part of the gorge called Gardeau, now part of Letchworth State Park. Her grave lies at the Seneca Council Grounds, near the inn.

57

Don't miss the drive down into the steep gorge to the **Middle Falls Area.** Here you can park near the river and walk an easy half-mile section of the **Gorge Trail.** The trail links 107-foot **Middle Falls** with **Upper Falls,** which tumble 70 feet from beneath a soaring railroad trestle. Those with more time and energy can follow this sometimes steep trail downstream to the **Lower Falls Bridge** and beyond for 5 miles.

Camping and Lodging

Letchworth has 270 tent or RV sites (mid-May–mid-Oct.), with showers; 82 cabins (some year-round). Reservations advised in season; call 800-456-2267. Camping fee. The Glen Iris Inn offers 15 rooms, and meals are available; call 585-493-2622.

Letchworth State Park, Castile, NY 14427; 585-493-3600; www.nysparks.com/parks

Allegany

7 miles south of Salamanca, off I-86

Thunder Rocks

- 65,556 acres - Year-round - Entrance fee
- 2,200-foot peaks
- Hiking, boating, biking, cross-country skiing, horseback riding, snowmobiling

It's tempting to lose yourself among the steep valleys, thick forest, and stream-carved mountains of this park. Popular with campers and leaf peepers, Allegany is actually more dramatic in winter, when snow squalls sweep through the hollows, leaving fresh powder for skiers, snowmobilers, and alpine romantics.

Since its origins in 1921, the park has shared a common border with the Seneca Reservation. Their struggle against the federal government's nearby Kinzua Dam Project is reported at the **Seneca-Iroquois National Museum** *(794-814 Broad St. 716-945-1738. Feb.–Dec.; adm. fee),* just outside the park in Salamanca.

PARK TIP: *Visit Bridal Falls after a good rain and enjoy the music of the rushing waters.*

The park's best views come from the **Stone Tower** at the Summit Cabin Area, near the north entrance. After a stop here, head south for the 25-mile auto tour. Driving in a clockwise direction, continue south on Park Route 2 and stop at **Thunder Rocks** to see the house-size boulders. Then your route leads through oil and gas fields along the state border, past **Science Lake,** and on to the **Old Quaker Store Museum,** where exhibits highlight park history. On your way back north, visit **Stony Brook Overlook** for autumnal vistas, and **Big Basin** for 220-year-old hemlocks.

If you have more time, consider a swim at **Quaker Lake,** renting a boat at **Red House Lake,** or hiking the popular 1.5-mile round-trip **Bear Caves Trail.** There are 45 miles of equestrian trails, used for snowmobiling when the snow falls. Also in winter, skiers will find excellent trails and rentals.

Camping and Lodging

The park has 423 tent and RV sites, with showers; 10 full-service cottages; 364 cabins (some open for year-round use). Reservations advised in season; call 800-456-2267. Camping fee.

Allegany State Park, 2373 ASP Rte. 1, Suite 3, Salamanca, NY 14779; 716-354-9121; www.nysparks.com/parks

58

Connetquot

On N.Y. 27 (Sunrise Hwy.), near Oakdale

- 3,473 acres ▪ Year-round ▪ Entrance fee ▪ Access by permit only
- No pets ▪ No camping ▪ Gristmill and tavern ▪ Trout hatchery
- Stocked streams ▪ Hiking, fly-fishing (license required)

An oasis of wetlands, meandering trout streams, and pine-barren forest in the middle of suburban Long Island, Connetquot preserves what F. Scott Fitzgerald called the "old island here that flowered once for Dutch sailors' eyes—a fresh, green breast of the new world." To visit Connetquot is to enter a sanctuary with deer, hawks, owls, eastern bluebirds, brown creepers, and winter wrens. Anglers share the fishing with ospreys and great blue herons.

The site of an 18th-century gristmill and the Snedecor Tavern (circa 1820), **Connetquot River** has long been valued for its resources and beauty. In 1866 a group of sportsmen formed a club to maintain the river area for the propagation of game birds, fish, and animals, and the State Park Service has continued the tradition since 1973.

Only visitors over 60 years old or those with handicaps can drive to the hatchery, so come prepared to walk. Start by the millpond dam at **Snedecor Tavern,** enlarged as the sportsman's club, and the **Nicoll Gristmill.** The buildings *(631-581-1072. By appointment)* house exhibits on milling, hunting, and fishing, as well as mounted animals.

If you have the time for an easy 2-mile walk, follow the **Yellow Trail** through the woods to the trout hatchery. From here, cross the bridge and return along the river and pond via the **Red Trail.** While walking the trails, keep an eye out for trailing arbutus and orchids in their natural habitat. For information on nature programs, call 631-581-1072.

The park requires a permit, obtained in advance, for hikers (good for one year), and reservations for fishing sites and boats. Requests should be sent to the address below; include your name, address, telephone number, and number of people to be included in the permit.

Connetquot River State Park Preserve, P.O. Box 505, Oakdale, NY 11769; 631-581-1005; www.nysparks.com/parks

59

Fishing the Connetquot River

Ohiopyle

15 miles west of Uniontown on Pa. 381

■ 20,499 acres ■ Year-round ■ Wild river gorge ■ Ferncliff Natural Area ■ White-water rafting ■ Hiking, biking ■ Hunting, fishing (license required for both) ■ Snowmobiling, horseback riding, cross-country skiing ■ Rock climbing

Youghiogheny River

The Native American word *ohiopehhile,* meaning "white, frothy water," probably gave this park and the village it surrounds their names. They stand at the gateway to the rugged Laurel Mountains, where the Youghiogheny River has carved a 1,700-foot-deep gorge. Within the park, thick oak-and-maple forest rises on both sides of the "Yough" (yock), surrounding the gorge for more than 14 miles. The park's focal point is 20-foot Ohiopyle Falls, which spews foam and spray at the heart of the park and village, where the river carves a horseshoe through the gorge.

Across the river, high above the gorge on a peninsula formed by the bend in the river, stands Ferncliff Natural Area, a designated National Natural Landmark with scenic overlooks and nature trails. More than 100,000 white-water boaters a year launch here, making the Yough one of the most heavily used recreational rivers in the country.

PARK TIP: *For great views of the "Yough," hop on the bike trail at the train station.*

Although the state only began acquiring parklands here in the mid-1960s, Ohiopyle has been well known through the ages. Long ago the Delaware, Shawnee, and Iroquois used the area as a hunting ground. And in 1754, before the French and Indian War, George Washington came down the Yough looking for a water route to the Forks of the Ohio (near present-day Pittsburgh), but he turned back at the falls. In the 19th century, the Baltimore & Ohio Railroad followed Washington's path through the gorge to reach Pittsburgh and the West. By the beginning of the 20th century, the railroad was running summer excursion trains to the small resort that developed here.

What to See and Do

Start your visit at the well-marked **Visitor Center** in the train station on the north side of Ohiopyle village. Here pick up a map, brochures about park and local attractions, and information on river and mountain-bike outfitters.

The **Great Allegheny Bike Trail** going north toward Connellsville from the Visitor Center crosses two old train bridges that span the Youghiogheny River. Take a rest at both spots for beautiful and expansive views of the river.

If you are on a tight schedule, drive straight to **Ohiopyle Falls.** The falls span the river, causing clouds of mist, rainbows, and an eerie rumble. Take pictures from the observation decks or stroll along the river. Outfitters operate across the street; you can watch them launch raft loads of life-jacketed paddlers onto the Lower Yough from the ramp just downstream of the falls. To view the first set of rapids, follow the **Meadow Run Trail** to **Entrance Rapids.**

For a different view of the gorge, drive north across the bridge on Pa. 381 to **Ferncliff Natural Area.** Short, easy nature trails follow

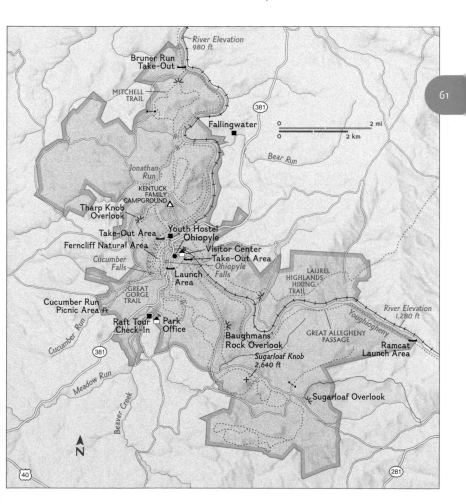

the rim of the Ferncliff Peninsula and afford bird's-eye vistas of the falls, gorge, and river runners careening through six sets of rapids. In June the trails bloom with rhododendron, mountain laurel, and partridge berry.

If you have time, head south to the top of **Cucumber Run,** where in April and May the ravine bursts forth in blankets of wildflowers, joined by blooming rhododendron in June. Walk the half-mile **Great Gorge Trail** to **Cucumber Falls,** or drive to a nearby lot. Cap your day with a hike or drive up to **Tharp Knob Overlook** to watch the sun set on the gorge.

Further Adventures

If day hikes are your thing, the park has 85 miles of trails for you to choose from. Both the **Sugarloaf Trail** and the **Baughman Trail** climb up about 900 feet, over 3.5 miles, through the woods from the gorge to the mountain-biking and snowmobile area near **Sugarloaf Knob.** If you are a serious backpacker, you can head north for 70 miles along the **Laurel Highlands Hiking Trail,** which starts here.

Hike or bike the popular **Great Allegheny Passage** that passes through the park as it follows an abandoned railroad bed paralleling the river. Mountain biking along part of the 28 miles of this trail is the best way to lose yourself to the power of the place. *(Bike rentals are available in Ohiopyle village.)*

The 9-mile **Middle Yough** upstream from the village has excellent canoeing water with some Class I and II white water. The Class III and IV rapids of the **Lower Yough,** a 7.5-mile segment below the village, challenge enthusiasts in white-water rafts, kayaks, and decked canoes. The popularity of the Lower Yough means all boaters must have a launch permit and shuttle token from April through mid-October. Reservations are recommended *(call 888-727-2757)* on weekends and holidays. *Note: The Lower Yough can be dangerous. Boaters without the services of one of the four authorized park outfitters should be experienced paddlers with proper equipment and thorough knowledge of the area.*

Camping and Lodging

The park has 212 tent or RV sites (March through antlerless deer season in late fall), with shower facilities; 4 camping cottages, 4 yurts, and 3 wall-tent sites. Call 888-727-2757 for reservations. Camping fee.

Ohiopyle State Park, P.O. Box 105, Ohiopyle, PA 15470; 724-329-8591; www.dcnr.state.pa.us/stateparks /parks/ohiopyle.aspx

FALLINGWATER: Architect Frank Lloyd Wright caught the drama of the Laurel Highlands forest gorges and rushing water within the design of his 1936 masterpiece, Fallingwater *(Pa. 381, 2 miles N of Ohiopyle. 724-329-8501. April–mid-Nov. Tues.–Sun.; adm. fee).* Acclaimed by the American Institute of Architects as the "best all-time work of American architecture," Fallingwater employs local stone, poured concrete, glass walls, and cantilever construction to blend with the wooded hillside and thrust above the waterfalls of Bear Run.

Presque Isle

4 miles west of downtown Erie on Pa. 832

■ 3,200 acres ■ Year-round ■ No camping ■ Coastal wilderness
■ Bird-watching ■ Boat tours ■ Swimming, boating, hiking, bicycling,
inline skating, ice skating, cross-country skiing ■ Hunting, fishing
(licenses required)

This 7-mile-long sand spit rises above the waves of Lake Erie just
brushing the lake's south shore. Built by the action of wind and waves,
Presque Isle is here because of a ridge of sediment deposited as a
glacial moraine 11,000 years ago. Since that time, breezes and surf
have driven the peninsula ever eastward. Home to green herons, bald
eagles, and American redstarts, Presque Isle has been identified as one
of the best birding areas in America.

According to legends of the Eriez Indians, who first inhabited
the south shore of Lake Erie, Presque Isle forms the silhouette of the
left arm of the Great Spirit who reached into the lake to shelter the
Eriez from a storm.

In the 1720s, French explorers named the land Presque Isle,
meaning "nearly an island." Later, during the War of 1812, Misery
Bay served as the home of Commodore Oliver Perry's fleet. His brig
Niagara is moored across Presque Isle Bay from the park at the **Erie
Maritime Museum** *(814-452-2744; Adm. fee)* near Dobbins Landing
in Erie. Recognizing the undeveloped peninsula's value as a wildlife
habitat and recreation area, the state designated the land a state park
and began developing it
during the 1920s.

63

What to See and Do

With camping facilities
nearby, Presque Isle lures
weekend visitors again
and again. Before start-
ing, stop at the **Tom Ridge
Environmental Center
(TREC)** atop the hill outside the entrance. Here
you can see interactive
exhibits that showcase
Presque Isle history,
ecosystems, and wildlife;
view a large-format film
in the Big Green Screen
Theatre; or take in spec-
tacular views from the
observation tower. Park
maps and information on
educational programs are
also available.

Cottonwoods along Lake Erie

"WE HAVE MET THE ENEMY..."
On Sept. 10, 1813, Commodore Perry and his fleet of nine ships defeated the British near Sandusky, Ohio. A turning point in British control of the Lakes region, the battle cost Perry 123 casualties and disabled his flagship, the *Lawrence*. Undaunted, Perry transferred to the brig *Niagara*, raised his "Don't Give Up the Ship" battle flag, and fought on. Afterward he wrote his famous dispatch to Gen. William Henry Harrison: "We have met the enemy and they are ours."

Inquire about the park's popular warm-weather attraction—the free pontoon boat tour *(Mem. Day–Labor Day)*. It departs from East Boat Livery landing and provides a 45-minute narration as it cruises through inland ponds. Along the way you may see wildlife such as great blue herons, painted turtles, muskrats, beavers, and deer.

Walk choices range from the 13.5-mile **Karl Boyes Multi-Purpose Trail** to the 1.25-mile **Sidewalk Trail** leading from the boat livery on Misery Bay to the lakeside and 74-foot-tall **Presque Isle Lighthouse.** Combine the pontoon boat tour with the Sidewalk to observe ecological zones ranging from marsh to climax forest to beaches.

Discover the savannah among the groves and forest as you walk along **Dead Pond Trail.** Here, the pines suddenly give way to a large open grassland with a sandy trail crossing it. The colored grasses make for a spectacular fall hike. The tracks and scat of coyotes indicate their presence in this habitat, but they are elusive and seldom seen by humans. (To reach the grasslands, hike on the Dead Pond Trail for about a mile from the trailhead or for a shorter route, hike in from B-Trail and make a left onto Dead Pond Trail where a short walk takes you to the savannah.)

Don't miss the lake vistas from the **Sunset Point** and **Budny Beach** shores at the northeast end of the park. From here, you can walk the easy 1.5-mile **Gull Point Trail** loop, which stops at an observation platform overlooking the restricted management area of Gull Point. From this vantage point, birders can spot concentrations of migratory shorebirds and waterfowl, including wood ducks and tundra swans, as well as easily witness migrating falcons preying on the shorebirds.

If you have the time for some serious leisure, 11 beaches beckon you for a lakeside picnic or a swim *(swimming permitted Mem. Day–Labor Day)*. Or launch your boat and tie up at the nearly 500-slip **Presque Isle Marina.** If you didn't bring your own, motorboat, pontoon boat, kayak, and canoe rentals are available at the Livery

PARK TIP: *Discover the surprising color of the grasslands or savannah area along Dead Pond Trail.*

(814-838-3938. Mem. Day–Labor Day). For information on scenic boat tours, call 800-988-5780.

You can end your visit with a trip across the bay via the ferry from the Waterworks ferry dock *(Mem. Day–Labor Day. Call the park or stop by the Tom Ridge Environmental Center for schedule. Fare),* or visit the new bike rental facility.

Presque Isle State Park, 301 Peninsula Dr., Ste. 1, Erie, PA 16505; 814-833-7424; www.dcnr.state.pa.us/stateparks/parks/presqueisle.aspx

Cook Forest

12 miles north of I-80/Brookville on Pa. 36

- 8,500 acres ▪ Year-round ▪ Sawmill Craft Center and Theater
- Canoeing, tubing, hiking, swimming, cross-country skiing
- Fishing, hunting (license required for both)

Picture 200-foot-tall stands of virgin timber on gentle slopes, and you will grasp the lure of Cook Forest and how it came to be nicknamed the Black Forest of Pennsylvania. The first Pennsylvania state park acquired to preserve a natural landmark, Cook Forest lies south of the Allegheny National Forest, where an upheaval of the Earth's crust created open valleys and rounded hills reaching 1,600 feet. Once a primary means of shipping rafts of timber south to Pittsburgh, the shallow Clarion River has carved the valley that bounds the park to the east.

In the 1800s, the need for lumber made Pennsylvania the largest producing state in the Union. The boom persisted into the 20th century, when most stands of old-growth forest had been cleared from the northern highlands. Beginning in 1910, environmentalists bent on saving the remains of these woods campaigned to buy the forest from the A. Cook Sons lumber company on the grounds that "the East possesses few scenes more impressive than this magnificent area of primeval white pine surrounded by giant hemlocks and hardwoods." In 1927 Cook Forest became a state park, and by 1934 President Roosevelt's Civilian

Forest Cathedral

Conservation Corps had set up camp here and begun building roads, trails, and cabins. They were also working to save the giant white pines from blister rust, a serious fungal disease.

What to See and Do

Cook Forest is a place to feel humble in the face of nature. If you only have a short time, go straight to the **Log Cabin Inn Environmental Learning Center** (*Mem. Day–Labor Day*) and pick up a park map. A mile of easy walking will take you to the heart of the **National Natural Landmark old-growth forest.** Following the **Longfellow Trail** (1.2 miles one way) from the Learning Center, you will traverse a forest floor of pine needles. Giant hemlocks and white pines loom above the gently sloping trail until you arrive at a glade known as the **Forest Cathedral.** A canopy of eastern hemlock and white pine more than 300 years old, this is a place where you hear nothing but the songs of wind and bird.

PARK TIP: *The Longfellow Trail is a must for all who visit the Forest Cathedral National Natural Landmark.*

Next, pause at the **Sawmill Craft Center and Theater** about a half-mile west of the Learning Center. Here, craftspeople display and sell their creations and offer demonstrations and classes in arts ranging from bird carving to quilting. The theater hosts plays and musicals each weekend of the summer.

Don't miss a trip through the woods on **Forest Drive** as it swings northeast, joins Coleman Run Road, and meets the **Clarion River.** The river got its name from surveyors in 1817, who thought "the ripple of the river sounds like a distant clarion," or trumpet call. Your drive follows this slow-moving river as it twists south for 5 miles to the park office and Cooksburg Bridge. Picnickers, anglers, waders, and canoeists love this section of the park. For those so inclined, outfitters in Cooksburg can supply canoes (*ask park for information*).

Before you leave, climb up the **Cook Forest Fire Tower** (Fire Tower Rd.) for photographs of the Clarion River Valley from 1,600 feet, the park's highest point. Here at **Seneca Point** you will also see a site where erosion has exposed beds of massive sedimentary rocks as large as houses.

Camping and Lodging

Ridge Camp has 210 tent or RV sites (mid-April–mid-Dec.), with shower facilities; 18 rustic cabins (mid-April–mid-Dec.). For reservations call 888-727-2757. Camping fee.

Cook Forest State Park, P.O. Box 120, Cooksburg, PA 16217; 814-744-8407; www.cookforest.com

HOW MUCH WOOD CAN A WOODHICK LOG? More than 100 years ago, when A. Cook Sons lumber company ruled over the Clarion Valley, the woods echoed with the sighs of saws and thousands of men—many unemployed Civil War veterans—who sought a living as "woodhicks," or loggers. Life in the logging camps began at 5 a.m. and ended at 9 p.m. Men worked six days a week, 11 hours a day. But room and board were free, and a man could earn $1.50 a day . . . if he didn't get his head snapped off by a hemlock bucking as it fell.

Ricketts Glen

30 miles north of Bloomsburg on Pa. 487

- 13,050 acres
- Year-round ▪ Glens
- Waterfalls ▪ Giant trees ▪ Lake
- Fishing (license required), boating, swimming, hiking, cross-country skiing

Stairway to Harrison Wright Falls

Ricketts Glen, an undiscovered gem of Pennsylvania parks, is, from the south, recognizable by its escarpment spanning part of the Allegheny Front and rising up to 1,200 feet above the surrounding hills. Here you find **Lake Jean** and the **Glens Natural Area,** where waterfalls and giant trees epitomize the "forest primeval." The park is named for former owner Col. Robert Bruce Ricketts, who fought at the Battle of Gettysburg.

To visit beautiful **Adams Falls,** pick up a map at the park office and follow Pa. 487 and Pa. 118 to the south side of the park. The falls are near the parking lot. Most sites, however, are not this easy to reach. For the full effect of the glen area, you need the stamina to hike steep trails for a minimum of 3 miles, as they follow **Kitchen Creek**'s 1,000-foot plunge.

Start south of the park office and take the **Falls Trail** through Ganoga Glen to 94-foot **Ganoga Falls,** the highest in the park. Along the way, you will pass a score of named cascades as you descend among giant pines, hemlocks, and oaks. Where the creek branches join at Waters Meet to form **Ricketts Glen,** the trees, some older than 500 years, can span 4 feet in diameter. The return climb is equally rewarding, as it loops through **Glen Leigh** and skirts eight more falls.

Lake Jean offers quieter waters, where you can bring your own registered nonpowered or electric-powered boats, rent a canoe or a rowboat lakeside, or swim at the beach *(Mem. Day–mid-Sept.).*

Camping and Lodging

There are 120 tent or trailer sites, with showers, and 10 cabins. Cabins and some campsites available year-round. Walk-ins available, but reservations strongly recommended at 888-727-2757. Camping fee.

Ricketts Glen State Park, 695 State Route 487, Benton, PA 17814; 570-477-5675; www.dcnr.state.pa.us/stateparks/parks/rickettsglen.aspx

67

Island Beach

On N.J. 35, in Seaside Park

- 3,000 acres ■ Year-round ■ Entrance fee ■ No camping ■ Barrier island ■ Surf fishing ■ Bird-watching ■ Swimming, canoeing, kayaking

Goldenrod and dune grasses

This protected place on the Jersey Shore thoroughly transports you back to a time before humans ruled the world. The last significant remnant of the barrier island ecosystem that once existed along more than 150 miles of the state's Atlantic coast, Island Beach stands as an oasis amid massive coastal development. The park stretches for more than 9 miles, sandwiched between the Atlantic Ocean and Barnegat Bay, a collage of white beaches, dunes, and marsh constituting the southern tip of the barrier island that ends at Barnegat Inlet.

While summer heat draws crowds of bathers, the guarded bathing area covers less than a mile of the beach, leaving the rest of the park to wildlife, surf fishermen, beach walkers, and birders drawn to observe the large populations of migratory fowl as well as the state's largest osprey colony.

For centuries, Island Beach has defied human encroachment. Henry Hudson steered clear of the island, noting large shoals in his log of 1609. In 1735 the British king ceded a large holding, including Island Beach, to the First Earl of Sterling … who kept his distance. During the 19th century, a few squatters shared the island with the U.S. Life Saving Service. Then, in 1926, Andrew Carnegie's partner, Henry C. Phipps, purchased the land with the intent of developing an exclusive resort. After Phipps built three model homes, the Depression brought an end to that dream. The state bought the property in 1953, opened the park in 1959, and today Ocean House, in the Northern Natural Area, serves as summer residence for the governor of New Jersey.

> FLYING LITMUS TEST: Because ospreys are at the top of the food chain in estuaries such as Barnegat Bay, their prevalence correlates with the health of the environment. Ospreys suffer from poor reproductive rates because they feed on fish contaminated by chemical pollutants. Before the elimination of DDT, Island Beach's osprey population had dwindled to five nesting pairs. Today, the Sedge Islands are home to 30 nesting pairs, and the fishing is good.

What to See and Do

Make your first stop the **Aeolium Nature Center** *(732-793-1698)*, about a mile inside the park entrance. Here, pick up a map and study the host of brochures highlighting park flora, fauna, geology, and the various special programs. If you are lucky enough to visit during July or August, or on a weekend in spring or fall, someone at the center will tell you how to join one of the naturalist-guided birding and marine life tours. Naturalists also lead free canoe tours *(Mem. Day–Labor Day Tues., Thurs., & Sun.)* of the Sedge Islands, where the ospreys nest and fish. Space on these three-hour tours is limited, so call ahead for reservations.

If you don't have time for a canoe tour, drive to the south end of the park and walk the short **Bird Blind Trail** through the bayberry until you reach the blind. You might see bold red foxes along the way, and this is the best place in the park to watch nesting and fishing ospreys. And, when the marigolds bloom here in early September, waves of migrating monarch butterflies arrive to feast.

For a dramatic beach hike, head south from the parking lot in the Southern Natural Area to **Barnegat Inlet.** The 1.5-mile trek through soft, white sand lands you in view of the 172-foot-high **Barnegat Lighthouse** across the inlet, marking treacherous shoals offshore. If you come here during the winter, expect to see gray and harbor seals. Dolphins arrive to feed when the herring run in May.

Surf anglers enjoy the wild beaches of the Northern Natural Area, where you can fish for striped bass right outside the governor's front door.

Island Beach State Park, P.O. Box 37, Seaside Park, NJ 08752; 732-793-0506; www.njparksandforests.org/parks/island.html

High Point

On N.J. 23, in Sussex

■ 15,000 acres ■ Year-round ■ Entrance fee (Mem. Day to Labor Day)
■ Veterans Memorial ■ Appalachian Trail ■ Bird-watching ■ Hiking,
swimming, fishing (license required), nonmotorized boating,
cross-country skiing

On the way to High Point

The crown jewel of the Delaware Water Gap region, High Point
State Park sits in the northwest corner of the state atop the tallest
knob in New Jersey (1,803 feet), attracting leaf peepers, hikers, cross-
country skiers, migrating birds, and bears. On a clear day you can
see 220-foot High Point Monument from 40 to 50 miles away, towering like the Bunker Hill Monument above the forest on Kittatinny
Ridge. And from the monument's observation deck you can see even

farther … to the steep Catskill Mountains in the north and the Pocono plateau to the west. But it's the view to the south that takes some people's breath away. Here, where the Delaware River flows through a wide river valley for more than 40 miles, state and federal lands on both sides preserve an unbroken swath of hardwood forest filling hundreds of square miles.

High Point had its first serious fling with humans in 1890, when the plush High Point Inn was developed on the shores of Lake Marcia. But by 1909 the resort had gone bankrupt and Col. Anthony Kuser picked up the mortgage, making High Point his summer home before handing the property over to the state in the 1920s.

What to See and Do

High Point attracts a crowd each October to traverse its forest, alive with autumn colors of maple, oak, and sassafras. Whether or not leaf-peeping is your reason for visiting, stop at the **park office** on the south side of N.J. 23 and pick up current maps, trail guides, and brochures. Then head north on **Scenic Drive** to the **High Point Monument,** dedicated to New Jersey war heroes. The 1930s monument is recently renovated and has spectacular views.

With a little more time for nature, take the easy 2.5-mile **Cedar Swamp Trail** from the end of Cedar Swamp Road. This loop leads through the boggy remains of a 30-acre glacial lake, where you find a rare upland growth of Atlantic white cedar. The trail guide *(available at the park office)* will tell you what you are seeing, and you can enjoy a rest on the benches along the way and, in spring, listen to the songs of migrating warblers. Deer, porcupines, and black bears pass this way, too, so keep your eyes open.

The 4.5-mile **Iris Trail** is the first choice of many day hikers. Many backpackers join the Appalachian Trail in the park, following it 42 miles south to the Water Gap. Take the Appalachian Trail to the north through hemlock gorges into old agricultural fields for views of the surrounding countryside and the High Point Monument off in the distance. Each winter, ski and snowshoe rentals, and some 10 miles of groomed trails, draw cross-country skiers and snowshoers who later lounge before the fire in the lodge at Lake Marcia. This is also a popular spot for swimmers during the summer.

PARK TIP: *The sunsets and western view are unmatched where the short, but steep, Blue Dot Trail tops the ridge.*

Camping and Lodging

The park has 50 tent sites (April–Oct.), showers available. Two group sites, 2 family cabins, and a group cabin are open mid-May to mid-Oct. Reservations accepted up to 11 months in advance; call 973-875-4800. Camping fee.

High Point State Park, 1480 N.J. 23, Sussex, NJ 07461; 973-875-4800; www.njparksandforests.org/parks/highpoint.html

71

Ringwood

Off County Rd. 511, in Ringwood

- 6,196 acres ▪ Year-round ▪ Vehicle fee (Mem. Day to Labor Day)
- No camping ▪ Botanical gardens ▪ Historic manors ▪ Hiking, boating ▪ Hunting, fishing (license required for both)

Winter at Ringwood Manor

Driving up the winding road toward the stone tower and Gothic windows of Skylands Manor, visitors may have the sense of venturing into the threshold of novelist Emily Brontë's *Wuthering Heights.* Thickly wooded, rugged, and windy, the terrain of the Ramapo Mountains looks like Brontë's Yorkshire. And like the setting for Brontë's novel, Ringwood State Park defines itself by the juxtaposition of two manors divided by a wilderness as well as social ranking. Beginning in 1936, the estates began a slow merger to form this unusual park, which includes the 96-acre **New Jersey State Botanical Gardens** and the 74-acre **Shepherd Lake,** where you can rent a boat or take a swim when lifeguards are on duty.

The best place to start seeing the natural and material splendor that money can buy is **Ringwood Manor.** From Sloatsburg Road, you can spot the mansion on the slopes above Sally's Pond. Embracing several architectural styles, this 51-room manor house is part of a National Historic Landmark District; it was home to some of America's most powerful ironmakers for nearly 200 years. Furnished with a collection of Americana, 21 of the rooms have been restored and opened for tours *(Wed.–Sun.).* The grounds make a baronial picnic site.

PARK TIP: *You'll find the nicest waterfall along the Ringwood-Ramapo Trail to Shepherd Lake, a must see in spring and early summer.*

After learning about Ringwood's history, head east through the forest and follow Morris Road to **Skylands Manor** *(open first Sun. of month).* The palatial facade of this 44-room Jacobean mansion, a stockbroker's fantasy from the 1920s, makes a dramatic focal point for the Botanical Gardens. Pick up a map at the park headquarters, and head off to explore your favorite gardens. Come in late May to see the magnolias, crab apples, lilacs, and tulips in flower.

Ringwood State Park, 1304 Sloatsburg Rd., Ringwood, NJ 07456; 973-962-7031; www.njparksandforests.org/parks/ringwood.html

Allaire

4 miles west of Spring Lake, on County Rd. 524

■ 3,068 acres ■ Year-round ■ Parking fee (weekends Mem. Day to Labor Day) ■ 19th-century ironmaking village ■ Narrow-gauge railroad ■ Hiking, canoeing ■ Hunting, fishing (license required for both)

If you like prowling around relics of the past, enter this park in the heart of a forest, where the narrow Manasquan River meanders toward the sea. On the river's north bank sits the remains of a company town that thrived by smelting bog iron ore over a century and a half ago. Yet from the looks of the carpenter shop, blacksmith shop, general store, bakery, chapel, and houses, the citizens just left on the train you might hear chuffing through the woods to the west.

Allaire village *(weekend fee)* traces its roots to an early 19th-century iron forge. During the second quarter of the 1800s the property was rebuilt and expanded by then owner James P. Allaire into a community of 400 people. But when the iron business closed in 1846, the town declined. During the 1940s, the state began to develop the park and preserve the historic village, and in the 1960s railroad buffs interested in steam railroading set up operations at the park, resulting in the 3-foot-gauge **Pine Creek Railroad.**

On weekends in spring and fall and Wednesday through Sunday in summer, Allaire village *(weekends, fee)* comes alive with historical interpret-ers. The season for the Pine Creek Railroad *(fee)* is a little longer *(April–Oct. weekends, and daily July & Aug.)* when it carries pas-sengers twice around a 0.75-mile loop. Nature lovers might best see the park by canoeing or hiking along the river in the spring, when the floodplain blooms with violets, ginseng, and white Dutchman's-breeches.

Allaire village wash day

Camping

There are 45 tent and RV sites, with shower facilities; 4 yurts and 6 shelters. No RV hookups. Call the park, 732-938-2371, for reservations. Camping fee.

Allaire State Park, 4265 Atlantic Ave., Farmingdale, NJ 07727; 732-938-2371; www.njparksandforests.org/parks/allaire.html

Cape Henlopen

1 mile east of Lewes, off Del. 9

- 6,000+ acres ▪ Year-round ▪ Entrance fee ▪ No fires on beach
- Wild maritime landscape ▪ Bountiful wildlife ▪ Dune trail ▪ Bird-watching ▪ Hiking, biking ▪ Surf fishing, hunting (license required)

Phragmite at sunset

Jutting out into the sea, the thumb-like projection of Cape Henlopen separates the Atlantic Ocean from Delaware Bay—a discernible landmark since the Spanish first identified it around 1544. Though the Dutch in the next century founded a small fort on this wild, wind-swept land, and the military maintained one of its key posts here during World War II, no permanent settlement took root. So today Cape Henlopen—preserved in 1964 as a state park—appears much as it did centuries ago.

Rimmed by a wide, sandy beach and containing sand dunes and forests of pine, cherry, oak, and cedar, Cape Henlopen has a dynamic, ever changing landscape. Though the cape itself has existed for thousands of years, winds and waves have tirelessly chipped, chiseled, and resculptured its profile, slowly changing its shape. The peninsula's seashore is creeping westward, while the tip marches north about 50 feet a year.

Despite this continually changing environment, life holds on. You may not see the velvet ants, pine lizards, hairy wolf spiders, rabbits, snakes, mice, or voles—they stay mostly hidden by day— but look for their tracks that etch the sand early in the morning. The birdlife, however, is awesome. A stop along the Atlantic fly- way, the cape lures hundreds of species each year: sanderlings, red knits, ruddy turnstones, pelicans, eider ducks, even bald eagles and ospreys, to name just a few.

Of all the cape's wildlife, however, two species put on the most intriguing seasonal displays. In spring, horseshoe crabs—a species unchanged for 300,000 years—sidle onto the bayshore, where they dig shallow holes and lay tiny, pea green eggs. Half- starved migrating shorebirds, somehow timing their arrival just right, swarm to the scene, jab the sand for eggs to devour, and double their weight in two weeks. For months after, thousands of helmetlike crabs, stranded at high tide, litter the beach like the aftermath of a battle.

Between mid-April and mid-August, the piping plover— sweet little shorebirds the color of dry sand—nest among the dunes. Endangered, these little birds are protected by park rangers (access to the dunes and Cape Henlopen Point is limited during nesting season).

As you approach the park on Del. 9, passing condomini- ums and high-rises, you may doubt a lonely, isolated realm could beckon ahead. Just before the fee booth, the road forks; to the right are campgrounds, hiking trails, and the Observation Tower, while straight ahead lie the nature center, hiking trails, and access to the point—some of the most beautiful, desolate land around.

What to See and Do

Begin at the small **Seaside Nature Center** *(302-645-6852),* full of aquariums displaying local denizens. This is a good place to pick up park information and trail brochures, and to perhaps sign up for an interpretive program. Then, to sample the cape's diverse habitats, take three short trails through beach, pine forest, and dune environments. The first, the 0.7-mile **Seaside Nature Trail,** begins next to the nature center and wanders through low dunes

Cape Henlopen's oceanside

dotted with markers keyed to a brochure available at the nature center. The trail comes to the sandy shores of gentle Breakwater Harbor and follows the bayshore a bit before looping back through the woods.

Consider stopping at the **Observation Tower** built on an old military bunker. At the top awaits an extraordinary vista: a mosaic of pinelands, marshes fingered with tidal creeks and piney ridges, the endless blue Atlantic, and rippling sand dunes.

Just down the road is the start of the **Walking Dune Hiking Trail,** offering an intimate look at "walking" dunes—mounds of sand blown by the wind, moving forward bit by bit. The dunes once traveled 60 feet a year, but the growth of vegetation has hampered their speed. Look closely: The "dwarf" pines along the sandy peaks may actually be the topmost branches of 30-foot trees!

For another panoramic vista, drive to the end of the southern park road, where **Herring Point Overlook** takes in a sweeping scene of the crashing Atlantic. A short trail leads down to the beach, where you can picnic, swim, or sunbathe.

WAR STORIES: Standing atop the 83-foot concrete Observation Tower, it's easy to understand the cape's strategic importance to shipping along the Atlantic. That's why the Army built Fort Miles Military Reserve in the early 1900s, and why, during World War II, soldiers here kept watch for enemy activity offshore. Indeed, more than 400 Allied ships were sunk by German U-boats. And, in one of the last actions of the war, a German submarine, *U-858,* surrendered here five days after V-E Day. The lands have since been returned to the state.

Further Adventures

Hardy hikers won't want to miss the 1.8-mile **Beach Loop Trail** *(closed during piping plover nesting March– Sept.),* beginning from The Point parking lot and following the cape's contour around its lonely, easternmost point. Be forewarned: Walking on sand is tiring; only those in good shape should attempt this hike. Wandering along the bayshore, where a lighthouse overlooks placid **Breakwater Harbor,** the trail heads east past sand dunes inhabited in summer by nesting piping plover, black skimmers, and least and common terns. You soon reach the wide open point where land and bay and ocean meet. Just offshore, a lighthouse flashes warnings to ships and boats. Chances are, flocks of shorebirds, and perhaps a brown pelican or two, will be the only signs of life. Return along the ocean, where the Atlantic surf rolls onto a wide, seashell-strewn beach.

Camping

Set among pine-covered dunes are 159 tent and RV sites (March–Nov.). Call 302-645-2103 for information and 877-987-2757 for reservations. Camping fee.

Cape Henlopen State Park, 42 Cape Henlopen Dr., Lewes, DE 19958; 302-645-8983; www.destateparks.com/chsp/chsp.htm

Trap Pond

5 miles east of Laurel via Del. 24 and East Trap Pond Rd.

■ 3,300 acres ■ Year-round ■ Entrance fee May through Oct.
■ Bald cypress trees ■ Nature Center ■ Hiking, biking, canoeing,
fishing (license required)

Among the rows of corn
and soybeans on the Eastern
Shore rises a great stand
of bald cypress trees, their
moss-draped limbs and but-
tressed trunks reminiscent of
a southern bayou. The remnants of an ancient swamp-
land that once covered much
of the Atlantic coastal plain,
these relics of another time
form the heart of the park.

In the late 1700s, colo-
nists discovered that the
rot-resistant bald cypress
wood was ideal for building
boats, posts, and shingles.
They excavated Trap Pond
to power their mills ... and
down came the tall, shaggy
trees. As more trees toppled,
opening up the tree canopy,
the sun dried the underlying
peat bogs, making the whole
swamp susceptible to fire.
One 1930s blaze raged for
eight months.

The cypress of Trap
Pond evoke an aura of
mystery. In winter, flocks of
overwintering Canada geese
and whistling swans sit by

Trap Pond morning

the water's edge, and the trees stand locked in ice—quite a sight to
behold. Acquired by the federal government in the 1930s, Trap Pond
and its surrounding forest became Delaware's first state park in 1951.

What to See and Do

Stop by the **Bald Cypress Nature Center** *(302-875-5163)* in the park's
main section to learn about Trap Pond's natural history and pick up
park literature and a schedule of interpretive programs. Then hop
in your car, exit the park, and proceed down Trap Pond Road to the
first road you come to (Goosenest Road); turn right and in about 100
yards enter the campground. Head for the other side of the pond and

the **Cypress Point Trail,** the park's most intriguing hike. Just a mile long, the trail wanders beside the shore, where bald cypress congregate in all their splendor.

PARK TIP: *The bridge crossing the Terrapin Branch, off the Loblolly Bicycle Trail, is a great place to take in the sights, sounds, and smells of the cypress swamp.*

The point where a short boardwalk juts out across the tea-colored waters offers a good spot to examine these odd deciduous conifers with their "knees" poking above the standing water like probing periscopes. Watch for wildlife, too: eastern painted and spotted turtles sunning on gnarled logs, bull frogs, and green tree frogs. One resident, the carpenter frog, is also known as the bog frog because of its preference for the sphagnum wetlands of cypress swamps. Birders will see a wide variety of southern birds, including prothonotary and parula, as well as the elusive Swainson's warbler, one of the least known of North America's birds because it favors dense swamps. After about half a mile, the trail returns through woods embracing 12 different species of oaks and four different pines.

The new 4.9-mile, hard-packed **Loblolly Bicycle Trail** weaves its way through the forests and swamps showcasing the park habitat. This trail is equally suited to hiking and is friendly to both wheelchairs and strollers. Visitors may bring their own bikes or take advantage of the park's "Loan-a-Bike" program.

While hiking provides a good introduction to the cypress swamp, nothing beats a canoe trip through a labyrinth of flared trunks and knobby knees. *(Canoes may be rented in summer season from the park concessionaire.)* Try the popular trail leading southeast from Trap Pond to Records Pond along the **James Branch River,** deep into the swamp's interior. Floating silently past stands of cypress, including one giant more than 500 years old, you'll feel like you've traveled into centuries past.

AMPHIBIAN SYMPHONY: As night falls on the springtime swamp, a small reedy voice breaks the silence, soon joined by more voices: humming trills and bassline grunts and plunks like twanging rubber bands. It's the amphibian symphony—an integral part of the frog and toad courtship. Each species has its own sound, enabling males to call across the darkness for mates.

End your exertions by dropping a fishing line. A largemouth bass, crappie, or bluegill might accept your invitation. Shaded by loblolly pines, picnic tables dot the shore, and there are several other hiking trails you may explore.

Another way to experience the swamp is to hop aboard the pontoon tour boat. Relax and take in the turtles, wading birds, beaver, snakes and ospreys. Call the Bald Cypress Nature Center for a schedule *(fee).*

Camping

The park has 142 tent or RV sites (March–Nov.), with showers. Call 877-987-2757 for reservations. Camping fee.

Trap Pond State Park, 33587 Bald Cypress Ln., Laurel, DE 19956; 302-875-5153; www.destateparks.com/tpsp/tpsp.htm

Fort Delaware

Via ferry from end of Clinton St., Delaware City

- 285 acres ▪ Wed.–Sun. mid-June–Labor Day, weekends late April to mid-June ▪ No pets ▪ No camping ▪ Historic fort ▪ Heronry

A 10-minute ferry ride *(fare)* brings you to **Pea Patch Island**—named for an 18th-century legend concerning a boatload of spilled peas— and **Fort Delaware,** complete with a moat. Built between 1848 and 1868 to defend the Delaware River entrance to Philadelphia, and later garrisoned during WW I and II, the bastion is best known for its role in the Civil War, when it imprisoned Confederate soldiers. Fort Delaware remains a well-preserved Civil War fortress. Interpreters dressed in period garb *(daily in season)* march, demonstrate weapons, and chat about those trying times when 16,000 people were jammed onto the island.

Cattle egret

The **Prison Camp Trail** loops through the island's north end, with markers keyed to a brochure *(available at gift shop)* detailing prison life. Midway, an observation platform looks out on one of the largest heronries north of Florida—as many as 5,000 herons and egrets nest here *(April–July)*. Watch the great birds glide over the marshlands; with binoculars you can pick out their large nests in the trees.

Fort Delaware State Park, P.O. Box 170, Delaware City, DE 19706; 302-834-7941; www.destateparks.com/fortdelaware

White Clay Creek

2 miles northwest of Newark on Del. 896

- 3,614 acres ▪ Year-round ▪ Entrance fee (Mar.–Nov.) ▪ Primitive, youth group camping only ▪ Bird-watching ▪ White-tailed deer ▪ Hiking, biking, fishing, hunting (license required) ▪ Frisbee golf

Showcasing the beauty of Delaware's piedmont, this park has three different entrances accessing 35 miles of trails that explore lush farm valleys and thick woods. Take the Hopkins Road entrance for the **Nature Center.** Nearby, the 2.1-mile **Preserve Trail Loop** traverses a stone-strewn creek. And the 2-mile **Possum Hill Trail,** off Smith Mill Road, wanders through rolling farmland, passing a weathered Mason-Dixon Line monument. Take the 4.5-mile **Twin Valley Trail** into the hardwood forest and unique flora of the valleys.

White Clay Creek State Park, 425 Wedgewood Rd., Rte. 896, Newark, DE 19711; 302-368-6900; www.destateparks.com/wccsp

79

Wild horses of Assateague

Assateague

8 miles south of Ocean City via US 50 and Md. 611

■ 1,000 acres ■ April through Nov. (Day use of area open year-round) ■ Entrance fee (Mem. Day to Labor Day) ■ Nature Center ■ Wild horses ■ Bird-watching ■ Swimming, boating, fishing

Created and dominated by the sea, Assateague Island is a narrow barrier island of golden sand stretching 33 miles off the coasts of eastern Maryland and Virginia. A stark contrast to the neon lights of nearby Ocean City, its wild, natural beaches and bird-filled marshes are virtually undeveloped.

One of thousands of barrier islands and spits protecting the Atlantic coast from the ocean's brutal onslaught, Assateague is a sandy, vulnerable place of constant change—growing and shrinking and moving as the sea adds sand here, washes it away there. Many geologists believe the barrier islands were created after the last Ice Age. As glacial ice melted, rivers carried ice-scoured rocks and sands to coastal estuaries, where offshore currents and waves redeposited them in new configurations along the shoreline.

Humans have tried to possess this difficult land, from early-day colonists to modern entrepreneurs, who built roads and buildings in hopes of creating a beachfront resort. Nature won out: The great March storm of 1962—also dubbed the Ash Wednesday Storm—blew away every last hope for human habitation, leaving the island to revert to its natural state. In most summers, however, the ocean is calm, the beaches warm. Created in 1964 and one of Maryland's most visited parks, the state park joined two other entities in preserving the entire island: Assateague Island National Seashore, which encircles the

state park, and Chincoteague National Wildlife Refuge, lying at the southern part of the island.

What to See and Do

The park's premier attraction is, of course, the beach. Less crowded than Ocean City, the 2-mile sandy shoreline lures thousands each summer to swim, collect shells, picnic, go clamming, and simply bask in the sun's warm rays. Check out the **Nature Center,** which has aquariums full of local species, as well as innovative interpretive programs.

Along quieter parts of the beach—especially to the north—you glean a true sense of what the Eastern Seaboard was like centuries ago: Churning surf rolls onto empty sand, tall oatgrass rustles in a salty breeze, and pines and bayberry shrubs create a dense thicket along the island's spine. Keep walking north and you'll cross into Assateague Island National Seashore, void of any signs of 20th-century life. Here the wildlife is out in full force. You may not see the nocturnal red foxes, hognose snakes, or wolf spiders, but in early morning you can spot their tracks in the sand. And you can't miss the fabled wild horses. Legend dictates that the ancestors of these small creatures swam ashore after a Spanish galleon sank in the 1700s. But they more likely descend from horses that were placed on the island in colonial times for free grazing and to avoid paying taxes on them.

PARK TIP: *Don't miss seeing the sun rise—it's one of the highlights at the park.*

And then there are the birds. More than 200 different species have been spotted on this rest stop along the Atlantic flyway—ranging from the common gull to herons and egrets to endangered peregrine falcons and bald eagles. Birders come from all over to watch the show: Terns dive-bombing the water to catch fish, gulls dropping clams to break them open on a paved road, flocks of sandpipers flirting with the surf on long, strawlike legs, and protected piping plover nesting in the sand dunes. The best viewing times are spring and autumn, during the annual migrations. Don't forget the binoculars.

Further Adventures

Consider hopping in a canoe and paddling down **Sinepuxent** and **Chincoteague Bay.** You glide past golden marshes filled with wading birds—egrets, herons, perhaps even a brown pelican or two. In early morning, muskrats and white-tailed and sika deer feed near the water's edge. The National Park Service also operates four backcountry canoe-camping sites along the way.

For a primer on the island's three ecosystems—dune, forest, and marsh—drive (or bike) south about 3 miles along Bayberry Drive to the developed area on **Assateague Island National Seashore** *(410-641-1441. Vehicle fee),* with campsites and several excellent, short hiking trails. There's also a recently added, handicap-accessible hiking and biking path that connects the campground with Assateague Island National Seashore. The **Life of the Dunes Trail** explores the ever shifting world of sand, teaching how different plants have adapted to the harsh, unstable dune conditions, where temperatures can reach more than 120°F. For example, the leaves of dusty miller, a gray-green plant with yellow flowers, are covered with thick white "hairs," which serve as heat insulators. The **Life of the Marsh Trail** offers a good chance of spotting wild horses, their stomachs bloated by salty marsh grass. *(Remember: It's illegal to feed and pet them.)* And the **Life of the Forest Trail** visits a maritime forest inhabited by the Delmarva fox squirrel, an endangered subspecies twice the size of its common gray cousin, with foxlike ears.

The fascinating **Chincoteague National Wildlife Refuge** *(757-336-6122. Vehicle fee; no camping)* lies 50 miles away. (You'll have to exit the island, drive south to Va. 175, and re-enter the island via Chincoteague.) Established in 1943, the refuge's 14 freshwater impoundments provide a haven for shorebirds. In winter, thousands of greater snow geese descend, offering one of the most breathtaking natural spectacles around. The Wildlife Loop, closed to cars until 3 p.m. daily, gives hikers and bikers a chance to spot birdlife up close.

ASSATEAGUE'S INLETS: Early explorers noted that the island of Assateague extended some 60 miles along the coastline. Great storms have since whittled through the weak spots, forming inlets. The most recent break occurred in 1933, when the power-packed Inlet Storm severed present-day Assateague from Fenwick Island, site of Ocean City. Nature would probably have closed the inlet since, had humans not intervened by building a jetty.

Camping

The park has 350 tent and RV sites, with showers. Reservations highly recommended in summer. For reservations, call 888-432-2267 or visit the website. Camping fee.

Assateague State Park, 7307 Stephen Decatur Hwy., Berlin, MD 21811; 410-641-2120; www.dnr.state.md.us /publiclands

Gunpowder Falls

3 areas in Baltimore and Harford Counties

■ 18,000 acres ■ Year-round ■ Scenic river valley ■ Hiking, biking, swimming, boating

Surprisingly close to Baltimore, this state park embraces the banks of a beautiful river and its two tributaries as they cross a mosaic of open meadows and gentle forested slopes, encountering rocky bluffs, a freshwater marsh—and no waterfalls. The term "falls" dates back to colonial times, when swift-moving streams that emptied into a tidal river were considered that river's falls; in this case, Big and Little Gunpowder Falls flow into the tidal Gunpowder River. Established in the late 1950s, Maryland's largest state park is scattered across three different recreation areas. Make a point to get a map from the Visitor Center in Kingsville.

Canoeing the Big Gunpowder Falls

The **Hammerman Area** near the Chesapeake Bay contains picnic tables and a swimming beach *(Mem. Day–Labor Day; adm. fee)*. For a fee, motorboats may be launched from Dundee Creek Marina, and paddlers may explore the marsh at the river's mouth—a birder's paradise. Try entering this world of giant cattails and wild rice in early morning, when deer, raccoons, and muskrats feed along the river's edge.

In the more remote **Hereford Area,** 35 miles upstream, 100 miles of hiking trails await. A rocky, 1.5-mile segment of the **Gunpowder Falls South Trail** *(off Mount Carmel Rd.)* showcases **Big Gunpowder Falls.** Here the fast-moving water supports a large population of trout.

PARK TIP: *The best-kept secret is the Mill Pond Cottage, a cozy bungalow, for rent, nestled in the Hereford area.*

The 19.7-mile **Torrey C. Brown Trail** allows hikers and bikers to meander north from Ashland into Pennsylvania, through plush green pastures and rural towns. Pick up a map at the Monkton train station.

Camping

The park has 22 primitive sites on Hart-Miller Island (Mem. Day–Labor Day) in Chesapeake Bay; accessible only by private boat. No showers. Available first come, first served. Camping fee.

Gunpowder Falls State Park, P.O. Box 480, Kingsville, MD 21087; 410-592-2897; www.dnr.state.md.us/publiclands

Patapsco Valley

5 different areas; call for directions

Bridge over Patapsco River in Hollofield Area

- 16,043 acres
- User fee ▪ Scenic river valley ▪ Hiking, biking, canoeing, hunting, fishing (license required)

A long, skinny wilderness area, the Patapsco River winds 32 miles from its source near Woodbine to the Baltimore Harbor, as lovely as it was when Capt. John Smith first set eyes on it in 1608. It wasn't always so. Early in the last century, lumbermen denuded the area; then in the 1970s, the dumping of sewage and industrial waste turned the river into a cesspool. Thanks to clean-water legislation, fish once again swim its depths, songbirds fill the tree canopy, and coyotes roam the forests. The state created the narrow park in 1907.

PARK TIP: *On a hot day, check out the pool at Cascade Falls along the 2.2-mile Cascade Falls Trail.*

Patapsco Valley encompasses five different entities and manages two natural areas. Three areas—**Hollofield, Pickall,** and **Hilton**—are for picnicking and camping; the **Avalon-Orange Grove, Glen Artney,** and **Mckeldin Areas** stand out for their hiking and biking trails. Stop by **park headquarters,** on US 40 near Ellicott City, for information.

The Avalon Area includes the 1.6-mile **Grist Mill Trail,** a paved path that winds along the floodplain. Along the way, bikers and hikers visit the ruins of the 1856 **Orange Grove Flour Mill** and the landmark steel-and-cable **swinging bridge.** To explore the surrounding forested ridges, take the 1-mile **Valley View Trail,** with overlooks of the silvery ribbon of water far below. For more hiking and biking, head for the Mckeldin Area, 20 miles upstream. The popular 4-mile **Switchback Trail** sashays between dense woods and the Patapsco.

Camping

Hollofield has 73 tent and RV sites (late-April–late-Oct.), Hilton has 6 cabins and 14 tent sites (late-March–Oct.), both with showers; group campsites are also available at Hilton and Mckeldin. For reservations, call 888-432-2267 or visit the park website. Camping fee.

Patapsco Valley State Park, 8020 Baltimore National Pike, Ellicott City, MD 21043; 410-461-5005; www.dnr.state.md.us/publiclands

Swallow Falls

7 miles northwest of Oakland, off US 219

■ 257 acres ■ Year-round ■ Entrance fee ■ Pets permitted
(Labor Day–Mem. Day) ■ Camping ■ Hiking ■ Picnic area

The Youghiogheny River flows through Swallow Falls State Park, spilling over two falls and through a deep, rocky canyon before continuing its tempestuous journey across the Appalachian plateau. Muddy Creek Falls, Maryland's largest, can be found on Muddy Creek, a tributary of the Youghiogheny. Surprisingly, this striking scene is not what led to the formation of the state park. On the river's bank stands a magnificent grove of virgin hemlock and white pine, never logged thanks to the foresight of one Henry Rug, who owned the forest at the turn of the 20th century. The 40-acre grove and surrounding forest were donated to the state in 1906, and around this gift the Civilian Conservation Corps developed one of Maryland's earliest state parks.

People come from far and wide to walk the 1.25-mile **Canyon Trail** along the river gorge. The hike begins from the main parking area, delving deep into regal hemlocks. Follow the sign to **Muddy Creek Falls,** which splashes 52 feet over a wide stone ledge into a big green pool. From here, a wooden staircase leads down to a narrow cliff-shaded path winding beside the furious, churning river. Ahead stands two-tiered **Swallow Falls,** flanked above and below with large flat boulders; sun worshippers dot them in summer. Note the large plinth below the falls, where thousands of cliff swallows once nested, lending the park their name.

85

Most people stick by the river, but for the hardy, a 5.5-mile hiking trail—marked by white blazes—winds through sylvan woods, connecting Swallow Falls to nearby **Herrington Manor State Park** *(301-334-9180).* A small lake with boat rentals and swimming beach make for a quiet respite.

Camping

The park has 65 tent and RV sites (mid-April–mid-Dec.), with shower facilities. Reservations recommended in summer; call 888-432-2267 or visit the park website. Camping fee.

Swallow Falls State Park, 222 Herrington Ln., Oakland, MD 21550; 301-334-9180; www.dnr.state.md.us/publiclands

Youghiogheny River

Grayson Highlands

Between Damascus and Independence, on US 58

- 4,822 acres ■ Year-round ■ Entrance fee ■ Alpine scenery
- Access to Appalachian Trail and Mount Rogers NRA ■ Horse camping ■ Hiking, fishing (license required), mountain biking, cross-country skiing

Sitting high atop the Appalachians in southern Virginia, Grayson Highlands crowns lofty Haw Orchard Mountain, offering some of the most spectacular alpine scenery around. Flanked by the state's two highest peaks—5,729-foot Mount Rogers and 5,520-foot Whitetop Mountain—this is the northern realm of red spruce and fir, Ice Age relics that still flourish in the high elevation and abundant moisture. Trout-filled streams roll off the mountainside, wild horses graze flower-dotted meadows, and blooms of purple and white rhododendron festoon the understory in June and July. With its cool summer temperatures, sophisticated horse-camping facilities, and miles of hiking trails, it's surprising that just 160,000 people visit this scenic corner annually.

Jones Homestead

Long before the park was established, hardy pioneers of Scotch-Irish descent settled the region. They left behind their names in such park features as Massie Gap and Wilburn Ridge. Celebrating this heritage is a fall festival held in late September, complete with live bluegrass music and molasses-making.

What to See and Do

From the contact station at 3,698 feet, follow Grayson Highland Lane up Haw Orchard Mountain, with supreme mountain vistas in every direction. At **Buzzard Rock Overlook,** about halfway up, a short walk is rewarded with a splendid vista of farm fields cradled by rows and rows of towering, tree-covered ridges. As you climb higher, the forest around you changes to northern hardwood. The temperature here may be 10 degrees cooler than at the contact station, and you may very well be in the clouds. The **Virgil J. Cox Visitor Center** *(Mem. Day–Labor Day)*, located at 4,958 feet, remembers the region's rich heritage with exhibits on pioneer life, including such items as hand tools, moonshining apparatuses, and musical instruments; there are also natural history exhibits. Local artisans sell their handicrafts—quilts, musical instruments, and delicate art glass, among others—at the adjacent **Mountain Crafts Shop** *(late May–Sept.)*.

PARK TIP: *Look for a yellow birch tree growing atop a large boulder 0.4 miles down the Twin Pinnacle Trail; it's called the "magic tree" because of all the folk tales it has inspired.*

The popular 1.6-mile-loop **Twin Pinnacles Trail** leaves from behind the Visitor Center. Hiking through mountain ash, yellow birch, and spine-covered hawthorns—which gave the mountain its name—you soon come to Little Pinnacle, an igneous rock outcrop with 360-degree views of surrounding crags, including regal Mount Rogers. Hike a half-mile farther and you'll reach the top of Big Pinnacle, with views down into Massie Gap.

To visit a restored homestead, drive down the hill to the picnic area and walk the 2-mile **Rock House Ridge Trail.** Wandering through a pretty meadow, you'll soon come to the **Jones Homestead,** complete with oak-log cabin, spring house, cane mill (to grind sorghum), and an old cemetery surrounded by a crumbling rock wall.

Further Adventures

Adjacent to the spectacular **Mount Rogers National Recreation Area** *(276-783-5196),* Grayson Highlands provides the shortest hike to the top of **Mount Rogers**—4.3 miles from Massie Gap via the Rhododendron Gap and Appalachian Trails. The hike shows off the area's beauty to perfection—overlapping mountains marching off into the distance, grassy balds, thickets of sweet blueberries (ripe in August), and acre upon acre of Catawba rhododendron, quite a sight when they bloom in June. Keep an eye out for wild ponies. Dense with the state's only spruce and fir forest and often fogged in, the summit itself has no views; but mosses and ferns, which thrive in this moist environment, create a dark, magical realm.

Camping

The park has 73 tent and RV sites, with showers; 23 horse-camp sites adjacent to horse barn (March–Nov.). Call 800-933-7275 for reservations or visit www .reserveamerica.com. Camping fee.

Grayson Highlands State Park, 829 Grayson Highland Ln., Mouth of Wilson, VA 24363; 276-579-7092; www.dcr.virginia.gov/state_parks

MOUNTAIN BALDS: Gazing across the panoramic sweeps of mountains in the southern Appalachians, you'll note rocky, treeless spots among the forested slopes. Called balds, some are said to have been created by Native Americans who set fires for game clearings, while others resulted from logging in the 1800s. For hikers, these balds can be a source of revelation: In spring many balds become blooming gardens of deep-pink rhododendron.

87

Douthat

7 miles north of Clifton Forge on Va. 629

■ 4,546 acres ■ Vehicle fee ■ Spectacular mountain setting ■ Nature programs ■ Hiking, fishing (license required), boating, swimming

White-tailed deer

88

Driving deep into the Allegheny Mountains, the cars thin out, massive ridges crop up, and a splendid sense of isolation envelops you. Hidden in this lofty mountainous realm lies Douthat State Park, where forested, windswept peaks ring an indigo-colored lake—the domain of black bear and white-tailed deer, wild turkey, and whippoorwill. This park isn't meant for a whirlwind tour; spend at least a weekend here, sampling the 43 miles of hiking trails, fishing in the trout-filled lake, or simply gazing into the night sky at extremely bright stars.

The park was named for Robert Douthat, who obtained a land grant for the area in 1795. Douthat was placed on the National Register of Historic Places in 1986 and is a veritable memorial to the Civilian Conservation Corps, which built most of the park's rustic cabins, its restaurant, and two lodges. The Depression-era artistry of its 600 workers still is evident in such details as hand-carved doors and hinges.

What to See and Do

From Clifton Forge, Va. 629 winds beneath a canopy of oak and hickory along clear-running Wilson Creek, providing a taste of what lies ahead. Beyond the entrance gate, stop by the **Park Office**, register, and pick up park maps and information; check to see if any park sponsored programs might be of interest.

The park has more than 40 miles of wooded hiking trails ranging from easy to strenuous walks. The 1.3-mile **Blue Suck Falls Trail** is the perfect choice for the moderate hiker. You will stroll past one of the park's vernal pools and up the trail beside rock-riven Blue Suck Run. The woodsy path highlights many of the park's trees, which are typical of the Appalachians: dogwood, black oak, white oak, white pine, sassafras, American chestnut, hemlock, and the tulip poplar—decorated in spring with yellowish-green blooms the shape of tulips. Here, as elsewhere in the park, mountain laurel and rhododendron form the understory—adorning the forest with brilliant blooms of pink and white in spring.

> **PARK TIP:** *Hikers who wander up to Tuscarora Overlook will be rewarded with magnificent views from a small cabin built by the Civilian Conservation Corps in the 1930s.*

The easy 0.8-mile **Heron Run Trail,** beginning inside Lakeside Campground, hugs the shoreline of Douthat Lake, a perfect vantage to admire the shimmering reflections of high mountain peaks and maples crowding the shoreline. Along the beginning of the trail stands a magnificent stand of dark-green hemlocks. Walk quietly: You have a good chance of spotting a beaver or two. The narrow trail wends to the dam, at which point you'll have to retrace your steps or continue on the **YCC Trail** around the lake.

If you'd like a different perspective on the park and have a lot of stamina, drive to the Douthat Lakeview Restaurant and the trailhead for the 5.6-mile loop formed by the **Buck Hollow, Mountain Top,** and **Mountain Side Trails.** This rugged, hilly hike winds through a pretty hollow to the top of Beards Mountain, offering far-off views of rumpled ridges extending as far as the eye can see. Then, continuing on the mountain's other side, you spy Douthat Lake, a little sparkling gem nestled far below at the base of the mountains. Along the way, tree-filled coves burst into flames of color in autumn.

After all this hiking, you're probably ready for a swim. Head for **Douthat Lake,** where a sandy beach occupies a small cove, which also holds an amphitheater with weekly programs *(Mem. Day– Labor Day).* The Boat Dock rents paddleboats, johnboats, canoes, funyaks, and hydrobikes. You can fish here, or at nearby **Wilson Creek.**

Camping and Lodging

The park has 74 tent and RV sites, with showers, in 3 areas; 30 cabins and Creasey and Douthat Lodges. (March–Nov.) Whispering Pines Campground is expected to open in 2011. Call 800-933-7275 for reservations or visit www.reserveamerica .com. Camping fee.

Douthat State Park, 14239 Douthat State Park Rd., Millsboro, VA 24460; 540-862-8100; www.dcr.virginia.gov /state_parks

AUTUMN COLOR: The heralding of autumn begins at Douthat in late September with the slightest hints of color—a few precocious maples or oaks flashing gold or red. Then, at startling speeds, the whole forest explodes in a brilliant mosaic: Flowering dogwoods turn crimson and sassafras burnt orange; poplars and birches become yellow; while oaks blaze in yellows, oranges, or bronzes; and sugar maples—the forest highlight—glow with intense scarlets, oranges, and golds.

False Cape

5 miles south of Sandbridge, southeast of Virginia Beach.
No vehicular access

- 4,321 acres ▪ Year-round ▪ Entrance fee to Back Bay NWR
- No cars ▪ No pets ▪ Beautiful barrier spit ▪ Hiking, biking,
swimming, fishing (license required)

Primitive, windswept, and wildly beautiful, False Cape isn't easy to get to; you must hike or bike 5 miles to reach its gates. But isolation is also one of its virtues. Located along a mile-wide barrier spit between the Atlantic Ocean and Back Bay, the unspoiled coastal environment embraces beach, dunes, marshlands, and maritime forest as pristine as they were centuries ago.

The park's most exceptional feature is its abundant wildlife: red foxes, white-tailed deer, feral pigs and horses, raccoons, nutria, and hundreds of loggerhead turtles—the only sea turtle that nests in Virginia. Birders are in paradise at this remote perch along the Atlantic flyway, where up to 300 species—egrets, swallows, flocks of ducks, trumpeter swans—stop by each year.

False Cape first became known as a shipping graveyard; sailors aiming for Cape Henry just north often became confused by this landmass—hence the cape's name—and sank their ships in shallow waters. Using cypress-wood debris, the survivors of one such wreck in 1895 built the fishing community of Wash Woods, which thrived until sand engulfed it in the 1950s. The least-visited of Virginia's state parks, False Cape opened in 1980.

Be forewarned: There is no food service or drinking water in the park; carry at least one gallon of water per person, per day.

Wind-rippled dunes

Mosquitoes and biting flies are pesky in summer, so bring repellent.

The only access to the park is through Back Bay National Wildlife Refuge *(757-721-2412. Entrance fee; trails closed Nov.–March),* and cars are prohibited in both the refuge and the park; park at the Back Bay visitor contact station, don your walking shoes or hop a bike, and head south into the refuge. *(You can also enter along the beach or by canoe along Back Bay. Contact the park for information.)*

What to See and Do

Back Bay is a glorious refuge, a wonderful introduction to life on a barrier spit. Mostly marshland, it harbors abundant birdlife. Follow signs along the dike road; by the time you reach the state park, you'll have entered the maritime forest; live oaks, hollies, and loblolly pines. The scenery indicates that you're on the spine of the barrier spit, where vegetation has managed to take root in the sandy soil. To the west, toward Back Bay, lies marshland; to the east, golden dunes undulate to the Atlantic and an endless beach. Continue straight ahead on the park's only road, which splices the spit. You'll soon reach the **contact station,** where you can pick up brochures and maps, as well as a guide to the 2.4-mile **Barbour Hill Interpretive Trail.** This nature loop explores the different features of the barrier spit, including loblolly pines, walking dunes, and thickets full of wildlife.

LIFE OF A LOGGERHEAD: Most common to Florida's beaches, endangered loggerhead turtles nest as far north as False Cape—a ritual that can be observed between May and October. After dark the female loggerhead crawls ashore, where she digs a nest and buries about 110 leathery eggs, then heads back to the water. Hatchlings pop through the sand 50 to 70 days later, and with flailing flippers race for the waves. The next time anyone sees these little guys they're 4 inches long and living somewhere near the Azores. Researchers have suggested that the loggerheads may return to their birth site to nest—commencing the cycle all over again.

Now you have a choice. If you've had enough exercise, take the 0.7-mile **Barbour Hill Beach Trail** to the Atlantic Ocean—and a beautiful, desolate beach sprinkled with shells. Or continue 2.4 miles down the main road to **False Cape Landing,** with pretty views of **Back Bay.** On the east side of the road, the 0.6-mile **False Cape Landing Trail** provides another chance to reach the Atlantic. Two miles farther down the main road lies **Wash Woods,** site of an educational center *(visit by advance reservation only)* and a tangle of short trails. Try the 0.5-mile **Cemetery Trail,** which visits the remains of the early settlement: a church steeple and shaded cemetery dotted with crumbling tombstones.

From here, head to the beach on the **Wash Woods Interpretive Trail;** or delve even deeper into solitude along the 3-mile **Dudley Island Trail** *(hikers only).* Wandering to the North Carolina line, this trail promises good odds for sighting some of the region's wild horses, and perhaps even a red fox.

Camping

The park has 12 primitive sites, with no showers. Camping fee. Reservations required. Call 800-933-7279.

False Cape State Park, 4001 Sandpiper Rd., Virginia Beach, VA 23456; 757-426-7128; www.dcr.virginia.gov/state_parks

First Landing

US 60 at Cape Henry, in Virginia Beach

Bald cypress swamp

- 2,889 acres ▪ Year-round
- Vehicle fee ▪ Cypress swamp
- Varied ecosystems ▪ Hiking, biking, boating

Tucked between high-rises on the tip of Cape Henry, this park boasts an astonishing medley of northern and southern ecosystems, including cordgrass-filled marshlands, forested dunes, and a bald cypress swamp.

Lacking fertile farmland, much of the cape was settled only recently. Indeed, when Capt. John Smith landed here in 1607—memorialized in the park's name—he chose to push farther up the James River to found America's first permanent English settlement, at Jamestown. In 1936 nearly 3,000 acres of the pristine land became one of Virginia's first state parks, now the state's most visited.

On the south side of US 60, the **Bald Cypress Trail** runs along a boardwalk above tannin-stained waters, where bulbous-trunked bald cypress stand draped in Spanish moss. You may glimpse pileated woodpeckers or the endangered chicken turtle, whose neck extends longer than the length of its shell. Extend the hike with the 3.1-mile **Osmanthus Trail,** wandering beneath olive trees with ample blueberry bushes along the trial. The longer, less crowded, 5-mile **Long Creek Trail** moves through bird-filled salt marshes, prime habitat for egret and blue heron. The 6-mile **Cape Henry hiker-biker trail** cuts across the park to the **Narrows** *(accessible by auto via 64th St.)* and its small beach. There's a boat launch here, but no swimming. To cool off, head to the bay shore. Don't forget the 1.2-mile **Osprey Trail** that follows the Broad Bay shoreline where it's rumored the pirate Blackbeard hid from his enemies. The new **Live Oak Trail** connects the campground to the picnic area and main trail system.

PARK TIP: *Along Cape Henry Trail there's a replica Chesapeake Indian Village with five longhouses and one sweatlodge.*

Camping and Lodging

The park has 222 tent and RV sites, with showers and hookups (March–Dec.); 20 housekeeping cabins (open year-round). For reservations, call 800-933-7275 or visit www.reserveamerica.com. Camping fee.

First Landing State Park and Natural Area, 2500 Shore Dr., Virginia Beach, VA 23451; 757-412-2300; www.dcr.virginia.gov/state_parks

Westmoreland

40 miles east of Fredericksburg, off Va. 3

- 1,300 acres ▪ Year-round ▪ Entrance fee ▪ Fossil-filled cliffs
- Hiking, swimming, boating, bird-watching ▪ Picnic area

Overlooking the Potomac River on Virginia's Northern Neck, Westmoreland's multihued Horsehead Cliffs provide more than a scenic backdrop for visitors who come to swim, boat, fish, and sun. Embedded with billions of fossils of sea creatures dating back 15 million years, the cliffs recall a time when porpoises, sharks, and whales cavorted in a warm, shallow sea. Protected for millions of years by sand and silt, these relics are only now being exposed through erosion. Cast upon the rocky beach, they're here for finding and keeping.

Beyond the cliffs, the park's pretty woodlands cover deep-gouged ridges, and frogs bellow in a cattail-filled marsh. Crisscrossed with 6 hiking trails, this forested realm lures more than 100 species of birds, including wild turkeys and—soaring above—ospreys and bald eagles.

Get an introduction to the area at the **Visitor Center** (*Mem. Day–Labor Day*), located in the heart of the park. Be sure to check out the fossils—so you know what to look for later on. From here it's a short walk to the park's most popular spot, the beach. The easy 0.4-mile **Beach Trail** leads to a rocky expanse on the Potomac. Families picnic, kids splash, and everyone keeps their eyes peeled for that coveted fossil. (*Fossil collecting is permitted along the beach between the cliffs and marsh; digging in the cliffs themselves is illegal and dangerous.*) Or try out the nearby paved 0.5-mile **Rock Springs Trail** for use by the disabled and bicycles.

To explore the marsh and woodlands, take the interpretive **Big Meadows Nature Trail,** located half a mile east of the Visitor Center. About midway (0.3 mile), a short spur leads to the river and a view of the cliffs. Farther along is **Yellow Swamp,** cloaked in spring with the tender shoots of cattails. The path ends at the **Turkey Neck Trail;** you can either backtrack or make a loop by turning right. Don't miss the new 1.5-mile **Conservation Corps Trail** adjacent to the park's entrance.

Camping

The park has 138 tent and RV sites, with showers and hookups; 27 cabins and 6 camping cabins (March–Nov.). Call park or 800-933-7275 for reservations. Camping fee.

Westmoreland State Park, 1650 State Park Rd., Montross, VA 22520; 804-493-8821; www.dcr.virginia.gov/state_parks

Pipestem Resort

12 miles south of Hinton on W. Va. 20

■ 4,026 acres ■ Year-round ■ Bluestone River Gorge ■ Mountain scenery ■ Nature Center ■ Horse rentals and trails ■ Hiking, tennis, swimming, golf, boating, mountain biking

In one aspect a wilderness oasis with remote hiking trails, a clear-running river, and plenty of wildlife, Pipestem is also a "resort" state park—with golf courses, restaurants, swimming pools, and conference facilities. Whether hiking or golfing, you can't miss the park's spectacular setting. Sitting prettily on a plateau high above the

Springtime profusion on a Pipestem ridge

Bluestone River Gorge, the surrounding ridges roll off in every direction, changing moods with the time of day. White-tailed deer nibble bushes along the park road, wild turkeys rummage the understory, and the occasional golden or bald eagle soars in the blue sky above everything where a sense of splendid isolation pervades.

In summers long past, Algonquin, Shawnee, and Iroquois came to this remote spot in the Appalachians to fish and hunt. These people were probably the first to use the hollow, woody stems of the native "pipestem" bush (known as meadowsweet) to fashion their pipes, a practice that continued with later European colonists. The region's beauty was threatened around the turn of the 20th century, when the Bluestone River ran black with the coal dust of nearby industries—a blemish that since has been cleaned up. The park opened its gates to the public in 1970.

What to See and Do

With all the activities and facilities, you could easily spend a week at Pipestem and still have lots to do. If time is short, begin near the entrance station with the popular 0.33-mile walk to **Pipestem Knob Tower,** which offers a sweeping view of scattered farms and lush green mountains. Next, drive along the 3-mile **park road,** which bisects the plateau, extending the length of the park. Several pullouts provide a chance to pause and take in the spectacular mountain setting.

Along the way you pass the **stables** *(closed Mon. after Labor Day–Mem. Day; fee),* where horses may be rented. If you plan to spend more than a couple of days here, consider signing up for an overnight trail ride into Bluestone Canyon. The ride comes complete with a cookout beneath the stars and a berth in a primitive 1910 cabin. The overnight **Trout Wrangler ride** includes a stream crossing, modern lodging, and a professional fly-fishing guide in addition to a cookout *(reservations required).*

You should also make a point to visit the **Canyon Rim Center,** which is located near park headquarters. Housing the **Mountain Artisans Shop,** full of locally made handicrafts, the center serves as the upper terminus for an **aerial tramway** *(May–Oct.; fare)* that shoots into 1,200-foot Bluestone Canyon to **Mountain Creek Lodge** *(May–Oct.),* a romantic getaway that also features an elegant restaurant. The views alone are worth the trip, though the portion of the **River Trail** that wanders along the rugged, rock-strewn river at the bottom is first-rate.

If you don't take the tramway (or even if you do), don't miss the hike along the 0.75-mile **Canyon Rim Trail,** which leaves from the center and drops 500 feet off the plateau to Heritage Point. This large sandstone outcropping juts out over the gorge,

NEW RIVER: Flowing northwest from Hinton to Fayetteville, the New River Gorge National River promises some of the East's best white-water rafting, drawing floods of thrill seekers from mid-March to October. Lesser known are the river's landside treats: mountain biking, rock climbing (1,400 different course choices), plus 25 hiking trails that explore waterfalls, geological formations, and old coal and railroad towns. Stop by the Sandstone Visitor Center *(304-466-0417)* or the Canyon Rim Visitor Center *(304-574-2115)* in Lansing for the best views of the gorge, as well as exhibits that describe its geological and cultural history. You can also obtain information on how to arrange a white-water rafting trip.

offering sweeping views of pure mountain scenery. Along the way, sassafras and dogwood, maple and oak shade the rocky trail.

Just before you reach McKeever Lodge along the park road, leave your car and walk the short, steep trail to **Long Branch Lake,** a serene body of water nestled in the woods. Stocked with trout, the lake is popular with fishermen, canoeists, and paddleboaters *(rentals available at dock near Long Branch Lake Dam).*

At the end of the park road, seven-story **McKeever Lodge** sits on the lip of the canyon, offering stupendous views as well as an extravaganza of facilities. Even if you're not staying here, at least take a cup of coffee in the window-walled restaurant—preferably early in the morning, when purplish peaks float above gossamers of fog.

Further Adventures

Hardy hikers should consider taking the 4-mile one-way **River Trail,** an old road that begins near McKeever Lodge and winds to the bottom of Bluestone Gorge through a thick canopy of tulip poplar, oak, black locust, hemlock, and rhododendron. The trail passes the remains of a long-gone farmstead and offers plenty of chances to spot squirrels and white-tailed deer. Birders will appreciate the abundance of birdlife: 161 species have been spotted at Pipestem, including tundra swan, Bonaparte's gull, American wigeon, black-bellied plover, and 24 types of warblers. In September, hawks and other migratory raptors fly by. The fun part comes at the bottom of the canyon, where you must wade across the cool, green river *(before starting, check with park staff to see if the river is running high).* Walk downstream to Mountain Creek Lodge, and let the aerial tram whisk you back up to the canyon rim.

Another popular, albeit arduous, trail traces a rugged and unspoiled segment of the **Bluestone Gorge,** protected as the Bluestone National Scenic River. Hike the 8.5 miles to lovely 2,100-acre **Bluestone State Park** *(304-466-2805),* where misty mountains ring boat-dotted Bluestone Lake, and watch for great blue herons and kingfishers, which favor the warm-water stream. (During summer, park rangers sometimes lead groups on this beautiful foray into the wilderness.)

If you're not up to the hike, drive to Bluestone via W. Va. 20 and sample the lake's beauty along one of the park's short trails, through stream-laced woods inhabited by wild turkey flocks, white-tailed deer, woodchuck—and the elusive bobcat. The popular 2-mile **Boundary Trail** ambles to a cave in the forest.

Camping and Lodging

The park has 82 tent and RV sites, with shower facilities; and 26 housekeeping cabins. Camping fee. McKeever Lodge offers 113 rooms; the rustic Mountain Creek Lodge has 30 rooms (summer only; tram access). Call 304-466-1800 or 800-225-5982 for reservations.

Pipestem Resort State Park, P.O. Box 150, Pipestem, WV 25979; 304-466-1800 or 800-225-5982; www.pipestemresort.com

Blackwater Falls

Off W. Va. 32, near Davis

■ 2,456 acres ■ Year-round ■ Blackwater River Canyon ■ Hiking, cross-country skiing, fishing (license required), mountain biking ■ Petting zoo

Blackwater Falls

One of the most dramatic gorges east of the Mississippi slices through the Potomac Highlands in this park. Half a mile wide and 8 miles long, the canyon was cut by the Blackwater River, whose five-story-high falls are justifiably famous. Hugging the canyon rim, the park provides endless views of the gorge, and trails lead you close enough to the falls to feel their cool, misty breath on your face.

One of West Virginia's signature "resort parks," Blackwater boasts a beautifully situated stone-and-wood lodge overlooking

97

the canyon and an active Nordic center, with 20 miles of cross-country skiing trails, as well as dark West Virginia skies for prime star gazing for amateur astronomers.

What to See and Do

Obviously, **Blackwater Falls** are the park's major attraction, and maps available in the lodge information center list a number of relatively short trails weaving down into the gorge. The most accessible and therefore the most popular is the paved 0.25-mile **Gentle Trail,** which begins on Blackwater Falls Road before reaching the lodge and leads to an observation platform above the falls. Or, if stairs don't bother you, you can follow the more than 200 steps from the Trading Post parking lot to the roaring water. A final platform at the base of the falls offers a good sense of their power and beauty.

PARK TIP: *West Virginia's most photographed view—Lindy Point Overlook—is located at the end of a half-mile trail.*

The distinctive red-brown river water is stained by leaching from upcountry hemlocks and spruce. Rhododendron also frill the canyon edges, buffeting them in greenery year-round. In winter, mist from the falls veils the surrounding greenery in a lace of ice.

Two other trails worth following lie just west of the lodge on Blackwater Falls Road. If you take the mile-long **Balanced Rock Trail,** you'll come to a large sandstone boulder that seems to perch precariously on a smaller rock. As you leave the rock, you can take the trail spur to your left and make a quick loop around the **Rhododendron Trail,** especially appealing in summer. The nearby **Elakala Trail** will take you down to a footbridge across the **Upper Elakala Falls.** From here you weave back through a garden of huge boulders and equally impressive hemlocks. For hikers looking for something a little more challenging, pick up the 8-mile (one-way) **Blackwater/Canaan Trail** at the horse stables and follow it south through mountain scenery and into the wide-open Canaan Valley Resort State Park.

In the northwest corner of the park, **Pendleton Lake** offers a cooling alternative to mountain hiking, and keeps boaters occupied all through the summer months. In winter, cross-country skiers flock to the park to take advantage of evergreen-overhung trails and the area's predictably abundant snowfall. A toboggan run and rope tow *(fee)* provide more winter sport.

Camping and Lodging

The park has 65 tent and RV sites (May–Oct.), with shower facilities. Camping fee. Blackwater Lodge offers 54 rooms and 26 cabins. Reserve far in advance by calling the park at 304-259-5216 or 800-225-5982, or by visiting the website.

Blackwater Falls State Park, P.O. Drawer 490, Davis, WV 26260; 304-259-5216 or 800-225-5982; www.blackwaterfalls.com

Autumn-bedecked country road

Canaan Valley Resort

10 miles south of Davis, off W. Va. 32

■ 6,014 acres ■ Year-round ■ Mountain-ringed valley ■ Interpretive programs ■ Skiing, ice skating, hiking, swimming, golf

Gazing for the first time upon Canaan Valley's rugged beauty, a group of fur traders in the 18th century were reminded of Canaan, the promised land of milk and honey. Hunters who later ventured into the valley, however, formed a different opinion: Filled with bears, panthers, tangled growth, and dangerous cliffs, the place literally swallowed humans whole. These days, visitors here still feel like explorers, enduring narrow, winding, mountainous roads to reach this isolated pocket in central West Virginia. But those who persevere discover a mecca for outdoor recreation, and in the heart of it all sits Canaan Valley Resort State Park.

PARK TIP: *The Summer Tube Park with 5 lanes and a 1,000-foot drop is a family fun activity suitable for all ages.*

The main reason people come here is to ski in winter and play in summer. Cradled by tall peaks of the Alleghenies, the valley—actually the largest and highest plateau (3,200 feet) east of the Rockies—catches storms and collects an abundance of snow, heralding long winters and skiing from Thanksgiving into April. The state park boasts a ski area with 34 runs, plus a cross-country ski center and many miles of trails. Mountain biking, hiking, golfing, and canoeing on the Blackwater River take precedent in other seasons.

The charm of Canaan lies in its undisturbed wilderness, where animals outnumber the people. The thick stands of red spruce that

WINNOWING WOODCOCKS: The wetlands of Canaan Valley are the courtship grounds of the woodcock—a bird typically found much farther north in Canadian peatlands. From March into June, at dawn, dusk, and night, the males fly high into the sky and then dive-bomb the ground, their swept-back wings creating an odd humming sound loud enough to be heard—even by humans—half a mile away. A bird repeats this "winnow" up to eight times before dropping beside the female of his choice.

once filled the valley are long gone, thanks to loggers in the 1920s; but in their wake flourishes a realm of meadows, balsam swamps, marshes, ponds, and bogs that swarm with such wildlife as black ducks, green herons, minks, raccoons, and skunks, to name just a few. Beech, birch, and maple cloak the surrounding mountain ridges—the domain of white-tailed deer and snowshoe hare, coyote and black bear.

What to See and Do

If you're game for exploring the valley beyond the ski lifts, take the **Deer Run Trail,** which begins near the lodge (*ask for trail map at front desk*) and wanders for 1.5 miles through hemlocks, thickets of rhododendron and mountain laurel, and a balsam swamp. Watch for white-tailed deer and red squirrels (locally called "fairy diddles"), as well as golden-crowned kinglets, hermit thrushes, vireos, and warblers. At trail's end, you can visit the **Nature Center and Ski Touring Center,** then loop back to the lodge via the **Abe Run** and **Mill Run Trails.** Another easy hike, the 1-mile **Blackwater River Trail** (*trailhead at golf course parking lot; request a guide from the Nature Center*), ambles along the slow-moving Blackwater River, past some of the park's most beautiful big-toothed aspen.

Those wanting a more rugged experience—hiking or cross-country skiing—should head for the **Bald Knob Trail.** (From the lower lot of ski area, cross the road and walk up gravel drive to smaller parking area and the trailhead.) The steep, 1.25-mile climb through hardwood forest brings you to 4,308-foot Bald Knob, offering a stupendous view of the entire Canaan Valley. (For an easier route, pay a few dollars for the ski lift, which brings you to the ridgetop, then hike a short way to the knob.)

Another option is the **Canaan/Blackwater Trail** (8 miles one way), which climbs up and over Canaan Mountain to Blackwater Falls State Park, a popular trek especially among cross-country skiers. But be forewarned: The terrain is quite difficult. It is suggested that you stop by the Nature Center for additional information. At the end of the day, put up your feet at the lodge, which beckons with a snapping fire, hearty meals, whirlpool bath, and perhaps some live entertainment.

Camping and Lodging

The park has 34 tent and RV sites, with shower facilities. Camping fee. The Canaan Valley Lodge offers 250 rooms and 23 cabins. Call 304-866-4121 or 800-622-4121, or visit the website for reservations.

Canaan Valley Resort State Park, HC 70, Box 330, Davis, WV 26260; 304-866-4121 or 800-622-4121; www.canaanresort.com

Watoga

17 miles south of Marlinton, 3 miles east of US 219

■ 10,100 acres ■ Year-round ■ Hiking, fishing (license required), cross-country skiing

West Virginia's largest state park, Watoga sprawls across the Appalachian highlands near the Virginia border. Established in 1934, the park was developed by the Civilian Conservation Corps, and the quaint cabins they built still stand; a small museum details the CCC's efforts in the area. The shallow **Greenbrier River** that meanders along the park's western boundary accounts for its name: "Watauga" is Cherokee for "river of islands." Ensconced in lush, green hardwood forest, the park's 11-acre **Watoga Lake** is a classic West Virginia paradise. Most park facilities are in the northern half. The southern portion, adjacent to the vast Monongahela National Forest and the Calvin Price State Forest, remains wild.

PARK TIP: *Black bears are frequent summer guests along with white-tailed deer, river otters, wild turkeys, ruffed grouse, beavers, gray and red foxes, and the occasional bobcat at night.*

Pick up information at the park's rustic headquarters; then, for a long overview of the park, head up to the **T. M. Cheek Overlook.** For hikers and tree-lovers, the **Brooks Memorial Arboretum** offers several walks through forests of birch, hemlock, maple, beech, and tulip trees. A 6-mile round-trip bike ride on the **Ann Bailey Trail** will take you to a lookout tower with views of the Greenbrier Valley. Along the way listen for the unmistakable thrumping of wild ruffed grouse hidden in the forest. Take a row across the wide open waters of Watoga Lake, or try your hand at a little fishing, perhaps at **Laurel Run.** Evenings are good times to stroll along part of the **Greenbrier River Trail,** a 77-mile-long corridor following the path of the former C & O Railroad.

Camping and Lodging

The park has 100 tent and RV sites (mid-April–Nov.), with showers; 34 cabins (10 open year-round). Call 304-799-4087 or 800-225-5982 for reservations. Camping fee.

Watoga State Park, HC 82, Box 252, Marlinton, WV 24954; 304-799-4087; www.watoga.com

Flame azalea

SOUTHEAST

TENNESSEE

Fall Creek Falls
Roan Mountain
Pickett
Reelfoot Lake

KENTUCKY

Cumberland Falls
Natural Bridge
Carter Caves
John James Audubon

NORTH CAROLINA

Hanging Rock
Stone Mountain
Hammocks Beach
Fort Macon

103

MISSISSIPPI

Tishomingo
Winterville Mounds
Natchez
Percy Quin

ALABAMA

DeSoto
Cheaha
Joe Wheeler
Gulf

GEORGIA

Stephen C. Foster
Tallulah Gorge
Fort Mountain
Cloudland Canyon
Providence Canyon

FLORIDA

John Pennekamp
   Coral Reef
Myakka River
Wekiwa Springs
Paynes Prairie
St. Joseph Peninsula

SOUTH CAROLINA

Mountain Bridge
Devils Fork
Huntington Beach
Hunting Island

Sunrise at John Pennekamp Coral Reef State Park, Florida

Hanging Rock

4 miles northwest of Danbury, on Hanging Rock Park Road

▪ 7,040 acres ▪ Year-round ▪ 300-foot cliffs ▪ Waterfalls ▪ Hiking, rock climbing ▪ Boating, fishing (license required), swimming ▪ National Historic Landmark

View from Hanging Rock

Exposed knobs, peaks, and high rock cliffs characterize this rugged park lying in the Sauratown Mountains. Named for the Saura Indians, the range rises some 20 miles east of the Blue Ridge, hence the nickname "mountains away from the mountains." Hanging Rock, Moore's Wall, Wolf Rock, and other outcrops are supported by a foundation of quartzite. The resulting stone caps and ridges climb to 400 feet and range nearly 2 miles long on a mountain system that towers more than 1,500 feet above the countryside.

Nearby mineral spring resorts attracted visitors in the decades after the Civil War, but they were devastated by fires in the years leading up to the Great Depression. In 1936, a citizens group donated land for the creation of a park, and later in the decade the Civilian Conservation Corps started putting in a road, trails, a stone bathhouse, and a beach to accompany the 12-acre lake formed by damming Cascade Creek.

What to See and Do

Drive to the **Visitor Center** and pick up a trail map. The 0.7-mile **Chestnut Oak Nature Trail** offers a quick primer on the local forest as it gently winds along the lake under a canopy of oak and pine. More than 300 species of flora grow in the park, including rhododendron, mountain laurel, galax, azalea, and numerous ferns. At higher elevations you'll find delicate wildflowers such as lady's slipper, bird's-foot violet, and fire pink.

For waterfalls, park in the first lot and walk 0.3 mile to **Upper Cascades,** retrace your steps and take **Indian Creek Trail** down to **Hidden Falls** and **Window Falls** (0.6 mile from parking lot). The trail continues downhill, crossing the stream on big rocks, and pushing through the rhododendron understory 3 more miles to the Dan River. (To return, you must retrace your steps or have someone pick you up on the dirt road at trail's end.)

To get a good look at the park's signature rock formations, try **Hanging Rock Trail,** a 2.6-mile up-and-back hike that takes you to the top of the 200-foot cliff for which the park is named. From here, savor views of the surrounding country:

> PARK TIP: *Don't miss the spectacular Lower Cascades waterfall. Here you can walk to the base and dangle your feet in a pool of cool water.*

Moore's Knob shows itself to the west, and Winston-Salem is visible on clear days due south. If time allows, take the more strenuous, 4.3-mile **Moore's Wall Loop Trail,** which provides wonderfully close encounters with Moore's Knob and Balanced Rock, and offers a rewarding mountain vista from a 30-foot **observation tower.** Rock climbers test their agility and strength on Moore's Wall as well as on nearby **Cook's Wall.**

Hanging Rock Lake has a snack bar, stone-and-timber bathhouse, beach, and diving platform. In the summertime, chill out in the roped-off swimming area or fish for bass and bream. You can rent a rowboat or canoe and paddle around enjoying views of encircling forest and distant Moore's Knob. Also, check for regularly scheduled ranger programs on geology and mountain flora and fauna. You may be lucky enough to see a white-tailed deer, gray fox, or eastern screech owl. Wild turkey can be seen throughout the year, and on occasions, peregrine falcons can be heard during the winter nesting season.

LAYERED LOOK: As you walk the park's trails and gaze up at its sheer cliffs, you can read the rock walls for a history of time and movement of the Earth. Sand and mud from an inland sea were packed down to sandstone and shale, then metamorphosed with tremendous pressure and heat into hard quartzite and mica schist. Piled up like a stack of papers, the layers—each with its own color and texture— were then rumpled and bent, the stress so great that here and there they fractured.

Camping and Lodging

The park has 73 tent and RV sites, with showers, available by reservation. Eight group campsites offer more primitive arrangements; reservations required. Camping fee. There are also 10 cabins. For reservations, call the park at 877-722-6762.

Hanging Rock State Park, 1790 Hanging Park Rd., Danbury, NC 27016; 336-593-8480; www .ncsparks.gov/visit/parks/haro .main.php

Stone Mountain

7 miles southwest of Roaring Gap, off N.C. 1002

■ 14,100 acres ■ Year-round ■ 600-foot granite dome ■ Hiking ■ Waterfalls ■ Rock climbing, trout fishing (license required) ■ Historic structures

Rock climbers on face of Stone Mountain

More than 300 million years ago, molten lava blistered up under the Earth's surface and hardened into a 25-square-mile mass of igneous rock here in what would become the edge of North Carolina's mountain region. Part of that mass, Stone Mountain swells 600 feet high, its rounded bald front obscured from view until you are well into the park. The forces of erosion continue, rivulets of water clawing dark grooves down its face and standing pools leaving potholes on the top. Surrounding Stone Mountain, a forest of oak, maple, hickory, and pine gives cover to a host of wildlife, while a network of streams carves out valleys, in one case growing from a high trickle to a series of plunging falls.

Little is known of the area's earliest inhabitants, the Catawba, but the later white settlers made their living here by farming and logging. The mountain folk used to point out scars on the rock face and claim that they were made by the devil's chariot; a split in a gigantic boulder, they said, was caused by a shaking of the Earth on the day Christ was crucified. Long aware of the beauty and natural resources of the area, locals in the 1960s campaigned for the formation of a state park. At their prompting, the North Carolina Granite Corporation—owner of much of the desired property—donated 418.5 acres that included Stone Mountain, and agreed to sell more to the state. Thus, Stone Mountain State Park came into being in 1969 and was designated a National Natural Landmark six years later.

What to See and Do

Begin at the **Visitor Center,** a small but up-to-date facility loaded with interesting displays on pioneers and natural history. Among the exhibits are an 1865 muzzle loader, an 1870s loom, a 1930s mail-order banjo with calfskin head, and a copper moonshine still. A deck offers a fine view of the mountain. Pick up a map here and drive 2 miles down to the parking lot, where a 0.5-mile hike affords splendid views of the broad southwest face of Stone Mountain.

Try to make time for **Stone Mountain Trail.** The gorgeous 4.5-mile loop opens with an adrenaline-raising sign: "Area contains hazards associated with rocks, steep slopes and cliffs. Injury or death possible. Stay on Marked Trail!" You then ascend a precipitous trail, shooting up through the forest and out across tremendous slabs of granite. In less than a mile you're at the top, taking in magnificent panoramas. You could turn around and go back down, but staying with the loop brings you to **Stone Mountain Falls,** a 200-foot cascade. A series of steps and boardwalks offers safe viewing. Continue around to the base, fringed with pinewoods and high-grass meadows. At this point you can take another trail up to **Cedar Rock** (1 mile) and **Wolf Rock** (1.5 miles) granite outcrops. Or head back, passing the 1855 Hutchinson Homestead with its log cabin and outbuildings.

Hone your fly-fishing technique on one of the managed sections of Bullhead and Rich Mountain Creeks, where a limited number of anglers are allowed to fish on a catch-and-release basis *(fee).* Other streams in the system are open for take-home fishing. Finally, if you take the gravel road out, you'll drive past the quaint 1898 Garden Creek Baptist Church, one of the oldest churches in Wilkes County.

Camping

The park has 88 tent and RV sites, with showers; 6 backcountry sites. Available first come, first served. There are also 4 primitive tent sites suitable for groups; for reservations contact the park. Camping fee.

Stone Mountain State Park, 3042 Frank Pkwy., Roaring Gap, NC 28668; 336-957-8185; www.ncsparks.gov/visit/parks/stmo/main.php

107

BUG LADY: Betty Lou Wallace of nearby Mountain Park began collecting insects in the fourth grade. Pretty soon she was winning awards in state and national science fairs. Her butterflies, moths, and other insects—caught mostly in the 1950s—eventually numbered 9,000. Calling herself the "buggiest" girl in the state, Betty Lou raised many of her catches from egg to larva to pupa to adult. Part of her collection is on display in the Stone Mountain State Park Visitor Center; the handsome cases were built by her father, cabinetmaker I. O. Wallace.

Hammocks Beach

4 miles south of Swansboro, via N.C. 1511 and passenger ferry

▪ 1,160 acres ▪ Year-round ▪ Ferry fee ▪ No pets on ferry ▪ Barrier island ▪ Canoe trail ▪ Swimming, shelling, fishing

Located on unspoiled Bear Island, Hammocks Beach offers estuarine creeks, salt marshes, high dunes, and white-sand beaches. The 3.5-mile-long slip attracts nesting loggerhead turtles, while egrets and herons stalk the tidal creeks, and bottlenose dolphins sport offshore. Originally named Bare Island for its lack of vegetation, the island was a haven for pirates in the early 18th century. During World War II, the Coast Guard patrolled here against U-boats. Donated to a black teachers organization, the island became a "blacks only" park in 1961. After the Civil Rights Act of 1964, it opened to the general public.

A 15-minute ferry *(Mem. Day–Labor Day daily, May & Sept. Wed.–Sun., April & Oct. Fri.–Sun.; fare)* or a water taxi runs from the mainland. Once on the island, it's a 15-minute walk to the **beach**—bring good shoes, a hat, insect repellent, and plenty of sunscreen. A seasonal concessionaire sells drinks and snacks, and the bathhouse has showers and changing rooms. You can fish for flounder, trout, bluefish, and puppy drum. Stroll along the beach, take a swim, or just park yourself on the sand and soak up the sun.

Camping

The park has year-round backcountry sites, 14 with capacity for 6 people, 3 with capacity for 12. Reservations required; call 877-722-6764. Camping fee.

Hammocks Beach State Park, 1572 Hammocks Beach Rd., Swansboro, NC 28584; 910-326-4881; www.ncsparks.gov/visit/parks/habe/main.php

Bear Island dunes

Fort Macon

4 miles east of Atlantic Beach on N.C. 58

- 424 acres ■ Year-round ■ No camping ■ Civil War–era fort
- Ocean swimming, fishing

On the eastern tip of Bogue Banks, where the Atlantic crashes into Bogue Sound, a young Lt. William Eliason engineered the construction of a huge masonry bastion called **Fort Macon** to guard Beaufort Inlet. Earlier forts on the same site dated back to 1756. The present fort built between 1826 and 1834 was named for a North Carolina senator. On April 25, 1862, Union batteries bombarded the Confederate-held bastion for 11 hours, their rifled cannon pounding the fort. The Confederate surrender underscored the futility of 1820s defenses against 1860s technology.

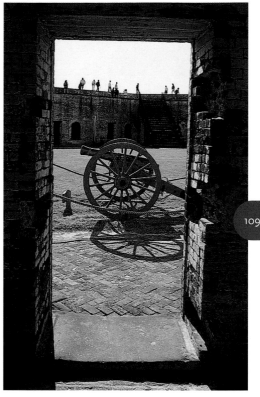

Fort Macon

After the war, Fort Macon served as a military and civil prison for about ten years, then was regarrisoned during the Spanish-American War. Abandoned for two decades, the fort was sold to North Carolina for one dollar in 1924 for use as a park. During World War II, coast artillery troops once again occupied the old fort. Since 1946, it has functioned as a major tourist draw, North Carolina's most visited state park.

Guided tours *(mid-April–mid-Oct.)* of the pentagonal fort explore local military history and ramble through the vaulted casemates, gunpowder magazines, and counterfire galleries. You can also pick up a self-guided tour brochure at the fort entrance.

Don't miss the new Coastal Education and Visitor Center, offering a greater understanding of North Carolina's fragile coastal ecology. And there are picnic shelters and outdoor grills. If you go fishing, you're likely to catch flounder, bluefish, or spot.

Fort Macon State Park, P.O. Box 127, Atlantic Beach, NC 28512; 252-726-3775; www.ncsparks.gov/visit/parks/foma/main.php

Mountain Bridge

Jones Gap Station: 25 miles northwest of Greenville, off US 276.
Caesars Head Station: 30 miles northwest of Greenville on US 276

Rock pinnacle, Caesars Head Station

■ 11,130 acres ■ Year-round ■ Waterfall ■ Mountain vistas ■ Hiking, fishing (license required)

Tucked into the state's mountainous northwest corner and linked by trails, Caesars Head and adjacent Jones Gap State Natural Areas were in 1996 combined into one entity—Mountain Bridge Wilderness Area. This is where the Blue Ridge suddenly drops 2,000 feet to South Carolina's piedmont, forming a high rock escarpment that gives wonderful views of the foothills to the south. Low-lying Jones Gap embraces the Middle Saluda River Valley, home to more than 600 plant species, while Caesars Head spreads over the highlands, its granite out-crop namesake somewhat resembling the Roman emperor's profile.

One of the earliest settlers here, planter and merchant Col. Benjamin Hagood, bought 500 acres just before the Civil War. Hagood herded livestock up the mountain in spring and stayed in his cabin until fall. Another pioneer, Solomon Jones, is said to have laid out a road in the 1840s without surveying instruments, relying instead on his instincts for contours and grades. The Jones Gap toll road went from River Falls to Caesars Head and on to Cedar Mountain, North Carolina. Now used by hikers, it's the easiest foot-path from Jones Gap to Caesars Head.

From the 1860s to the early 1900s, the toll road stayed busy with guests of a Caesars Head resort hotel. A journalist in 1895 wrote that "the way up is torturous, and possibly could be improved, but it is no child's play to build a road through these gorges and along the precipitous mountain sides." Nevertheless, one "finds rich compensation in the bracing atmosphere and the boundless views." People came from as far away as China for those views, and for dancing, dining, tennis, and swimming. Only the views remain—the hotel burned in 1954, and the old dance hall is now a private club just down from the Visitor Center. The parkland was privately owned until the state bought it in the late 1970s.

What to See and Do

Both Jones Gap Station and Caesars Head Station lie off the beaten tourism path, and most people come through for a quick look or for serious hiking or backpacking. If you want to look up at towering cliffs, go to Jones Gap; for views out from the clifftops, drive up the twisty road to Caesars Head.

Jones Gap Station

Starting with Jones Gap, from the hiker check-in station, a footbridge crosses the Middle Saluda and leads to a wide, shady picnic area and the pools of the old Cleveland Fish Hatchery, which operated here from 1931 to 1963. The rainbow, brook, and brown trout swimming in the pools provide a visual sample of what you might catch in the streams. Look up from here to the heights—forested mountains and steep rock walls rising more than 1,500 feet from the valley floor. Directly ahead looms Cleveland Cliff, a towering stone bulwark.

    Walk to the **Learning Center,** a stone-and-log building that sits on what used to be the fish hatchery superintendent's house. Take in the

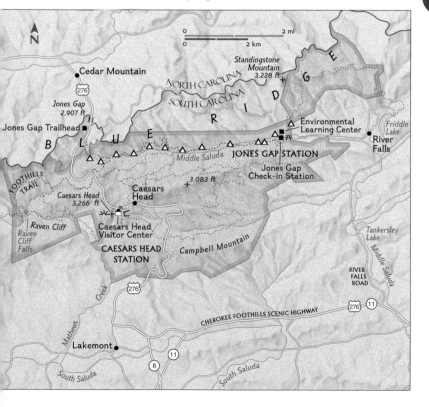

nature exhibits now located on the kiosk by the front pond. If you're backpacking, check on trailside campsites. Among the many trails from here, **Hospital Rock Trail** zigzags up Standingstone Mountain and east around to Friddle Lake—4.4 miles one way (then another 2 miles back along the road). It's a tough 1.2 miles up to Hospital Rock itself, a 30-foot-long shelter that was reputedly used by Confederates to stash medical supplies. For closer views take **Rim of the Gap Trail,** then connector #22 to **Pinnacle Pass Trail,** a 6-mile round-trip.

The easiest way from here up to Caesars Head is to hike west on the **Jones Gap Trail,** then hook up with connecting trails. Considered very strenuous, the **Rim of the Gap Trail** is a 5-mile walk up to Caesars Head, which affords excellent views of the mountains to the north. Unless you're in extremely good condition and want to walk back, have somebody drive around and meet you at the top.

Caesars Head Station

As you crest the mountain from the south, the parking lot for Caesars Head appears abruptly on the left. There's only one entrance before you start heading down the other side of the mountain, so drive slowly. The **Visitor Center** has a gift shop and interesting photographs from the resort hotel days. From here it's a short scramble out to the overlook atop the **Caesars Head promontory,** at an elevation of 3,266 feet. The panorama takes in Table Rock to the southwest, Table Rock reservoir, and long stretches of undulating hills that subside to plains. Hawks and ravens glide over this vast space.

Take the wooden stairway down through a crevice in the rock, a cool passageway known as **Devil's Kitchen.** Another viewpoint from down here allows you to look up at the profile of Caesars Head. If you can't see it, don't worry. The chin fell off 50 years ago, and actually, some people say, the mountain was named for a hunting dog that fell to its death.

If you have time for only one hike, drive a mile north and park at the trailhead for **Raven Cliff Falls,** a moderately difficult walk of 2 miles (one way). The effort brings you to a series of cascades that plummet a total of 420 feet down a narrow valley. Wildflowers you may see along the way include columbine, showy orchids, and jack-in-the-pulpit.

Camping

There is primitive trailside camping only. Call 866-345-7275 for reservations or visit www.southcarolinaparks.reserveamerica.com. Register at either station. Camping fee.

Mountain Bridge Wilderness Area, 8155 Geer Hwy., Cleveland, SC 29635; 864-836-6115; www.southcarolinaparks.com

Devils Fork

4 miles northeast of Salem, off S.C. 11

■ 644 acres ■ Year-round ■ Wilderness area ■ Boat rentals ■ Lake swimming, fishing (license required), hiking ■ Entrance fee

One of a string of parks just off the Cherokee Foothills Scenic Highway (S.C. 11), Devils Fork hugs the shore of Lake Jocassee, a 7,565-acre reservoir created in 1973 by Duke Power Company for hydroelectric energy. The park nudges into the Blue Ridge mountains, giving added pleasure to lake activities. Named for an area creek, the park dates from 1991. The neighboring **Jocassee Gorge** wilderness protects an additional 33,000 ecologically significant acres.

Lake Jocassee

Stop in first at park headquarters for information and a trail map. From here take the 1.5-mile **Oconee Bell Nature Trail** through pine and hardwood forest. The trail is named for a wildflower that blooms white in March; about 95 percent of the plant's total population grows here. From the picnic area, the moderate 2.5-mile **Bear Cove Trail** courses through mountain laurel and rhododendron thickets to a view of the lake and surrounding mountains. Wild turkey and white-tailed deer are common, as are bloodroot, trout lily, and other wildflowers. Bird species include the recently reintroduced peregrine falcon, while songbirds such as red-eyed vireo and scarlet tanager fill the woods with music.

The park's focal point, **Lake Jocassee** has a 75-mile shoreline and deep, clear water just right for boating and fishing; among likely catches are brown and rainbow trout, and smallmouth bass. The lake holds four state fishing records, including a brown trout of nearly 18 pounds. There are also five waterfalls that are accessible by boat only. Boat rentals are available at Lake Jocassee Outdoor Center *(0.5 mile before park entrance);* they'll deliver and pick up the boat. Swimming in the park is at your own risk.

Camping and Lodging

There are 84 tent and RV sites, with showers and laundry; 20 villas for more luxurious accommodations. Call 866-345-7275 for reservations. Visit the Jocassee Outdoor Center for boat rentals.

Devils Fork State Park, 161 Holcombe Circle, Salem, SC 29676; 864-944-2639; www.southcarolinaparks.com

Huntington Beach

3 miles south of Murrells Inlet on US 17

- 2,500 acres ▪ Year-round ▪ Day-use fee ▪ Beach ▪ Marsh boardwalk
- Nature trail ▪ Historic house

114

Wind-rippled dunes at Huntington Beach

One of the best preserved stretches on popular Grand Strand, Huntington Beach occupies 3 miles of gorgeous beach washed by warm seas. Extensive dunes and salt marsh shelter a variety of plants and animals on this length of South Carolina coast. In 1930 sculptor Anna Hyatt Huntington and her husband, railroad heir Archer Milton Huntington, bought a large tract of land that once belonged to four rice plantations. When the Huntingtons made their purchase, the property was a hunting and fishing preserve. Their idea was to study and protect the local flora and fauna as well as to build a winter home and studio on the beach—the Moorish-style Atalaya (Spanish for "watchtower") is open for tours.

The Huntingtons returned here regularly until 1947. After Mr. Huntington's death in 1955, Mrs. Huntington moved her studio across the highway to Brookgreen Gardens and most of the furniture to New York, where she died in 1973. The Trustees of Brookgreen leased the 2,500-acre parcel to South Carolina in 1960.

PARK TIP: *Take the Kerrigan Trail from the visitor's center to Mullet Pond observation deck—a premier bird-watching and alligator-viewing locale.*

What to See and Do

The park road starts in dense forest, then emerges to a lovely cause-way. On your right, a freshwater **lagoon** plays host to coots, marsh hens, grebes, and migratory ducks. Cattails, duckweed, and other plants edge this impoundment. Pull off after you cross the causeway and look for alligators lurking in the water. On the other side of the road, the saltwater **marsh** with its tall grasses and rushes is where you can spot snowy egrets, great blue herons, and other waterfowl.

Take the road to the right and drive a short way to the main park area. Here a park store sells supplies, and a two-story beachside pavil-ion has changing rooms. Although the low-lying gray building to the south may look somewhat forbidding, it's actually the Huntingtons' unique winter home, **Atalaya.** Acting as his own Civilian Conserva-tion Corps, Huntington hired local labor during the lean years of the early 1930s to construct Atalaya and Brookgreen Gardens. The 30-room mansion forms a square surrounding an courtyard planted with Sabal pal-mettos and Phoenix palms. You might imagine you're in a Mediterranean villa, its pierced brick walls, crumbling in places, covered with fig vines. The 40-foot tower held a 3,000-gallon water tank that, with the help of grav-ity, supplied the house with water. The rooms around the courtyard include Mrs. Huntington's spacious studio on the southern wing; a 25-foot skylight flooded the room with natural light.

> **SCULPTURE BY THE SEA:** Directly across from the park lies one of the South's greatest cultural trea-sures. Started by Archer Milton and Anna Hyatt Huntington in the 1930s, Brookgreen Gardens *(US 17. 843-235-6000. Adm. fee)* now displays more than 500 works of American sculpture in landscaped settings defined by lily pools, azaleas, dog-woods, and mossy live oaks. The rearing horses at the entrance are by Mrs. Huntington.

115

After touring Atalaya, walk up to the **beach.** If you want neigh-bors, stay close; if you want a whole beach, walk north or south.

Taking a left after the causeway brings you to the Education Center and the **boardwalk,** which extends 500 feet out to a covered deck for wildlife viewing. Across the road, the 1.5-mile **Sandpiper Pond Nature Trail** goes into the woods opposite the marsh. Following a 100-year-old abandoned road, the path enters a forest of live oak and loblolly pine, then leads to the brackish environs of Sandpiper Pond. To get a look at the park's various ecosystems, drive down the park road to the beach access and continue 1.2 miles to the jetty at the north end. There's a picnic area, and the jetty fishing is good for flounder, spottail bass, and croaker, or just enjoy the marine birds.

Camping

The park has 133 tent and RV sites, with showers and available by reservation by calling 866-345-7275, or online at www.south carolinaparks.reserveamerica.com. Camping fee.

Huntington Beach State Park, Murrells Inlet, SC 29576; 843-237-4440; www.southcarolinaparks.com

Hunting Island

16 miles east of Beaufort on US 21

- 5,000 acres ▪ Year-round ▪ Beach ▪ Historic lighthouse
- Nature Center ▪ Nature trails ▪ Fishing

A semitropical barrier island spreads its ample skirt of sandy beach for 4 pristine miles along the Atlantic shore, while back in its salt marsh mussels and fiddler crabs hide in mudflats, and herons and egrets (two of the 175 species of park birds) pose in tall cordgrass. Nearby plantation owners gave the island its name when they started the tradition of deer hunting here in the early 18th century, a tradition that continued until the island became a public park in the 1930s. Despite the hunting, deer remain abundant.

In 1938 the Civilian Conservation Corps began the task of constructing a 2-mile causeway over the marshes connecting Hunting

Island to the mainland. Fierce mosquitoes, a forest fire, and a hurricane hampered, but didn't defeat, their efforts. During World War II the Coast Guard moved in. The park reopened to the public after the war, and in the 1950s electricity and segregated bathhouses were installed. In 1966 all the park facilities were desegregated.

Though the causeway remains, nearly all the original CCC buildings have been wiped out by hurricanes and erosion. As coastal sands shift north to south, some 15 feet of island land is lost each year. Large shoals in St. Helena Sound just to the north claim much of the sand that would otherwise flow down to Hunting Island. To counteract the inevitable forces of wind and waves, more than four million

Palms at sunrise on Hunting Island

PARK TIP: *Visit the lagoon—
a staff favorite—where you're
bound to see a pelican perched
on a stump or discover a quiet
fishing spot.*

cubic yards of sand have been pumped in from offshore since 1968, but nature continues to make quick work of such stopgap efforts. Erosion happens so quickly in places that you can see tree skeletons standing in the surf where forests once grew. A prominent island landmark, the 1875 lighthouse was first located in a place now awash with breakers; the earlier light was destroyed during the Civil War.

What to See and Do

Entering the park, you drive through a dense forest of live oak, slash pine, and palmetto. The boardwalk across a freshwater pond to the **Visitor Center** is one of the best places for spotting alligators. The center itself has exhibits on cultural history, beach habitats, and the lighthouse. To make sure you don't miss it, drive around to the **Hunting Island Lighthouse** *(fee),* a 135-foot sentinel that operated until 1933. You can climb to the top and enjoy views of the beach, the ocean, and the island shoreline.

From here it's a short walk to the beach, but the dunes' prickly sand spurs make shoes a necessity. A picnic shelter, restrooms, and a beach shop are handy to the swimming area. Shells common along the beach include coquina clams, cockles, lettered olives, and knobbed and channeled whelks.

Just off the park road, a **nature trail** winds a 6-mile loop through an maritime forest. If you encounter alligators, give them a wide berth —they're unpredictable. The trail meanders for a while along the lagoon, once a freshwater marsh but now connected with Fripp Inlet. Across the highway, a short **marsh boardwalk** gives you access to what many call the island's beautiful side. Come at sunset for an enchanting view of golden grasses and long-legged birds.

To cast for whiting, spot, sea trout, and other saltwater fish, take Sea Island Parkway down to the southern end of the island, where a fishing pier extends 1,120 feet into the inlet. The **Hunting Island Nature Center** is located at the foot of the pier and offers visitors an interactive look at the many creatures found on this barrier island.

Camping and Lodging

The park has 200 tent and RV sites, with showers; one cabin is also available. Camping fee. For reservations, call 866-345-7275.

Hunting Island State Park, 2555 Sea Island Pkwy., Hunting Island, SC 29920; 843-838-2011; www.southcarolinaparks .com

117

TIDAL CHANGE: The Carolina marshes, dreamy backwaters fringed with rich mud and cordgrass, change character depending on the time of day—or, more accurately, on the tide. At low tide, fiddler crabs scurry out of their holes, while egrets and raccoons take advantage of low water to catch a meal. When the waters of high tide stream in from the ocean, the marsh becomes still and smooth as a mirror. But underneath is a food-chain hierarchy of microscopic nutrients, as well as shrimp, blue crabs, and even bottle-nosed dolphins.

Stephen C. Foster

18 miles northeast of Fargo on Ga. 177

■ 80 acres ■ Year-round ■ Fee for wildlife refuge ■ Okefenokee Swamp tours ■ Boardwalk nature trail ■ Boating, fishing (license required)

Bald cypress

Tall cypress trees dripping with Spanish moss make mirror-perfect reflections in the clean, black waters of an ancient swamp visited by alligators and water moccasins, bears and otters. An anhinga breaks the surface of the water, a fish speared on its beak, and flies to the nearest tree … then all is still again. Named for the songwriter who penned the line "Way down upon the Swanee [sic] River," the park occupies 80-acre Jones Island, which lies entirely inside the 396,000-acre **Okefenokee National Wildlife Refuge** *(912-496-3331).*

PARK TIP: *Don't be surprised if you see a black bear munching on acorns or palmetto berries in the fall.*

More of a watershed than a swamp, the Okefenokee is a shallow basin from which an inland sea retreated long ago, leaving a reservoir of water that gives rise to the Suwannee River on this (west) side and the St. Marys on the east. That original basin of water collected enough dead vegetation over thousands of years that layers of peat several feet thick began to form. As seeds blew onto these floating mats, aquatic plants and trees took root and islands appeared. Unlike most islands, these actually hang above the swamp floor; the thinner ones are spongy and shake if you walk on them, hence the Indian name Okefenokee ("land of the trembling earth").

The swamp was once owned by the Hebard Cypress Company, which drove 20-foot pilings deep into the muck and laid 35 miles of railroad track through the swamp. From 1908 to 1927 it harvested virgin cypress, employing 2,000 men and creating a lively community. In 1937 the wildlife refuge that now covers more than 90 percent of the 700-square-mile swamp was established. The state park was created on Jones Island within the national wildlife refuge in 1954.

What to See and Do

A good way to explore the swamp in spring and summer is by taking the 90-minute **boat tour** *(fare)*; sign up at the park office as soon as you arrive. Traveling the lily-speckled waterways, you'll see gators, egrets, herons, turtles, and stands of cypress. The tannic acid from decayed vegetation gives the water its dark color.

While waiting for a tour, or after, walk across to the **Museum** and adjoining **Interpretive Center.** The museum focuses on local flora and fauna, while the center holds exhibits on moonshining, turpentining, beekeeping, and other activities of the past.

From here, take the 1.5-mile **Trembling Earth Nature Trail** out behind the park office. An elevated **boardwalk** weaves 2,100 feet into the swamp, past mossy cypress, freshwater ponds, and wetlands. You'll probably see alligators and herons, and have a chance to spot deer, egrets, and sandhill cranes as well. In all, there are 234 species of birds in the refuge, and a resident population of 12,000 alligators. Interpretive markers punctuate the loop, and a covered pavilion

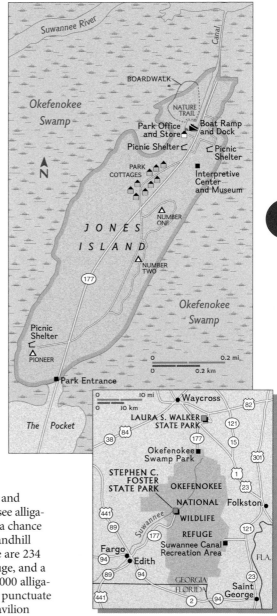

DOWN THE DRAIN: In 1890 an Atlanta lawyer named Capt. Harry Jackson had the bright idea of draining the Okefenokee Swamp. He bought up half the swamp and planned to dig a series of canals that would direct the water down the St. Marys River, leaving a dry Okefenokee worth millions in timber and fertile land. Not until a few years into the project did Jackson realize the enormity of the undertaking. By 1895 an 11.5-mile main canal and about 8 miles of branches were complete, but Jackson estimated it would take 300 miles to do the job. With funds drying up quicker than the swamp, Jackson gave it up and died shortly thereafter.

makes a fine perch for resting and studying the primordial scene.

Further Adventures

If you want to venture into the swamp on your own, there are 20 miles of marked waterways. Motorboat or canoe rentals are available for the day; the boat basin adjoins the park office and information center. While there, you can purchase supplies and pick up a trail map.

A canal leads from the boat basin out to **Billy's Lake,** the largest of the 60 named lakes in the Okefenokee. The 2-mile-long lake measures only 300 to 750 feet wide. If you go east on Billy's Lake, you come to **Billy's Island** *(3 miles from boat basin)*. You can tie up at the dock and take a 0.75-mile walking trail. The Hebard Cypress Company bought the island from a pioneer family and used it as their main interior camp. Houses sprang up on the 4-mile island, as well as streets, a hotel, and a movie theater. Lush new growth has erased nearly all signs of civilization, making it hard to imagine a thriving community of 600 people existing on this jungly outpost. But you can see an old cemetery, a couple of Indian mounds, a railroad bed, and a curiosity—the rusting frame of a car with a right-hand steering wheel.

To the north of Billy's Island lies **Minnie's Lake** *(4 miles from boat basin),* which connects to another finger of water called **Big Water Lake** *(5 miles farther)*. Big cypress punctuate the narrow waterway, which opens to a grassy prairie. Then at Big Water, you see more cypress and scrub underbrush. In addition to alligators and herons, look for red-shouldered hawks, vultures, and otters. There are two rest-stop shelters along the way for the paddle weary.

Camping and Lodging

The park has 64 tent and RV sites, with showers; 9 cottages. Reservations advised in season; call 800-864-7275. Fee.

Stephen C. Foster State Park, 17515 Hwy. 177, Fargo, GA 31631; 912-637-5274; www.gastateparks .org/info/scfoster

Boating on the Suwannee River

Tallulah Gorge

On US 441, in Tallulah Falls

▪ 2,711 acres ▪ Year-round ▪ Parking fee ▪ Wild gorge ▪ Rim trail, overlooks ▪ Lake swimming, tennis

A stream that drops as sharply as the Tallulah River can do a lot of landscaping over thousands of years. In less than a mile it plunges 500 feet, sawing its way through quartzite and leaving a legacy of rock formations and cascades. The Cherokee translation of "Tallulah" means "the cry of the frog." As you stand on the edge of the 2-mile-long Tallulah Gorge and peer 1,000 feet down to the river, it's as though you are looking back to the earliest rock.

The human history, by contrast, is relatively recent. A few decades before the Civil War, about the time the area's Indians were being forced out, the first white sightseers began coming to look at the gorge. By the late 19th century, the town of Tallulah Falls boasted 20 hotels, making it one of the most popular resorts in the South. Against protests of early environmentalists, a dam was installed above the falls in 1912 to generate electricity for Atlanta and other towns. As the novelty of the gorge wore off, resorts waned and by 1921 fires had virtually wiped the town off the map. For years, the area remained almost empty of tourists; and movies like *Deliverance* portrayed a

Tallulah River

place of untamed and dangerous beauty. In 1992 the Georgia Power Company leased acreage to the Georgia Department of Natural Resources, and the state park was born.

What to See and Do

If you're traveling north, follow signs to the right for the **Jane Hurt Yarn Interpretive Center.** Here, pick up maps and information and spend an hour browsing exhibits on the area's cultural and natural history. Highlights include a bird-watching station; information on persistent trillium, an endangered wildflower; panels and dioramas on the park's eight distinct ecosystems; and a must-see 15-minute film with footage of rock climbers and kayakers.

Approximately a mile long, the **North Rim Trail** has six overlooks and takes about one hour to walk both ways. The trail leads to breathless views of plunging waterslides, blue-green pools, and vertiginous cliffs where birds tilt and wheel in a wide chasm of air. The west end of the trail provides a fine vista of the spillways of **Tallulah Dam,** just beyond the east end where rock climbers go *(permit required; 20 issued per day).*

There is a trail almost the same length on the **South Rim,** which has five overlooks. Connecting the two trails is a dramatic 200-foot suspension bridge. Hikers must be prepared for the 531 steps from the north rim, 547 from the south rim, and an additional 25 from lower Hurricane Falls platform to gorge floor. You will need a permit *(100 issued per day)* if you plan to hike to the bottom of the gorge; check at the Interpretive Center.

If you want to bike or take a longer walk, inquire about the other 20 miles of trails, including the 10-mile off-road trail from the center to **Tugaloo Lake.** There is also a handicapped-accessible path to an overlook with views of **LaDora Falls.**

Five weekends *(April & Nov.)* the power company releases enough water to turn the river into a frothing rampage suitable for expert kayaking. For those who prefer more peaceful waters, the 63-acre **Tallulah Falls Lake** has a beach with a guarded swimming area.

WALKING ON AIR: Tallulah Gorge made it into the national news on July 18, 1970, when Karl Wallenda walked across it on a 2-inch-thick steel cable stretched 750 feet above the river. Some 35,000 spectators turned out to watch the 65-year-old circus family patriarch make the 1,000-foot crossing. During a high-wire stunt eight years later in Puerto Rico, Wallenda fell to his death. The remains of the towers from which the cable was suspended are visible on the north and south rims. Local lore has confirmed that Wallenda was not the first—a Professor Leon ropewalked across in 1886.

Camping

The park has 45 tent and RV sites and 5 tent-only sites, with showers. Reservations advised in season; call 706-754-7979. Camping fee.

Tallulah Gorge State Park., P.O. Box 248, Tallulah Falls, GA 30573; 706-754-7981; www.gastateparks.org/info/tallulah

Fort Mountain

8 miles east of Chatsworth on Ga. 52

- 3,711 acres ▪ Year-round ▪ Parking pass fee ▪ Mountain wilderness
- Hiking, swimming, fishing (license required)

Some of Georgia's prettiest scenery can be found in the hills, farms, and meadows of the Chattahoochee National Forest, where Fort Mountain crests to 2,800 feet at the southern end of the Appalachians. On this prominent lookout is a mysterious 855-foot-long rock wall built by Woodland Indians around 2,000 years ago. Framed by cliffs, the wall snakes around the mountain's south slope. In 1934 Dalton resident Ivan Allen donated 1,930 acres of land, including the wall, to the state, and the Civilian Conservation Corps developed the area into a park.

Autumn at Fort Mountain

Stop at the office for maps and information, then proceed to the parking lot for the **Old Fort Wall.** An overlook provides a good view of the ruin, or you can take the 1.8-mile **Old Fort Trail** around the structure and to a 50-foot stone **lookout tower.** Though tower views are obscured by tall trees, there's an overlook of the Cohutta Mountains to the west. Just before the parking lot, **Cool Springs Overlook** faces east over the Cohutta Wilderness Area.

PARK TIP: *Rise early to take in Georgia's best sunrise at the Cool Springs Overlook.*

Back at the main park area, the 0.7-mile **Big Rock Nature Trail** diverts out to a westward view of low-lying mountains rippling into purple haze. The trail follows the creek that issues from **Fort Mountain Lake.** You can take the **Lake Loop Trail** 1.2 miles around the lake, then head down to the beach *(May–Sept.).* Or rent a paddle or fishing boat. If you feel the need for a really good workout, head for the 8.2-mile **Gahuti Backpacking Trail** that loops nearly the entire park.

Camping and Lodging

The park has 70 tent and RV sites, with showers; 4 walk-in tent, 4 backcountry, 6 squirrel nest, and 3 pioneer sites, plus 15 cabins. Reservations advised in season; call 800-864-7275. Camping fee.

Fort Mountain State Park, 181 Fort Mountain Park Rd., Chatsworth, GA 30705; 706-422-1932; www.gastateparks.org/info/fortmt

123

Cloudland Canyon

8 miles southeast of Trenton on Ga. 136

- 3,485 acres ▪ Year-round ▪ Parking pass fee ▪ Hiking trails
- Tennis courts, disk golf

A gift of endless space characterizes this rugged mountain park. Standing at the canyon overlook where the ground drops away 1,000 feet, you feel the immense power of nature to make massive changes over time. Here at the western edge of Lookout Mountain, streams have chiseled away at the layers of shale and sandstone over the eons to create a deep gorge embellished by craggy cliffs and cascading waterfalls.

The state began acquiring land from local owners in 1938 for the establishment of a park; the completion of Ga. 136 the following year meant visitors no longer had to travel through Alabama or Tennessee to reach the canyon.

If you have just a short time at Cloudland Canyon, park at the **Canyon Overlook** (the Point) and in just a few steps enjoy the finest view in the park. Bear Creek (on your right) and Daniel Creek (left) join in the gorge below to form Sitton Gulch Creek, or Cloudland Canyon. Peering north out to the wide open valley—the direction of the streams—you look toward the oldest rocks in the area.

With more time you can take the **Waterfalls Trail** to the left, down into Daniel Creek Canyon. You pass through rhododendron, laurel, and hemlock along walls of sandstone—in places deeply undercut by the more easily eroding shale. Two prominent waterfalls are about a mile from the parking lot; the one to the right drops nearly 100 feet. Over time, these cascades will wear down their rock ledges and retreat farther upstream, eventually disappearing altogether as the slopes gradually smooth out. You can return to the parking lot, or continue up and along the west rim of Cloudland Canyon through hemlock, dogwood, and mountain laurel and back around for a 4.8-mile loop.

After your journey into the natural world, drive south from the parking area. Here the family can enjoy the swimming pool or tennis courts. A short walk from the courts is a wildlife-viewing area planted with clover, wheat, rye, and other goodies to tempt the appetites of deer, turkeys, rabbits, quail, and more. From the 16-foot observation tower you can watch animals enjoy hassle-free garden raiding and listen to the music of the eastern towhees and tufted titmice. Late afternoon is prime time for feeding.

Camping and Lodging

The park has 72 tent and RV sites, with showers; 30 walk-in tent sites; 16 cottages; and 11 backcountry sites. Reservations for all advised in season; call 800-864-7275. Camping fee.

Cloudland Canyon State Park, 122 Cloudland Canyon Park Rd., Rising Fawn, GA 30738; 706-657-4050; www.gastateparks.org/info/cloudland

Providence Canyon

7 miles west of Lumpkin on Ga. 39C

■ 1,108 acres ■ Year-round ■ Parking pass fee ■ Hiking

Thank the area's early settlers for Georgia's "little Grand Canyon," a striking network of 16 fingerlike gullies etched deep into the red-clay hills. Those early 19th-century farmers had no idea that clearing the trees for fields would set up an unstoppable erosion process. By 1850 water had cut ditches 5 feet deep in the soft, sandy soil. Today, there are 16 canyons in the park ranging from a quarter of a miler to 1.5 miles. The state park was created in 1971 to preserve and protect the canyon's unusual beauty.

Providence Canyon

Forty-three different colors of the castellated ridges and naked walls, including bright oranges, reds, violets, and whites, make an arresting sight, particularly in summer when wildflowers such as the rare plumleaf azalea add to the scene. Then hike along the rim for views into the gullies. If you only have a short time, drive to the picnic area and take the **rim walk** to the left for the best overlooks. You'll see where watercourses have planed the canyon walls. Sunrise and sunset fine-tune the scarlet tones.

You can hike into 9 of the 16 canyons from the 3-mile **Canyon Loop Trail.** The 7-mile **Red Blaze Backcountry Loop** takes you into the forested area overlooking the canyons.

Camping

The park has 6 backpack sites and rustic campsites for groups. Reservations advised in season; call the park or 800-864-7275. Camping fee.

Providence Canyon State Conservation Park, 8601 Canyon Rd., Lumpkin, GA 31815; 229-838-4706; www.gastateparks.org/info/providence

John Pennekamp Coral Reef

Mile Marker 102.5 on US 1, in Key Largo

- 63,845 acres ▪ Year-round ▪ Living coral reef ▪ Glass-bottom boat tours ▪ Scuba/snorkeling tours ▪ Nature and canoe trails ▪ Boat rentals ▪ Aquarium

Scuba diver at the reef

One of the great natural treasures of the Southeast, John Penne-kamp's coral reef flashes with color in the Straits of Florida. Almost 95 percent underwater, the park stretches approximately 25 miles along the shore and 3 miles into the ocean, protecting a portion of the only living coral reef offshore the continental United States. Trade winds and warm waters of the Gulf Stream bless this invaluable ecosystem, as well as the park's other intriguing communities—the sea grass beds, mangrove swamps, and tropical hammocks.

If you take a boat out to the patch reefs, you'll behold an undersea garden that has taken from 5,000 to 7,000 years to grow. The reefs are actually complex communities formed by living animals called polyps that secrete a limestone substrate around themselves. Over several generations, these substrates develop into a large, hard mass that not only anchors new polyps but shelters sponges, crabs, shrimps, and nearly 600 species of fish.

Early visitors to the reef could not resist taking home souvenirs in the form of live corals and seashells; what they couldn't break off, they went after with hammers, chisels, even dynamite. As the demand for marine trinkets increased, commercial vendors stepped up the harvest. At a biological conference in 1957, Dr. Gilbert Voss of the Marine Institute of Miami predicted that without restricted access the reef would soon be dead. An assistant editor for the *Miami Herald,* John Pennekamp, became the reef's most outspoken champion. Pennekamp had helped in the creation of Everglades National Park, and now he and Voss set out to marshal support from local government. So began a three-year battle against commercial businesses that depended upon plunder from the reef. The real winner was the reef itself, and in 1960 the country's first undersea park was dedicated.

What to See and Do

First off, head to the **Main Concession building** *(305-451-6300)* and check out boat tour times. If the weather is good, there are usually three glass-bottom and three snorkeling tours *(fee)* a day. Tours last about 2.5 hours; the snorkeling tours offer about 90 minutes in the water. Heading out to the reef, these tours show you the highlight of the park—the kaleidoscope of tropical life under the surface. Among the most colorful fish you'll see are angelfish, parrot fish, snapper, and triggerfish. Brain and star corals are accented by softer corals such as sea fans, plumes, and whips. In all, the reef harbors 40 different kinds of coral, and on days of good visibility, you can see for more than 100 feet underwater.

Above the surface is worth a look, too. The park and adjacent Key Largo portion of the **Florida Keys National Marine Sanctuary** *(305-852-7717)* cover a total of 178 square nautical miles, a dazzling sheet of blue-green water lined by mangroves. The park stretches nearly the entire length of Key Largo, longest of the keys.

CHRIST OF THE DEEP: Graced by pillars of sunlight, the most well-known landmark at the adjacent Florida Keys National Marine Sanctuary stands on the seafloor under 20 feet of water, its uplifted arms and flowing robe a familiar sight to hosts of snorkelers and fish. A 1961 gift from the Underwater Society of America, the nine-foot bronze is a copy of "Il Christo degli Abissi," placed in the Mediterranean Sea near Genoa as an inspiration to those who work or play in the ocean.

127

If you're stuck on land waiting for a tour, walk over to the **Visitor Center.** In addition to its friendly and knowledgeable staff, the center has a 30,000-gallon saltwater aquarium filled with a rainbow spectrum of fish, coral, sponges, and other marine life. You can study the exhibits and watch films here to get a feel for what you'll see out in the water. One worthwhile display, a tank of dead coral littered by trash, underscores the need to treat the fragile reef system with care; touching or standing on coral can harm it and is against the law.

After a boat tour, you'll probably be ready to idle away the rest of the day. You can rent snorkeling equipment at the concession building, then head over to **Cannon Beach** on Largo Sound. The rocky beach is typical of the Upper Keys, where the reef traps sand before it reaches the shore. You won't see much coral this far in, but there are tropical fish of all colors and shapes. A reconstructed Spanish shipwreck lies in shallow water about 130 feet offshore, complete with an anchor and cannons. Another fun thing to do is to rent a canoe or kayak at the main concession and explore the network of mangroves and tidal creeks on a 2.5-mile canoe trail that leads to the **Far Beach** area. There are showers and a swimming area here. *(Note: If you swim outside the designated swimming areas, you must display a Diver Down flag—available at Dive Shop.)*

Three short walking trails are easy to fit into a busy day and will give you an appreciation for the variety of Keys vegetation. The **Wild Tamarind Trail** loops through a hardwood hammock that includes tropical plants such as thatch palm, strangler fig, gumbo-limbo, and West Indian mahogany. Over near the water, the **Mangrove Trail** follows a boardwalk through red, black, and white mangroves, trees that can actually live in saltwater. Their cagelike roots provide sanctuary to young fish and help stabilize the shoreline.

Further Adventures

If you want to try scuba diving, the dive shop at the marina *(305-451-6322)* offers scuba tours both for novices and experienced divers. A noncertification resort course has you diving down to 20 feet within four hours, and an open-water certification class takes three to four days to complete.

To accommodate those wishing for more deep-sea adventure, the marina rents fishing boats. You need to study your navigation charts and know what the channel markers mean. Canoe and kayak rentals are also available.

Camping

The park has 47 tent and RV sites, with showers. Reservations are highly recommended; call 800-326-3521 or visit www.reserve america.com. Camping fee. Mid-fall through spring is the busy season.

John Pennekamp Coral Reef State Park, Mile Marker 102.5, P.O. Box 487, Key Largo, FL 33037; 305-451-1202; www.floridastateparks.org /pennekamp

Myakka River

9 miles east of I-75 on Fla. 72

- 37,000 acres ▪ Year-round ▪ Entrance fee ▪ Boat and tram tours
- Hiking, bird-watching, fishing (license required), biking

Cabbage palms along Myakka River

One of Florida's oldest and largest state parks spreads along the banks of the gentle Myakka River for 12 miles, presenting a wonderfully varied landscape of marsh-fringed lakes, oak and palm hammocks, pine flatwoods, and palmetto prairies. In general, as you drive the park road, deep woods lie to your right, while to your left are open views of marshes and Upper Myakka Lake. Deer, bobcats, and wild turkeys find good cover in the hammocks; alligators, turtles, and wading birds may be spotted out in the wetlands to the left.

129

The state purchased the land in 1934, and for the next seven years the Civilian Conservation Corps and the U.S. Army, with guidance from the National Park Service, developed the park with trails and facilities. Opened to the public in 1942, the park preserves one of Florida's most diverse natural areas. In 1985 the state legislature declared the Myakka a state wild and scenic river, giving special protection status to a 34-mile section and making it one of only three rivers in the state so designated. South of the highway sprawls the 7,500-acre wilderness preserve, a portion of the park completely unspoiled by any development.

What to See and Do

Myakka is a big park, and even though it's very popular—particularly on weekends—you can find a quiet corner without going to much trouble. You'll be handed a brochure and a tour schedule at the entrance gate. If you want more specific information—for instance, on backpacking, horseback riding, or the wilderness pre-serve—stop at the Visitor Center. If you need more details on tours and rentals, you'll get plenty of help down at the **Boat Basin.**

Park Drive winds 7 serpentine miles along the edge of the river and lake. The drive is itself a major attraction, affording fine views of the marshes and hammocks and offering plenty of turnouts for further study. Most drivers travel below the 25-mph limit. Just after the road crosses the river, pull over to the right for an unmarked **fisherman's trail.** This sandy path under rattling cabbage palms and moss-hung oaks follows the river downstream about a mile back toward the highway. Few people seem to be aware of this lovely trail that offers good views of the peaceful river and wetlands. A bit farther down the road is a designated 1-mile **nature loop.** The trail explores a pretty section of open forest, and interpretive markers provide interesting commentary on local flora and fauna. Along this walk discover one of the park's newest attractions—the **Myakka Canopy Walkway.** Suspended 25 feet above the ground, the board-walk extends 85 feet through the treetop canopy to a 74-foot tower with views of the "high frontier."

As you continue down the road, you'll see several places along the right to pull off for more hiking. The trails, nearly 40 miles total, loop out under dense hammocks and across dry prairies. You can walk out as far as you like, but to really get into the wilderness you'll need to backpack.

The busiest area in the park, the **Boat Basin,** lies about 3.5 miles from the entrance. Sign up here for the highly popular

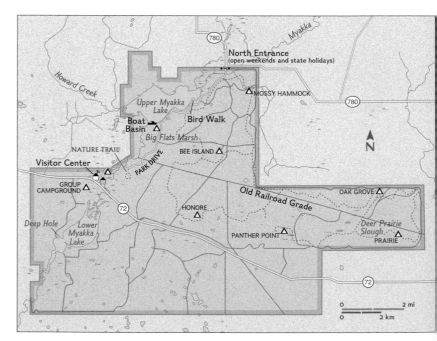

airboat tours *(fee)* and **tram safaris** *(fee),* running several times a day. The 70-passenger boats cruise around Lake Myakka for about an hour, while a guide outlines the ecological scene. The trams carry up to 50 passengers through the forested areas, and provide a running narration. To help you explore on your own, the Boat Basin rents canoes and kayaks, and the store sells picnic, fishing, and camping supplies. An invasion of hydrilla, an exotic weed, has reduced fish catches somewhat, but you can paddle quietly along the edges of the lake or downstream and observe alligators and long-legged birds.

A good alternative is to rent a bike here and pedal up to the north entrance (3.5 miles). The road is flat and scenic, and traffic is light. After about 2 miles, turn left for the **bird walk,** a boardwalk out to a viewing platform in the grassy marshes. Panels here help you put names to the birds you see, such as great blue herons, snowy egrets, roseate spoonbills, and various ducks. Just before the north entrance, you can turn right into a picnic area by a creek called **Clay Gully.**

Further Adventures

Considered one of the most beautiful places in the park, **Deer Prairie Slough** lies 10 miles to the east, its groves of giant maple and oak forming a high ceiling for a lush garden of ferns and subtropical plants. But since it's 6.5 miles one way from the trailhead, only hardy backpackers *(primitive campsites available)* and bikers get to see it. In the wet season (late spring to early fall) the ground soaks up a lot of water (bring plenty of socks).

If you don't want to camp out, you can still experience primitive Florida by heading across the highway to the **Myakka River Wilderness Preserve.** More than a quarter of the park's total acreage lies in this sanctuary of marshes and hammocks around **Lower Myakka Lake.** A limited number of visitors are allowed in each day; register at the Ranger Station (entrance gate) and drive over to the parking area. A dirt track leads 1.5 miles down to the lake; from here it's another half mile to **Deep Hole,** a 140-foot-deep sink favored by anglers.

Camping and Lodging

The park has 90 tent or RV sites, with showers. Majority available by reservation. Camping fee. There are also 5 log cabins. For cabin and campground reservations, call 877-444-6777; for backpack sites, 941-361-6511.

Myakka River State Park, 13208 Rte. 72, Sarasota, FL 34241; 941-361-6511; www .floridastateparks.org/myakkariver

131

SMART BURN: Florida's steamy inland prairies, vast grasslands dotted with wildflowers and saw palmettos, began to disappear as a result of fire exclusion practices encouraged early in the last century and implemented only until recently. The absence of fire nearly spelled disaster for Myakka's prairie. Without natural fires, trees and shrubs crept in on the prairie's turf, and animals dependent on this system vanished. To restore the open range, the park uses frequent prescribed burns and removes the feral pigs that are destroying prairie plants and animals.

Wekiwa Springs

3 miles north of Apopka, off Fla. 434 or Fla. 436

■ 8,000 acres ■ Year-round ■ Natural springs ■ Swimming, canoeing, hiking

Canoes on Wekiwa Springs

Birds call from unseen perches and fish flap the surface of the water as your canoe glides through an ancient wilderness. From the low swamps to the dry sand ridges, this inviting park presents a picture of Florida's wild and jungly interior almost as it looked before the arrival of Europeans. The presence of eight shell mounds in the park indicates that Timucuans—early hunter-gatherers— lived here on abundant fish and shellfish. The park takes its name from the Creek word for "spring of water." To complicate matters, Wekiwa (we-KI-wa) Springs forms the headwaters of Wekiva (we-KI-va) River, Creek for "flowing water."

White settlers began moving here in the 1840s, following the Second Seminole War. They cut down the cypress and farmed cotton and other crops, using the river to ship their goods and turn their grist- and sawmills. It was not long before tourists discovered the springs with their soothing mineral waters, and by the 1890s a resort hotel was in full swing in a town called Clay Springs. The Great Depression killed off the tourism trade and the town ceased to exist. After the hotel burned in 1953, it gradually melded back into the wilderness as locals began scavenging. What remains from that era are railroad grades used by loggers, and hundreds of large cypress stumps. But you won't see many cypress trees; the loggers were very thorough.

The Apopka Sportsmen Club bought the land in 1934 and held it as a fishing and hunting preserve until 1969. About that time, local developers were envisioning subdivisions, but the state stepped in, purchased the property, and opened it as a park in 1970. The adjacent Rock Springs Run State Reserve and Lower Wekiva River State Preserve, combined with Wekiwa Springs, make a total of more than 40,000 acres collectively called **Wekiva River Basin State Parks** (see sidebar).

What to See and Do

The entrance **Ranger Station** will get you started with brochures and maps. Most people come to paddle or take a dip in the spring waters, which maintain a temperature of 68° to 72°F. The **Wekiwa Springs** bathing area is enhanced by a boardwalk, ramp, and steps, the 3-acre swimming hole has a shallow and deep end. You can swim down toward the cave from where the water issues; the spring is so forceful it pushes you away. Afterward, spread a blanket on the grassy area and grab a snack. The nearby **Visitor Center** outlines the natural and cultural history of Wekiva Basin.

For a nice, leisurely outing, rent a canoe or kayak and paddle down **Wekiwa Springs Run** to Wekiwa Marina, have lunch, then head back. Allow two hours' paddling time for the 2-mile round-trip. The park also has a concession that offers canoe trips. You can paddle to Katie's Landing about 4.5 hours away, and they'll pick you up. For a longer excursion, drive to King's Landing (407-886-0859), rent a canoe and paddle 8.5 miles (about 6 hours) down **Rock Springs Run** to the marina. The King's Landing operators will pick you up here. *Remember: The park is a wilderness area and a map and potable water are necessities.*

PARK TIP: *Take a trail through the Sandhill area, where fall wildflowers flourish, especially after prescribed burns.*

If you want to give your arms a rest, try some of the 13.5-mile **Main Hiking Trail**. A shorter loop, the 5.3-mile **Volksmarch Trail,** offers much of the same scenery—riparian wetlands, then a climb up to pine flatwoods and a sandhill area, the remnants of dunes from before the last Ice Age.

Camping

Wekiwa Springs has 60 tent or RV sites, with showers. For reservations, call 800-326-3521. There are also 2 canoe camps and 2 backpack camps; call the park. Camping fee.

Wekiwa Springs State Park, 1800 Wekiwa Circle, Apopka, FL 32712; 407-884-2008; www.floridastateparks.org/wekiwasprings

Paynes Prairie

1 mile north of Micanopy on US 441

■ 22,000 acres ■ Year-round ■ Entrance fee ■ Hiking ■ Fishing (license required)

One of Florida's most significant natural areas sprawls over an 8.5-mile-wide basin created by the sinking of the terrain's limestone foundation. The ponds, marshes, wet prairie, and pinewoods that characterize the preserve are home to large numbers of alligators, wading birds, and otters, as well as wintering sandhill cranes and bald eagles. In 1774, naturalist William Bartram described the basin as the great Alachua Savannah. The preserve takes its name from King Payne, a Seminole chief.

PARK TIP: *Join a ranger-led hike to see Alachua Sink in action, while observing alligators and many of the 270-plus species of birds.*

Start at the **Visitor Center** *(352-466-4100),* which has a window onto the marshy prairie once home to bison. Although the basin fills with water from time to time, during a late 17th-century dry period the largest cattle ranch in Spanish Florida operated here. Two centuries later, during a wet spell, there was enough water to form a lake that served as a steamboat route. You can gain a broader perspective by taking the 0.3-mile **Wacahoota Trail** out to a 50-foot observation tower.

Also here, **Lake Wauberg** features a boat ramp and picnic area. You can fish for bream, bass, and speckled perch, but you'll need your own boat *(electric motors only).* Across the park road, **Chacala Trail** makes a loop of about 6 miles through pine flatwoods and shaded hammocks.

In the North Rim area, stop off at the **Bolen Bluff** trailhead (US 441). This pleasant 2.5-mile walk goes to a wildlife viewing platform. The **North Rim** has an Interpretive Center and the 3-mile **LaChua Trail,** which provides scenic views of the marsh, Alachua Sink, and Alachua Lake.

Camping

The park has 35 RV and 15 tent sites, with showers; for reservations, call 800-326-3521 or visit www.reserveamerica.com. Camping fee.

Paynes Prairie Preserve State Park, 100 Savannah Blvd., Micanopy, FL 32667; 352-466-3397; www.florida stateparks.org/paynesprairie

White ibises

St. Joseph Peninsula

*26 miles west of
Apalachicola on
State Rd. 30E*

- 2,716 acres - Year-round - Beaches
- Nature trails, boardwalk - Bird-watching

Sand dunes and sea oats along the Gulf shore

A long fishhook off the elbow in Florida's panhandle, the remote, rarefied beauty of St. Joseph cuts into the Gulf of Mexico. More than 9 miles of white quartz sand drape the park's Gulf shore, while a 10-mile bay side embraces mudflats, tidal marsh, and more sandy beach. Early Indians lived on shellfish from these warm waters. A Spanish fort was established here in the 17th century. But, except for U.S. Army training during World War II, the peninsula has remained fairly peaceful over the centuries.

Bird-watching—serious and incidental—is one of the favorite activities here. In addition to the usual resident long-legged shore- and wading birds, thousands of hawks fly through during fall migrations. You can see dozens a day, flying north as they follow the peninsula's hook back toward the mainland. They then arc down the Gulf Coast toward Mexico. Monarch butterflies and peregrine falcons wing their way through in fall.

Three nature trails, totaling about 5 miles, offer a look at the various coastal communities—beach, bay shore, dunes, flatwoods, and sandpine scrub. One of these paths explores the large dune system and its sea oats, yaupon holly, saw palmetto, rosemary, and other plants, passing tracks of the nocturnal raccoons and cotton mice. If you want to poke around the shallow bay area, rent a canoe from businesses just outside the park. And if you really want to get away from it all, a protected wilderness on the peninsula's north end makes up nearly two-thirds of the park's total acreage. You can pitch a tent out here, walk on 6 miles of trails, and absorb the sanctity of an untamed seashore.

Camping and Lodging

The park has 119 tent or RV sites (90 percent may be reserved), with showers, and 8 cabins. Call 800-326-3521. Camping fee.

St. Joseph Peninsula State Park, 8899 Cape San Blas Rd., Port St. Joe, FL 32456; 850-227-1327; www.floridastateparks.org/stjoseph

135

DeSoto

8 miles northeast of Fort Payne on County Rd. 89

- 3,502 acres ▪ Year-round ▪ Day-use fee ▪ 22-mile canyon drive
- 15 waterfalls ▪ Hiking ▪ Lodge ▪ Swimming, mountain biking

As you approach DeSoto State Park from the resort town of Mentone to the north, you'll take County Rd. 89, part of the scenic Lookout Mountain Parkway that stretches from Chattanooga to Gadsden. Vacation cottages and country stores intersperse with parkland, making it hard to tell when you're actually within park boundaries.

Seven miles before you reach the main park, signs direct you left (east) to DeSoto Falls, where Arthur Miller, a self-educated engineer, built a dam in the mid-1920s to supply power to nearby towns. Though no longer generating electricity, the project was a marvel of mountain community resourcefulness. Miller and a partner bought 300 acres of land surrounding the falls and planned to develop a vacation resort, divided into 266 building lots. But the Depression brought that dream to a halt.

The Civilian Conservation Corps arrived here in 1935, and put in cabins, a lodge, trails, and other facilities. Named for the Spanish explorer who made forays into the area in 1540 on a search for gold, the state park was dedicated in May 1939.

What to See and Do

DeSoto, an old-style park, does not have the slick visitor center, but it does have an extensive roster of interpretive activities. You need to make inquiries at the **Country Store** or **Lodge** *(256-845-5380 or 800-568-8840),* and pick up maps and brochures. The maps, however, are

DeSoto Falls

not to scale and can present a confusing tangle of roads and trails. Instead of describing neat loops, the trails meander all over the main park area, and are called by their corresponding blaze (Blue, Orange, Gold). Ask for suggestions on hikes and drives, then get specific directions. The challenge is well worth it—DeSoto offers a sense of rare untamed wilderness.

The 8 miles of trails wind along unusual geological formations, past endangered plant life, and over rustic footbridges. Start by walking along the bluff just behind the lodge. You can hike about as far as you like and get good views of Little River and its high rock cliffs. The **rhododendron trails,** located along here, take you past Indian Falls and other falls, and in May and June the rhododendron and mountain laurel burst into a pageant of color. The 0.25-mile Azalea Boardwalk Trail is handicapped accessible.

Back at the Country Store area you can swim in the Olympic-size pool (*Mem. Day–Labor Day*), or picnic in a stone shelter. This is also the play area—check out volleyballs, horseshoes, and

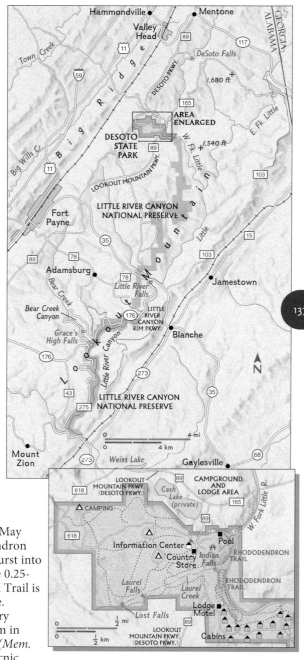

GRANNY DOLLAR: People around here still recall the legendary woman who was born in the 1820s and lived until 1931. Local papers back then found good material in Granny Dollar, the pipe-smoking part-Cherokee whose father had two wives and 26 children. She could remember her father hiding in a cave to avoid the 1830s Indian Removal. Near the end of her life she looked back with sadness: "Another race has taken our fields, our forests and our game ... The trouble with the white race is that they lay up so much for old age that they quit work at 50 and 60 years. When they stop working, they get out of touch with nature; all wear shoes in summer which keeps them from God's good earth; then they begin to fail, and soon they are dead."

other recreational equipment at the store. Next door the **Doyle Benefield Interpretive Center** *(Mem. Day–Oct.)* has mounted animals, live snakes, and displays on the area's history. From here drive 6 miles north to spectacular 100-foot-high **DeSoto Falls.**

Further Adventures

Riding the back of long, flat Lookout Mountain, **Little River Canyon National Preserve** *(256-845-9605)* sprawls some 40 miles north to south, its forest laced by streams slashing through the deep canyon along the park's eastern border. Union Gen. Andrew May tried crossing the timber-laden canyon in 1864, leading his troops to join Sherman in Georgia. Confederate snipers on his rear encouraged him to find a quick route across.

The **Little River Canyon Rim Parkway** twists for 22 miles, dipping around the river bends and the boundaries of the preserve. One of the deepest canyons east of the Mississippi, it descends 700 feet in its 16-mile run, its sheer walls and churning cascades a boon to rock climbers and whitewater enthusiasts. If you plan to climb or boat, contact the preserve.

Those who prefer to explore by car should drive 5 miles down County Rd. 89 from the Country Store; at Ala. 35 turn left, and travel 5 miles to the start of the parkway, Ala. 176. Here get out for a look at **Little River Falls,** a 60-foot plunge at the head of the canyon. After the first few miles, you'll find yourself pulling over every few minutes to gaze down into the gorge and out to the layered cliffs. The road at one point cuts far to the northwest to maneuver around **Bear Creek Canyon,** a tributary gorge adorned by **Grace's High Falls.**

The parkway's first 12 miles are on a good gravel-and-asphalt road. After that, the going gets rougher, with patches and potholes to slow you down. You can bail out after 12 miles (follow Ala. 176 west) and return on back roads to the lodge area.

PARK TIP: *Take the old CCC roadbed to the "unfinished bridge" meant to span Straight Creek and be part of the original DeSoto Parkway.*

Camping and Lodging

There are 94 tent and RV sites, with showers and hook-ups; 22 primitive sites; 22 cabins; and 25 lodge rooms. Camping fee. For reservations, call 256-845-5380 (campsites) or 800-760-4089.

DeSoto State Park, 13883 County Rd. 89, Fort Payne, AL 35967; 256-845-5075; www.alapark.com/desotoresort

Cheaha

20 miles south of Anniston on Ala. 281

- 2,719 acres ▪ Year-round ▪ Entrance fee
- Mountain vistas
- Hiking, biking
- Swimming, fishing (license required)

Little has changed at this easygoing state park since the early 1940s, when the Civilian Conservation Corps finished building the lodge and disbanded. The CCC started work here in 1933 when only a mule trail went to the top of Cheaha (CHE-ha) Mountain, the highest point in the state. After putting in a road, they erected an observation tower using only native stone and hand tools, then turned to building cabins and a 50-foot-long dam for

Wild Cheaha Mountain

139

a reservoir. The park still has the same benign charm and the same fine mountain views that attracted the earliest visitors. You can still spend a night in the lodge or cabins and walk the trails laid out by those industrious young men in the 1930s.

Creek for "high," Cheaha makes a final exclamation point in the Appalachian Mountains as they peter out in northern Alabama. Chestnut oaks and scrub pines cover the summit, and in autumn the red maples fire up the woods. Since Cheaha is located within Talladega National Forest, the overlooks give a sense of almost unlimited wilderness in all directions. Looking out from the cliffs, you may see turkey vultures and red-tailed hawks circling the heights.

What to See and Do

First stop by the park office or **Country Store** for a park map. Return to the park's entrance gate and drive the 2.5-mile **Bunker Loop** around the top of Cheaha Mountain. Along the way you'll want to stop for walks and overlooks, particularly for the 50-foot **Observation Tower** on the state's highest point. The 1930s stone tower beckons with terrific views of timbered hills rolling into the hazy distance; the 2,407-foot elevation may not sound like much, but you're so far above the surrounding landscape that you'll feel high up. The adjoining **CCC Museum** displays photos and tools of their camps.

Continue around to **Bald Rock Trail,** a 1-mile handicapped-accessible boardwalk loop through boulder-strewn woods on a high ridge. For the best overlook, you need only walk 0.25-mile out to a cliff with a grandstand vista of the soft green hills and hollows. Down the road, **Pulpit Rock Trail** is another nice short walk out to a similar westward exposure, but you also have a good southern vantage here and a view down to the park lake. This makes a fine place to picnic, or sit with the sun on your face and the scent of pine in the air.

TALLADEGA SCENIC BYWAY: One of the state's prettiest drives winds along Ala. 281 from just north of I-20 down through the park, then to Adams Gap. Sprinkled with views similar to those on Cheaha Mountain, the 27-mile byway follows the narrow ridge of Horseblock Mountain south toward the tail end of the Appalachians. You have fine views of the Coosa River valley to the west before the steep climb up Cheaha. The 100-mile Pinhoti Trail parallels the route and is the southern connection to the Appalachian Trail.

Another walk up here, the 0.25-mile **Rock Garden Trail,** brings you to fine overlooks of a cliff favored by rock climbers and rappelers. This trail continues as the Lake Trail for a mile, down to **Cheaha Lake** (or you can drive around). From May through August the lake and sandy beach are open for swimming, sunning, and fishing. Bring your own bait and tackle; paddleboats are available for rent. Further adventures may be found on the challenging new 6-mile **Cheaha Mountain Express Bike Trail,** which is open to hikers as well.

PARK TIP: *The 6-mile single-track Cheaha Mountain Express Bike Trail provides an ideal opportunity to see the native plants and animals.*

Camping and Lodging

The park has 73 tent or RV sites, with showers. Camping fee. There are also 11 cabins and 5 chalets; a 30-unit motel; plus 30 beds at the lodge. Reservations advised in season; call 205-488-5115 or 800-846-2654.

Cheaha State Park, 19644 Ala. 281, Delta, AL 36258; 256-488-5111; www.alapark.com/cheaharesort

Joe Wheeler

2 miles west of Rogersville, off US 72

▪ 2,550 acres ▪ Year-round ▪ Day-use fee ▪ Lake ▪ Golf, tennis, biking, swimming, fishing (license required) ▪ Convention/meeting facility

Named for a Confederate cavalry commander whose house stands nearby, this well-developed resort park hugs the shores of **Wheeler**

Lake, a 74-mile-long reservoir created by a dam that stretches more than a mile across the Tennessee River. Activities focus around the lake and the handsome stone-and-redwood **Resort Lodge,** complete with a dining room that overlooks the lake. A pool and swimming area in the lake are reserved for lodge guests only.

If you're not staying overnight, a special day-use area *(fee)* near the wooded campground offers a beach, bathhouse, picnic tables, tennis courts, and 5 miles of hiking trails. To get out on the lake, go up past the lodge to the marina and rent a paddleboat, fishing boat, or pontoon boat. There's also a 4-mile multiuse trail that has recently opened in the cabin area.

Camping and Lodging

The park has 116 tent or RV sites, with showers and hookups; 10 riverside cottages; 40 primitive tent sites. Reservations advised; call 256-247-1184. Camping fee. For reservations at the 27 cabins, 2 group lodges, and 75 units at Resort Lodge, call 256-247-5461.

Joe Wheeler State Park, 201 McLean Dr., Rogersville, AL 35652; 256-247-5466; www.alapark.com/joewheeler

Gulf

Just east of Gulf Shores on Ala. 182

▪ 6,150 acres ▪ Year-round ▪ Day-use fee ▪ Gulf of Mexico beach
▪ Golf, swimming, tennis

The wide welcome mat of this sunny park, a white-sand beach, runs for 2.5 miles along the Gulf of Mexico. First developed by the CCC in the 1930s, Gulf State Park was upgraded to resort status with new facilities in the 1970s.

Starting on the beach side of the highway, walk out onto the 1,512-foot **fishing pier** *(fee),* the longest in the Gulf. A bit farther east, the beach pavilion is the place to go if you just want an afternoon on the sand.

Across the highway, Lake Shelby offers freshwater fishing and swimming. The Nature Center here has exhibits on shore ecology and live animals from the area. You can take your own boat east through a canal to the smaller **Middle Lake,** where a campground sprawls on the north shore. There are over 7 miles of trails through the woods that connect the park with the surrounding cities.

Camping and Lodging

The park has 496 RV and tent sites, with showers. Camping fee. There are also 20 cabins and 11 cottages. For reservations, call 251-948-6353 (campsites only) or 800-252-7275 (for all).

Gulf State Park, 20115 Ala. 135, Gulf Shores, AL 36542; 251-948-7275; www.alapark.com/gulfstate

Tishomingo

2 miles south of Tishomingo, off Miss. 25 (or milepost 304 off Natchez Trace Pkwy.)

- 1,530 acres - Year-round - Day-use fee - Indian artifacts - Float trips
- Hiking, swimming, fishing (license required)

142

Dogwood at twilight on Haynes Lake

An old-fashioned state park, Tishomingo nestles in the Appalachian foothills on the border of Alabama, presenting a rugged contour unusual in this low-lying state. Tremendous sandstone cliffs vie for attention with moss-covered boulders strewn about the hillsides, while woodland trails explore cool glades lined by ferns and colorful wildflowers.

Named for a Chickasaw chief, the park was the site of paleo-Indians as early as 7000 B.C. The Indians relied on the high-quality chert and sandstone for making tools, and they used the local clay for ceramics.

The park straddles the Natchez Trace Parkway, the fabled highway extending nearly 500 miles from Nashville to Natchez that began as a bison trail followed by prehistoric hunters. By the early 18th century, the Trace was well worn by Indians, French and Spanish traders, trappers, soldiers, and missionaries. Cutthroats and vagabonds found easy prey on the long, lonely stretches darkened by tree tunnels, prompting early travelers to call the road the "devil's backbone."

The Civilian Conservation Corps started building a park here in the mid-1930s, putting in trails and facilities with rock quarried in the park. The pond just south of the Trace was created for the park's main water supply, and if you continue a bit farther on the park road, you can see the remnants of the old CCC camp off the trail on the right. Other reminders of their work can be found here and there throughout the park, including the swinging bridge across Bear Creek. In 1997, the park sponsored a crew from the service organization AmeriCorps to refurbish trails and facilities.

What to See and Do

After you arrive, stop first at the **park office,** where you can pick up a brochure and trail map. Then get some exercise outside on the 13-mile system of trails that range from short loops to sections 6 miles long. One of the best ways to acquaint yourself with the terrain and its subtle interplay of rocky ridges and shallow defiles is to take the **Bear Creek Outcroppings Trail** that begins on the swinging bridge near the pool. Cross the 186-foot-long bridge, suspended high above frothy, boulder-tossed Bear Creek, and continue up through the woods. You can get a drink from a cool, clean spring, and take a look at the park's largest rock shelter, the 62-foot-high **Jean's Overhang.** (The park's many overhangs average 25 to 30 feet.)

Though the park in general lacks overlooks and broad vistas, it specializes in close-ups; look carefully and you'll see a spectacular variety of plant life. Among more than 600 kinds of ferns and wildflowers are rare purple cliff brake and walking ferns, delicate fire pinks, spring beauties, and mayapple mandrakes, their blossoms like little umbrellas. In spring look for the blooms of oak-leaf hydrangea, wild azalea, and mountain laurel.

DULCIMER DAYS: They come from the mountains of Tennessee and the foothills of Alabama, from the hollers of north Georgia and the lowlands of Mississippi—everybody toting his or her own dulcimer and raring to play. Two weekends a year, in spring and fall, Tishomingo hosts an event that brings about 50 musicians. An informal jam session Friday night is followed by a full day of fine hillbilly music. Many of the players make their own instruments and bring extras to sell, and they'll show you how to start hammering out your own dulcet tunes. *(For information contact the park.)*

143

Returning along Bear Creek, the path offers fine views of cypress knees bent at the water's edge and the stream rushing and churning northward, building momentum on its way to the Tennessee River.

You can also walk on the other side of the creek, heading all the way up across the Trace to 45-acre **Haynes Lake** (2 miles from the pool). About halfway along this pretty walk, a trail to the left leads across the park road to a copy of an 1840s log cabin, donated by local families in the late 1970s. A short trail loops the old CCC pond behind the cabin. Popular with photographers, the scenic pond is edged with wildflowers and lilies, and it flows to a waterfall set about with boulders. Of course, if you prefer not to walk, you can drive up to the lake. Though there's no swimming here, you will find that the fishing here is good for catfish, bream, crappie, and bass.

Whereas the lake area dates from the 1960s, the **Horseshoe Bend** area was the work of the CCC in the 1930s. In addition to the cabins, the CCC built the old **Loochapola Lodge** of wood and native Highland Church sandstone, which serves as a focal point for various activities. Part of the rustic scenery, the people you see rocking on the wide front porch are locals who partake in an elder care program. In operation for some 30 years, the program doesn't just provide meals, it keeps seniors busy with quilting, pitching horseshoes, and the like. In addition to the elder care, the lodge serves as a rental facility for family reunions, church groups, Boy Scouts, and so forth.

Further Adventures

To cool off on a hot day, take a swim in the pool *(Mem. Day–Labor Day; fee)*, or sign up at the park office for a canoe trip

Paddling the Horseshoe Bend area

down **Bear Creek** *(mid-April–mid-Oct. Reservations strongly recommended through park; fee)*. The three-hour excursions begin 6.25 miles upstream *(transportation provided),* then meander back to the swinging bridge, offering pleasant, woodsy scenery. It's mostly a lazy float, but there are some Class I ripples that give you a chance to get wet. Offered once a day in season, the trips take up to 16 canoes.

Camping and Lodging

The park has 62 RV sites, with showers. There are also primitive tent and group cabin sites. Camping fee. Also available are 6 cabins; reservations advised in season. For information and all reservations, contact the park at 662-438-6914.

Tishomingo State Park, P.O. Box 880, Tishomingo, MS 38873; 662-438-6914; http://home.mdwfp.com

Winterville Mounds

6 miles north of Greenville off Miss. 1

▪ 42 acres ▪ Year-round ▪ Donation ▪ No camping ▪ Prehistoric
Indian mounds ▪ Museum

One of the numerous ceremonial settlements strung along the
Mississippi River, the village that flourished near here about a thousand years ago traded, farmed, fought, and played until it began to
disperse around the year 1450. Of the villagers' activities, one of the
most fascinating to modern civilization was their mound building.
Ten of the original earth mounds remain, including the 65-foot-high
Temple Mound. Villagers constructed most of the original 23 mounds
during the Mississippian period from 1200 to 1250 by hauling millions of cubic feet of dirt from as far as 16 miles away to create these
mounds in the form of an ellipse. The mounds were apparently part
of the religious system and the site of sacred ceremonies. While
many of the Winterville people were farmers and lived outside of
the mounds, it is believed that ranking tribal leaders and others lived
at the mound. Archaeologists believe that the general population of
Winterville began to decline after a great fire erupted and destroyed
the original building on the Temple Mound in 1300. Both mound
building and maintenance of existing mounds stopped after the fire.

Based on archaeological evidence, this civilization may have
been very similar in structure and tradition to that of the Natchez
Indian tribe of Mississippi, as documented in the early 1700s by
French explorers.

Originally at least 23 in number, these archaeological gold
mines were damaged or destroyed by modern farmers and highway
construction engineers, who bulldozed them flat when they were in
the way. But in some cases, the farmers accidentally preserved them
from erosion by planting them with hay and other crops.

In 1939 a community effort was led by the Greenville Garden
Club to purchase and protect this site. The first modern archaeological studies of Winterville were conducted by Harvard University and
the National Park Service in the 1940s. Winterville operated as a state
park from the mid-sixties to 2000, during which time it was officially
designated a National Historic Landmark. Today it is administered
by the Mississippi Department of Archives and History.

Built in the shape of a mound, the **Winterville Mounds Museum**
displays a dugout canoe, pottery, ax heads, spear points, bone and
stone tools, pipes, and bead and shell ornaments. Exhibits outline
Mississippian trade, agriculture, and daily life, focusing on the
culture that existed within the immediate vicinity. Interpretive programs help re-create a world far removed from ours. Take a short
trail that leads to the top of the Temple Mound (Mound A) for great
views of the flat delta terrain.

Winterville Mounds Historic Site, 2415 Hwy. 1N, Greenville, MS 38703;
662-334-4684; www.mdah.state.ms.us

Natchez

10 miles north of Natchez, off US 61

- 3,411 acres ▪ Year-round ▪ Entrance fee ▪ Deep South scenery
- Lake ▪ Fishing (license required) ▪ Nature trail ▪ Picnic area

Along the Natchez Trace

Located near the southern terminus of the Natchez Trace, this secluded, peaceful park dates from 1979. The park's visitors generally fall into two categories— tourists from Natchez and serious anglers. The sun-worshiping Natchez Indians lived in a nearby village until the arrival of the French in 1716. By the early 19th century, not only were the Indians and French gone, so were the later-arriving English and Spanish. The era of spiral staircases and sky-high ceilings was at hand. Built by rich cotton planters, dozens of the region's neoclassic mansions have survived and are on tour year-round.

Built in 1985, the 230-acre **Natchez State Park Lake** was stocked with bass, bluegill, red-ear bream, crappie, and catfish. That one time was enough to produce the state record 18.15-pound largemouth bass. You'll need your own fishing gear, but if you don't have any, you can still get out on the lake and paddle around the 50 acres of open lake water; the rest consists of standing dead timber and stumps. Rental cabins hide among the woods at lake's edge. The lake and nearby areas provide a home to alligators, water moccasins, and rattlesnakes. And you might want to note that in summer it's a good idea to bring insect repellent.

There are no set loop trails here, but you can wander old logging roads as far as you like. The terrain supports oak, hickory, poplar, and gum trees, and you may catch a glimpse of a deer or wild turkey.

Camping and Lodging

The park has 50 tent and RV sites, with showers and hook-ups; 10 cabins. Reservations advised in season; call the park at 601-442-2658. Camping fee.

Natchez State Park, 230 B Wickliff Rd., Natchez, MS 39120; 601-442-2658; http://home.mdwfp.com

Percy Quin

6 miles south of McComb, off I-55

■ 1,700 acres ■ Year-round ■ Entrance fee ■ Deep South scenery
■ Lake ■ Watersports ■ Fishing (license required), golf, swimming,
tennis ■ Nature trail ■ Conservation center

During the Great Depression, a local newspaper editor stirred
up interest in buying devalued land for the creation of a state park.
By 1935, a brigade of 200 Civilian Conservation Corps laborers,
working for a dollar a day, had begun cutting timber for the construction of a lodge and cabins. Within three years the work was
done, a dirt dam erected with wheelbarrows and shovels. Several
of the original structures built by the CCC still stand today, including the Visitor Center. Looking closely, you can still see the marks
of hand tools in the exposed beams of the building.

The park was named for U.S. Congressman Percy Edwards
Quin, whose ancestors were original Pike County settlers. In
1942, the dam that had been built with backbreaking labor broke,
and the lake dried up for three years, until $75,000 was raised
for rebuilding.

Percy Quin centers around 700-acre **Lake Tangipahoa,** edged
by loblolly pines and magnolias amid peaceful rolling hills. The best
way to get a feel for this Deep South park is to take part or all of the
8-mile nature trail that circles the lake. The trail offers the opportunity for spotting a variety of wildflowers and birds. Also notice many
of the more than 22 species of trees within the park, including black
cherry, spruce pine, red maple, water oak, white oak, and southern
chestnut oak.

Most people want to get right onto the lake. Park next to the
public boat ramp; the marina is for people who want to store their
own boats, and you'll need your own if you want to water-ski. A
public swimming area is located near the lodge, positioned near the
park entrance, and you can pick up information here. Nearby are the
swimming pool *(fee)* and archery range.

Stop for lunch at one of the many picnic sites, or take advantage
of the sports fields and playgrounds. There are five tennis courts and
a game room at the lodge.

For those who need to follow through on their swing, there
are 27 holes of golf at the Quail Hollow Golf Course *(601-684-2903.
Mem. Day–Labor Day; greens fee)*. The course offers a challenge for
any golfer with a variety of signature holes and flowing greens across
hilly terrain.

Camping and Lodging

The park has 101 RV and 40 tent sites, with showers; group sites;
and 27 cabins. Reservations advised; call 601-684-3938. Camping fee.

Percy Quin State Park, 2036 Percy Quin Dr., McComb, MS 39648;
601-684-3938; http://home.mdwfp.com

147

Fall Creek Falls

14 miles northwest of Pikeville on Tenn. 284

■ 25,300 acres ■ Year-round ■ Waterfalls ■ Hiking ■ Lake ■ Nature Center ■ Scenic drive ■ Resort lodge ■ Golf, tennis ■ Swimming, horseback riding, biking

Tennessee's largest and most popular state park lies on the western edge of the Cumberland Plateau, a forested area sliced by giant gorges and tumbling waterfalls. Though developed into a resort park, Fall Creek Falls maintains more than two-thirds of its acreage in a natural state; you can behold some of Tennessee's spectacular scenery just off a scenic drive along Cane Creek Gorge.

The rock layers you see exposed were laid down 250 to 325 million years ago, the remains of ancient dunes, tidal plains, and swamps.

Fall Creek Falls

The park's Cane Creek then began cutting through the terrain, leaving flat-topped hills. The three towering falls here were formed when tributaries eroded soft shales underlying sandstone ledges from which the water now cascades. The park's centerpiece, Fall Creek Falls, plunges 256 feet.

In 1935 the National Park Service made the place a recreation demonstration area, with the Civilian Conservation Corps and Works Progress Administration adding bridges, trails, and facilities. Old farmlands reverted to forest, while other large fields were planted with pines. Turned over to the state in 1944, the area began a period of steady growth and popularity. The state park officially opened as a resort in 1972.

What to See and Do

Whichever park entrance you use, well-marked signs direct you to the **Information Center** and visitor's lounge. Pick up trail maps and park literature here and plan your visit. If you're staying at the Fall Creek Falls Inn or one of the cabins, you may want to check in. At any rate, driving around that way (west) will take you across the dam and provides fine views of **Fall Creek Lake.** Nestled beside the lake, the three-story concrete inn may not have great visual appeal from the outside, but the rooms are quiet and comfortable. The spacious dining room serves good country buffets at reasonable prices; picture windows look onto the lake and its resident geese.

Just up the road, turn right for the 6-mile **Gorge Scenic Drive,** a wonderful

PARK TIP: *Explore the old homesteads and small waterfalls on your way to the Prater Place.*

loop that goes past the park's highlights. The first turnout is for **Fall Creek Falls** itself, where a short walk ends at a thrilling cliffside overlook. Nature must have been proud of her falls to have created this perfectly situated viewing platform. From here you look down on a semicircular amphitheater of stone over which the water plummets to a big plunge pool. Continuing around, pull over again for breathtaking views of the 800-foot-deep gorge, as wide as a mile in places. The sound of wind and water thunder up from the valley floor, and sundown tints the rock walls russet and ash. A good place to watch birds soaring the updrafts is from **Millikan's Overlook,** named for a naturalist who fell to his death climbing here in 1947.

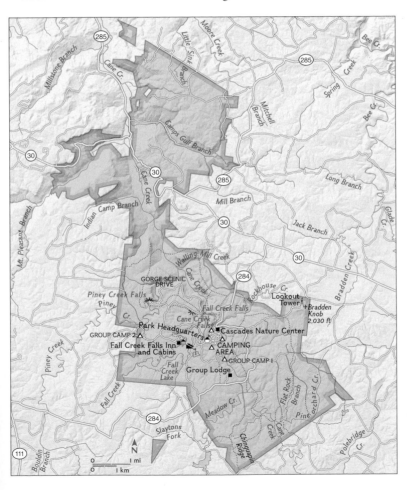

At **Piney Creek Falls Overlook,** two short paths lead out to another impressive waterfall, this one a 75-foot plunge. Virgin stands of eastern hemlock, yellow birch, and yellow poplar surround this secluded redoubt of stone terraces and pulpits. The path on the left takes you over a suspension bridge on the upper creek.

Hiking trails begin at the **Nature Center.** First, take a look inside at the exhibits on local geology, flora, and fauna. Choices are a live honeybee hive, taxidermic animals, and several films—the 14-minute film on the park gives you a good overview. Then take a walk. A bouncy suspension bridge over Cane Creek brings you to trailheads for Fall Creek Falls. The easy **Woodland Trail** is the quickest way there—about 20 minutes. Or you can swing out on the **Gorge Trail,** which takes a little longer because of its many overlooks. Both trails end up at the same overlook for Fall Creek Falls that you had on the scenic drive. If you have time and stamina, continue down a switchback trail for a little less than half a mile to the base of the falls. A good option is to head out on Gorge Trail and return on Woodland, for a total walk of about 90 minutes. A longer, yet easier stroll, the 4.6-mile **Paw Paw Trail** starts at the Nature Center, pauses for views of **Cane Creek Falls** and Fall Creek Falls, and winds back through the forest.

WINTER WORLD: The 256-foot Fall Creek Falls are perhaps at their magical best in the dead of winter. Frozen to a trickle, the mighty falls take on a strange silence, the high ledge hung with fangs of ice two stories tall, the plunge pool turned into an immense iceberg. In winter, you have nearly the whole park to yourself. Rhododendron leaves droop, curling in the cold, while the mist of creek water rimes low shrubs that clatter like heavy wind chimes as you push past. And a warm noontime sun can send 10-foot icicles crashing to the valley floor.

Further Adventures

If you have all day to hike, or want to do an overnight backpack, the **Cane Creek Lower Loop** courses around the gorge for about 12 miles. There are two designated camping areas *(permit required).* For another workout, the 13-mile Cane Creek Upper Loop offers an in-depth exploration of the creeks and forest of the park's southeastern corner.

Four miles of paved trails skirt the lake from the inn to Fall Creek Falls and out to Piney Creek Falls. Fall Creek Lake is stocked with bass, bream, and catfish. You can rent paddleboats, canoes, and boats from the boat dock, but you need to bring your own motor and battery.

Camping and Lodging

The park has 240 tent and RV sites, with showers; 30 cabins; 4 group camps with cabins or lodges. Some reservations taken; call 800-250-8611. To reserve rooms at the 145-room inn, call 800-250-8610. Camping fee.

Fall Creek Falls State Resort Park, 2900 Village Camp Rd., Pikeville, TN 37367; 423-881-3297; www.state.tn.us/environment/parks/fallcreekfalls

Roan Mountain

20 miles southeast of Elizabethton on Tenn. 143

- 2,006 acres ▪ Year-round ▪ Natural rhododendron garden
- 6,285-foot peak ▪ Hiking, swimming, camping

Every June, the top of Roan Mountain bursts into brilliant purples, pinks, and reds as the rhododendron garden on the 6,285-foot peak comes into blossom. Catawba legend claimed that the shrubs would bloom red after a bloody battle. In the 18th century a famous botanist, John Fraser, made a journey to the summit and reported back on the "new plant," *Rhododendron catawbiense.*

Such was the appeal of Roan Mountain that in 1877 Gen. Thomas Wilder erected a 20-room inn on the mountaintop, replacing it a mere eight years later with the 166-room Cloudland Hotel. Carriages ferried guests from the railroad station up to the hotel. Early advertising beckoned visitors to "magnificent views above the clouds where the rivers are born."

151

Rhododendron adorning Roan Mountain

Buying large tracts of land on area mountains, Wilder mined the hills for iron ore. By 1900, the mines had played out, Wilder sold his holdings; and the hotel was abandoned. Stands of mature balsam fir and spruce were cut down, and the rhododendron was dug up for sale to nurseries.

Left alone, the natural gardens began coming back to life, as thick and healthy as ever. In 1941 the U.S. Forest Service acquired the mountaintop acreage and began to manage the gardens, controlling the surrounding 850 acres of Fraser fir and spruce and thinning the rhododendron when necessary. Today the annual Rhododendron Festival, held the third weekend in June, draws crowds of admirers.

PARK TIP: *Stand on the Cate's Hole footbridge and gaze at the water flowing over the boulders with the Great White Laurel Rhododendron bushes lining the streamsides.*

Dave Miller Homestead

What to See and Do

Start your time in the park with a trip to the **Visitor Center,** which has displays on area culture and natural history. You can sit in a rocking chair on the porch to plan your visit. Then spend some time exploring the newly renovated Interpretive Center, or browse the expanded gift shop.

Stretch your legs on the 1-mile **Cloudland Nature Trail,** and get a taste for the mountain air before driving to higher elevations. Among the 150 species of wildflowers—which are in bloom from early May to early fall—are orchids, trilliums, and larkspur. The adjoining 0.4-mile **Peg Leg Mine Trail** takes you past a Doe River mill wheel and then back to the site of a 19th-century ore production works.

It's a 10-mile drive south to the top of Roan Mountain. On the way up, stop off at the **Dave Miller Homestead** (*Mem. Day–Labor Day Wed.–Sun.*), a farm with a log house, root cellar, and other dependencies dating from 1870 to 1919. Continue to the parking and picnic area on your right. Here you can play tennis, swim (*fee*), and run the kids through the playground. Trails from here include the delightful **Raven Rock Overlook,** a 0.6-mile walk through hemlocks and rhododendrons to views down to the pool and out upon the mountains to the west.

Drive on up to Carver's Gap, where the road intersects the Appalachian Trail. Turn right for Roan Knob and the rhododendron gardens. You're now actually beyond the park boundary and into **Pisgah National Forest** (*828-682-6146*).

ROAN MYSTERIES: No one knows how the mountain got its name. One version maintains that Daniel Boone left a roan horse up here, while some folks hold it was called after a "rowan tree" that grows bright red berries in late fall. Another enigma is the eerie music sometimes heard on the mountain. Scientists speculate that electrically charged air currents brush each other near the summit, filling the air with the sound of buzzing bees.

Camping and Lodging

The park has 86 tent or RV sites and 20 tent-only sites, with showers; 30 cabins. Reservations advised in season; call 423-772-3030. Camping fee. No tent camping mid-Nov. to mid-April.

Roan Mountain State Park, 1015 Hwy. 143, Roan Mountain, TN 37687; 423-772-0190 or 800-250-8620; www.state.tn .us/environment/parks/

Pickett

12 miles northeast of Jamestown on Tenn. 154

- Forest and park: over 20,000 acres; Park only: 900 acres ▪ Year-round ▪ Natural bridges and overhangs ▪ Hiking ▪ Lake swimming ▪ Fishing, hunting (license required for both)

Bobcat

Set in a secluded corner of Tennessee, Pickett holds some of the state's most striking geological features. Natural arches, cavelike overhangs, and graceful waterfalls await those who venture just off Tenn. 154 into the hilly forests.

In the early 1800s, white settlers began moving into the area that had once sheltered prehistoric Indians. By the early 1930s, the Civilian Conservation Corps had arrived, putting in trails, a boathouse, office, picnic shelters, rustic cabins, and a lodge made with locally quarried stone. The park opened to the public in 1940.

What to See and Do

Stop at the park office for trail maps and information. If you're short on time, take two or three of the shorter trails that lead to the park's many arresting geological points of interest. Driving just past the office and over Thompson Creek a quarter mile, you come to a turnout on your right. This is the trailhead for the vigorous, 10-mile **Hidden Passage Loop,** but a walk of just over a mile takes you to **Crystal Falls.** Mountain laurel and rhododendron line the trail, and if you hike quietly you have a good chance of surprising a deer. Since the release of black bears into the adjacent Big South Fork back-country, many have made the park home.

Even shorter trails are just off Tenn. 154 between the office and the park entrance: a 0.25-mile (one-way) trail leads to **Indian**

Rockhouse, a tremendous overhang, used by prehistoric Indians; on the other side of the road, **Hazard Cave**—the park's largest overhang—was named for CCC officer James E. Hazard. If you move far enough back in this cavernous auditorium of rock, the opening seems to close down like a giant eyelid. Walk back up to the road, or continue on until you link up with the network of trails around the lake and cabins. Driving toward the lake, pull over for **Natural Bridge.** You can walk across and under this 50-foot-long stone arch.

PARK TIP: *Look for the Hazard Cave glow worm, a gnat larva that in June produces a faint shine at night.*

Down at the boat dock, you can rent a canoe or rowboat and paddle around 15-acre **Arch Lake.** There's an unsupervised swimming area and fishing for trout and other species. From the park office, you may check out equipment for horseshoes, tennis, and volleyball. During the summer, a naturalist conducts free guided tours and campfire programs.

Be sure not to miss the new **Civilian Conservation Corps Museum,** which highlights the contributions made by the CCC in Tennessee.

Camping and Lodging

The park has 34 tent and RV sites. Available first come, first served. A group camp can handle up to 144 persons. Camping fee. The park also has 5 villas, 5 chalets, and 10 cottages; for reservations, call 931-879-5821 or 877-260-0010.

Pickett State Park, 4605 Pickett Park Hwy., Jamestown, TN 38556; 931-879-5821; www.state.tn.us/environment/parks/pickett

BIG SOUTH FORK: On Pickett's eastern border, the Big South Fork National River and Recreation Area *(Visitor Center on Tenn. 297, 15 miles west of Oneida. 423-286-7275)* encompasses a sprawling 119,000 acres in Tennessee and Kentucky. Over the ages, the Cumberland River's Big South Fork carved a rugged wonderland of spires, pinnacles, and sheer cliffs. Once ransacked by logging and mining operations, nature has begun reclaiming this gorgeous back-of-beyond. In addition to the many trails, adventurous souls seek out the 80 miles of streams, ranging from placid to dangerous white water.

Reelfoot Lake

5 miles southeast of Tiptonville on Tenn. 21

▪ 280 acres ▪ Year-round ▪ Boat cruises ▪ Bald eagle tours ▪ National Wildlife Refuge ▪ Wildlife drives ▪ Nature centers ▪ Hiking ▪ Fishing, hunting (license required for both)

Named for a legendary Indian, this appealing lakeside park is composed of ten segments situated among the 25,000-acre Reelfoot Lake Wildlife Management Area, 60 percent of it water and wetlands. Ancient cypress haunt the margins of Reelfoot Lake, while waterbirds and eagles add to a picture of primitive beauty. Only

5 miles from the Mississippi River, the lake was born during the New Madrid earthquakes in the winter of 1811-12, when violent landslides and sinks reshaped the area's topography.

Reflections of bald cypress

The **Reelfoot Lake Visitor Center** *(731-253-9652)* is a good place to familiarize yourself with the area and its offerings. Take in the excellent exhibits on the lake's formation and the area's natural history. Included here are a Native American exhibit and a boardwalk out through a cypress forest. Narrated pontoon boat tours *(fee)* operate May through September. Pick up an auto tour map and plan your itinerary. The 37-mile drive loops the lake and offers several miles of side excursions, plus 10 miles of hiking trails.

Next drive northeast on Tenn. 22 to the Visitor Center *(731-538-2481. Mon.–Fri.)* for the **Reelfoot Lake National Wildlife Refuge** where you can learn more about local flora and fauna. Some 125,000 Canada geese and 215,000 mallard ducks stop here during winter migrations. A 5-mile round-trip excursion from here, by car or foot, brings you to an observation platform on **Grassy Island,** a great place for viewing wildlife and sunsets.

Continuing back around to the Visitor Center, you can arrange to join an eagle-watching tour *(Jan.–early March; tour fee),* or there are also several possibilities for short hikes, including the **Keystone Trail,** which edges the lake for about 1.5 miles through old-growth cypress and offers views of waterfowl and wading birds.

If you have your own boat with you, you can fish for crappie, bream, largemouth bass, catfish, bluegill, and many other kinds of fish in **Reelfoot Lake,** one of the largest natural fish hatcheries in the country.

155

PARK TIP: *Plan to greet daybreak at the Visitor Center boardwalk. Sunsets are best enjoyed at the south campground.*

Camping

The park has two camping areas with 100 tent and RV sites, with showers. Available on a first-come, first-served basis. Camping fee.

Reelfoot Lake State Resort Park, 2595 State Rte. 21E, Tiptonville, TN 38079; 731-253-9652; www.state.tn.us/environment/parks/reelfootlake

Cumberland Falls

15 miles southwest of Corbin on Ky. 90

- 1,657 acres - Year-round - Hiking - Swimming, fishing (license required), horseback riding - Waterfalls - Moonbow - White-water rafting

On a boulder-tossed bend in the Cumberland River, a curtain of water 125 feet across drops nearly seven roaring stories, spraying the gorge with so much mist that on moonlit nights an eerie arc of light shimmers out from the falls. The only regularly occurring moonbow in the Western Hemisphere, the rare phenomenon works best during a full moon on a clear night. You should be able to catch a glimpse at least five nights a month (if the weather cooperates). But even if you miss the moonbow, there's still plenty to do.

Named in 1750 for the Duke of Cumberland by Kentucky explorer Dr. Thomas Walker, the river found itself the center of controversy in the 1920s, when above the falls a power dam was proposed. Delaware politician T. Coleman DuPont, who had summered here, offered to buy the whole area, including the falls, and donate it to the state. Suspicious that DuPont had an interest in the local utility, the legislature took three years to accept the offer. By then DuPont had already died, but his heirs made good on the offer, and Cumberland Falls State Park was dedicated on August 21, 1931. The ubiquitous CCC built the original DuPont Lodge and 15 cabins in 1933.

> **SWING TIME:** Put on your checkered shirts and cowboy boots, grab your partner, and head down to the poolside dance pavilion. A time-honored tradition at Cumberland Falls, square dancing takes place several nights a week during the summer. It's all right if you don't know a do-si-do from an electric slide; the caller will set you straight.

What to See and Do

If you arrive from Corbin, stop off first at the **DuPont Lodge** for brochures and maps. But if you can't wait to see the falls, continue on to the parking lot and walk the paved path out onto the rock slabs. The sight of pounding froth, the light mist on your skin, and the rush in your ears will keep you absorbed for a long time. A waist-high cable prevents you from straying too close to this tempting force of nature. To see the moonbow (at night), look just downstream from the base of the falls—the bow begins here, rising up about 50 feet and curving

Rafters in spray of Cumberland Falls

slightly down river. Your brochure will tell you when the phenomenon occurs.

The **Moonbow Trail** leads 10.7 miles downstream to the mouth of Laurel River, but the trail continues (as Sheltowee Trace) the entire length of the Daniel Boone National Forest. To make a 7-mile loop, in less than 2 miles cut right and up from the river on the **Cumberland River Trail.** After crossing Ky. 90, follow the road east for 25 yards, then head back into the woods and down an old logging road to the river; take the trail downstream about 2 miles back to the parking lot. The **Eagle Falls Trail** on the other side of the river, about 3 miles round-trip, offers views of Cumberland Falls and Eagle Falls.

PARK TIP: *Around lunch-time on a sunny day, you might see a single or double rainbow at the waterfall in place of a moonbow.*

You can take a guided rafting trip *(May–Oct.; fee),* or arrange for canoe or kayak rentals with a local outfitter. There are Class III rapids below the falls, and Class I and II above. For further cooling off, take a dip in the Olympic-size pool *(fee).*

Camping and Lodging

The park has 50 tent and RV sites (April–Oct.), with shower facilities. Make reservations by calling 888-459-7275 or online at www.reserve america.com. Camping fee. There are also 25 furnished cabins and 51 historic lodge units; call the park or visit the park's website to reserve.

Cumberland Falls State Resort Park, 7351 Hwy. 90, Corbin, KY 40701; 606-528-4121 or 800-325-0063; www.parks.ky.gov/findparks/resortparks/cf

Natural Bridge

2 miles south of Slade on Ky. 11

- 2,500 acres ▪ Year-round ▪ Sandstone arch ▪ Skylift ▪ Hiking
- Nature Center ▪ Lodge ▪ Lake, swimming pool

Natural Bridge

Less than an hour from Lexington, this popular park showcases several sandstone arches, rock shelters, and other impressive geological features. Existing for at least 100,000 years, Natural Bridge was originally a rock shelter with a solid back wall that water, wind, joint fractures, and gravity broke away, creating the arch. One of the area's massive arches, Natural Bridge has a mean width of 24 feet. (There are more than 150 arches found within a 5-mile radius, formed in different ways.)

PARK TIP: *Canoe or kayak the frequently overlooked Mill Creek Lake, a 50-acre body of water with massive sandstone cliffs surrounding.*

Early Indians discovered the area around 1500 B.C., taking up residence in the rock shelters and carving figures into the walls. Explorers heading from the Bluegrass arrived here in the mid-1700s, but the steep valleys and narrow ridges made settlement difficult. Railroads put in by lumber companies were bringing tourists here by the turn of the 20th century. In 1926 the Louisville & Nashville Railroad deeded the land to Kentucky, and the state park came into being.

What to See and Do

Start out at the **Activities Center;** the lower floor has a Nature Center with exhibits on the area's flora and fauna. After your orientation, pick up a map of the park's 10 trails and head out to **Natural Bridge.**

Blazed in the 1890s by the Lexington & Eastern Railroad, the **Original Trail** is your easiest bet—a 0.5-mile hike up through a forest of rhododendron, hemlock, yellow poplar, and white pine. A natural fracture on the other side of the bridge allows access to the top. For a more challenging and scenic walk up, take the 0.75-mile **Balanced Rock Trail,** which starts with a series of limestone steps and goes up past a cave. Continue up and around to Balanced Rock, a tremendous sandstone boulder that appears perched on a cliff. Walk along the base of the cliff, and eventually you arrive at the wooden shelter on top of a ridge near the arch.

A more leisurely walk up is available on the 1.75-mile **Rock Garden Trail.** For a four-hour hike, you can take the Balanced Rock Trail up to Natural Bridge, then take **Hood's Branch Trail** 4 miles around to the **Skylift** parking lot. Or ride the lift *(mid-April–Oct.; fee)* either to Natural Bridge and take Rock Garden Trail back to the lodge or Activities Center or connect with the new **Low Gap Trail** to the skylift parking area. If you can work in **Laurel Ridge Trail,** only three-fourths of a mile, you'll be rewarded with wonderful views of Natural Bridge and Middle Fork canyon. Just north of the Mountain Parkway, the 29,000-acre **Red River Gorge Geological Area** *(606-663-2852)* has some 60 miles of additional trails leading to impressive rock formations.

You can rent paddleboats *(Mem. Day–Labor Day)* for the small pond, and putter around **Hoedown Island,** where weekly square dances take place on an outdoor patio during the summer. Other recreational venues include a swimming pool *(fee for camping guests only)* and a miniature golf course.

Camping and Lodging

The park has 87 tent and RV sites, with showers; 12 primitive tent sites. All sites open April through Oct. For reservations, call 888-459-7275 or visit www.reserveamerica.com. Camping fee. Hemlock Lodge has 35 units, plus 11 one- and two-bedroom cottages; call 606-663-2214 or 800-325-1710 to reserve.

> **SILVER IN THEM THAR HILLS:** Generations of treasure seekers have been lured into the eastern Kentucky mountains by tales of an adventurer named John Swift, who allegedly found a Shawnee silver mine in the 1760s. In England to raise funds for a large expedition, Swift was jailed for his colonial sympathies during the Revolution. He later returned, a blind old man, and with his journal descriptions—which match with details in the Natural Bridge area—led believers on a search. They never found the silver, but just before his death Swift encouraged them, "Don't ever stop a lookin', boys. It's there and it'll make you and Kentucky rich." They didn't stop looking, and the unfortunate result was the destruction of many aboriginal sites.

Natural Bridge State Resort Park, 2135 Natural Bridge Rd., Slade, KY 40376; 606-663-2214 or 800-325-1710; www.parks.ky.gov

Carter Caves

8 miles northeast of Olive Hill on Ky. 182

■ 2,000 acres ■ Year-round ■ 20 caverns ■ Natural bridges ■ Hiking
■ Golf, tennis, swimming, horseback riding, fishing (license
required) ■ Fieldstone lodge ■ Flashlight required for each person
on some cave tours

A hilly country carved by the narrow, meandering Tygart's
Creek, Carter County is pitted with caves and graced by arches
and other natural features produced by thousands of years' erosion
of the limestone layers that underlie a hard sandstone cap. Open
to tourists since the 1880s, the commercial caves changed hands
a number of times until private donors deeded the land to the
state in 1946.

Start your visit by driving to the **Welcome Center** and making
a reservation to take a guided tour of one or two of the caves
open regularly *(fee)*. Considered the park's most scenic, **Cascade
Cave** *(75-minute tour)* is one of the largest of the 200 caves in the
county. Noteworthy are the spacious rooms, fantastic formations,
and 30-foot waterfall. The **X Cave** *(45-minute tour),* named for its
crossing passageways, also contains a number of large decorations.
Other caves in the park include the historic **Saltpetre Cave,** a source
of gunpowder material during the War of 1812, and the **Laurel
Cave** and **Horn Hollow** caves. Thousands of endangered Indiana
bats hibernate in **Bat Cave** and Saltpetre Cave during the winter.

From the Welcome Center, a 0.5-mile loop trail takes you to
Natural Bridge; the 180-foot-long tunnel through the hill is strong
enough to support a paved highway. It's also a good idea to take
as much of the 3.25-mile **3 Bridges Trail** as you're up for. Coursing
around the main part of the park, this gentle trail passes many
geological highlights, including **Fern Bridge**—a sandstone arch 90
feet high and 120 feet wide—and **Smokey Bridge,** the state's largest natural bridge at 90 feet by 220 feet. The 0.75-mile **Box Canyon
Trail** passes such striking features as Cascade Natural Bridge, Box
Canyon, and the Wind Tunnel.

Long and narrow **Smoky Valley Lake** offers 45 acres for fishing.
Guided canoe trips are offered in the summer *(fee)*. Another way to
see the park is on horseback along the 10.5-mile **Kiser Hollow Trail.**
The loop trail is open for daytime rides *(no trailside camping permitted)*. Horse rentals available Memorial Day to Labor Day *(fee)*.

Camping and Lodging

The park has 89 tent and RV sites (some open in winter), with
showers. To reserve, call 888-459-7275 or go to www.reserveamerica
.com. Camping fee. There are also 11 cottages and 28 lodge units;
call 800-325-0059 for reservations.

Carter Caves State Resort Park, 344 Caveland Dr., Olive Hill, KY 41164;
606-286-4411; www.parks.ky.gov

John James Audubon

On US 41N, in Henderson

- 705 acres ▪ Year-round ▪ No pets in nature preserve ▪ Art museum
- Nature Center ▪ Hiking, golfing, bird-watching, paddleboats

The great naturalist and artist John James Audubon (1785–1851) lived with his wife and children in Henderson, a small Ohio River town, from 1810 to 1819. On the Mississippi flyway, the town held irresistible appeal to the artist, his devoted wife noting, "I have a rival in every bird." Later, Audubon spent his life traveling the land from Florida to Labrador, meticulously and obsessively painting birds and other animals in their natural settings. His masterpiece, *The Birds of America,* was published in 1838.

Beech-maple forest

The park was crafted in the late 1930s by the Civilian Conservation Corps (CCC), who built six cottages, installed gardens, dug Recreation Lake by hand, and constructed the **John James Audubon Memorial Museum and Teahouse** in the style of a French-Norman inn to honor Audubon's French heritage. The museum features the world's largest collection of Audubon artwork and boasts a hands-on nature center, bird observatory, and public art gallery. You can join in naturalist-led nature talks and walks.

PARK TIP: *Hike the back-country trail in early March when spring wildflowers and migrating warblers appear.*

Several short trails totaling about 5.5 miles traipse about the nature preserve and to the wildlife lake; more than 20 species of warblers visit here every spring. To make a 3.3-mile circuit, walk from the Nature Center on Warbler Road until it joins with the **Back Country Trail.** Then take the **Wilderness Lake** and **Coffee Tree Trails** back to the center. Rent some clubs and hit the nine-hole golf course. Then rent a paddleboat or fish at the recreational lake *(Mem. Day–Labor Day).*

Camping and Lodging

There are 69 tent sites, with showers. Call 888-459-7275 to reserve or online at www.reserveamerica.com. Camping fee. Also, 6 cottages.

John James Audubon State Park, P.O. Box 576, Henderson, KY 42419; 270-826-2247; www.parks.ky.gov

GREAT LAKES

MINNESOTA

Itasca
Forestville/Mystery Cave
Tettegouche
Soudan Underground Mine
Blue Mounds

WISCONSIN

Devil's Lake
Peninsula
Rock Island
Copper Falls

MICHIGAN

Mackinac Island
Porcupine Mountains
Fort Wilkins
P.J. Hoffmaster
Hartwick Pines

163

ILLINOIS

Giant City
Fort Massac
Starved Rock
Mississippi Palisades
Ferne Clyffe

INDIANA

Brown County
Spring Mill
Falls of the Ohio
Indiana Dunes

OHIO

Hocking Hills
Hueston Woods
Kelleys Island
Maumee Bay

Grand Hotel, Mackinac Island, Michigan

Hocking Hills

12 miles west of Logan and US 33 on Ohio 664, in Hocking Hills

■ 2,331 acres ■ Year-round ■ Waterfalls, caves, and hollows ■ Hiking, swimming, biking, fishing (license required)

Old Man's Cave

Richard Rowe so loved the overhangs along the creeks of the Hocking Hills he moved into one, or under one, which became known as Old Man's Cave. Almost two centuries later, the recesses of the twisting gorge where Rowe lived (and is buried) still tempt those seeking refuge.

Water cutting through the Blackhand sandstone of these hills created a cluster of streams that drop through potholes and waterfalls, beribboned with ferns and hemlocks. Trails rise from the side to top cliffs and then tunnel beneath overhangs. The park is comprised of six separate areas, each with a distinctive feature: Rock House, Cantwell Cliffs, Cedar Falls, Conkles Hollow, Ash Cave, and, of course, Old Man's Cave. These units fit into a patchwork of state forest and natural areas that comprise more than 10,000 acres, linked by trails and roads.

Glaciers never flattened these hills, but they crept close to narrow and choke the canyon outlets, leading nearby Indian tribes to name a local river Hockhocking, or "bottle river." By the mid-19th century, non-Indian settlers had discovered the area's beauty. The CCC laid out trails, hewed steps and handholds into the sandstone, built stone bridges, and tunneled through obstacles in the gorges.

Dress warmly for the damp, cool climate of the gorges, and spot the red-backed salamanders in the rock crevasses as you roam among the giant hemlocks, birches, and yews.

PARK TIP: *For solitude take the 0.5-mile loop off the Gorge Trail to Broken Rock Falls. Here, the waterfall's mist nourishes flora and fauna.*

What to See and Do

Hikes in Hocking Hills are neither difficult nor long, but if you have time for a few, include **Ash Cave** and **Old Man's Cave.** The first trail, about 2 miles long, leads to a huge recess cave beneath a towering ledge. The cave's mouth yawns 90 feet tall and its rear wall lies 100 feet deep. Large ash piles were found inside, along with flints, pottery bits, and corn cobs—presumably left by a prehistoric barbecue.

You can hike trails that run up and down the gorge around Old Man's Cave, from **Upper Falls** and **Devil's Bathtub** at the north end to the **Lower Falls, Rowe's Cave,** and the **Sphinx Head** to the south. The eastern rim trail has splendid overlooks, but hike down into the gorge to feel the embrace of the tree-shrouded canyon and appreciate the arched stone bridges and recessed rock stairs. The **Visitor Center** at the trailhead has exhibits on the hills' geology and human inhabitants.

If you have more time, tackle **Conkles Hollow,** a canyon with tall trees and spring wildflowers. The rim trail, dangerous in slick conditions, leads to a falls overlook. **Rock House,** an extraordinary cave halfway up a 150-foot cliff, has a 25-foot ceiling and a 200-foot corridor, with arches at each end. Water and wind erosion have widened the sandstone cracks to form windows, and columns support the roof.

If you can, take a look at all six sections of the park. You may also want

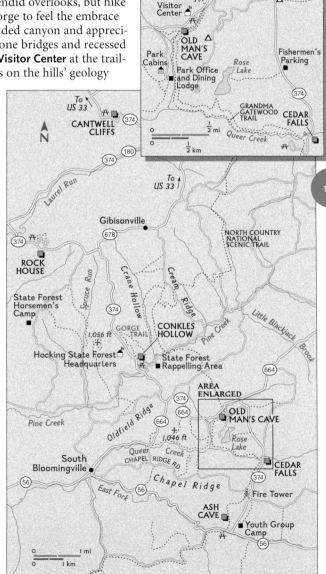

165

Cedar Falls

to check out the lodge and swimming pool near Old Man's Cave.

Further Adventures

In winter, the waterfalls are replaced by hanging ice, turning gorges into crystal palaces. Ice at the Ash Cave Waterfall builds like a stalactite, eventually forming a column 90 feet high. Hikers are particularly cautioned to stay on the trail. For 40 plus years, park rangers have led an annual hike the third Saturday in January from Old Man's Cave to Ash Cave.

Spring-fed **Rose Lake** offers ice fishing in winter and, in summer, serves up rainbow, golden, and brown trout (often fished out by midsummer), as well as bass and catfish.

The ambitious **Grandma Gatewood Trail** cuts through state forest land to link three Hocking Hill areas: Old Man's Cave, Cedar Falls, and Ash Cave. The 6-mile route is part of the North Country National Scenic Trail, which will run from New York to North Dakota when completed.

Surrounding the park, 9,238-acre **Hocking State Forest** *(740-385-4402)* provides additional opportunities, such as 40 miles of horse trails, with a horse camp near Rock House. The forest also hosts a mile-long rock-climbing area near Conkles Hollow, where climbers test themselves on 100-foot-high faces. Because the rock is sandstone, they anchor ropes to trees and top rope.

Camping and Lodging

The park has 172 tent and RV sites, with showers (about half available through winter), and two primitive walk-in camp areas (one for youth groups). Available by reservation. Camping fee. There are also 40 two-bedroom modern cabins with fireplaces, available year-round; call 888-644-6727 to reserve.

Hocking Hills State Park, 19852 S.R. 664, Logan, OH 43138; 740-385-6841; www.ohiodnr.com/parks

SLUMP BLOCKS: The canyon walls in Hocking Hills expose layers of an ancient sea, eons of fine sand compacted by the enormous weight of water and sediments that settled or were washed down when the Appalachian Mountains rose to the east. Overhanging cliffs form when water cuts through harder layers and reaches the easily eroded softer sandstone. As streams take their twists and turns, they gouge recess caves into the cliff faces. Eventually, the weight of the overhang is too much, and it breaks off and falls. One of these big chunks of stone, called a slump block, is in the middle of the Gorge Trail below the falls at Conkles Hollow.

166

Hueston Woods

45 miles west of Dayton, off Ohio 732

■ 3,596 acres ■ Year-round ■ Nature preserve, Nature Center, interpretive programs ■ Pioneer Farm Museum ■ Fossils ■ Hiking, swimming, fishing (license required), boating, miniature golf ■ Golf

The beech-maple forest that once stretched across Ohio survives here near the Indiana border. While most of the region's once vast forest was felled for farmland, soldier Matthew Hueston bought land along Four Mile Creek in 1797 and kept the axes away. Today, the virgin forest of the "Big Woods" is protected along Acton Lake's south shore.

The park caters to a range of recreational interests. There is golf, both standard and miniature, a man-made lake with marina and rentals, and a lodge with tennis courts and pools.

Creature comforts like these lure crowds, but they have not overshadowed more traditional park attractions. There are 10 miles of hiking trails, several fossil collection areas, and the Pioneer Farm Museum tucked within the golf course. The Nature Center has live animal exhibits and naturalist programs, and lovers of wildlife can visit the nearby Raptor Rehabilitation Education Project, a homeless shelter for injured or orphaned birds of prey.

167

Pioneer Farm Museum

What to See and Do

Pick up a map at the **Nature Center** and walk into the 200-acre **Big Woods,** where the shade of oaks, beeches, and maples shelters flowers and wispy ferns on the forest floor. Historians suggest the Hueston family saved these trees to tap them for sugary sap; each March naturalists set out to do just that, boiling the sap in the lakeside sugar house. Across the lake, **Cedar Falls Trail** (1 mile) is a favorite spring hike, when wildflowers blossom and the falls tumble down a series of shelves cut in shale and limestone.

The rocks of Hueston Woods are so riddled with marine fossils that visitors are free to dig up and pocket the remnants of whatever

RAPTOR REHAB: In Ohio, when a fledgling hawk falls out of a nest, or a barred owl runs into a power line, the bird may soon be vacationing at a state park. At Hueston Woods, the Raptor Rehabilitation Education Project takes in battered birds from all over the state and nurses them back to health. Visitors can tour the cages and flight pen at the center for a close look at these injured birds of prey, from turkey vultures to golden eagles. Many of the birds can't make it back to the wild, and become permanent residents at Hueston Woods State Park.

sea snails and octopuses they find. The tropical sea that covered the area 500 million years ago left buried in its sediments an enormous variety of ancient species. A booklet and map available at the Nature Center explains what bryozoans and trilobites are, and maps some of the better areas to collect.

The park has an area at the lake's west end for mountain biking *(bicycles are not allowed on hiking trails),* ranging from fairly relaxed loops to steeper, wilder trails. Bike rentals are available. There's a fishing pier near the sugar house on the south shore, and anglers also troll the 625-acre lake with boats of 10 horsepower or less, trying to snag bass, bluegill, and catfish. In summer, an active small craft sailing contingent can be seen tacking back and forth, and canoes, pontoon boats, and powerboats can also be rented *(513-523-8859).*

PARK TIP: *Watch life in the woods surrounding Acton Lake the easy way—from the lodge windows.*

Camping and Lodging
The park has 490 tent or RV sites (75 open in winter), with showers. Available on a first-come, first-served basis. Camping fee. There are also 3 camper cabins, with equipment provided; a yurt, a group camp; and a horse camp and arena at the north end of the park with 28 sites, 15 with electricity, (closed in winter). The park rents 59 cabins and offers a 94-room resort lodge, with a restaurant; for reservations, call 800-282-7275.

Hueston Woods State Park, 6301 Park Office Rd., College Corner, OH 45003; 513-523-6347; www.ohiodnr.com/parks

Kelleys Island

Ferry from Marblehead

▪ 676 acres ▪ Year-round ▪ Glacial grooves ▪ Boating, fishing (license required), hiking, swimming beach ▪ Nature preserve ▪ Ferry (419-798-9763)

Though Kelleys Island first became widely known for its wine in the 1830s, the park was established primarily to preserve the enormous grooves, among the largest in the world, dug by glaciers moving across the island more than 20,000 years ago. In places, the tracks are worn smooth as glass, as deep as 15 feet and 400 feet long. The glaciers' path can be viewed from an observation point north of the campground. Look for coral and shell animal fossils.

A short bike ride *(bikes & golf carts available for rent)* across the island leads to **Inscription Rock** and petroglyphs created by Native Americans some 500 years ago. Now faded by erosion, the art was copied in 1850 by Colonel Eastman. The park also offers 5 miles of hiking trails, a swimming beach, and naturalists available to discuss the unique vegetation.

Camping

The park has 129 tent or RV sites, with showers (May–Oct.); a group youth camp; two island yurts (getaway rentals); and two rent-a-camp sites. For reservations, call 866-644-6727 or check occupancy sign at the ferry. Camping fee.

Kelleys Island S.P., 1169 N. Buck Rd., Lakeside-Marblehead, OH 43440; 419-734-4424; www.ohiodnr.com/parks

169

Glacial grooves at Kelleys Island

Maumee Bay

9 miles east of Toledo via Ohio 2, then north on North Curtice Rd.

■ 1,400 acres ■ Year-round ■ Nature Center ■ Wetlands, marshes ■ Boating, golf, sledding

This is a remnant of the Great Black Swamp, the wetlands that covered the plains south of Lake Erie after the glaciers receded and the lake shrank to its present shore. The swamp was drained and logged a century ago and much is now farmland, but preservation of the habitat here provides a home to slithery things as well as a variety of birds.

Many visitors, however, are here for golf on the "Scottish Links" course, for entertainment at the amphitheater, perhaps a little walleye fishing *(license required),* or swimming at the beach along Erie.

Trautman Nature Center has maps, a naturalist on duty, and a new monarch butterfly exhibit. A 2-mile boardwalk trail explores the wetlands to the east, with interpretive signs and an observation blind.

Camping and Lodging

The park offers 256 tent or RV sites, with showers. Camping fee; call 866-644-6727 to reserve. Quilter Lodge has 120 rooms, 20 cottages, and a restaurant; call 800-282-7275 for lodge or cottage reservations.

Maumee Bay State Park, 1400 State Park Rd. #1, Oregon, OH 43618; 419-836-7758; www.ohiodnr.com/parks

Mackinac Island

Ferry from St. Ignace or Mackinaw City, or fly into Mackinac Island Airport (906-643-7165)

▪ 1,800 acres ▪ Year-round, Fort Mackinac May through Oct.
▪ No cars ▪ No camping ▪ Historic hotel ▪ Carriage rides ▪ Arch Rock ▪ Interpreters ▪ Biking, hiking ▪ National Historic Landmark

Mackinac Island's peaceful shoreline

Hiking to the high point of the island above Fort Mackinac, it's hard to understand how the British maintained their concentration and aimed their cannon at the Americans below during a sneak attack on the fort during the War of 1812. The views from 320 feet above the lake are distractingly spectacular in all directions. Back in 1812, however, the island was coveted as a key strategic military post, guarding the Straits of Mackinac. The British quietly rowed ashore at the island's north end and marched under cover of darkness along Mackinac's spine.

Today, it's the beauty of this Shangri-la most visitors hope to capture. Within the 2,200-acre island is the gem of Michigan's state parks. Here soldiers costumed in American uniforms now play music on the parade ground and load and fire the cannon at Michigan's only Revolutionary War fort. Interpreters re-create military life in the 1880s, and if this is any indication, life at the outpost wasn't bad. Even then, Mackinac was a popular vacation spot, renowned for its beauty, its luxurious hotel, and swept clean by the lake breezes, a lack of irritating insects.

What to See and Do

Start at the **Visitor Center,** which sits by the boat slips just west of the marina, looking up at Fort Mackinac across **Marquette Park.** (There is also an information kiosk on Huron Street.) Here you can get maps and advice, and see an audiovisual program about the island.

Before starting your trek up to the fort, you might want to visit some downtown attractions, from the **Benjamin Blacksmith Shop** on Market Street—note the scarifying tools for repairing horses' teeth— to the 1830 **Mission Church** on Huron (Main) Street (and don't miss the famous fudge shops). There are also various buildings dating back to the 1820s, when the American fur trade was centered here. Continuing east along the lake, you pass beautiful old hotels and summer houses.

The gleaming white ramparts of **Fort Mackinac** stand grandly 150 feet above the town, approached by a wide ramp up the hillside behind Marquette Park. There are 14 historic buildings within, from the Soldiers' Barracks (which now house a museum shop) to the Officers' Stone Quarters, where you can drink tea while taking in a view of the straits from the terrace and the Mackinac Bridge on the lower level. Music and musket fire by period-costumed guides take place on the vast parade grounds at the fort's center, and a comprehensive exhibit covers the area's history.

In today's mechanized age, the lack of autos on the island is one of its chief distinctions. Numerous island vendors rent bicycles of various capabilities, and this is how many folks tour, stopping along the routes for short hikes to particular features. You can also hire a carriage or, if you like mini-marathons, run the 8.5-mile shore circuit. On the east shore, hardy souls climb the steep stairs to **Arch Rock,** while others take a less arduous route there by bicycle above the fort. You might see a sailboat on the lake framed in the arch, which spans 50 feet, while a seagull poses on top. **Sugar Loaf,** a limestone outcrop, is not far away.

From British Landing you can either continue along the sunny western shore or take the route of the invading soldiers up along the island's spine. The high road leads back to the south side of the island, where you can veer west by the Jewel Golf Course for a visit

171

to the 1887 **Grand Hotel** *(800-334-7263. Mid-May–Oct.)*, which keeps its Victorian nose in the air by requiring that men wear jackets and ties and that women "not be attired in slacks" after 6 p.m. You can't miss seeing the 660-foot veranda as you approach the island by ferry, but if you want to stroll along it, you'll either have to rent a room or pay a fee … and dress correctly.

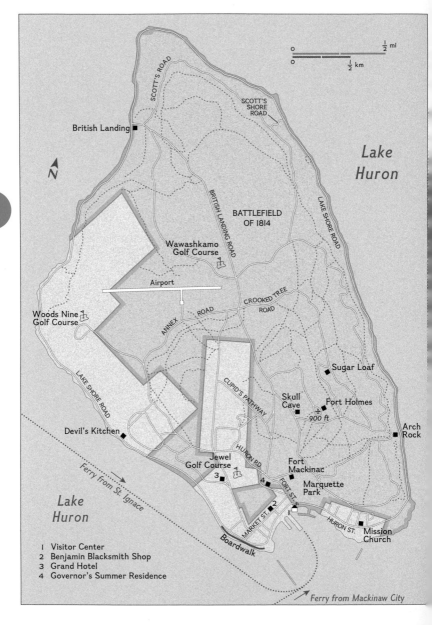

1 Visitor Center
2 Benjamin Blacksmith Shop
3 Grand Hotel
4 Governor's Summer Residence

Further Adventures

Only about 500 people live on the island year-round, so it's a much quieter place when the fort and other sites reduce their hours after Labor Day. Other park facilities are open from mid-May to mid-October for a taste of fall color. Visitors can wander the island any time of the year, but getting there after the ferries stop in January is no easy feat. Locals snowmobile to the mainland 3.5 miles away on an ice bridge lined with discarded Christmas trees, but visitors may want to try a private plane or the small commercial airline service that flies to the island. A few small hotels stay open for winter visitors, who can ride horse-drawn sleighs and ski on groomed cross-country trails.

Nearby Sights

The history of Mackinac Island is closely linked to other events on the Straits of Mackinac, and the Mackinac State Historic Parks manages related sites, **Old Mackinac Point Lighthouse, Colonial Michilimackinac,** and **Historic Mill Creek** *(231-436-4100)*. The three are located across the straits on the northern shore of the Lower Peninsula, near Mackinaw City. Colonial Michilimackinac re-creates a fort occupied in the 18th century first by the French and then the British, who were vying for control of the regional fur trade. Within the reconstructed fort interpreters dressed as British Redcoats show what life was like in a remote military outpost in the 1770s. The historic 1892 lighthouse was active until 1957 when the lights on the bridge rendered it obsolete. Also located here is the 1907 fog signal building.

ANCIENT ISLAND: About 11,000 years ago, as the last of the great glaciers retreated to the north, Mackinac Island poked above the surface of Lake Algonquin, a huge body of water that included what are now Lakes Michigan and Huron. The high shelf at the center of today's island—about a half mile long and a quarter mile wide—is called the Ancient Island. Lake levels gradually fell as the glacier gouged a deeper trough to the north, until at one point Mackinac was not an island, but a highland peninsula jutting out from the Michigan mainland. Then the basins filled again, and Lake Nipissing rose to again submerge part of the island. A sharp geological eye can pick out six distinct terraces carved by erosion during the various ups and downs of the lake.

East along the north shore is Mill Creek, where one water-powered sawmill supplied much of the lumber for building on Mackinac Island during the boom years of the fur trade. The site, rediscovered by amateur archaeologists with a metal detector in the 1970s, has an 18th-century reconstructed sawmill powered by a 4-foot flutter wheel propelled by water; the saw moves up and down a hundred times a minute. The park includes 625 acres of forest, nature trails, and a growing number of reconstructed buildings, based on findings in the archaeological digs.

Mackinac State Historic Parks, P.O. Box 370, Mackinac Island, MI 49757; 231-436-4100; Chamber of Commerce 906-847-6418 or 800-454-5227; www.mackinacparks.com

Porcupine Mountains

18 miles west of Ontonagon on Mich. 107 or 1 mile east of Wakefield, off Mich. 28

■ 60,000 acres ■ Year-round ■ Entrance fee ■ No pack animals or motorized vehicles in backcountry ■ Waterfalls ■ Lake of the Clouds ■ Cross-country and downhill skiing ■ Fishing (license required), hiking

Autumn color along the Carp River, Porcupine Mountains

Forget the small, huddled stands of tall pines found in pockets of virgin forest around the Midwest. If you want a real wilderness, the Porcupine Mountains are bristling with thousands of acres of forest never touched by the logger's ax, as well as remote lakes, wild trout streams, and panoramic views of Lake Superior, the wildest of the Great Lakes.

The "Porkies," named by Ojibwa Indians for the forested ridges resembling a porcupine's back, are the largest stand of old-growth forest between the Mississippi River and the Adirondacks. For wilderness-starved Midwesterners, the park offers 85 miles of trails, with towering hemlock, dozens of waterfalls, bald eagles and black bears, and yurts and rustic cabins *(to rent call 800-447-2757 or visit www.mi.gov/porkies)*. While the vast majority of visitors make only a brief stop at the spectacular Lake of the Clouds escarpment, others who take a few days to trek the Mirror Lake Trail or the Lake Superior shoreline are richly rewarded.

Timber companies that had stripped much of Michigan by the 1930s had their eyes on the Porkies, but, propelled by a national conservation campaign (there was even consideration of a national park designation), Porcupine became a state park in 1945. Over 35,000 acres of shaggy old-growth forest forms the beating heart of the park, including some maples with 3-foot-wide trunks. The park supports healthy black bear and gray wolf populations and has occasional moose-sighting reports.

What to See and Do

Visitors who come only for a day follow an enjoyable, if predictable, routine: A stop at the **Visitor Center** *(mid-May–mid-Oct.)* at the east entrance of the park for exhibits on the park's geology, wildlife, and history; a drive to the **Lake of the Clouds** escarpment for a sky-high view across the lake of steep forested ridges and Government Peak; and a stop at the sandy beach at **Union Bay** for a picnic and a dip.

For those with more time and sturdy hiking boots, trails at the Lake of the Clouds escarpment head west before dropping down to the Big Carp River, south to **Mirror Lake,** or north to the lakeshore, where you can hike a section of the 16-mile **Lake Superior Trail.** Cabins at Mirror Lake, Lily Pond, and Lake of the Clouds are all equipped with boats.

The west side of the park, less busy than the east, features exciting stretches along the **Presque Isle River.** Hikers can take a loop trail from the river's mouth a mile upstream past three waterfalls, cross a bridge, and return on the other side of the river. The Presque Isle River is considered one of the Midwest's most challenging streams for kayakers. In spring and fall, wading fishermen run as thick as the steelhead and salmon returning to spawn.

175

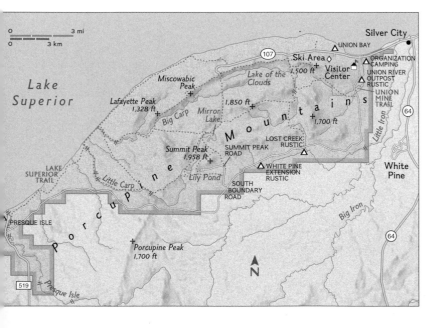

Winter attracts skiers of both the downhill and Nordic variety to 26 miles of groomed double tracks and a downhill ski area near Union Bay. Three ski-in overnight cabins and four yurts are for rent along the Nordic trail system, and snowmobiles are allowed on 32 miles of park roads.

Further Adventures

The 16-mile **Lake Superior Trail** is the longest trail in the park, and it is best done with a vehicle dropped at either end, unless you have enough time—at least five days—to loop inland from the lakeshore and return through the backcountry to your starting point. The trail moves in and out from the shore, crossing steep ravines near the west end. A short hike inland along the Big Carp River brings you to Shining Cloud Falls, a two-stage drop, the largest waterfall in the interior of the park.

The highest mountain peak in the park, at 1,958 feet above sea level, is **Summit Peak,** and from the observation tower at the top of the peak, you can see the park in all directions. You can drive to within a half mile of the top on Summit Peak Road.

History buffs will certainly want to spend some time exploring the 45-minute **Union Mine Trail,** which is located a mile south of the Visitor Center. The stamp mill, blacksmith shop, and big machinery may be gone, but the mine shafts are still visible, and markers tell the story of this unsuccessful attempt to hit copper pay dirt 150 years ago. More than 45 mines were sunk into the Porkies—10 of them fairly deeply—but the fine consistency of the copper, the remoteness of the mining locations, and the turbulent nature of copper prices all combined to thwart success.

COPPER FEVER: In the 1840s, when many Americans heard the siren call of mineral wealth from the western wilderness, copper miners were attracted to the Porcupine Mountains. They discovered some significant copper deposits in the sandstone, and inspired by the story of a huge copper mass sitting along the Ontonagon River just east of the mountains they dug 10 mines, looking for something better. Ontonagon boulder was first discovered by Alexander Henry in the 18th century, and later rolled to the river mouth by entrepreneur Julius Eldred. It eventually ended up at the Smithsonian Institution in Washington, D.C. Luckily for the wilderness, another was never found.

Camping and Lodging

The park has one modern campground with 99 sites. You are advised to make reservations in season; call 800-447-2757 or visit www.mi.gov/porkies. Camping fee. There are also 4 rustic "outposts" with 64 campsites and 16 hike-in cabins available (May–Nov.; fee for cabins must be paid in advance). Backcountry campers must register but may camp trailside.

Porcupine Mountains Wilderness State Park, 33303 Headquarters Rd., Ontonagon, MI 49953; 906-885-5275; www.michigan.gov/dnr

Fort Wilkins

1 mile east of Copper Harbor on US 41

■ 700 acres ■ Year-round, buildings mid-May to mid-Oct. ■ Day-use permit ■ Lake Superior shore ■ Costumed interpreters ■ Historic lighthouse ■ Fishing (license required), hiking

Soldiers were posted at Fort Wilkins to quell expected conflicts between the Ojibwa and the copper miners who came to Michigan's northernmost region, the Keweenaw Peninsula, in the 1840s. As it turned out, the only problems they had to deal with were their own—harsh winters, isolation, and loneliness. Today, costumed interpreters help visitors experience life in what was once an outpost frontier.

Explore the park by hiking the 2-mile **nature trail** that begins near the east campground, skirts the park's perimeter, with views of both Lake Superior and Lake Fanny Hooe, and ends up at the historic fort, where 12 of the buildings are original.

On the jutting peninsula enclosing the east side of Copper Harbor is **Copper Harbor Lighthouse** *(adm. fee),* one of the oldest lighthouses on Lake Superior, first constructed in 1848 and rebuilt in 1866. Taken out of service in 1933, the old light is now part of the park, visited by excursion boat from Copper Harbor. Inside the yellow brick station, period furnishings re-create the life of light-house keepers, and exhibits cover lighthouse history and shipwreck lore. A newer steel tower stands nearby and still guides boats safely to the harbor.

Camping and Lodging

The park has 169 tent or RV sites (mid-May–mid-Oct.), with showers. Reservations advised; call park. Camping fee. There is also a small cabin; call 800-447-2757 for reservations.

Fort Wilkins State Park, P.O. Box 71, Copper Harbor, MI 49918; 906-289-4215; www.michigan.gov/dnr

P.J. Hoffmaster

10 miles south of Muskegon on US 31 and Pontaluma Rd.

■ 1,183 acres ■ Year-round ■ Entrance fee ■ No off-road vehicles ■ Sand dunes ■ Nature Center ■ Swimming beach ■ Hiking

Out the big window at the Gillette Visitor Center, a huge dune looms … and it's moving easterly. Not to worry. Much too slowly for the eye to see, the dunes along the Lake Michigan shore are changing shape. Many park visitors come to enjoy the beach at the north end of the park, but there are opportunities for solitude hiking among the wooded sand dunes that have been anchored here by trees that have taken root. The viewing platform atop the **Dune Climb Stairway** offers a magnificent vista of the blue lake and the dunes all around, a view

Dunes along Lake Michigan

increasingly rare along this coast as the park has become an island of natural beauty along a shore fringed by development.

Partly because they are young and changing rapidly, the dunes along Lake Michigan have played a major role in scientists' understanding of plant succession—the way the family of plants and trees evolves from the first seeds to take root to a climax plant community that may be quite different. When naturalists at Hoffmaster take groups for walks among the dunes, they take note of these ongoing changes—for instance, whether the decline of the trillium that once blanketed areas of the dunes is due to lower levels of water or the increase of browsing deer driven to the park as a refuge from surrounding development, or both.

What to See and Do

Stop first at the modern two-story **Gillette Visitor Center,** where a nine-projector slide show explains Lake Michigan's evolving shoreline, the largest expanse of freshwater dune shoreline in the world. Then take

DUNE DIALECT: Here are a few choice terms in dune dialect so you can hold your own, like a foredune.
Blowout: Saucerlike dune depression carved by wind, usually where vegetation has been destroyed.
Foredune: A dune running parallel to the shore, the first dune established.
Fulgerite: Fused grains of sand in the shape of a tube, caused by a lightning strike.
Marram grass: Grass species that builds dunes by trapping sand and stabilizing with its roots.

the 0.5-mile **trail** to the shore, noting as you descend between dunes how the sand blocks the wind and other sounds. Along this trail is the 165-step climb to the dune overlook platform, thoughtfully equipped with benches.

There are 10 miles of hiking trails winding along the 3 miles of shoreline and through the dunes, many clothed now by beech and maple forest. In summer, the soft sandy beach at the park's north end is popular for swimming and sunning. In winter, the park opens 3 miles of cross-country skiing trails at the south end of the park. There is a shelter with a fireplace at the trailhead, but no equipment rental.

In order to protect the delicate ecology of the dunes, bicycles are allowed only on paved roads.

Camping

The park has 293 tent or RV sites, with showers. Reservations advised in season; call 800-447-2757. Camping fee.

P.J. Hoffmaster State Park, 6585 Lake Harbor Rd., Muskegon, MI 49441; 231-798-3711; www.michigandnr.com/parksandtrails/parks andtrailssearch.aspx

Hartwick Pines

5 miles north of Grayling on Mich. 93

▪ 7,694 acres ▪ Year-round ▪ Entrance fee ▪ Pine forest ▪ Logging camp museum ▪ Fishing (license required), hiking, cross-country skiing

From the farmhouses on the Great Plains to the railroad ties that crisscross the prairies, America's expansion in the early 19th century was largely built of white pine from Michigan's northern forest. One of the few stands of tall timber unfelled exists here. The tall 150-foot pines in this virgin forest are estimated to be around 350 years old.

The **Michigan Forest Center** hosts exhibits on the ecology of the forests and the economy of the timber harvest. Take the self-guided **Virgin Pines Foot Trail** for an hour-long trek that shows you the trees of the North Woods and leads to a **logging camp museum** *(May–Oct.)*. The steam-powered sawmill chugs back to life on several summer weekends *(fare)*.

Hiking trails lead to **Hartwick Lake** and the **East Branch Au Sable River,** a good trout-fishing stream. On the west side, biking trails are groomed for cross-country skiing.

Camping and Lodging

The park has 100 tent and RV sites, showers, and a rustic cabin (mid-April–Nov.). For reservations, call 800-447-2757. Camping fee.

Hartwick Pines State Park, 4216 Ranger Rd., Grayling, MI 49738; 989-348-7068; www.michigan.gov/dnr

Brown County

2 miles south of Nashville, via Ind. 135 and Ind. 46

■ 15,696 acres ■ Year-round ■ Entrance fee, except weekdays in winter ■ Scenic views ■ Covered bridge ■ Swimming pool ■ Historic inn ■ Nature Center ■ Trail rides ■ Hiking, mountain biking, fishing (license required), cross-country skiing

The old covered bridge at the north entrance to this venerable preserve aptly symbolizes the rural, old-timey atmosphere of the park and surrounding hills. This country has been called the "Little Smokies" for the mists that rise from its steep and wooded ravines, and there is an Appalachian ring to the place-names of towns tucked into the hills, such as Beanblossom and Gnaw Bone. Along a particularly scenic network of ridges sits the largest state park in Indiana.

Once isolated by poor roads and forested hills, the region around Brown County State Park is now a tourist mecca with a concentration of craftspeople and artists. After a half day in the galleries of Nashville, travelers are often ready for a peaceful walk or picnic at one of the park's overlooks. In addition to its bridle and hiking trails, the park offers such comforts as a large swimming pool and the rustic Abe Martin Lodge. Many park facilities—including shelters, trails, and lookout towers—were the work of the Civilian Conservation Corps. But the CCC also contributed by

Old Brown County fence

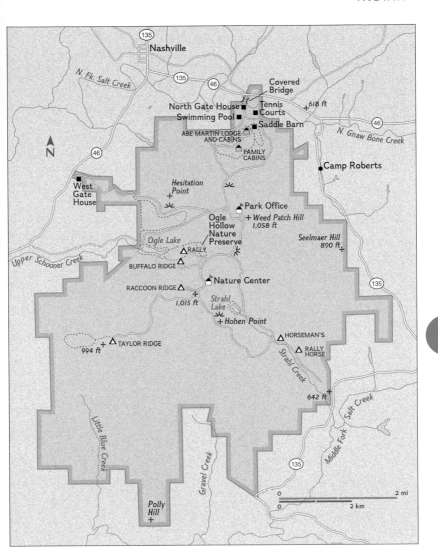

planting some of the black locust, black walnut, pine, and spruce in the park to help prevent erosion.

Fall colors in the Brown County hills are a rich mosaic of orange, gold, and red, out of which can sometimes be heard the gobble of wild turkeys. Spring, too, is a good time to visit, when forest highlights include white serviceberry buds, flowering dogwoods, and redbuds in bloom. Deer are the most commonly spotted large animals.

What to See and Do

If natural beauty ranks higher than services in your mind, use the park's west entrance, which almost immediately brings you to a lookout tower and **Hesitation Point,** with views of canyons and hills so densely wooded they resemble a head of broccoli. Untouched by the glaciers that flattened much of the Great Lakes region, the ridges and valleys here were cut by streams through an ancient ocean bottom.

Or take the north entrance, crossing Salt Creek on a two-lane covered bridge that dates back to 1838. An Olympic-size swimming pool is just inside the entrance, along with tennis courts, a saddle barn, and an amphitheater. The **Abe Martin Lodge,** a Depression-era structure built with native stone and hand-hewn oak timbers from the park forests, waits just up the road.

However you enter, head for **Weed Patch Hill,** the high ground at the center of the park and the location of the park headquarters, campgrounds, Nature Center, and interesting trails.

The **Nature Center** displays crosscuts of park trees such as beech, locust, and elm, and a mounted gray fox, great horned owl, and hawks. The timber rattler and copperhead snakes sometimes found in the glass case are alive—they are released in winter—and bird feeders attract goldfinches, cardinals, and other birds to a viewing window. Interpretive programs such as walks, talks, and hikes are held daily from May through October, and weekends in winter. In addition, the Nature Center remains open all winter, when visitors come to ice fish at **Ogle Lake** or cross-country ski on ungroomed trails and closed roads.

From the Nature Center, hike down to **Strahl Lake,** or go the other direction, past the Buffalo Ridge Campground, to the **Ogle Hollow Nature Preserve.** This 41-acre area, with a mile-long, self-guided nature trail running through it, provides a rare view of what the forests of Indiana were like before farmers, loggers, and livestock arrived. The steep, shady hillsides sustain a small population of yellowwood trees—delicate, gray-barked trees with wisteria flowers, rarely found north of the Ozarks.

Over 70 miles of bridle trails run through the roadless parts of the horse-friendly park's southern and eastern areas. You can bring your own horse or rent from the stable at the park. The trails provide hitching posts and mounting blocks along the well-marked paths. Ten miles of mountain biking trails, regarded as some of the best in the Midwest, ranging from easy to rugged are also open to hikers. When winter arrives cross-country skiing is available on the ungroomed trails.

Camping and Lodging

The park has 429 tent and RV sites with showers (105 open in winter, no showers); and a 204-site horse camp. For reservations May through Oct., call 866-622-6746. Camping fee. Abe Martin Lodge offers 84 lodge rooms, 76 cabins, and restaurant (year-round); call 877-563-4371 for reservations.

Brown County State Park, P.O. Box 608, Nashville, IN 47448; 812-988-6406; www.in.gov/dnr

Spring Mill

3 miles east of Mitchell on Ind. 60

▪ 1,319 acres ▪ Year-round ▪ Entrance fee April through Oct. ▪ Pioneer village ▪ Caves ▪ Astronaut memorial ▪ Nature preserve ▪ Operating gristmill ▪ Hiking, fishing (license required), swimming, mountain biking

183

Historic village of Spring Mill

Back in 1815, the spring streams that still spout from openings in the cave-riddled limestone of southern Indiana attracted soldier Samuel Jackson, Jr., to build a crude water-powered mill. The site became the town of Spring Mill, and later owners built bigger mills to accommodate area farmers.

You can still buy a sack of cornmeal ground at Spring Mill, but the mood today is more nostalgic than entrepreneurial. The village, abandoned in the late 19th century after the railroad chose a northern route, has been restored to its 1833 period of prosperity. Summer craftspeople put on 19th-century clothes and pick up the old tools to re-create village life. In spring and fall visitors are offered special workshops on chair caning, fiddle making, or log cabin building.

PARK TIP: *Look for the hidden monument dedicated to Alexander Wilson, father of American ornithology, along Trail 4 below Donaldson Cave.*

An eccentric Scotsman, George Donaldson, had the foresight to protect the beauty and rarity of the forests and caves on his property. His reserve of virgin forest, now part of the park, offers a primordial kind of history, the type that couldn't be re-created if lumber companies had taken their cuts.

What to See and Do

This park's variety is a good match for visitors with wide-ranging curiosity and time to try different adventures. Start at the **Grissom Memorial** near the park entrance for maps and information. The memorial has a small museum featuring the *Molly Brown*, a Gemini III space capsule, and exhibits on the life and work of astronaut "Gus" Grissom from nearby Mitchell. Grissom used to fish in the park as a boy. The second American to fly in suborbital space, he perished in the Apollo I launchpad fire in 1967.

The southeast corner of the park features the **Donaldson Woods Nature Preserve,** 67 acres of the kind of forest that once covered most of Indiana. Although a road skirts the edge of the preserve, it's more rewarding to walk through the huge tulip poplars and white oaks on **Trail 3,** looping from the Twin Caves parking lot around to **Donaldson Cave** and back to the Grissom Memorial. You can enter Donaldson Cave and walk a short way beside the rich blue stream that pours from it, or join a naturalist-led tour for a deeper journey.

In the northwest corner of the park is **Pioneer Village,** not far from where another stream emerging from Hamer Cave provides the water that drives the gristmill. The mill itself creaks and groans to life for ten minutes every hour from May through October. Within you can purchase cornmeal and the work of village artisans. Early residents' log houses decorated with period furnishings are also open. The **Nature Center** with displays on park history and a big wildlife observation window faces Spring Mill Lake, into which the cave streams drain.

Take a **Twin Caves** boat trip *(fee)* led by park personnel—a popular activity, so reserve early in the day. The trip takes about 20 minutes and goes 500 feet into a pitch-black cave. Eight to twelve people ride in each aluminum boat, with a guide to tell them about bats, crayfish, and blind cave fish. After heavy rains, when the volume of water in the cave rises, trips may be canceled.

Offered on the east side of the park near the outdoor pool and showers, evening hayrides *(fee)* leave from the camp store May through October.

Camping and Lodging

There are 234 tent and RV sites, some with showers, and a youth group tent area. Reservations advised weekends Mem. Day through Oct.; call 866-622-6746. Camping fee. Spring Mill Inn has 74 rooms; call 877-977-7464 to reserve.

Spring Mill State Park, P.O. Box 376, Mitchell, IN 47446; 812-849-4129; www.in.gov/dnr

NIGHT OF THE TROGLOBITES: In the dark recesses of the limestone caves at Spring Creek lives a pale scaly critter known as the northern cave fish. When visitors to Twin Caves flash their lights in the water, these fish can't even blink—they don't have eyes. Animals that never leave the dark of the cave—called troglobites (cave dwellers)—include these blind cave fish as well as blind crayfish, their neighbors. While they are often smaller than distant cave-dwelling relatives with eyes (called troglophiles), the troglobites, scientists say, have acutely developed their other senses and do quite well in the dark.

Falls of the Ohio

1 mile west of Interstate 65 and Jeffersonville on Riverside Drive

■ 144 acres ■ Year-round ■ Fee for Interpretive Center ■ No camping
■ Fossil beds and cliffs ■ Dam ■ Bird-watching ■ Kayaking, fishing
(license required), hiking ■ Parking fee unless visiting Interpretive
Center

If you find it far-fetched that the hilly country of southeastern
Indiana once lay beneath an ocean, watch the award-winning docu-
mentary shown in the Interpretive Center. It takes you underwater
for a look at a primitive sea like the one that was here 387 million
years ago. Then walk along the Ohio River just below the long dam
that crosses the river near Louisville, and look at the limestone
rocks around you. You are walking through the Devonian period,
sometimes called the age of fishes, and the fossils seen everywhere
are corals, sponges, trilobites, and brachiopods. There are so many
unique fossils exposed in such numbers that it's hard to walk around
without putting your sole on a coral, crinoid, or brachiopod—creatures that were buried in ocean-bottom sediments eons ago.

Early explorers found it tough going when they reached this part
of the Ohio, as the exposed bedrock formed cataract falls, blocking
upstream travel and "grat[ing] harshly" on the bottoms of boats going
downstream, as Walt Whitman put it after a bumpy ride. Because
many had to portage, it was a natural place for settlement. Gen.
George Rogers Clark, who founded Louisville and Clarksville, chose
lands nearby as his reward for service in the Revolutionary War.

Though early settlers certainly noticed the fossil beds when the
water was low—particularly after a long dike was built in the late
1800s to divert some of the water around Goose Island—today we
know what an extraordinary paleontological find this is. Visitors
today, like their forebearers, wander around informally, picking up
the odd coral for a closer look (just don't take it out of the park!).

What to See and Do

The first thing you see as you drive into the park is the **Interpretive
Center,** its circular central hall banded with Indiana limestone and
brick to look like the strata of the fossil beds below. In the lobby
are full-size models of a woolly mammoth, fish, and early Native
American inhabitants, who hunted near the falls. In addition, a video
in the center's auditorium vividly re-creates the ancient tropical sea.

Go exploring on you own or join a naturalist for a guided tour
on the **fossil beds** from May to October. When the fossil beds are
exposed (typically summer and fall), you can walk on an ancient
seafloor and see corals and sponges covering every inch of limestone.
About 200 of the 220-acre fossil bed are readily accessible when the
gates on the dam are closed (mid-Aug.–mid-Oct. if river conditions
permit). On several Saturdays this time of the year three-hour foot
and canoe hikes are offered. The outer fossil beds by **Goose Island**
are where a greater number of outstanding fossils can be seen.

Evidence indicates that for 10,000 years Indians enjoyed the area's rich wildlife, an abundance still evident today. The 1,404-acre **Falls of the Ohio National Wildlife Conservation Area** set aside by the U.S. Army Corps of Engineers includes the islands in the river below McAlpine Dam, adjacent to the park. Bird-watchers will spot great blue herons and killdeer, as well as migratory birds. Anglers cast lines from the shore or boats into the waters below the dam, fishing for bass, sauger, and catfish.

The half-mile **Woodland Loop Trail,** just downriver from the Interpretive Center, gives hikers a look at diverse stream-side vegetation, from honey locust trees to the sunchokes that were staples in Indian diets. A longer hike on top of the levee leads to the **George Rogers Clark homesite.**

Kayakers have a perpetual motion machine in the Falls of the Ohio: They put in below the Interpretive Center, ride an eddy back to the dam, then take off downstream for a mile before catching the eddy upriver again. Depending on the season, the water can be calm, or churned up to Class IV rapids.

Falls of the Ohio State Park, 201 West Riverside Dr., Jeffersonville, IN 47131; 812-280-9970; www.fallsoftheohio.org

> **BIRDMAN OF INDIANA:** While visitors to the Falls of the Ohio today come to see ancient life-forms encrusted in riverbed outcroppings, painter and naturalist John James Audubon came in 1807 looking for living creatures. The artist spent three years sketching the birds at the falls, producing more than 200 renderings, a large part of his early work. Copies are on display at the Interpretive Center, where an observation window looks out on bird feeders that attract Audubon's friends for today's artists.

Indiana Dunes

2 miles north of Chesterton on Ind. 49

■ 2,182 acres ■ Year-round ■ Entrance fee, except weekdays Oct. to May ■ Nature Center ■ Swimming beach ■ Sand dunes ■ Marshes ■ Hiking, cross-country skiing

Nestled within the 14,000-acre Indiana Dunes National Lakeshore, this state park holds some of the prize scenery of a nonpareil lake-side landscape, including the highest dunes on the shore, dune "canyons" blown out by winds off Lake Michigan, and a popular swimming beach. There are live dunes that continue to move a few feet every year, and stabilized dunes anchored by an extraordinary range of plants. The shoreline was threatened by encroaching industrial development early in the century, and its preservation became one of the country's earliest conservationist causes, leading to the state's purchase of the parklands in 1925.

Most summer visitors make a beeline to the popular half-mile swimming beach. Those with an interest in the dunes' extraordinary ecosystem, however, will want to drive to the new **Nature Center,** visit the exhibits about dune creation and the diverse flora and fauna that thrive here, and then head off on a variety of trails.

Unless told otherwise, stay on the trail to avoid disturbing the fragile ecology of the dunes; there are a few places you can take off your shoes and plunge down a sandhill. Regardless, the trail system offers a great variety of lengths, views, and biota. **Trail 8,** a 1.5-mile route beginning near the Nature Center, climbs through wildflowers to the top of **Mount Tom,** the highest dune on the lakeshore, standing 192 feet tall in a small cluster of dune peaks. Fine views and interesting dunes are found along **Trail 9,** which goes east from the Nature Center around the **Beach House Blowout,** a sand canyon dug by lake winds. Abundant and unusual spring flowers can be seen on trails through a marsh and forest just inland from the dunes.

Don't miss the new 700-foot boardwalk running alongside Dunes Creek. On winter weekends with a snow base, trails are open to cross-country skiers.

Camping

The park has 140 tent or RV sites, with showers. For reservations, call 866-622-6746. Camping fee.

Indiana Dunes State Park, 1600 N. 25E, Chesterton, IN 46304; 219-926-1952; www.in.gov/dnr/parklake/2980.htm

High dunes of Lake Michigan

Giant City

12 miles south of Carbondale, off Ill. 13 onto Giant City Rd., or east off US 51

■ 4,055 acres ■ Year-round ■ Stone fort ■ Sandstone formations ■ Observation platform ■ Historic lodge ■ Rare plants ■ Horseback riding ■ Hiking, fishing (license required)

Along Stone Fort Nature Trail

Names have been carved in the soft sandstone walls of Giant City, recording the visitors who came to this area even in the years before the Civil War. This is not surprising given the sights: Slabs of sandstone 40 feet tall stand like closely packed buildings spaced by narrow alleyways. But these rocks certainly pre-date both skyscrapers and the Civil War; the Makanda sandstone is about 200 million years old.

In this park, astonishing works of nature stand out, but there are also notable man-made works. A stone fort wall runs along a bluff near the main northwest entrance, the work of an ancient people who somehow maneuvered 200-pound stones up from the creek below. And, more recently, the Civilian Conservation Corps built the handsome Giant City Lodge using massive white oak timbers and local sandstone.

Such achievements put some of the park's smaller wonders in the shade ... where they thrive. A forested nature preserve protects rare plants and provides a retreat for amateur botanists, bird-watchers, and people out for a peaceful stroll.

What to See and Do

Entering from the north you have a choice: a short hike to the **Stone Fort,** or a visit to the **Fern Rock Nature Preserve.** Do both. The **Stone Fort Nature Trail,** a short, steep hike around a bluff with three unscalable sides, reaches a head-high wall guarding the one humanly possible approach. Evidently this wall provided refuge from enemies for the Native Americans in the late Woodland period, who inhabited this region between A.D. 600 and 900.

The 2-mile **Trillium Trail** through the nature preserve travels over bluff and through forest typical of the Shawnee Hills, but with the distinction of several rare flowers: Forbes' saxifrage, Grove blue-grass, and white-flowered mints. For a more challenging hike, try the 12-mile **Red Cedar Hiking Trail.**

Whether or not you stay at **Giant City Lodge,** do take a look. Similar to many CCC buildings, the lobby has a tall beam ceiling and native rock walls centered around a large fireplace; it manages to be monumental yet intimate. Outside, climb the stairs to the 50-foot viewing platform on the bulbous water tower for a view of the rolling, thickly forested hills, or take in the recently constructed CCC statue commemorating the Illinois CCC workers. Nearby you can embark on various short trails, to **Devil's Standtable, Giant City,** and **Indian Creek,** and a handicapped-accessible trail to **Post Oak.**

From May through October, a trail circling through the park is open to riders who either bring their own horses or rent them from Giant City Stables *(618-529-4110).* Guided trail rides are also available. **Little Grassy Lake,** bordering the park's east side, is actually part of the Crab Orchard National Wildlife Refuge, and many park visitors go there to swim or canoe. There are boat launching ramps for anglers interested in bass, bluegill, and crappie.

Up the road from Giant City, you may spot a group of teens navigating across a wobbly rope ladder strung between two tall poles —one of several challenges offered by the **Touch of Nature Environmental Center** *(618-453-1121),* a 3,100-acre preserve adjacent to the park. Surrounding the park, refuge, and environmental center is the **Shawnee National Forest** *(618-253-7114).* Combined, these various preserves provide wildlife, and humans, with lots of habitat variety.

Camping and Lodging

The park has 85 tent and RV sites, with showers; and 14 hike-in tent sites. Available first come, first served. Camping fee. There is also a horse camp (May–Oct.), and a youth group camp. Giant City Lodge has 34 cabins (Feb.–mid-Dec.); for reservations, call 618-457-4921.

Giant City State Park, 235 Giant City Rd., Makanda, IL 62958; 618-457-4836; www.dnr.state.il.us/land/landmgt/parks/index.htm

189

Fort Massac

East side of Metropolis, off US 45

- 1,499 acres ▪ Year-round ▪ Ohio River ▪ Re-created fort ▪ Museum
▪ Boating ▪ Fishing and hunting (license required)

Fortifications at Fort Massac

190

The Ohio River that flows by Fort Massac hardly seems to warrant the unyielding timber stockade and blockhouses of this riverside fort, but back in the 18th century this area was a key juncture in the struggle for North America. Today, you can safely visit the reconstructed fort and its interesting museum, and walk through the blockhouses and along scenic **Hickory Nut Ridge Trail** as it loops along the river. Every October, a weekend encampment draws a huge crowd of latter-day frontiersmen and gawkers. People dress in period costume, a marching military band plays, and craftspeople make and sell their wares. Various events throughout the year involve demonstrations of old tools and weapons, often by costumed interpreters. A boat ramp into the Ohio River is also available, and the fishing for catfish and bass is plentiful.

Camping

The park has 60 tent and RV sites, with showers (mid-April–mid-Dec.); reservations at www.reserveamerica.com. Camping fee.

Fort Massac State Park, 1308 E. 5th St., Metropolis, IL 62960; 618-524-4712; www.dnr.state.il.us/land/landmgt/parks/index.htm

Starved Rock

1 mile south of Utica on Ill. 178

- 3,205 acres ▪ Year-round ▪ Canyons ▪ Historic lodge ▪ Horseback riding ▪ Fishing (license required), boating, hiking

A good place to start a visit to Starved Rock is across the river at the **Illinois Waterway Visitor Center** *(815-667-4054),* an operating lock and dam on the north bank of the Illinois River. From there you get a good view of Starved Rock, a tall shelf of pale sandstone collared by woods that color up gorgeously in the fall. The park runs for 7 miles on the river's south shore, its bluffs cut by 18 canyons reaching to the riverbank. Having viewed it from afar, drive to the park and hike to the top of the park's namesake butte.

The sandstone has been shaped into a number of canyons and high overlooks, reached along 12 miles of trails that run along the river, snaking back and climbing for dramatic views. The steep-sided bluffs are ribboned with waterfalls during heavy rains.

Starved Rock itself is big enough on top that the French built Fort St. Louis there in 1682 to oversee this key stretch of river rapids, hoping to protect their lucrative fur trade. Legend says native peoples had been in the area for centuries before, and after the French military left, Starved Rock continued to be a meeting place for traders and various tribes. In the 1760s, legend says when Ottawa Chief Pontiac was slain by an Illiniwek at a council meeting, Pontiac's allies chased the assassin's outnumbered band up onto the bluff. There the band held out, thwarted when they attempted to drop baskets on ropes to haul water from the river, succumbing eventually to starvation.

What to See and Do

The most crowded part of the park is the middle, site of a boat ramp, lodge, Visitor Center, and play areas. From there, trails run east along the river, riding the bluffs or skirting the riverside. Once you've put in a mile or so, hiking can be a peaceful and solitary adventure. Metal maps at the trailheads and color-coded markers keep you on track. You'll want to turn up one or more of the canyon trails, particularly when there's been rain or melting snow. Journey up **St. Louis Canyon,** where the steep walls suddenly open and you find yourself at the bottom of a high-sided rock bowl, with sandstone shelves and green tendrils. The sky above is framed by canyon rims like a blue arrowhead, its edges feathered by pine and cedar.

Autumn at Starved Rock

191

The **Starved Rock Lodge** was built in the 1930s by the Civilian Conservation Corps. Though modernized, the lodge retains much of its old rock-and-log charm, particularly in the high-beamed Great Room, with its huge stone fireplace. Notice the wood sculpture, including outdoor "chainsaw" wildlife carvings.

The **Illinois River** has catfish, bullhead, bass, walleye, and crappie for anglers. A boat ramp at the park's far west end has canoes for rent from Memorial Day to Labor Day; stay clear of tricky currents near the dam just below Lover's Leap.

The **Visitor Center** itself has displays on French and Native American history, the geology, flora and fauna, and a model of the fort that once stood here. There are guided hikes throughout the year and special annual events featuring canoeing, wildflower viewing, and autumn leaf-peeping. Nearby **Matthiessen State Park** *(815-667-4868)* offers horse camping and cross-country ski rentals.

Camping and Lodging

The park has 133 tent or RV sites, with shower facilities. Reservations by mail only. Camping fee. Starved Rock Lodge has 22 rooms; call 815-667-4211 for reservations.

Starved Rock State Park, P.O. Box 509, Utica, IL 61373; 815-667-4726; www.dnr.illinois.gov

Mississippi Palisades

3 miles north of Savanna on Ill. 84

- 2,550 acres ▪ Year-round ▪ Limestone cliffs ▪ Boating, hiking
- Fishing, hunting (license required for both) ▪ Bird-watching
- Rock climbing

Bald eagle

To get the awesome proportions of the Mississippi River right and to gauge both its powerful inscription on the landscape and its peaceful grace, you have to see it from above; the towering Mississippi Palisades provide this vantage. Thickly forested limestone cliffs open to magnificent overlooks near where the Apple River joins the Mississippi. Down below, across the highway, the park maintains a dock where boaters can put in on a wild stretch of what Mark Twain called a "monstrous big river."

If your legs and lungs are in reasonably good working condition, hike the trails at the southern end of the park, which wind through dense forests—brightly colored in the fall—to the rims of bluffs above the Mississippi. Where the mile-long **Sentinel Trail** reaches the rim, a huge finger of dolomite points toward the sky, looking like you might push it loose with a good kick (you can't). These unprotected trails run right to the edges, so watch your footing. Southern end trails also visit erosion-carved **Indian Head Rock.** The northern end of the park offers easier hiking and camping areas. You'll see the white bark of paper birch and some of the huge gouges taken out of trees by pileated woodpeckers—you might even see one of the big birds. Early in the morning, flocks of wild turkeys sometimes gobble about.

Outside of an occasional passing barge or powerboat, the big river that braids and twists below shows few marks of man, because it's protected as part of the **Upper Mississippi River National Fish and Wildlife Refuge** *(815-273-2732).* In January and February, keep an eye out for bald eagles fishing for channel catfish, perch, bass, and walleye. Boaters like the fishing here, and sometimes picnic or camp on the islands.

Camping

The park has 240 tent or RV sites, with shower facilities available May through Oct. Available first come, first served. Camping fee. There are also 3 primitive walk-in sites and a youth camp.

Mississippi Palisades State Park, 16327-A Illinois Rte. 84N, Savanna, IL 61074; 815-273-2731; www.dnr.state.il.us/land/landmgt/parks /index.htm

193

Ferne Clyffe

12 miles south of Marion, off Ill. 37

■ 2,430 acres ■ Year-round ■ Waterfalls ■ Caves ■ Hiking ■ Fishing (license required)

The hiss of falling water, whisper of fern fronds, and hollow echoes in large shelter caves are the sounds of this park. Among Ferne Clyffe's 18 trails, the 0.75-mile-long **Big Rocky Hollow Trail** travels to an intermittent 100-foot waterfall in a tree-shrouded canyon landing on moss- and lichen-decorated rocks. Another 0.5-mile-long trail leads to **Hawks' Cave,** where a 100-foot ledge overhangs an echo chamber with a pulpitlike formation. Swimming and boating are prohibited on the man-made Ferne Clyffe Lake, but anglers cast from its banks.

Camping

The park has 60 RV sites; 20 primitives and 3 primitive hike-in camps. Reservations at www.reserveamerica.com. Camping fee.

Ferne Clyffe State Park, P.O. Box 10, Goreville, IL 62939; 618-995-2411; www.dnr.state.il.us/land/landmgt/parks/index.htm

Devil's Lake

3 miles south of Baraboo, off US 12 and Wis. 123

■ More than 10,000 acres ■ Year-round ■ Vehicle fee ■ 500-foot bluffs ■ Native American mounds ■ Nature Center ■ Rock climbing, hiking, fishing (license required), swimming beaches

A century ago, Victorian travelers arrived at Devil's Lake daily on passenger trains that steamed along the lakeshore to elegant hotels, where formal dress was required for dinner and couples danced to orchestra music. Today, bands of glacial till, not trumpets, attract visitors to the lake, formed by retreating glaciers that cut off and rerouted the Wisconsin River 12,000 years ago. The hotel era ended in 1904, and few traces remain.

PARK TIP: *Looking for a way to cool off? Head for the depressions along the Grottoes Trail, where the air is cooled as it filters through the rock and settles into crevices.*

Now the state park is one of nine units in the Ice Age National Scientific Reserve, an indication of the park's commitment to putting the natural environment before creature comforts. The park's popularity suggests that this suits modern visitors, who hike the tall bluffs around the lake to landmarks such as Balanced Rock and the Devil's Doorway, or boat on the 360-acre lake with fishing line dangling.

What to See and Do

Begin at the **Visitor Center** at the north end of the lake; pick up maps, tour brochures for trails, and information on the park's animal-shaped mounds. Also check the schedule of naturalist programs. Close by is the **Nature Center,** where dioramas tell the geologic story behind the lake's formation, and exhibits describe the area's human history, including photographs from the posh resort era.

Trails run on both sides of the lake. The 1.5-mile **West Bluff Trail** offers magnificent vistas of the lake and the Baraboo Valley to the north. Examine closely the colorful—often purple—quartzite that is the primary material of the bluffs. With a brochure in hand, you can identify features left by upheaving mountains, a long-ago sea that buried the peaks in sediment, and the gradual erosion by rivers that uncovered the Baraboo Hills again.

CANYON GREEN: One place at Devil's Lake where climbers can't play on the rocks is Parfrey's Glen, in the eastern corner of the park. The delicate ravine walls are mostly fragile sandstone and conglomerate, and visitors today must stay on the trails. In the past there were sawmills, gristmills, and flumes, and over a century of visitors who came to picnic near the tumbling water, sandstone cliffs, dense woods, ferns, and mosses. On a hot summer day the canyon is as much as 15 degrees cooler than the rest of the park, supporting vegetation normally unseen this far south, including the tangled roots of yellow birches. Parfrey's Glen was named as the first State Natural Area in Wisconsin and is one of four within the state park. It can be reached with a short hike from a small parking area along County Road DL in the park's east corner.

Begin the 1.5-mile **East Bluff Trail** from the lake's south end, a short drive from the Information Station on South Shore Road. The trail is a sometimes steep climb that takes you to grottoes and such aptly named sights as Elephant Cave and Devil's Doorway. Also along the East Bluff is a pygmy forest of oak, hickory, and cedar stunted by thin soil and the elements. For a longer hike, travel part of the **Ice Age Trail,** which traces the glacier's historic edges from the state's southeast corner to the northeast.

There are two swimming beaches, and concessionaires at **Devil's Lake** rent canoes, kayaks, paddleboats, and rowboats. Though the trout are stocked, some big browns have been caught, as well as bass, walleye, northern pike, and panfish. Scuba divers and snorkelers enjoy 20-foot visibility at depths up to 45 feet. A mountain-biking trail shared with hikers loops east of the lake.

The bluff's outcrops are about as mountainous as Wisconsin gets, but rock climbers find challenges here. Quartzite is a good climbing rock because it's hard and withstands weathering.

In winter, 9 miles of cross-country ski trails are groomed for all skill levels. Ice fishing and snowshoeing are popular, but snowmobile use is limited.

Climbing to Balanced Rock

Camping

The park has 409 tent and RV sites, with shower facilities; 25 winter camping sites; and 9 group campsites. Reservations recommended in season; call 888-947-2757. Camping fee.

Devil's Lake State Park, S 5975 Park Rd., Baraboo, WI 53913; 608-356-8301; www.dnr.state.wi.us/org/land/parks

195

Peninsula

25 miles north of Sturgeon Bay on Wis. 42

■ 3,776 acres ■ Year-round ■ Green Bay views ■ Cliffs and caves
■ Eagle Bluff Lighthouse ■ Summer theater ■ Beach ■ Golf, hiking,
biking ■ Nature Center

Like the New England coast, the image of Wisconsin's Door County peninsula has evolved from a remote countryside of storm-whipped fishing villages to a vacationland of quaint guest houses and art galleries. Peninsula State Park embodies these contrasts, encompassing a vast acreage of hardwood forest and cliff-edge scenery along Green Bay, as well as an 18-hole golf course and summer theater.

The park's raison d'être, though, is its Green Bay coast, best seen from atop the peninsula's soaring bluffs. With a fresh onshore breeze

Sunset over Green Bay

and gulls wheeling above, you can drive the roads or walk the trails and gaze at ships big and small. For all its natural beauty, Peninsula's managers had attractions and entertainment in mind from the park's beginning in 1909. Golfers were putting on sand greens in the 1920s, and the first superintendent encouraged minstrel shows, a viewing tower, a ski jump, and a small zoo. While the accent today is on nature, you can still swing your nine-iron, and climb Eagle Tower for a terrific view.

What to See and Do

The 75-foot **Eagle Tower,** ostensibly built as a fire lookout, has from its beginning attracted hikers who climb the peninsula's highest bluffs and then want to climb another 110 steps to scan the horizon.

Accessing the park through its east entrance, your first stop—unless you've reserved an early tee time *(920-854-5791)*—is likely to be the **Information Center** at Eagle Terrace. From there hike the steep 2-mile Eagle Trail along the shoreline and up the bluffs to the tower.

The living quarters at **Eagle Bluff Lighthouse** have been restored to give visitors a sense of the lonely life of the lightkeeper's family. The stone light tower, automated in 1926, still orients ships entering the east passage into Green Bay.

Many prefer to take in the sights driving **Shore Road** around the park's perimeter from Eagle Harbor to Nicolet Bay to Welcker's Point and on to the south entrance near the village of Fish Creek—or the reverse. There are many turnouts. Bicyclists, who sometimes share the road, also have 19 miles of bike trails, some graveled, that crisscross the park. **Skyline Road** offers more panoramic views from an even higher vantage on the Niagara dolomite, the same tilted bedrock that forms Niagara Falls.

On sunny summer days you'll find **Nicolet Bay** busy with swimmers and sunbathers. Canoes, sailboats, and kayaks are rented here, with lessons available. On summer evenings, the popular **American Folklore Theatre** *(920-854-6117)* presents original musical comedies with regional themes six nights a week.

Green Bay is popular with people who like to fish, and it's made a comeback from the impact of pollution and overfishing in the 20th century. Coho salmon are prized, and other catches include trout (brown, rainbow, and lake), walleye, smallmouth bass, and perch. Not far from Nicolet Bay is **Horseshoe Island** (you can guess its shape), with a dock.

The **White Cedar Forest Natural Area,** in the park's southwest corner, is a damp, 53-acre preserve containing water-loving cedars, beautiful wildflowers (including the rare Dwarf Lake iris), and herons, ducks, and a chorus of frogs. The separate **White Cedar Nature Center,** located off Bluff Road in the center of the park, describes the park's natural history, and a 0.5-mile nature trail brings it to life.

FISH BOIL: A Door County fish boil is a festive affair, and good eating, too. It features the whitefish, a plentiful Great Lakes fish with a blue-collar reputation for feeding fishermen's families. At a traditional fish boil, a big iron kettle is placed over an open fire, and the whitefish is boiled with potatoes and onions. As the sun drops in the west, ladlefuls of butter are poured over the fish, with coleslaw on the side. Then, when you're about to expire from an excess of fish and festivity, someone sneaks up with the coup de grace: a fat slice of Door County cherry pie, which, of course, you are too polite to refuse.

Camping

The park has 468 tent or RV sites (100 with electric hookups), with showers, in 4 campgrounds; and 3 tent-only group camps. Campsites can be reserved up to 11 months in advance by calling 888-947-2757. Camping fee.

Peninsula State Park, P.O. Box 218, Fish Creek, WI 54212; 920-868-3258; www.dnr.state.wi.us/org/land/parks; www.folkloretheatre.com

197

Rock Island

Ferry (920-535-0122) from Jackson Harbor, on Washington Island

- 905 acres ▪ May through Nov. ▪ No motorized vehicles
- Historic house ▪ Beach ▪ Hiking

This remote and undeveloped island so reminded inventor Chester Thordarson of his native Iceland that he bought it in 1910 to preserve its beauty. A few of his distinctive buildings survive today. Long before Thordarson, however, the island was a stopping point for Indian travelers and French explorers, including Jean Nicolet in 1634. Visitors who trek around the island are particularly struck by the sounds of the lake and the gulls; with no motorized vehicles allowed, this kind of quiet is a rare experience.

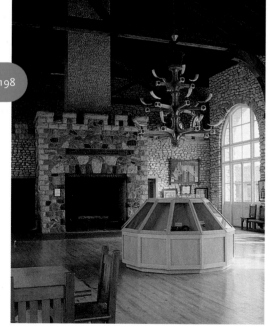

198

After two ferry rides (one to Washington Island, one to Rock Island), you arrive on the southwest shore of the little island, where visitors can enter the handsome stone **Viking Hall,** built by Thordarson as a boathouse. Inside, take a look at photo displays and exhibits on the island's ecology. Naturalist-led programs leave from Viking Hall, and the sandy south shore beach is a friendly swimming spot in good weather.

Ten miles of trails crisscross the island, and make a 6-mile loop around its shoreline. On the tall bluffs at the island's northern end stands the **Pottawatomi Lighthouse,** the first light station in Wisconsin, rebuilt in 1858 and still operating. These are dangerous waters, famous for shipwrecks. Steps below the lighthouse lead to the shore.

Viking Hall

Camping

The park has 40 tent sites and 2 group sites. Reservations advised in summer; call 888-947-2757. Camping fee.

Rock Island State Park, P.O. Box 118A, Washington Island, WI 54246; 920-847-2235; www.dnr.state.wi.us/org/land/parks

Copper Falls

2 miles northeast of Mellen on Wis. 169

- 3,068 acres - Year-round - Ancient lava flows - Waterfalls - Canyons - Hiking, bird-watching, fishing (license required) - Vehicle fee

The falls of the Bad River and Tyler Forks cut a geologic window in the layers of rock at Copper Falls. Sandstones and conglomerates, lava beds, granite, and sea-bottom sedimentary layers were exposed by the sagging of Lake Superior Basin and the downcutting of the rivers. The result is a series of spectacular waterfalls, including 20-foot **Copper Falls** and 30-foot **Brownstone Falls.**

The name of the park and falls is a misnomer: The water's brown tint is due not to minerals, but leaching from cedar and tamarack bogs upstream.

It's a short 1.7-mile round-trip hike from the picnic area to Copper Falls, the **Tyler Forks Cascades, Devil's Gate,** and Brownstone Falls, where the Bad River and Tyler Forks shoot through a series of rapids. Hikers can continue downriver to the **North Country National Scenic Trail,** which passes through the park on its way from upstate New York to North Dakota. Fishermen catch trout in the rivers, and hook pike and largemouth bass in **Loon Lake,** near the

Junction of the Bad and Tyler's Fork Rivers

199

park's south entrance. Swimmers enjoy the beach. And bird-watchers scan the skies for the 200-plus species of birds in the park, including songbirds such as wood thrush, red-eyed vireo, and warblers.

New mountain-biking trails are part of the park improvements, which also include a **Visitor Center** near the south entrance. Some 6 miles of bike trails become part of an 8-mile network of cross-country skiing trails in winter.

PARK TIP: *Check out the bridges, stairways, and buildings constructed by the World War I veteran doughboys, the WPA, and the CCC.*

Camping

The park has 54 tent or RV sites, with showers; backpack camp and 1 group camp. For reservations, call 888-947-2757. Camping fee.

Copper Falls State Park, 36764 Copper Falls Rd., Mellen, WI 54546; 715-274-5123; www.dnr.state.wi.us/org/land/parks

Itasca

20 miles north of Park Rapids on Minn. 71

- 32,698 acres ■ Year-round ■ Vehicle fee ■ Mississippi Headwaters ■ Virgin pine wilderness ■ Naturalist-led boat tours ■ Historic lodge ■ Fishing (license required), biking, swimming ■ Snowmobiling, cross-country skiing, snowshoeing

Lake Itasca, source of the Mississippi River

Old Man River, the mighty Mississippi, begins its life rippling between stepping-stones at the outlet of Lake Itasca. Explorers of North America had been guessing at the source of the river for 300 years when Henry Rowe Schoolcraft, led by Ojibwa guide Ozaawindib (Yellow Head), found the headwaters in 1832. Though some dissenters still point to Elk Lake above Itasca's west arm, experts affirm Schoolcraft's claim that Lake Itasca is the uppermost collection basin where the river begins its 2,500-mile journey to the Gulf of Mexico.

PARK TIP: *If you're interested in eagles, ask where to find the nests and watch adults catching fish to take back to their young.*

In 1965 a 2,000-acre wilderness with a virgin stand of enormous white and red pine was set aside on the west side of the park, looped around by Wilderness Drive and threaded with hiking trails. Park facilities are concentrated along the lake's east arm. Self-guided tours cover the wide variety of historic and natural landmarks in the park, and summer brings daily naturalist programs at various sites.

The loggers who changed the landscape of this region a century ago are long gone, but nature continues to make alterations, sometimes with help. After a severe windstorm in 1995 took down a number of the big old trees, the park added the 0.5-mile Blowdown Trail. Scientists now set controlled burns, duplicating what once occurred naturally and helping to regenerate the pine forest.

What to See and Do

If you enter the park through the north entrance, start your visit with a short walk to the **Mississippi Headwaters** at the lake outlet. The nearby **Mary Gibbs Mississippi Headwaters Center** describes the hydraulics of the great river system and the story of Lake Itasca's discovery. If you enter from the south or east, your first stop should be the **Jacob V. Brower Visitor Center** with its touchable relief map and exhibits on the park's natural and cultural history.

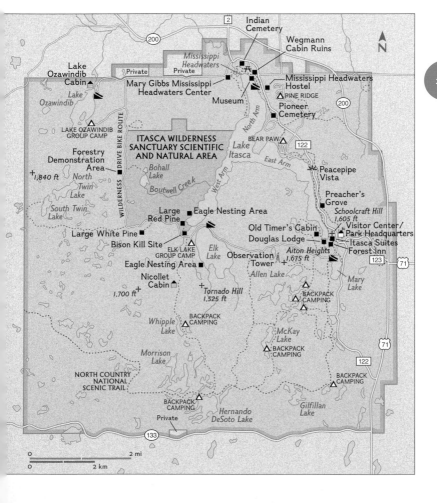

What you do next depends on your time; Itasca can occupy visitors for a week. The **Main Park Drive** runs along the east shore of the lake (there is also a bicycle path), with stops at the Indian Cemetery, swimming beach, Pioneer Cemetery, and among the 275-year-old pines at Preacher's Grove. **Douglas Lodge,** built in 1905 and offering rooms and meals, is the starting point for self-guided walks along a nature trail and among historic buildings such as the log-and-stone **Forest Inn.** In addition, the *Chester Charles II (218-732-5318. Mem. Day–Sept.; fare)* leaves from the pier below Douglas Lake for a 2-hour ride around the lake while a guide tells the park's human and natural history as the loons, bald eagles, and other wildlife glide by.

To experience these woods as they were before settlers arrived, take the 11-mile **Wilderness Drive** (also a bicycle route) west from the Mississippi Headwaters and loop around the **Itasca Wilderness Sanctuary Scientific and Natural Area.** The 0.5-mile **Bohall Trail** passes through groves more than 200 years old on its way to Bohall Lake. Orchid varieties also grow here, including the pink-and-white or snowy lady slipper, the state flower. The 0.3-mile **Landmark Interpretive Trail** has signs that explain forest features such as spring ponds, porcupines, and windfalls. Beavers, which have returned since being trapped nearly to extinction around 1900, may be found along the 3.9-mile **Deer Park Trail,** Allen Lake, and near Elk Lake.

Bicyclists can make a 17-mile loop that circumnavigates the park, around the lake and the sanctuary. If you haven't brought your own, rent gear in the park at Itasca Sports Rental *(218-266-2150. May–mid-Oct.),* where they also offer canoes, pontoons, and motorboats. Fishing tackle and bait are sold for anglers after crappie, northerns, walleyes, or bluegill.

Camping and Lodging

Itasca has 234 tent or RV sites, with showers; limited number open in winter. Reservations advised July and Aug. Camping fee. There are also 11 backcountry sites and 2 group camps. Also in the park, Douglas Lodge offers 7 rooms and 16 cabins; Itasca Suites has 12 units (open year-round); Bear Paw Campground has 6 cabins; and the 10-bedroom "Clubhouse," built in 1910, is rented to groups. All open Mem. Day to early autumn. Call 866-857-2757 to reserve. The Mississippi Headwaters Hostel is open year-round; call 218-266-3415 for reservations.

202

NAME GAME: The name "Itasca" comes from:

1. A legendary Indian girl whose tears for a lost lover began the Mississippi River.
2. A combination of the Latin words for "truth" and "head."
3. A water carrier in discoverer Henry Schoolcraft's favorite Verdi opera.

ANSWERS:
1. A legend by Mary Eastman, but untrue.
2. True. Schoolcraft combined Latin words "veritas" and "caput" to make the name.
3. False. Verdi hadn't written any operas in 1832.

Itasca State Park, 36750 Main Park Drive, Park Rapids, MN 56470; 218-699-7521; www.mnstateparks.info

Forestville/Mystery Cave

7 miles south of Wykoff via Minn. 16

■ 3,222 acres ■ Year-round ■ Vehicle fee ■ Largest cave in Minnesota ■ Historic village with interpreters ■ Spring-fed trout streams ■ Horseback riding, cross-country skiing

In 1910, when Thomas Meighen closed the dry goods store in fading Forestville, the shelves were still stocked. That, along with detailed account books, helped interpreters re-create life in this farm town, circa 1899. The buildings of Historic Forestville, a key feature in the state park, survive despite its fairly brief history—the town's population peaked at 200 in 1853 but declined after the railroad went elsewhere—thanks to the Meighen family, who owned the store and surrounding farmlands in the 1890s. Meighen's house was one of the buildings still standing when his descendants sold the property to the state.

In Meighen's time, locals were aware that a big portion of the South Branch Root River seemed to disappear into the ground west of town, but they didn't know where it went. The answer, discovered in 1937, is Mystery Cave, where a maze of linear passages visit shimmering pools, spiky stalactites, and distinctive formations with names such as Frozen Falls and Turquoise Lake.

What to See and Do

There are three distinct attractions to enjoy here: the restored past of Historic Forestville; the outdoor adventure of its forested river valley; and the geological wonders of Mystery Cave. Start at the **park office** near the west entrance, where you can get maps, schedules for interpretive programs, and advice.

Mystery Cave formations

If history is at the top of your list, drive through the park on County Rd. 118 to the parking areas south of the old steel bridge. Cross the 1899 bridge and you'll step into another era, meeting characters from the past portrayed by costumed interpreters, in **Historic Forestville** *(507-765-2785; www.mnhs.org/places/sites/hf)*. Among the restored buildings are the dry goods store, the Meighen residence, farm buildings, and historic garden and crop areas.

The park also has three blue-ribbon trout streams. Cast a line below the bridge or into nearby **Forestville Creek**, or hike along **Canfield Creek**, excellent for trout fishing, to **Big Spring**, which bubbles up near the park's south border. Throughout the park, bridle and hiking trails lead to streams and up the woody ridges. Hiking is rewarding in spring, when bluebells and other wildflowers bloom, wild turkeys gobble, and migrating warblers sing; or in fall, when the hardwood forests of oak, basswood, aspen, and sugar maple put on a color show. Bird-watching is a year-round favorite activity; among the 175 species spotted in the park there are nesting orioles, American redstarts, indigo buntings, and migrating eagles. There are also 15 miles of designated bridle trails—riders must not venture off them—and a special horse camp.

RESTORING NATURE: For the last 30 years, park staff have worked to restore natural features and communities both above and below ground. Tons of mud and rock fill were mined and dumped in Mystery Cave when it was first developed for tours in the 1930s and 1940s. The fill was painstakingly removed as the cave was renovated from 1988 through 1997, exposing numerous rare features. Prescribed burns have reinvigorated oak savanna, oak woodlands, and prairie. Many beautiful wildflowers and native plant communities are thriving again.

Then drive 5 miles west, following signs along County Rds. 118 and 5, to **Mystery Cave.** You don't have to crawl to get underground among the stalactites, flowstones, and dangling bats. Guided tours *(daily in summer; weekends in spring & fall; fee)* sample a small portion of the 13 miles of passageways—the longest known cave in the state. Tours through the **Historic Entrance** enjoy upright posture along well-lit passages on cement and metal grid walkways, while naturalists talk about cave geology and the biology of bats. The somewhat longer and more rustic tour from the **Minnesota Caverns Entrance** *(summer weekends)* 2 miles away requires visitors to carry their own lights. Bring a jacket; the temperature in the caves is 48°F year-round. Exhibits at the Visitor Center help interpret the cave.

Camping

The park has 73 tent or RV sites, with shower facilities, and a separate horse camp with 57 campsites. Reservations advised in season; call 866-857-2757. Camping fee.

Forestville/Mystery Cave State Park, 21071 County 118, Preston, MN 55965; 507-352-5111; www.dnr.state.mn.us/state_parks

Tettegouche

5 miles northeast of Silver Bay on Minn. 61

■ 9,346 acres ■ Year-round ■ Vehicle fee ■ Palisades ■ 60-foot waterfall ■ Hiking, rock climbing, fishing (license required)

A recent visitor to the top of towering Palisade Head arrived just in time to see a young man jump off the cliff above Lake Superior. For a moment his guts were in his shoes—then he saw a thick rope snaking over the edge. This 200-foot anorthosite cliff is a favorite rock climbing spot.

This park has two prominent rock headlands, along with many other attractions, including backcountry cabins, blue-ribbon fishing streams, a 60-foot waterfall, and spectacular autumn color.

The cabins are remnants of a fishing retreat built by Duluth businessmen in 1910. Various owners protected the area through the years before turning it over for a park in 1979. Today's visitors follow in the footsteps of the Duluth outdoorsmen, quite literally: This is a park for hikers, and its fishing lakes (as well as its cabins) are reached by walking the trails.

Basalt cliffs on Lake Superior's North Shore

What to See and Do

Travelers up Lake Superior's North Shore often are enthralled by the scenery that shows itself at every turn of Minn. 61. For those who can't bear to leave the lakeshore, Tettegouche offers spectacular and accessible cliff-top views at 214-foot **Palisade Head** (off Minn. 61) and **Shovel Point** (1.5-mile round-trip hike from park office), both towering remnants of lava flows a billion years ago. The cliffs are favorites of the carabiner set, rock hounds who will tie off to a tree and bounce down the sheer faces. Keep a good grip on the children, as the edges are largely without guard rails or supervision. For those who don't like heights, there are trails down to pebbly lakeshore beaches.

PARK TIP: *Hungry? Try your hand at blueberry picking (late July–mid-Aug.); the staff may provide hints as to where to find the ripest berries.*

If you have time, leave the car and hoof it inland—the rewards are ample. From the trailhead parking lot, it's about 1.5 miles round-trip to **High Falls,** the tallest waterfall inside the state borders. Just above the falls, a suspension footbridge crossing the Baptism River is part of the **Superior Hiking Trail** running from Duluth to Canada. There are 23 miles of hiking trails winding up and down the Sawtooth Mountains from view to view, including a 3.5-mile hike from the trailhead parking lot to **Mic Mac Lake.**

A SUPERIOR HIKE: The North Shore of Minnesota now has a hiking trail that backpackers compare to California's Pacific Crest Trail or the Inca Trail in Peru. From Duluth to the Canadian border, the Superior Hiking Trail runs the ridges through Tettegouche, on footbridges, over tumbling streams, through aspen glades and evergreen forests, and along the flanks of the Sawtooth Mountains. There are still a few unopened gaps in the trail, but the footloose footslogger may prefer to tackle the trail in sections, given its length and variety. There is always the vast blue lake nearby, a view that makes this trail unique. A guide is available from the Superior Hiking Trail Association *(P.O. Box 4, Two Harbors, MN 55616. 218-834-2700. Fee)*.

To the southwest, **Palisade Valley** includes steep-walled **Bean** and **Bear Lakes,** both offering trout fishing. The **Palisade Valley Overlook** is a sheer cliff looking down the valley where Palisade Creek flows out of Tettegouche Lake, to Lake Superior. The wetlands below are good for moose-watching.

In winter, visitors make their way on skis and snowshoes along the park's 17 miles of groomed ski trails. Twelve miles of snowmobile trails connect the park to the **North Shore State Trail** in adjacent **Finland State Forest** *(888-646-6367)* and **Superior National Forest** *(218-666-5251)*.

Camping and Lodging

The park has 28 tent or RV sites, with showers (some open in winter); a handicapped-accessible, 6-person cabin at Illgen Falls; 6 walk-in sites; and 13 cart-in sites. Tettegouche Camp has 4 rustic backcountry cabins and a group lodge. Reservations advised; call 866-857-2757. Camping fee.

Tettegouche State Park, 5702 Highway 61, Silver Bay, MN 55614; 218-226-6365; www.dnr.state.mn.us/state_parks

Soudan Underground Mine

25 miles northeast of Virginia on Minn. 169

■ 2,245 acres ■ Year-round ■ No pets ■ No camping ■ Red-rock formations ■ Unusual mix of wildlife and plant life ■ Hiking

Riding the rattling, shaking "cage" half a mile down into the Soudan Mine *(Mem. Day–Labor Day; adm. fee),* visitors may want to remind themselves that a century ago this was one of the safest iron mines in the region, and miners begged to work here. The Soudan opened in 1882, the first iron ore mine in Minnesota, now famous for its iron ranges. The Soudan and the forest around it were donated to the state by U.S. Steel after the mine shut down in 1962.

Walk through the Visitor Center, then take a look at the massive cables and hoist wheels outside and in the engine house and headframe. Next, don a hard hat for a 90-minute tour down the shaft to the work areas, where interpreters explain how the job changed over the years. A second tour descends to an underground physics lab.

The park also features 5 miles of fairly steep hiking trails. In winter, 3 miles of snowmobile trails are groomed.

Soudan Underground Mine State Park, P.O. Box 335, Soudan, MN 55782; 218-753-2245; www.dnr.state.mn.us/state_parks

Blue Mounds

6 miles north of I-90 on Minn. 75

■ 2,028 acres ■ Year-round ■ Vehicle fee ■ "Blue" cliff ■ Tallgrass prairie ■ Bison herd ■ Swimming, bird-watching, snowmobiling, rock climbing

When the sun set on the prairies of 1800s Minnesota, pioneers trekking west saw a blue haze in an outcrop of Sioux quartzite and named the prominent landmark Blue Mound. This park is one of the rare places where today's visitors can see what the travelers in covered wagons saw: bison, blooming wildflowers, and in late summer bluestem grasses taller than a pioneer.

Prickly pear cactus and Sioux quartzite amid prairie grasses

The west entrance ranger station, open year-round, has maps. For wildflowers and a spectacular view, hike the **Upper Mound Trail,** which crosses the Rock Alignment, a 1,250-foot ridge arrayed in an east-west direction. Although the builders are unknown, they aligned it with the sunrise and sunset on the first day of spring and fall. Also atop the Mound, the 0.7-mile **Bur Oak Trail** runs through wooded habitat friendly to birds and butterflies.

The mounds extend about 1.5 miles, rising as high as 90 feet, with sheer faces on the east side that lure increasing numbers of rock climbers. Near the north entrance are 500-acre winter and summer enclosures for 75 bison, with an observation platform just south of the road, and a mowed trail around three-quarters of the enclosure. The auction of excess bison in late September is an annual event.

Camping
The park has 73 tent and RV sites, with showers; and 14 walk-in sites. Reservations advised in season; call 866-857-2757. Camping fee.

Blue Mounds State Park, 1410 161st St., Luverne, MN 56156; 507-283-1307; www.dnr.state.mn.us/state_parks

CENTRAL PLAINS

NORTH DAKOTA

Cross Ranch
Fort Abraham Lincoln
Lake Metigoshe
Icelandic

SOUTH DAKOTA

Custer
Fort Sisseton
Newton Hills

NEBRASKA

Fort Robinson
Lake McConaughy
Arbor Lodge

KANSAS

Lake Scott
Prairie Dog
Clinton
Elk City

IOWA

Backbone
Ledges
Maquoketa Caves
Stone

MISSOURI

Prairie
Ha Ha Tonka
Montauk
Meramec

Custer State Park, South Dakota

Cross Ranch

15 miles south of Washburn on west bank of Missouri River, off N. Dak. 200A

- 589 acres ▪ Year-round ▪ Vehicle fee ▪ River-bottom ecology
- Hiking

Cottonwoods and prairie above the Missouri River

The great Missouri River once flowed unchecked through North Dakota for some 360 miles, before dams turned most of the river's course into lakes. One of the remaining wild sections of the Missouri runs adjacent to this park and the abutting 6,000-acre preserve owned by the Nature Conservancy. Together they protect a portion of this river-bottom ecology.

PARK TIP: *For a treat hike the Ma-ak-oti Trail, where the mighty Missouri River serves as your constant companion.*

Cross Ranch's floodplain nurtures a lovely cottonwood forest—for now, at least. In order to regenerate, cottonwoods require occasional flooding and scouring of the landscape. With the construction of the Garrison Dam upriver, periodic floods no longer wash through to create habitat for the thirsty cottonwood seedlings.

Not a long-living tree in the best of circumstances, the cottonwood is gradually being replaced by ash, box elder, and oak.

What to See and Do

Begin at the **Visitor Center,** where informative displays highlight the Missouri River's effect on the countryside, forest succession, and changing river channels. There are also presentations on the early Indians, ranchers, trappers, and riverboaters, as well as the endangered and extinct wildlife of the area.

From here, hike out through the river-bottom forest, where more than 15 miles of trails offer a peaceful and scenic education about this vanishing environment. The paths double as cross-country skiing trails during the winter months, with some 10 miles groomed.

If time is limited, the 2.6-mile **Matah Trail** circles the campground and takes in a riverside stretch beneath towering cottonwoods. For those with more time, the **Matah, Cottonwood,** and **Bison Trails** lead 3.5 miles to the **Levis Trail,** which explores an accreted island, attached to the shore after Garrison Dam was built and the river course changed. The park's backcountry camping sites are located here. This 2.3-mile trail wanders along the boundary of the Nature Conservancy's **Cross Ranch Nature Preserve** *(701-794-8741),* where you may spot deer, a coyote, or perhaps even a secretive bobcat. Keep an eye out for the bald eagles that hunt over the river in spring and fall, and two endangered bird species—the piping plover and least tern—nesting on the sandbars in the river. During summer, the Nature Conservancy offers a self-guided nature trail, which can be done in different sections, one a 0.75-mile trip, the other about 2 miles.

211

Camping and Lodging

There are 42 tent and RV sites and 23 tent-only sites, with showers, as well as 5 backcountry sites. Mid-May–mid-Sept. Camping reservations begin in April; call 800-807-4723. Camping fee. There are 3 cabins; call park to reserve at 701-794-3731.

Cross Ranch State Park, 1403 River Rd., Center, ND 58530; 701-794-3731; www.parkrec.nd.gov/parks/crsp.htm

FORT MANDAN: On October 24, 1804, the Lewis and Clark Expedition camped across the river from what is now Cross Ranch State Park. From their Fort Mandan camp, Capt. William Clark described the area much as you still see it: "The land is low and beautiful, and covered with oak and cottonwood, but has been too recently hunted to afford much game." The party spent the ensuing very cold winter nearby, almost certainly returning to the Cross Ranch area to hunt. Today a reconstruction of Fort Mandan *(701-462-8129. Closed Mon.)* stands in Washburn, a few miles north of the park. The site of the original fort is believed to lie beneath the Missouri River.

Fort Abraham Lincoln

7 miles south of Mandan on N. Dak. 1806

- 1,006 acres ▪ Year-round ▪ Entrance fee ▪ Indian village
- Custer home ▪ Horseback riding ▪ Fishing

Earthen lodge, On-A-Slant village

Visitors to this state park are faced with a juxtaposition—the history of the Native Americans who lived here before white settlement, and the efforts of the U.S. Army to subdue their descendants.

Prior to European settlement, there were 27 Plains Indian tribes. Ten were settled agricultural people, not the nomadic hunters of cowboy tradition. About A.D. 900, the groups that later formed the Mandan tribe arrived in the Dakotas. By the 1600s, several villages had been established near the Heart and Missouri Rivers, including On-A-Slant, an agricultural settlement occupied from the 1570s to the late 1700s. In 1781, smallpox hit the village; the Mandan abandoned the site and moved about 70 miles north on the Missouri. In 1834, smallpox struck again, wiping out most of the remaining tribe. Portions of On-A-Slant village, including several large earthen lodges, have been reconstructed within the state park.

Fort Abraham Lincoln was built in 1872 and, beginning in 1873, served as the home base of Lt. Col. George Armstrong Custer and the Seventh Cavalry. As such, it was a primary staging area for the Indian Wars. In 1875, the Interior Department ordered all Indians to report to reservations by January 31, 1876. By February 1, many had not reported, and the job of enforcing the order was turned over to the military. In May 1876, Custer left Fort Lincoln to bring in the laggards. He and more than 225 soldiers under his immediate command were killed on June 25 in a skirmish at the Little Bighorn in Montana.

The **Visitor Center** provides excellent displays on the tribes, villages, and local customs, as well as exhibits about the cavalry history of the fort. A walk just up the hill leads to the reconstructed **On-A-Slant.** Here a guided interpretive trail gives you a feel for the Mandan way of life, from the cool interior of the lodges to the agricultural crops and techniques employed by the tribe.

North of the Visitor Center lies the **Cavalry Post,** dominated by the reconstructed Victorian home of George and Libbie Custer. Guided tours are available *(May–mid-Oct., by appt. rest of year).*

Camping

The park has 57 tent and RV sites and 37 primitive sites. April–Oct. For reservations, call North Dakota's centralized reservation system at 800-807-4723 or online at www.parkrec.nd.gov. Camping fee.

Fort Abraham Lincoln State Park, 4480 Fort Lincoln Rd., Mandan, ND 58554; 701 667-6340; www.parkrec.nd.gov/parks/flsp.htm

Lake Metigoshe

15 miles north of Bottineau on N. Dak. 43

▪ 1,554 acres ▪ Year-round ▪ Vehicle fee ▪ Swimming, boating, kayaking ▪ Hiking, cross-country skiing, snowmobiling

Hard by the Canadian border in north-central North Dakota, Lake Metigoshe is one of the state's popular year-round vacation spots. The Chippewa called the lake Metigoshe Washegum, meaning "clear lake surrounded by oaks."

The Chippewa also named the Turtle Mountains, home to the park. The thick woods of these low, rolling hills, dotted with intensely blue-black lakes, provide excellent cover for a variety of wildlife. Keep an eye out for the area's marquee mammal, the large and clumsy-looking moose, as well as the occasional bear and even rarely, a wolf wandering down from Canada.

Lake Metigoshe

What to See and Do

Visitors looking to explore this park should take the time to hike the **Old Oak Trail,** North Dakota's first National Recreation Trail. It takes about two hours to hike the full 3 miles. A self-guided brochure *(available at trailhead)* explains marked sites along the trail and provides excellent background to the history, wildlife, ecology, and geology of this glacier-formed region. In addition, the park offers worthwhile naturalist programs and guided hikes. Contact the park office for more information on the various topics and the specific schedules.

PARK TIP: *Smell the forest, listen to the coyotes howl at sunrise or sunset, and watch the Ruffed Grouse drum for his "special friend" as you walk the park trails.*

For the most part, visitors come to **Lake Metigoshe** for water sports—boating, waterskiing, Jet skiing, and swimming *(canoe and kayak rentals available).* There are boat launch facilities and a terraced swimming beach. Motorized boats drive most of the fishermen off the lake in the summer. If you have time, rent a canoe and explore **School Section Lake,** where motorized boating is prohibited. For the very hearty, an ambitious inter-lake trip involving some portaging is available between School Section and nearby **Lake Erimosh.**

North Dakota is famous for its bitter, snowy winter weather, and most people wouldn't dream of visiting in the cold months, when "forty below keeps the riffraff out" becomes a popular saying. But Lake Metigoshe State Park shines in these conditions, serving as a jumping-off point for the 250 miles of groomed snowmobile and cross-country trails that roam the Turtle Mountains. One—taking about three hours round-trip—travels to the **International Peace Garden** on the U.S.–Canada border. The lake grows a coat of ice thick enough to support a colony of ice-fishing sheds—and the trucks used to transport and access them—as well as skaters and sledders.

Camping

Lake Metigoshe offers 130 tent and RV sites, with showers; some sites with water and electricity; 3 year-round cabins with heat. Reservations available by calling North Dakota's centralized reservation system at 800-807-4723. Camping fee.

Lake Metigoshe State Park, #2 Lake Metigoshe State Park, Bottineau, ND 58318; 701-263-4651; www.parkrec .nd.gov/parks/lmsp.htm

MÉTIS: The land from Lake Metigoshe east to Lake Superior and north to Lake Winnipeg once comprised an improbable quasi-country, the rebellious province of the Métis. The Métis were descendants of Indian (mostly Chippewa) and French trappers in the 18th and 19th centuries. Indians in the area described them as "half man, half cart," after their constant companion, the wooden Red River cart with which they hauled trade goods. The wheels of the carts couldn't be greased because dust would cement them to the axle. The grinding wood made an interminable shriek, usually described as "hellish." In the latter half of the 19th century, Métis leader Louis Riel attempted to form a Métis country on lands in western Canada. The revolt was eventually put down and Riel was hanged in 1885 by the Regina government.

Icelandic

5 miles west of Cavalier on N. Dak. 5

- 912 acres ▪ Year-round
- Vehicle fee ▪ Prairie natural area ▪ Pioneer heritage museum ▪ Cross-country skiing

This state park combines the natural history of North Dakota with the cultural heritage of its early immigrants. The park also preserves some vanishing natural areas. When the glaciers melted at the end of

Moose

the last ice age, about 13,000 years ago, they left behind vast lakes. Glacial Lake Agassiz was the largest, stretching 350,000 square miles from Hudson Bay to North Dakota's southeastern corner. Lakes Winnipeg, Winnepegosa, and Manitoba, as well as Lake of the Woods, are remnants of that lake, and the Red River Valley in North Dakota and Minnesota is its former bed. Today, nearly every acre of this fertile valley has been conquered for agriculture, but at Icelandic you can see remnants of the primeval landscape. Located along what was the ancient lake shoreline, the park is underlain by 60 feet of sand in what is known as a sandgrass prairie.

Begin at the **Pioneer Heritage Center,** where a museum showcases the history of the early settlers. A short walk takes you to the **Gunlogson Homestead,** an 1882 two-story frame building, and a replica of a typical Icelander's homesteading log cabin. The beautifully restored **Akra Community Hall** provides an echo of community life, revolving around church, school, and communal dinners.

A short walk north lies the second heart of this park, the 94-acre **Gunlogson Nature Preserve.** Located along the Tongue River, the preserve provides a look at an undisturbed river valley ecosystem. A self-guided nature trail beginning at the homestead passes through lowland forests and marshes, several springs, and a peat bog.

Down the road next to the campgrounds, **Lake Renwick** offers swimming, fishing *(license required),* and boating. If you choose to visit in winter, you can try ice fishing for a real North Dakota experience.

Camping

There are 162 tent and RV sites, with showers; also primitive camping. Call 800-807-4723 or online at www.parkrec.nd.gov for reservations. Camping fee.

Icelandic State Park, 13751 Hwy. 5, Cavalier, ND 58220; 701-265-4561; www.parkrec.nd.gov/parks/isp.htm

Custer

4 miles east of Custer on US 16A

▪ 71,000 acres ▪ Year-round ▪ Entrance fee ▪ Needles Highway (closed in winter) ▪ Bison herd ▪ Rock climbing, mountain biking, fishing (license required), horseback riding, hiking

Cathedral Spires, viewed from Little Devils Tower

To see how many stars there really are in the sky, visit Custer State Park. Here crystal-clear night skies show thousands of glittering diamonds from Orion to the Pleiades in a profusion not often observed in this electrically lit nation. But the stars above are just a sidelight to the natural treasures below. This state park is located in the Black Hills, a geologic wonder of cracked limestone caves, dark forests, and craggy mountains. Known as Paha Sapa and sacred to the Lakota, the Black Hills are a combination of home of the gods, mecca of vision quests, and center of the world. It is hard to visit the area without sensing a world of mystery and spirit.

The hills are named for their dark appearance from a distance, a shade created by their thick covering of ponderosa pine. Geologically, they comprise an elliptically domed area about 125 miles long and 65 miles wide, stretching from western South Dakota into eastern Wyoming. The many caves in the area's cracked layers were created when the central crystalline portion uplifted through the limestone.

PARK TIP: *Feel the thunder as wranglers round up the park's 1,400 head of bison in late September.*

The Black Hills are a major year-round destination, famous for sublime natural wonders such as Custer State Park, Wind Cave, and Jewel Cave, and for man-made roadside attractions such as Mount Rushmore and the Crazy Horse Monument.

Custer presents its visitors with classic, relatively undisturbed Black Hills scenery and a variety of activities. Travel to the park's northern end to view steep, craggy rock faces and mountainsides black with ponderosa pine. Or check out the southern portion, a landscape of open plains and rolling, bare-topped hills that shine with new grass in spring and gleam a dormant red and brown in winter. Most of the park's famed bison herd roam these grasslands.

The park, established in 1913 as a game preserve, played a major role in the preservation of the American bison, which had been hunted nearly to extinction by the early settlers.

During the fires of 1988 and 1990, some 31,000 acres of Black Hills forest burned. But the positive role those fires played in the ecosystem is evident in the new, grassy meadows that provide habitat and food for a diversity of animals.

Spring is a special time in the park as the young grasses begin to emerge and act as a magnet to draw deer, bison, elk, and other large, park wildlife near the roads.

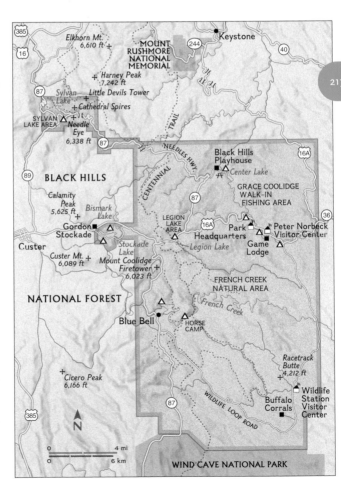

217

What to See and Do

A visit to Custer starts at the **Peter Norbeck Visitor Center,** which showcases the story of the park from its volcanic period through the activities of the CCC using full-scale dioramas. Be sure to visit the park's scenic high point, the **Needles Highway** *(closed in winter).* The 14-mile drive winds through sharp, needle-like granite formations to the popular **Sylvan Lake Area,** near Needles Eye, Harney Peak, and Cathedral Spires. Trailheads for several hikes may be found along this beautiful drive, including the 1-mile **Sylvan Lake Shore Trail;** the **Cathedral Spires Trail,** a one-way trail that spans the park's mountainous country; and the **Sunday Gulch Trail,** a 2.8-mile loop.

Grace Coolidge Creek

You can also travel part of the **Centennial Trail,** which extends 111 miles from Bear Butte State Park near Sturgis to Wind Cave National Park.

Back at the Visitor Center, pick up the 18-mile **Wildlife Loop Road** for a leisurely trip to see the park's other main drawing card, its herd of 1,400 bison. About 10 miles south along the winding, well-maintained road lie the **Buffalo Corrals.** But most of the bison will be out grazing on the plains somewhere along this drive. These animals may look slow and placid while munching grass on the prairie, but stay clear! Although a mature bison bull may stand 6 feet high at the shoulders and weigh a ton, it can turn with astounding agility while sprinting at speeds of up to 30 miles an hour.

On the last Monday of September, cowboys round up the park's bison, bringing them into the corrals. Typically 250 to 300 animals are sold at auction, and the rest are released back into the park after branding and vaccination. The sale of the culled bison, held on the third Saturday of November, attracts a large crowd.

Also loitering on the rolling plains is a herd of burros. Perhaps envious of the bison's status as the park's main mammal, the burros

218

attempt to take center stage by asserting personality. You are almost certain to run into a "burro jam," when visitors stop along the road to photograph these charming, outgoing quadrupeds. A burro may even stick its head into your car searching for a snack.

Farther along the Wildlife Loop lies a prairie-dog town. The animals are important to the diet of many western predators, especially birds of prey. Their burrows are easy to find; they look like tiny black volcanoes. You may also notice many other animals along this road, including pronghorn, deer, elk, and bighorn sheep. Your chances of seeing these large creatures increase if you travel in the early morning and at dusk.

Near Legion Lake, almost back at the Visitor Center, is another important stop: **Badger Hole,** named for Badger Clark, South Dakota's first poet laureate. Clark lived alone here from 1927 until his death in 1957. You can visit his small cabin and hike a short nature trail in the area.

Further Adventures

If you have more time, hike up **Harney Peak,** just outside of Custer's borders within the **Black Hills National Forest** *(605-673-9200).* At 7,242 feet, Harney is the highest point in South Dakota. The park maintains four trails that range from moderate to strenuous, all leaving from the Sylvan Lake Area. Plan on four to five hours to do a round-trip of 5 to 6.5 miles.

A second worthwhile effort is a hike through all or part of the **French Creek Natural Area,** a 12-mile-long stretch of relatively undisturbed canyon country along the creek of the same name. There are no formal trails, but you can follow the creek through a steep-walled and timbered canyon. Hikers must cross French Creek numerous times, so be prepared to wade.

> EAST COMES WEST: In 1874, Lt. Col. George Armstrong Custer led his famous Black Hills expedition into what is now the park bearing his name. Prospectors with Custer discovered gold along French Creek, bringing a rush of settlers to the area and triggering the Indian wars that eventually led to Custer's defeat and death. The park's second, somewhat lesser brush with national renown came in 1927, when President Calvin Coolidge, vacationing here at the State Game Lodge, gave reporters a note with this famous statement: "I do not choose to run again for President of the United States." He sent for his staff and ran the country from the lodge for the summer.

Camping and Lodging

Custer offers 8 developed campgrounds with 305 tent and RV sites, 50 camper cabins, and 30 tent-only sites, with shower facilities available April–Dec. The park also has 2 backcountry areas and a 27-site horse camp. Primitive camping year-round. Reservations recommended for all sites; call 800-710-2267. Camping fee. There are also 112 rooms in four lodges, May–Oct., and 109 cabins, some open year-round; call 888-875-0001 for reservations.

Custer State Park, 13329 Hwy. 16-A, Custer, SD 57730; 605-255-4515; www.custerstatepark.com

Fort Sisseton

22 miles north of Webster via S. Dak. 25

■ 125 acres ■ Year-round ■ Entrance fee

Fort Sisseton State Historic Park comprises a collection of buildings dating from its days as a military post—1864 to 1889. The park is located in the northern realm of the beautiful Coteau des Prairies, a plateau reaching an elevation of 2,000 feet.

PARK TIP: *Rent a canoe at Kettle Lake and cruise the shoreline. If you're lucky, you may see bald eagles, white pelicans, white egrets, or blue herons on or above the lake.*

The fort's construction was prompted by the Minnesota Indian Uprising of 1862. In 1866, Fort Sisseton's chief scout, Sam Brown, had to intercept his own incorrect message about an "Indian war party," which turned out to be peaceful Lakota. To prevent bloodshed, Brown set out on a return trip to the fort without resting and lost direction in a sudden, blinding, late spring snowstorm. Finding familiar landmarks south of Fort Sisseton, he arrived in the early morning after riding more than 150 miles and in time to correct his mistake. Exhausted, frostbitten, and unable to stand, he never took a natural step again after his hours in the saddle. (In the 1930s, the WPA restored 14 of the 45-plus original structures.)

The **Visitor Center** (*Mem. Day–Labor Day*) has excellent displays about life in the fort, and an entire barracks has been re-created in period style. Interpretive signs drawing on the diary of Andrew Jackson Fisk will guide you. Fisk joined the Second Minnesota Cavalry at age 14 and became the camp quartermaster by 16.

On the first weekend in June, the fort hosts a historical festival, complete with an encampment, shooting contests, drill parades, fiddlers, and other frontier amusement.

Camping

The park has 10 campsites, 3 camping cabins, and 3 tent sites, with showers. Reservations by calling 800-710-2267 or visit www.CampSD .com. Camping fee.

Fort Sisseton State Historic Park, 11907 434th Ave., Lake City, SD 57247; 605-448-5474; http://gfp .sd.gov/state-parks/ directory/fort-sisseton

Cannon in front of fort hospital

Newton Hills

6 miles south of Canton on County Rd. 135

Red-winged blackbird

■ 1,063 acres ■ Year-round ■ Entrance fee ■ Hiking, swimming, fishing (license required) ■ Cross-country skiing

For the visitor heading across the corn- and wheatfield country of South Dakota and Iowa, timbered Newton Hills pops up ahead in sharp relief, the legacy of glaciers from the last ice age. This park preserves native countryside on the southern edge of the Coteau des Prairies. Extending along the eastern border of South Dakota, the plateau marks the western edge of the geographical province known as the Central Lowlands. To the west begin the Great Plains, extending to the Rockies.

Inside the park thrives a native upland forest, primarily oak but laced with other hardwoods. To get a flavor of the park in a short time, hike the **Woodland Trail**, a 0.75-mile loop that travels along the Sergeant Creek drainage, then up a hill to a peaceful niche of beautiful old oaks interspersed with small areas of preserved native prairie. An excellent place for bird-watching, the park has recorded more than 200 species, including the peregrine falcon.

If you have time for another hike, consider the 0.5-mile **Coteau Trail,** an interpretive loop along the edge of the woods, where markers identify the various types of vegetation. Then travel to the southern edge of the park, where **Lake Lakota** offers swimming and fishing. If you are here in August, check out the Sioux River Folk Festival.

Camping and Lodging

Newton Hills has 128 tent and RV sites, with showers available April–Nov. Camping fee. Eight cabins and a group lodge are also available year-round. Reservations advised in season; call 800-710-2267.

Newton Hills State Park, 28771 482nd Ave., Canton, SD 57013; 605-987-2263; www.sdgfp.info/parks

221

Fort Robinson

3 miles west of Crawford on US 20

- 22,000 acres ▪ Year-round ▪ Vehicle fee ▪ Red Cloud Agency
- Bison herd and bighorn sheep ▪ Hiking, mountain biking, horseback riding, bird-watching, fishing

Horse-drawn tour

Fort Robinson, the largest of Nebraska's state parks, nestles beneath the stark rugged bluffs of the White River. Its main attraction is its military history, from its role in 1873 as an Indian agency to its use as a German prisoner-of-war camp during World War II. The park complex takes in the original site of the Red Cloud Agency, established as a reservation for the Sioux under Chief Red Cloud.

Fort Robinson and the agency were among the most important staging areas for the 19th-century Indian wars in the West, as the U.S. Army tried to entice the entire Sioux tribe to join Red Cloud on the reservation. Many Sioux refused, remaining on the plains with Crazy Horse and later joining the Cheyenne to defeat Lt. Col. George Armstrong Custer at the 1876 Battle of the Little Bighorn. When Crazy Horse eventually surrendered in 1877, he was taken to Fort Robinson and imprisoned in the guardhouse. This is also where a soldier fatally stabbed him.

Beyond the fort complex, the park's 22,000 acres include an extensive plains environment, complete with bison herd.

What to See and Do

The activities available at Fort Robinson can keep you busy for a week. A good way to get an overview of the park is to take a horse-drawn historical tour *(Mem. Day–Labor Day; sign up at the information booth).*

First on the list should be the fort's historic sites. The large 1887 **parade grounds** extend away from the main entrance, flanked by the **Adobe Officers' Quarters,** also dating from 1887. The restorations here show how officers of the period lived. The **Fort Robinson Museum** *(call the Historical Society for hours, 308-665-2919)* interprets military life at the fort from the Indian wars to World War II. The displays are colorful and informative, although here the focus is on the military side of the story. A second museum at the fort, the **Trailside Museum,** presents a comprehensive look at the geology and paleontology of Nebraska and includes a complete Columbian mammoth skeleton. After firmly grounding yourself on the fort's place in history, drive 1.5 miles from the main fort complex to the area that actually served as the Red Cloud Agency and the World War II prisoner-of-war camp.

Once you've explored these facilities, take the 6-mile **Smiley Canyon Scenic Drive,** which dips and dives through classic broken cattle country. A bison herd frequents these pastures. In 1981, the park introduced 6 bighorn sheep from the Custer State Park herd. Be on your lookout for them as you drive through the park.

If you have the time and the seat for it, an excellent way to see the park is on horseback. Trail rides of varying length and difficulty are available at the stables on the grounds *(Mem. Day–Labor Day; fee).* Or travel by foot or mountain bike along the 30 miles of trails.

223

Camping and Lodging

The park has 75 tent and RV sites, and tent-only sites, with shower facilities offered April to mid-Nov. Primitive camping available year-round. First come, first served. Camping fee. The park also has a 23-room lodge; 32 cabins; and Comanche Hall, which houses 60 people and is open April to mid-Nov. Lodging is available by reservation; call the park at 308-665-2900.

Fort Robinson State Park, P.O. Box 392, Crawford, NE 69339; 308-665-2900; http://outdoornebraska.ne.gov

CHEYENNE OUTBREAK: On September 9, 1878, 300 Northern Cheyenne left their Oklahoma reservation to return to their native lands around the White River. A band of 149 led by Dull Knife were eventually captured and taken to Fort Robinson, where the commanding officer tried to starve them into submission. A group of warriors including Dull Knife escaped on January 9, 1879, and managed to scale the bluffs nearby. They remained at large, without horses, for nearly two weeks, outmaneuvering the cavalry. After the soldiers found them, the warriors refused to surrender. In the ensuing fight, 64 Cheyenne and 11 soldiers were killed.

Lake McConaughy

9 miles northwest of Ogallala on Neb. 61

- 35,700 acres ▪ Year-round ▪ Vehicle fee ▪ Swimming, fishing (license required), boating, windsurfing

Lake McConaughy forms the core of this state recreation area, offering visitors white-sand beaches along much of its 105 miles of shoreline on the North Platte River. The North Platte and Platte Rivers—the Platte forming where the North Platte joins the South Platte—were major landmarks during the development of western America. The broad, flat river valley provided explorers and settlers with a fertile highway through what had become known as the Great American Desert.

Pioneers also followed the North Platte River to South Pass, a natural gateway through the Rockies. The first overland mail service, the telegraph, the Pony Express, and the transcontinental railroad all followed the Platte River.

Among the first things visitors do on entering the park is to take in the 3.5-mile-long, 162-foot-high **Kingsley Dam. Lake Ogallala,** the small lake below the dam, offers a bald eagle viewing area with heated blinds. In relative comfort, you can watch the eagles that congregate and feed here from mid-December until early spring.

The prime attraction of Lake McConaughy is as its name suggests: summertime water activities at Nebraska's largest lake. Your visit here will probably center in and near the water—fishing, swimming, boating, windsurfing, or simply sunning on the glistening sand. If you try your hand at the world-class fishing the lake offers, you may surface one of the dozen or so species of sport fish found here. Anglers have drawn state record-setting fish, including striper, rainbow trout, walleye, and tiger muskie from "Big Mac." In addition, extensive marshes at the lake's western end shelter a variety of birds, including sandhill cranes and Canada geese.

You may also wish to visit **Ash Hollow State Historical Park** *(US 26. 308-778-5651. Mid-May–Labor Day; adm. fee),* near the lake's west end. It was here in this shady grove of ash trees that Oregon Trail pioneers got a break from the trials of westward travel. Exhibits chronicle the area's Native American and pioneer history as well as the evidence of ancient visitors some 8,000 years ago.

Camping

The park has 325 RV sites, with showers, and unlimited primitive sites. Beach camping also permitted. Half the RV sites and all campsites available on a first-come, first-served basis; other half of RV sites reservable. For reservations, call the park or the reservation center at 402-471-1414. Camping fee.

Lake McConaughy State Recreation Area, 1475 Hwy. 61N, Ogallala, NE 69153; 308-284-8800; www.ngpc.state.ne.us/parks

Arbor Lodge

2600 Arbor Ave., Nebraska City

- 72 acres ▪ mid-April–mid-Oct. ▪ Entrance fee ▪ No camping
- Historic mansion

Arbor Lodge

Arbor Lodge is the birthplace of Arbor Day, begun in 1872 at the instigation of newspaperman Julius Sterling Morton. The mansion grew from a relatively modest four-room frame house built in 1855—at the time reputedly the only frame house between the Mississippi River and the Rocky Mountains—when Morton and his wife, Caroline, arrived to take over the *Nebraska City News.* The property was a barren, 160-acre homestead, so Julius and Caroline planted trees to mimic the greenery of their native Michigan. In 1872, as president of the State Board of Agriculture, Morton formalized his enthusiasm for tree planting by introducing a resolution calling for the celebration of Arbor Day on April 22 (which also happened to be his birthday). Over a million trees were planted in Nebraska on that first Arbor Day. The idea spread, and now nearly every U.S. state celebrates the holiday.

Morton served two terms as a territorial representative, a term as secretary and acting territorial governor, and finally as secretary of agriculture in the second Grover Cleveland Administration. He died in 1902. Meanwhile, the lodge's four major expansions were finally completed in 1903 by the Mortons' oldest son, Joy, founder of the Morton Salt Company. He donated the mansion and property to Nebraska in 1923.

The first and obvious stop is the 52-room neocolonial **Arbor Lodge,** with its terraced garden. Much of the Victorian and Empire furniture is original to the house. An ornate Tiffany skylight sparkles in the sun parlor, and the carriage house contains a large display of horse-drawn vehicles.

PARK TIP: *Sit on Monument Square's Whispering Bench, and notice how, when two people sit at each end of the half circle 50 feet away, they need only whisper to be heard.*

Then visit the 72-acre **arboretum,** with its more than 260 varieties of trees and shrubs. Walk along the 0.5-mile path beneath descendants of trees planted by the Mortons, then visit a dense grove of white pine, a log cabin memorializing the original settlers, and a bronze casting of Julius Morton.

Arbor Lodge State Historical Park, P.O. Box 15, Nebraska City, NE 68410; 402-873-7222; www.ngpc.state.ne.us/parks

225

Backbone

2 miles south of Strawberry Point, off Iowa W-68

■ 2,002 acres ■ Year-round ■ Roads within park closed in winter
■ Hiking, swimming, boating, fishing (license required), rock climbing, winter sports

This state park preserves one of the largest forested areas in Iowa—a state in which large forested areas are rare. The park's centerpiece is The Backbone, a high rocky ridge of dolomite that early inhabitants named after the devil's backbone. Its precipitous sides rise 80 to 100 feet above the Maquoketa River.

PARK TIP: *For the best trout fishing around, go to Richmond Springs, a natural spring that spills into two CCC-constructed ponds.*

The dolomite, sometimes called magnesium limestone, was deposited by a shallow tropical sea that covered Iowa some 430 million years ago. Dating from those times, The Backbone is studded with the fossils of extinct corals, occasionally measuring up to 20 inches in diameter.

Iowa's oldest state park, Backbone was established in 1919 and has remained largely free of logging. As a result, 80 percent of the park is forested, dominated in the upland areas by white and red oak, and along the river bottoms by walnut, box elder, cottonwood, and other species typical of the environment. These trees provide

Backbone trout stream

226

excellent habitat for migratory songbirds and game birds such as wild turkey and grouse.

The Maquoketa River runs through the park, and its sandy bottom draws people to wade, ride inner tubes, and play that popular Iowa sport, in-stream volleyball.

What to See and Do

First, visit the park's signature formation, **The Backbone.** Circumnavigate its quarter-mile length via a trail roughly a mile long, round-trip, watching for the Devil's Staircase, Big Oven, Little Oven, Rock Chimney, and other interesting shapes of stone. Below you on either side of the formation, the landscape drops away sharply to the Maquoketa River, offering spectacular panoramas.

If you have more time and energy, take a reliable flashlight to **Backbone Cave,** near the park's north entrance. This undeveloped cave slashes about 300 feet into the rock. There are no passages, just a single corridor through the rock, so there is no danger of getting lost. But be prepared to get dirty. A few stalactites and stalagmites remain, although most have long since been broken off and carried away as souvenirs.

If you have an interest in Depression-era history, take the time to explore the exhibits at Backbone's **Civilian Conservation Corps (CCC) Museum** *(Sat. Mem. Day–Labor Day).* Many buildings in this park—as in parks across the country—were built by the CCC in the 1930s. The corps also planted trees, built retaining walls, and installed telephone lines, among many other things. The museum commemorates their work in Iowa with artifacts and more than 1,500 uncatalogued photographs.

The park's extensive rock formations have proven a popular draw for rock climbers, even though few of the faces reach even 100 feet. Climbers scramble up **Razor's Edge** (40 feet) and **Slot Machine** (80 feet), among other formations, and rappel down. Backbone also contains 20 miles of hiking trails. The **East Lake** and **West Lake Trails** are open to mountain bikes.

BACKBONE STONE: The Silurian dolomite bedrock exposed in The Backbone Formation is among the most resistant bedrock strata found in Iowa. This tough formation created the face not only of Iowa, but of other prominent landforms in the U.S. In east-central Iowa, the Mississippi River bumps up against the dolomite, causing the river to trend eastward in the "nose" of the state between Dubuque and Davenport. The long sweep of this same bedrock forms the escarpments on the shores of Lakes Michigan and Huron, and the Niagara escarpment at Niagara Falls.

227

Camping and Lodging

Backbone has 127 tent and RV sites, with shower facilities. Available on a first-come, first-served basis. Camping fee. There are 16 cabins; for reservations, call 877-427-2757 or visit www.reserveiaparks.com.

Backbone State Park, 1282 120th St., Strawberry Point, IA 52076; 563-924-2000; www.iowadnr.gov/parks/index.html

Ledges

4 miles south of Boone, off Iowa 17

■ 1,200 acres ■ Year-round ■ Hiking ■ Bird-watching

The broken valley of the Des Moines River cradles Ledges State Park in an unusual Iowa landscape. Gold and gray sandstone bluffs form a sharp valley, dug out over the millennia by the normally inoffensive Pea's Creek. This narrowing stretches for about a mile along the creek, edged by sandstone bluffs rising to heights of 75 feet above the valley floor. The fragile sandstone was deposited by a swift-running river beginning about 300 million years ago.

The park showcases intriguing "concretion" formations —big chunks of sandstone that are more firmly cemented by the water than the surrounding rock, much like an oyster produces a pearl. The resulting large rocky gargoyles extend straight out from the valley's side walls and hover over the creek bed. These formations eventually weaken and fall off the rock face—one broke off during the flood of 1993—and leave shallow indented caves in the wall. You can see several concretions and evolving caves in the park.

The park also features several restored sections of prairie, tiny remnants of the shortgrass and tallgrass prairies that once dominated a quarter of the lower 48 states. The site at the top of the canyon near the campground was planted in 1950 as the first native prairie restoration ever attempted in Iowa. The adjacent site was reclaimed in 1987.

Ledges' prairies are dominated by four grass types— sideoats grama, Indian grass, little bluestem, and big bluestem. Big bluestem is sometimes called turkeyfoot because its blooming buds resemble a turkey's foot. Black-eyed Susans, purple coneflowers, blazing stars, and other wildflowers color the prairie in late spring and early summer.

The park's prairie and surrounding forest provide a favored habitat to more than 200 species of songbirds, promising good bird-watching.

What to See and Do

Your tour of the canyon carved through the sandstone is an experience that changes with the seasons. Spring brings wildflowers to the prairies, and in summer the valley provides a shady respite from the heat. Children especially enjoy playing in the pools near where the road fords shallow Pea's Creek. You can drive this road as it meanders down the center of the clearing, across several shallow fords. But your experience here will be greatly enhanced if you choose to walk some of the park's 13 miles of hiking trails, many of which run along the valley rim. In autumn the leaves of the oak-hickory forest crown the ridge in breathtaking color.

The **Lost Lake Nature Trail** leads to **Sentinel** and **Solstice Rocks,** where you stand 60 feet above the Des Moines River. Ledges has a rich history of habitation by the Mesquakie (Fox and Sac), and Solstice Rock is believed to be an observatory. The rock, which resembles the profile of an eagle's head, still has a red "eye" stained in berry dye. On the summer solstice, sunlight pours through a hole drilled in the rock, illuminating a small cavern behind it.

Davis Creek

Remember that the sandstone is highly susceptible to erosion, so climbing on the bluffs is prohibited.

Camping

The park offers 95 campsites with shower facilities (40 have hook-ups) open mid-April to mid-Oct. Half available on a first-come, first-served basis; half reservable at 877-427-2757 or www.reserve iaparks.com. Camping fee.

Ledges State Park, 1519 P Ave., Madrid, IA 50156; 515-432-1852; www.iowadnr.gov/parks/index.html

Maquoketa Caves

7 miles northwest of Maquoketa, off Iowa 428

- 323 acres ▪ Year-round ▪ Karst topography ▪ Cave exploration
- Hiking

This state park offers a primer on the karst processes that formed the 13 caves, sinkholes, and natural bridge along Raccoon Creek. Karst describes topography created when groundwater dissolves carbonate bedrock. The park also features rock caves formed when large blocks of stone slide down the face of rock walls, closing off areas behind.

Start at the **Visitor Center** *(Mem. Day–Labor Day Sat.–Sun.),* which opened in 1997 in the former Sagers Museum. It houses displays on the park's natural features, history, and archaeology.

Then head for the caves. Cave explorers should bring flashlights and very old clothes, and be prepared to get muddy. If you only have time to visit one cave—and want to stay relatively clean while doing so—choose **Dancehall,** the park's largest cave. Inside its upper entrance, just a short walk from the road, a paved and lighted walk explores its 1,100-foot length.

Located near Dancehall's upper entrance is another park attraction, **Natural Bridge,** a vast half-moon of craggy gray rock, overhung with ferns and clinging green finery. Eons ago, this was the entrance to Dancehall Cave, before the intervening sections collapsed.

If you have more time, an adventurous spirit, and a reliable flashlight, the other caves supply exotic experiences in the Iowa underground. Seven of the caves can be seen mostly standing up; six others require crawling. The trail system linking the caves totals about 6 miles, but the longest walk to any cave is only a half mile. Visitor Center staff can provide advice about which adventure is best suited for your group. In winter, water drips into some of the caves and freezes into icy columns, creating temporary

Natural Bridge

imitations of the stalagmites and stalactites formed by limestone deposits.

Camping

The park has 31 tent and RV sites, with showers available mid-April to mid-Oct. Available on a first-come, first-served basis, or for reservations, call 877-427-2757 or visit www.reserveiaparks.com. Camping fee.

Maquoketa Caves State Park, 10970 98th St., Maquoketa, IA 52060; 563-652-5833; www.iowadnr.gov/parks/index.html

Maquoketa Caves

Stone

Off Iowa 12, Sioux City

▪ 1,414 acres ▪ Year-round ▪ Loess Hills ▪ Hiking, biking, horseback riding

This park is located within the geologically distinctive Loess Hills that stretch from the Iowa–Missouri border through seven counties to Sioux City. In the last glacial period, glaciers crushed quartz silt into a fine powder. This rock flour was then carried downstream by summer snowmelt; when the river flow dried up, the broad floodplains were left covered with sediments. Some 12,500 to 150,000 years ago, prairie winds then deposited these sediments in what is now Iowa.

Iowa is covered with this fertile soil to a depth of several feet, but the Loess Hills consist of deposits more than 60 feet deep, and sometimes 200 feet deep. Loess (pronounced luss) landforms of this magnitude are duplicated in only one other place—along the Yellow River in the Kansu province of China.

The park's **Dorothy Pecaut Nature Center** offers a fine introduction to prairie ecology and wildlife, including some small aquariums of Iowa fish species, dioramas of bluff vegetation, and a walk-through display of what it's like under the loess. Two miles of hiking trails around the center provide an up-close look at the grassland and burr oak woods that make up this park.

Then drive the 3-mile **Stone Park Loop,** a narrow road that offers vistas of the region and examples of upland forest habitat. This route is but a section of the **Loess Hills National Scenic Byway,** 220 miles of designated roads through western Iowa.

Camping

The park has 30 tent and RV sites, with showers, and 2 camping cabins. Available either on a first-come, first-served basis, or make reservations at 877-427-2757 or www.reserveiaparks.com. Camping fee.

Stone State Park, 5001 Talbot Rd., Sioux City, IA 51103; 712-255-4698; www.iowadnr.gov/parks/index.html

231

Prairie

17 miles west of Lamar on US 160, near Liberal

▪ 3,964 acres ▪ Year-round ▪ Prairie ecosystems ▪ Wildlife ▪ Hiking

Sunset on the prairie

Tallgrass prairie once covered a swath of land stretching from central Nebraska to central Ohio, reaching as far north as Manitoba, Canada, and as far south as Texas. With the conquest of agriculture in the 19th century, the prairie disappeared bit by bit, until it all but vanished.

Where once there was 13 million acres of this prairie in Missouri, today there is only 65,000 acres. An island of tallgrass amid a sea of cultivation, Prairie State Park is the largest intact remnant prairie in Missouri, where more than 500 different plants and grasses can still be found.

Diaries of pioneers traveling west through the prairies often spoke of their covered wagons as ships in a sea of grass, noting a rocky cliff seen after many days amid the grasses as a sighting of "land." A little of that feeling can be recaptured in this park, where grasses often reach 6 to 8 feet in height. The park also has bison and elk herds. These animals can be dangerous. When you arrive, be sure to find out what areas are safe for hiking.

Prior to European settlement, fires swept through these prairies periodically, started either by lightning strikes or by Native American tribes. A healthy prairie requires fire. Without it, woody plants—trees and shrubs—gain footholds and choke out the grasses. So to preserve this park, the staff conducts controlled burns on one-third of its land each year, varying the season.

The park is home to a variety of wildlife, including at least 25 species listed as threatened or endangered—among them the northern harrier, grasshopper sparrow, and sedge wren. In addition, birds of prey abound; they sail through the skies, scanning the grasses below for a meal, or simply tumbling through the air in what appears to be an avian version of play.

What to See and Do

Begin with the **Visitor Center,** where you will find dioramas and displays explaining the prairie ecosystem as well as the cultural and social history of the area, including the early Osage residents and their predecessors. Ask the park naturalist where the bison and elk are grazing that day. To see these massive beasts, drive slowly along the dirt roads in the indicated section of the park. A major attraction, for those lucky enough to be here in the spring, is the new crop of pumpkin-colored bison calves. Check with the Visitor Center staff for details on bison locations or about naturalist-led programs, including wildflower walks, bird-identification workshops, and presentations on pioneer living history.

PRAIRIE SEAS: When Napoleon marched on Moscow in 1812, he had only to move his army 1,500 miles. The army of emigrants crossing the American West between 1840 and 1860 often went 2,500 miles, much of it through tallgrass prairie. Children who wandered away from pioneer wagons were "drowned" in the tall prairie grasses. A parent had to stand on the back of a horse to have any hope of sighting a missing young pioneer.

More than 13 miles of trails traverse the park, providing an introduction to the vastness of this colorful prairie plant life and the opportunity—for the quiet and patient—of spotting wildlife. The best time to enjoy these trails is in the early morning or evening. *(Beware electric fences used to control the park's bison.)*

To best experience the park, try the **Drover's Trail** (2.5 miles), the **Gayfeather Trail** (1.5 miles), the new **Coyote Trail** (3 miles), or the longer **Sandstone Trail** (4.8 miles). All the trails lead through the recently designated **Regal Tallgrass Prairie Natural Area,** which includes nearly the entire park.

Camping

Limited camping in the park. Two primitive campsites and a backpacking camp on the Coyote Trail. Camping fee.

Prairie State Park, 128 N.W. 150th Ln., Mindenmines, MO 64769; 417-843-6711; www.mostateparks.com/prairie.htm

Ha Ha Tonka

4 miles west of Camdenton, off US 54

▪ 3,709 acres ▪ Year-round ▪ No camping ▪ Castle ruins ▪ Hiking ▪ Karst topography

High on a bluff above the Lake of the Ozarks, the tall, white stone skeleton of a fire-ruined, 60-room mansion stands as a lonely reminder of an earlier age. Missouri's Ha Ha Tonka State Park preserves the remains of this grandiose turn-of-the-20th-century project, along with some of the finest karst topography nature has assembled in a single Midwestern place.

> PARK TIP: *Backpackers should try the 7-mile Turkey Pen Hollow Trail through Oak Woodland Natural Area.*

In the heart of the park stands the remains of the Snyder mansion, a castle with a commanding view of the valley below and the rolling Ozarks all around. The mansion was begun in 1905 by Kansas City businessman Robert Snyder, who had purchased 5,400 acres in the Ozarks as a vacation getaway. But a year after beginning construction, Snyder was killed in an automobile accident, and the partially built residence remained untouched for more than 15 years.

234

BAT WORLD: Globally, nearly a thousand kinds of bats comprise almost a quarter of all mammal species. They live in every habitat except the extreme desert and polar regions. They range in size from some Old World bats, with wingspans of up to 6 feet, to the tiny bumblebee bat of Thailand, which weighs less than a penny. Bats have been on Earth for more than 50 million years, yet today they are in severe decline nearly everywhere—primarily because of fear and misinformation. The endangered gray bats of Ha Ha Tonka are a great natural resource. Each bat may consume up to 3,000 insects a night, including mosquitoes. Gray bats are about the size of a human thumb, weigh 7 to 16 grams, and have a wingspan of almost 12 inches. The protection of this site has helped increase the population of these bats, from an estimated 200 in 1984 to as many as 30,000 in recent years.

In 1922, Snyder's sons finished the work, and their families used the beautiful place as a vacation retreat. Over time, the families came less and less often, and eventually leased it out as a hotel. In 1942 sparks from a fireplace ignited the roof, and the building, along with the nearby carriage house, was gutted. The stark exterior walls, all that remain, now stand sentinel over the lake.

Ha Ha Tonka possesses another legacy of the past—caves, natural bridges, sinkholes, and Ha Ha Tonka spring, all formed over thousands of years. The park's formations are the collapsed remains of a once extensive cave system. Whispering Dell sinkhole, for example, is 150 feet deep, one of a series of caverns whose roof collapsed. Its cool microclimate supports relict plant communities usually found at colder latitudes. The park also preserves more than 1,000 acres of oak and hickory woodlands.

What to See and Do

There aren't very many castle ruins in America, and when you have the chance to admire the remains of one as grand as Ha Ha Tonka, it's best to put it at the top of your visiting list. The skeletal remains of the **mansion** are a very short walk along a trail from the main parking lot, and there are two overlooks from which to see the striking views of the Niangua Arm of the lake below and the Ozark hills beyond.

Next, visit the large **natural bridge** soaring more than 70 feet above the cavern floor. Just down from the mansion ruins, the bridge was the original road access to the mansion. If you have time, hike from the parking lot along the **Dell Rim Trail** to the **Spring Trail,** leading down to a huge

235

Ruins of Snyder mansion

spring. A portion of the trail drops 200 feet, down 300 steps. At the base of the canyon, the spring issues 48 million gallons of water a day. The walk is strenuous. You can also reach the spring by driving to a parking area beside the lake and hiking in about a half mile.

Finally, **River Cave,** near park headquarters, is home to a growing population of gray bats, Indiana bats, and the blind grotto salamander. To protect the habitat, the cave may be explored by guided tour only. Check with the park office for information.

Ha Ha Tonka State Park, 1491 State Rd. D, Camdenton, MO 65020; 573-346-2986; www.mostateparks.com/hahatonka.htm

Montauk

21 miles southwest of Salem on Mo. 119

▪ 1,356 acres ▪ Year-round ▪ Fishing (license required), hiking

At the headwaters of the Current River, Montauk is a paradise for anglers. Here Pigeon Creek combines with the 40 million gallons of water spewing forth daily from the seven Montauk springs to provide blue-ribbon trout waters. During the 19th century, Montauk's considerable water power was put into the service of industry. Settlers built four different grist mills here. One, dating from 1896, still stands and is open for tours in summer.

The fast-flowing waters that once powered the mills provide an excellent habitat for rainbow trout, and this has made Montauk a popular sporting spot with anglers. Several trout derbies are held here each year. During the official trout season, from March through October, trout are stocked daily. In winter, when bald eagles hunt the streams and springs, catch-and-release fishing is allowed.

Montauk is managed as a fishing park, so this is the place to get a close-up look at some trout—preferably at the end of your fishing line. Fishing equipment can be rented in the park if you didn't bring yours. A portion of the stream is dedicated to fly-fishing and other sections allow artificial lures and bait; some areas are catch-and-release only.

PARK TIP: *If you're interested in seeing wildlife, the three-quarter-mile Lake Trail is a great place to stroll in the early evening.*

Montauk's location at the headwaters of the **Current River** has also made it a popular jumping-off point for canoeists. Although canoeing is not permitted within the park, just below it the Current is designated as part of the **Ozark National Scenic Riverways** *(573-323-4236)*, managed by the National Park Service. Canoe rentals are available from concessionaires at sites along the riverway. A half-day float along the fastest section of the river will take you from Inman Hollow to Cedargrove. Paddling down the Current, you'll see undercut banks, numerous springs, and high bluffs with vast square boulders tumbled like the dice of giants at their bases.

Bird-watchers, photographers, and nature lovers can also enjoy the park's scenic wonders. Two designated hiking trails offer many opportunities to explore flora and fauna, and a designated natural area, also within the park, showcases a splendid mature pine-and-hardwood upland forest.

Camping and Lodging

The park has 156 tent and RV sites, with showers. Some may be reserved by calling 877-422-6766. Camping fee. Cabins and a motel are also available; call 573-548-2434 for reservations.

Montauk State Park, c/o Missouri Department of Natural Resources, P.O. Box 176, Jefferson City, MO 65102; 573-548-2201; www.mostate parks.com/montauk.htm

Meramec

50 miles southwest of St. Louis, off I-44

▪ 6,896 acres ▪ Year-round ▪ 47 caves ▪ Cave tours ▪ Hiking, canoeing, swimming

Towering bluffs, gaping cave entrances, and massive overhanging trees furnish a picturesque backdrop for the alluring Meramec River. Within its clean spring-fed waters thrive the state's greatest variety of aquatic life, including a multitude of fish species. Several river miles flow through Meramec State Park's rugged Ozark landscape. Located within an hour's drive of St. Louis, Meramec is one of Missouri's most popular parks, especially as a cool respite from summer heat.

First, stop at the park's **Visitor Center,** which offers an introduction to the area through displays focusing on the river environment and the development of cave geology. A 3,500-gallon aquarium showcases the river's inhabitants.

Canoeing the Meramec River

If you have a chance, take the 90-minute guided tour of **Fisher Cave** *(call 573-468-6072 for times, updates, and fees),* the largest and some say most beautiful of the park's 47 caves. Using handheld lighting, the tours provide a sense of adventure. Fisher Cave shows you a wide variety of subterranean features, from massive columns more than 30 feet tall to intricate calcite deposits.

Hiking and backpacking the 16 miles of park trails can lead to rocky glades laced with wildflowers, serene corners of quiet solitude, and lush forests carpeted with ferns or ablaze in fall color. But in summer, most people spend their time drifting down the calm waters. Rent canoes, rafts, or inner tubes *(573-468-6519),* or bring your own.

Camping and Lodging

The park has 217 campsites, plus 3 group sites (April–Oct.). Reserve by calling 877-422-6766. Camping fee. There are also 20 cabins and 22 motel rooms that can be reserved by calling 888-637-2632.

Meramec State Park, 115 Meramec Park Dr., Sullivan, MO 63080; 573-468-6072; www.mostateparks.com/meramec.htm

Lake Scott

15 miles north of Scott City, off US 83

■ 1,020 acres ■ Year-round ■ Vehicle fee ■ Pueblo ruins ■ Hiking, swimming, fishing (license required)

Blooming yucca

Driving along the sweeping flat plains of agricultural Kansas, you could pass within a few hundred yards of this sunken canyon oasis without knowing it. But within Lake Scott State Park, rocky bluffs and walled canyons line Ladder Creek, leading north to the Smoky Hill River. The park sits in a long, narrow bowl, surrounded by high rocky hills, stony outcrops, and classic bluffs reminiscent in places of a Hopalong Cassidy movie.

PARK TIP: *Hunt for the place where the Ogallala aquifer bubbles to the surface. It's an ideal locale to sit and listen to the water or watch an occasional muskrat or beaver.*

In late summer, when the wheat on the Kansas plains has been cut and the browned stalks give the terrain a dusty look, drop over the canyon rim into the cool green of this park. Here, with the ivory blooming yucca, lies 100-acre Lake Scott encircled by steep, orange walls with such picturesque names as Horsethief Canyon, Timber Canyon, and Suicide Cliff—frequented by climbers and rappelers. According to popular folklore, the cliff was named for its supposed use as a bison jump by the Apache, or for a lovesick Indian suitor who jumped. Although romantic, both theories are unsubstantiated.

What to See and Do

The park's most remarkable feature is **El Cuartelejo Pueblo ruins,** the unlikely home of a band of 17th-century Taos Indians; the site is believed to be the northernmost pueblo in North America. The ruins were discovered in 1889, and reconstruction began in 1970. The foundation has been laid out as it would have been originally. Note the lack of doorways, indicating that entrance was gained via ladders from the roof. This park was the site of a number of Indian camps. The **El Cuartelejo Museum** (620-872-5912) in the nearby town of Scott City hosts interpretive displays of the artifacts found in the park.

The park has two trails. The 0.25-mile-long **Big Springs Nature Trail** near the park's main entrance passes natural rock steps over which spring water flows. A longer (7-mile) trail that accommodates hikers, horseback riders, and bikers encircles the lake. The early morning visitor might encounter wild turkeys, beavers, or bobcats or see a turkey vulture atop a nearby cottonwood.

For Kansans, the chief attraction of the state park is simply the presence of a lake in the water-starved western portion of their state. **Lake Scott** offers excellent fishing for bass, crappie, and channel catfish. A trout-stocked pond below Barrel Springs is a favorite fishing spot for children, and a swimming beach provides another happy option.

Outside the park boundary on the bluffs of Beaver Creek lies the site of the **Battle of Punished Woman's Fork,** where in 1878 the Northern Cheyenne, including Dull Knife and Little Wolf, fought the U.S. Cavalry in the last Indian battle in Kansas.

Camping

The park offers 60 RV sites and 80 primitive sites by reservation, with shower facilities, available mid-April to mid-Oct. Seasonal camping fee.

Lake Scott State Park, 101 W. Scott Lake Dr., Scott City, KS 67871; 620-872-2061; www.kdwp.state.ks.us/parks/parks.html

239

EL CUARTELEJO: In the 1660s, a group of Taos Indians fled Spanish rule in present-day New Mexico to the area now preserved as Lake Scott State Park. Here they built the pueblo that has become known as El Cuartelejo, meaning "old barracks" or "buildings." Although Spanish expeditions made forays into the area, the Taos inhabited the site—free of Spanish rule—until about 1730, when raids by the Comanche, Ute, and Pawnee forced them to return southward.

Prairie Dog

4 miles west of Norton on US 36

- 1,150 acres ▪ Year-round ▪ Vehicle fee ▪ Fishing (license required)
- Prairie-dog town

Prairie dogs on alert

A 1,500-pound carved limestone prairie dog greets visitors to this park. This once ubiquitous wild rodent of the Plains, the black-tailed prairie dog, had been poisoned nearly out of existence. When this park was established in 1967, there were none in residence. Early attempts by staff to introduce prairie dogs to their namesake park failed, but in 1982 a pair arrived from somewhere and took up residence.

The community has flourished since, growing from the original 2 to a population of more than 300. In fact, the park was named not for the little fellows, but for **Prairie Dog Creek,** which flows through the park, filling the adjacent 1,200-acre Keith Sebelius Reservoir.

When you visit the 38-acre park's prairie-dog town, you'll likely be greeted by an alert sentry sitting at the entrance to its burrow and emitting a high-pitched barking squeak when you approach. This watchdog-like barking, which signals fellow residents to zip back into their holes, is how this rodent came to be known as a "dog."

Your second stop should be the **adobe homestead** *(open seasonally or by appt.; call park for information),* down the paved road to the east of the prairie-dog colony. Built in the 1890s, this is the state's oldest surviving adobe structure that is open to the public. The interior walls provide graphic demonstration of mud-and-straw construction.

> **PARK TIP:** *While concentrating on the prairie dogs don't miss the white-tailed deer, pheasant, bobwhite, quail, wild turkey, coyote, and badger.*

Western Kansas has very few large bodies of water, and the **Keith Sebelius Reservoir** draws visitors from all over the state, especially for the fishing opportunities. Since 1992, high-water years have filled the reservoir beyond its original capacity—as evidenced by the skeletons of large drowned trees pointing skyward in mid-lake—creating the kind of habitat that grows record fish.

Camping

The park offers 60 campsites with hook-ups, and 100 primitive sites. Showers available mid-April through Oct. There are also four cabins, two primitive, and two with all the amenities. Call park at 785-877-2953 for reservations. Camping fee.

Prairie Dog State Park, P.O. Box 431, Norton, KS 67654; 785-877-2953; www.kdwp.state.ks.us/news/state_parks/locations/prairie-dog

Clinton

4 miles west of Lawrence, off US 10

▪ 1,455 acres ▪ Year-round ▪ Vehicle fee ▪ Swimming, boating, fishing (license required), biking ▪ Mountain bike skills course

Clinton's popularity stems from 7,000-acre **Clinton Reservoir,** devoted primarily to water sports and excellent angling and also popular for its beach. Wooded trails along the lakeshore have special appeal for mountain bikers.

The park oversees the restoration of the 19th-century **Barber School,** which was constructed of rubble stone, an unusual building material for the period. Due to the poor condition of the schoolhouse, a high fence has been placed around the building. Thomas Barber was an abolitionist and martyr during the "Bloody Kansas" pre-Civil War era. The park plans to restore some 40 acres of native prairie to a Civil War period appearance.

Camping

The park has 460 tent and RV sites (15 reserved), with showers. Two six-person cabins also available. Call 785-842-8562 for reservations. Camping fee.

Clinton Office, RR1, 798 N. 1415 Rd., Lawrence, KS 66049; 785-842-8562; www.kdwp.state.ks.us/news/state_parks

241

Elk City

5 miles northwest of Independence on US 75/160

▪ 857 acres ▪ Year-round ▪ Vehicle fee ▪ Hiking, fishing (license required), boating, swimming

Rimmed by the 250-foot-high **Osage Questas** bluffs, this park challenges the perception of a flat Kansas. These bluffs were formed by alternating beds of shale and limestone deposited by a shallow sea. They have eroded into a series of tilted hills that are steep on one side, sloped on the other, and covered with hickory and oak trees that are particularly colorful in fall. The park lies at the juncture of woodlands and bluestem prairie.

The county road and **Table Mound Hiking Trail** lead to overlooks offering views of **Elk City Reservoir,** prairie, and woodlands. Nearby, the lake attracts visitors to fish, boat, ski, swim, and watch waterfowl.

Camping

The park has 95 tent and RV sites and 55 primitive sites, with showers mid-April through Oct. Camping fee.

Elk City State Park, 4825 Squaw Creek Rd., Independence, KS 67301; 620-331-6295; www.kdwp.state.ks.us/news/state_parks

SOUTH CENTRAL

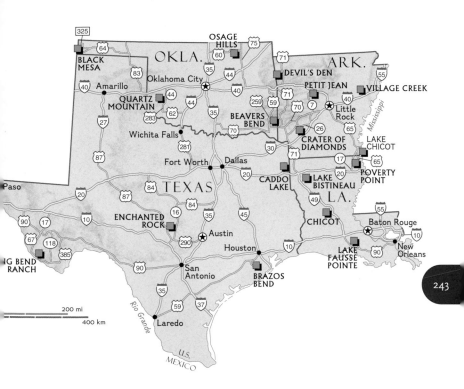

OKLAHOMA

Beavers Bend
Quartz Mountain
Black Mesa
Osage Hills

ARKANSAS

Petit Jean
Devil's Den
Village Creek
Crater of Diamonds
Lake Chicot

TEXAS

Big Bend Ranch
Enchanted Rock
Brazos Bend
Caddo Lake

LOUISIANA

Lake Fausse Pointe
Chicot
Poverty Point
Lake Bistineau

Rio Grande, U.S.–Mexican border

Beavers Bend

10 miles north of Broken Bow, off US 259

- 3,482 acres ▪ Year-round ▪ Rugged Ouachita Mountain terrain
- Mountain Fork River ▪ Broken Bow Reservoir ▪ Nature Center
- Hiking, nature trails

Paddlers on Mountain Fork River

The entrance road at Beavers Bend winds sinuously along a ridge top before dropping to the Mountain Fork River—a journey of only 3 miles that serves as a preview of this region, nicknamed the "Little Smokies." The Ouachita Mountains of eastern Oklahoma and western Arkansas were formed some 400 million years ago by tremendous tectonic forces that squeezed and folded the land, resulting in today's sometimes tortuous terrain of long, east-west ridges separated by steep-sided valleys and ravines. It's a rugged, intimate landscape, seen best from a hiking trail through open, pine woodland, or from a canoe on a clear, rocky river.

Mountain Fork was dammed in 1969 creating the 14,000-acre Broken Bow Reservoir; the park includes areas on the reservoir—campsites, lodge, and golf course *(580-494-6456. Greens fee)*—and on the river. The two areas are connected by road and by the 24-mile **David Boren Hiking Trail.** Beavers Bend lies within what was once Choctaw territory. Its name comes from Choctaw citizen John T. Beavers.

What to See and Do

To learn a bit about the history of forestry, stop by the **park office** and the **Forest Heritage and Education Center** *(580-494-6497),* which chronicles trees from the age of dinosaurs through the modern timber industry. While here, pick up a park map and trail guide.

At the **Beavers Bend Nature Center** you can learn about park programs on subjects from snakes to birds of prey to nature-related crafts. A naturalist may let you hold a king snake, and you can see specimens of local venomous species behind glass. Several live hawks and owls are usually on display here.

Walk down to the **Mountain Fork River** and admire the bluff on the opposite bank. In winter you may see a bald eagle perched in a streamside tree and ducks or double-crested cormorants paddling on the water. Bald cypress and sycamore line the river, while scrubby cedar and oak cling to the cliff.

Beavers Bend provides several reasonably short trails, all worth exploring. The **Cedar Bluff Nature Trail,** a fairly strenuous 1-mile loop, repays your effort with a splendid overlook above the river; the easier 1-mile **Dogwood Nature Trail** stays near the river for much of its length, wending through mixed woodland; the 1.1-mile **Forest Heritage Trail,** beginning at the park office, features interpretive signs on Ouachita forest ecology. To avoid confusion, the hiking trail is blazed white, while the nature trails are blue on white.

Although the trails and forest are appealing, most visitors focus on the beautiful Mountain Fork. Swimming, canoeing, and paddleboating are popular in summer; anglers wade the shallows throughout the year, testing their skills against trout. You may discover, though, that the best activity is no activity at all: Just find a flat rock at a quiet spot, lie back, and enjoy the sound of birdsong, the smell of pine, and the grand scenery of one of the prettiest places in Oklahoma.

SCENIC ROUTE: Sixty miles north of Beavers Bend, you'll find one of the region's most spectacular drives: the Talimena Scenic Byway in the Ouachita National Forest *(501-321-5202).* Called Hwy. 1 in Oklahoma and Hwy. 88 in Arkansas, it runs for 54 miles from Talihina, Oklahoma, to Mena, Arkansas. Following the high ridges of the Ouachita Mountains, Talimena offers all-encompassing vistas of heavily wooded hills and valleys. Queen Wilhelmina State Park Lodge *(479-394-2863),* 5 miles across the Arkansas state line, is a fine choice for a meal or overnight lodging.

245

Camping and Lodging

The park has 50 tent and 110 RV sites, with showers, and 47 cabins. Limited reservations; call the park at 580-494-6300. Camping fee. There are also 40 lodge rooms. For lodge reservations, call 580-494-6179.

Beavers Bend Resort State Park, P.O. Box 10, Broken Bow, OK 74728; 580-494-6300; www.oklahomaparks.com

Quartz Mountain

17 miles north of Altus via US 283 and Okla. 44

- 4,284 acres ▪ Year-round ▪ Rugged granite hills ▪ Lake Altus-Lugert
- Nature Center ▪ Diverse flora and fauna ▪ Hiking, bird-watching

On a clear day you may be as far away as 35 miles when you first see the red granite dome of Quartz Mountain on the horizon, rising from the southwestern plains. As impos-
ing as it and other Wichita Mountain peaks are, you're actually seeing only part of them: Millions of years of weathering have covered their bases with eroded rock to a depth of many thousands of feet, leaving only their tops showing above ground.

> **PARK TIP:** *Hike the Cedar Valley Trail through the box canyon—a nice way to view the inhabitants of the walnut, hackberry, and oak trees.*

Quartz Mountain is a strikingly attractive place, its rugged, boulder-strewn slopes in sharp contrast with the blue of Lake Altus-

Lake Altus-Lugert from Quartz Mountain

Lugert. This juxtaposition of rock and water, mountain and plains, produces great diversity in the wildlife and vegetation—which also shows the influence of the park's location in the country's midsection. You could, for instance, see an Eastern collared lizard sliding past a pecan or an Eastern redbud here, where, ecologically speaking, north meets south.

What to See and Do

Stop first at the **park office** for information or the **Nature Center,** where exhibits introduce Quartz Mountain's natural history. The area's granite, you'll learn, came to the surface as magma more than 500 million years ago; a shallow sea covered it in sedimentary limestone (long since eroded away), and it later was uplifted far higher than its present worn-down elevation. Kids will enjoy the touch table, where they can handle feathers, cattails, rocks, and—if they're brave enough—animal bones and skulls.

The short **Wichita Interpretive Trail** leads from the office to Live Oak Campground, crossing an intermittent stream. The muddy banks often reveal tracks of wild turkey, white-tailed deer, and even bobcats, which come down from the mountain to drink but are seen by only the luckiest visitors. The park's 0.5-mile **New Horizon Trail** begins at a parking lot just beyond the office. It heads rather steeply up Quartz Mountain to a lookout point about three-fourths of the way to the top; you're free to continue up and to pick another route back down. Be aware that rocky hillsides are a favored habitat of rattlesnakes; watch where you step. Another fearsome looking—but in this case harmless—reptile found here is the horned lizard, armed with sharp spines over its body. You may see this little "horned toad" sunning itself in sandy and rocky areas on hot days; it skitters away with surprising speed when you come too close.

Wildflower-lovers note that long-haired phlox, a species endemic to the Wichitas, can be seen here in spring—it's a great time to observe some of the park's 80 wildflower varieties, including coreopsis, larkspur, prickly pear cactus, and the beautiful Indian blanket or firewheel, a sunflower relative with red-and-yellow flowers.

In winter, **Lake Altus-Lugert** can host a dozen or more bald eagles; ask a naturalist about the best viewing locations. Another species seen on the lake in spring and fall, to the surprise of some visitors, is the white pelican; although many people think of it as a seabird, this bird migrates through the park on its way to and from breeding grounds in the northwestern United States and Canada.

247

Quartz Mountain also offers various activities, ranging from paddleboats (580-563-2465) on the river to golf (580-563-2520) to an off-road vehicle area (April–Sept.).

Camping

The park has 99 tent and 120 RV sites (some open year-round), with showers. For information, call the park, 580-563-2238. Camping fee. There are also 8 cottages and a lodge with 120 rooms; call 877-999-5567 or 580-563-2424 to reserve.

Quartz Mountain State Park, 43393 Scissortail Rd., Lone Wolf, OK 73655; 580-563-2238; www.quartz mountain.org

ON THE WILD SIDE: About 40 miles east of Quartz Mountain State Park, Wichita Mountains Wildlife Refuge (580-429-3222) holds a historic place in the national refuge system. Designated a national forest reserve in 1901 by proclamation of President William McKinley, it provides today's visitors the chance to see bison, elk, white-tailed deer, and Texas longhorn cattle up close along its 15-mile-long scenic drive. With nearly 60,000 acres of varied habitat, Wichita Mountains is well worth a side trip for anyone visiting southwestern Oklahoma.

Black Mesa

27 miles northwest of Boise City, off Rte. 325

▪ 349 acres, plus 1,460 acres in nearby nature preserve ▪ Year-round ▪ No bicycles permitted in the preserve ▪ Highest point in Oklahoma ▪ Flora, fauna, geology

For many travelers, Black Mesa State Park is only a stopping-off point on the way to Black Mesa itself, about 15 miles northwest. While the park offers pleasant camping, the nature preserve's combination of geological features, wildlife, and vegetation makes it one of Oklahoma's top natural history destinations. The flat-topped mesa is a remnant of an ancient lava flow that hardened into erosion-resistant basalt. Because of its height and its location in the far tip of Oklahoma's Panhandle, Black Mesa is more akin to the Rocky Mountain region than to the rest of the state.

PARK TIP: *Look closely while at the scenic overlook, near the group camp, and you'll find dinosaur tracks made by a juvenile Hadrosaur.*

Stop at the **park office** for maps and travel advice, then continue west on Rte. 325 to a paved road heading north. Follow signs to a parking lot at **Black Mesa Nature Preserve,** where a 4-mile trail leads up a short, rocky slope dotted with juniper and scrub oak. Allow at least four hours for the round-trip to the summit (more if you stop to bird-watch); be sure to wear sun protection and carry water.

On top of the mesa, more than 600 feet above the surrounding plains, you'll find a granite monument marking the highest spot in Oklahoma: 4,973 feet above sea level.

Black-billed magpies, golden eagles, and pinyon jays are among the western birds found at Black Mesa, and you may see mule deer, bobcats, or pronghorn as well.

Take time to enjoy the park's impressive views and unique environment, but keep an eye out for occasional thunderstorms, which can bring dangerous lightning.

Camping

There are 30 tent and 29 RV sites, with showers. Available first come, first served. Camping fee.

Black Mesa State Park and Nature Preserve, HCR-1 Box 8, Kenton, OK 73946; 580-426-2222; www.travelok.com

Rock Window

Osage Hills

11 miles west of Bartlesville, off US 60

■ 1,199 acres ■ Year-round ■ Rolling, wooded hills ■ Scenic creek, bluffs ■ Hiking

In his 1835 book, *A Tour on the Prairies,* Washington Irving wrote that traversing Oklahoma's Cross Timbers region was "like struggling through forests of cast iron." These north-south belts of woodland, stretching from Texas to Kansas, once grew so thickly and continuously that they presented a serious challenge to western pioneers. You'll find a modern-day sampling of this environment at Osage Hills State Park—but, unlike Irving, you're likely to find a visit far more a pleasure than a struggle.

Look-Out Lake

Trails wind through hills covered primarily in post and blackjack oak. Stop at the **park office** for a map, then drive through the campground to a road leading north, where an observation tower provides a good overview of the area.

Return and go south to the **Sand Creek Loop Trail** leading to bluffs along **Sand Creek.** Another popular path, the **Waterfalls Trail,** leads from the parking lot at the swimming pool to a series of small cascades. You'll likely see white-tailed deer and wild turkey along roads or paths; under park protection, both species have become accustomed to humans.

Osage Hills lies at the edge of what was once a great sea of tallgrass prairie covering 140 million Midwestern acres. Don't miss a chance to see a 37,000-acre expanse of this endangered habitat at the Nature Conservancy's **Tallgrass Prairie Preserve** *(918-287-4803),* north of nearby Pawhuska. Bison still roam and prairie chickens still dance here, just as they did when Washington Irving visited a century and a half ago.

Camping and Lodging

There are 27 tent and 20 RV sites, with showers. Available first come, first served. Camping fee. The park also has 8 furnished cabins. To reserve, call 918-336-4141.

Osage Hills State Park, HC 73, Box 84, Pawhuska, OK 74056; 918-336-5635; www.oklahomaparks.com

249

Petit Jean

20 miles west of Morrilton via Ark. 9 and Ark. 154

- 2,658 acres ▪ Year-round ▪ Indian bluff shelters ▪ Mountaintop panoramas ▪ Cedar Falls ▪ Hiking, swimming, boating, fishing (license required)

Arkansas River Valley from rocky outcropping

Petit Jean Mountain rises some 800 feet above the Arkansas River, its long silhouette like a rampart looming over the flat valley floor. But even in prehistoric times the mountain was a place more inviting than forbidding. Native Americans used its shallow bluff caves as shelters, and early settlers found in its breezy elevation some relief from sweltering summer temperatures in the lowlands.

In 1819, explorer and naturalist Thomas Nuttall wrote that "the hills of the Petit John appear conspicuous and picturesque," an observation that countless travelers have since echoed. Petit Jean's striking scenery, as well as the broad vistas from its perimeter cliffs, made it a natural choice when the first state parklands were acquired by Arkansas in 1923. Over the years it has remained a favorite spot for hiking, picnicking, camping, and weekend getaways.

PARK TIP: *If you're up to a long hike, try the path to the Grotto, off the Seven Hollows Trail, where a box canyon with a small waterfall and pool create a cool haven.*

Ark. 154 offers fine views as it winds up the mountainside—but it's wise to keep your eyes on the often twisty road. A turnoff at the summit leads to **Petit Jean's grave** (see sidebar), where you can take time to enjoy the panorama of river valley and hills.

Back on the highway, you'll soon pass **Lake Bailey,** a 100-acre impoundment on Cedar Creek, where anglers try their luck with bream, bass, and catfish, and the young in spirit scoot across the water on paddleboats.

What to See and Do

Get an introduction to Petit Jean's natural history at the park **Visitor Center** *(501-727-5441),* where you'll find exhibits on the area's flora, fauna, and geology. You can also pick up a schedule of interpreter-led hikes and special programs.

From here it's only a short drive to what is probably (and deservedly) the most popular spot on the mountain: **Cedar Falls,** a lovely waterfall nestled in a heavily wooded, steep-sided gorge. During dry summers the falls can slow to a trickle, but after rainy spells in spring and autumn, Cedar Creek cascades over a rock ledge and plunges spectacularly 95 feet to a pool encircled by sheer bluffs. It's one of Arkansas's most famous (and most photographed) sites, and no one should visit the park without taking it in.

The easy **Cedar Falls Overlook Boardwalks** *(handicap accessible)* leads from a parking lot off Ark. 154 to a viewpoint above the falls. Those who are able, though, should hike the more challenging **Cedar Falls Trail** to the pool below. The trailhead is located behind **Mather Lodge**—named for Stephen Mather, head of the National Park Service at the time of Petit Jean's founding—which perches on the edge of a bluff just west of the turnoff to the overlook. (If it's near mealtime, be sure to stop in at the lodge dining room, which is famed for its fabulous view of Cedar Creek Canyon.) The 2-mile round-trip hike requires a steep descent to Cedar Creek before turning upstream to the falls. The way back out is, of course, exactly equal in steepness, but it can seem far more strenuous, especially on a hot summer afternoon. Stops along the way provide welcome opportunities to appreciate the forest, wildflowers, and birds.

Woodlands in this part of the state are dominated by oak, hickory, and shortleaf pine, with maple, pawpaw, and dogwood among the many other accompanying species. Spring flowers, which begin their annual show as early as late February, include bloodroot, toothwort, mayapple, Solomon's seal, rue anemone, and trout lily. Later in the year daisies, asters, and milkweeds brighten the park's open fields and roadsides.

LEGEND OF PETIT JEAN: Several Arkansas localities possess French names, but none has such a fanciful origin as Petit Jean's. According to one legend that reads like a movie script, a young Frenchwoman disguised herself as a man—"Little John"—to accompany her boyfriend on an expedition to America. Not until after she became ill and died was her secret exposed. Petit Jean's supposed grave lies at a suitably romantic overlook on the eastern edge of the mountain; the view is well worth a visit—even if you take the story with a grain or two of salt.

251

Natural Bridge

Further Adventures

If you have more time, take the **Seven Hollows Trail;** this 4.5-mile loop is one of Arkansas's most rewarding hikes. Fascinating rock formations are the main attractions: **Natural Bridge,** for example, is a choice location for a "we were there" snapshot. The caves you see beside the trail were once used as shelters by early Indians.

The varied habitats along the way make for excellent bird-watching, especially when song is at its peak in the late spring. A walk just after dawn (when birds are most active, and most people are not) will likely bring sightings of such common species as Carolina chickadee, tufted titmouse, red-bellied woodpecker, pine warbler, and the brilliant-red summer tanager. Luckier finds might include a big, noisy pileated woodpecker, with its crimson crest, or a yellow-billed cuckoo, whose *cow-cow-cow* call is much more often heard than the singer itself is seen.

Red Bluff Drive, on the opposite side of Cedar Creek Canyon from Mather Lodge, leads to scenic overlooks and to the **Rock House Cave Trail.** Native Americans once lived in the bluff shelter at the end of this path. Imagine the dome-shaped cave here as a retreat from winter rains and summer sun. The renovated **CCC Barracks** serves as an interpretive center and meeting place for small groups.

Camping and Lodging

The park has 125 tent and RV sites (hook-ups), with showers. Reservations are accepted for 24 sites; call the park. Camping fee. There are also 32 cabins and 23 rooms at Mather Lodge. Reserve early; call 501-727-5431 or 800-264-2462.

Nearby Sights

The **Museum of Automobiles** *(501-727-5427. Adm. fee),* on the mountain just east of the park, displays a fine collection of antique cars. Fourteen miles west of the park, **Holla Bend National Wildlife Refuge** *(501-229-4300)* is one of Arkansas's best locations for viewing wildlife. Turkey, deer, bobcats, hawks, and a variety of songbirds are present all year; winter brings flocks of ducks and geese, as well as an impressive number of bald eagles. Reach the refuge by driving west on Ark. 154, and then turning north on Ark. 155.

Petit Jean State Park, 1285 Petit Jean Mountain Rd., Morrilton, AR 72110; 501-727-5441; www.petitjeanstatepark.com

Devil's Den

15 miles west of West Fork on Ark. 170

■ 2,500 acres ■ Year-round ■ Geological formations ■ Mountain
stream ■ Interpretive trails ■ Backpacking, biking, horseback riding

In the hundreds of millions of years since the Ozark Mountains of
northwestern Arkansas were uplifted from an ancient sea, creeks and
rivers have deeply dissected the soft, underlying sandstone and limestone, forming steep-sided valleys of striking beauty. Lying at the
bottom of one of these "hollers" (as the old-
time locals call them), Devil's Den State Park
offers visitors a microcosm of the Ozarks'
rugged terrain, dense hardwood forest, and
crystalline rivers.

PARK TIP: *Hike to the CCC
structure nominated for a
Pulitzer Prize—Yellow Rock
Overlook.*

What to See and Do

You'll experience this
eroded synclinal land-
scape (basically, a tilting
or folding of rock lay-
ers) as you wind down
Ark. 74 *(long trailers
use caution)* into the
park, arriving after
many switchbacks at
Lee Creek, the stream
traveling through the
park. Stop first at the
Visitor Center to pick
up trail brochures and
talk to the interpretive
staff about guided walks
and programs. If you're
interested in learning
about park flora, follow
signs to camping area
E and the 0.25-mile
Woody Plant Trail, where
signs identify native
trees and shrubs.

Next, return to
the Visitor Center and
the start of the 1.5-mile
Devil's Den Trail, the
park's most popular
hike. With a flashlight to
guide your way, you can
walk several hundred
feet into **Devil's Den,**

Rocky stream in autumn woods

253

the cave that gave the park its name; a little beyond is **Devil's Ice Box.** Both are "fracture" caves, formed by slippage of sandstone blocks. Air entering the Ice Box higher up the hillside is cooled in summer (and warmed in winter) by contact with belowground rocks that remain at a constant 55°–60°F. Park caves are temporarily closed; call 479-761-3325 for updates.

Ferns and wildflowers, and birdsong, make the Devil's Den Trail a spring delight. Watch for sassafras, a shrub or small tree once used to make tea; look for its mitten-shaped leaves. Watch, too, for birds such as the beautiful orange-and-black American redstart and the drab, greenish red-eyed vireo. The latter sings even in the heat of summer afternoons when other birds are silent.

For more geological exploration, drive to camping area A and walk the 1-mile **Lee Creek Trail.** The first half of the loop winds through a typical Ozark woodland, with occasional openings into old fields; the second part follows the streambed of Lee Creek. Examine the rocks here for fossils of sea creatures, including corals and crinoids (relatives of sea stars). Take time, too, to look into the creek itself, where you may spot a crayfish or a tiny, colorful darter.

BUTTERFIELD TRAIL: The Butterfield Hiking Trail at Devil's Den is named for the celebrated Butterfield Overland Mail stage line, which began carrying mail between St. Louis and San Francisco in 1858. Part of the trail traces a section of the historic route that connected mail stops in nearby Fayetteville and Fort Smith. The Butterfield line's life span was as short as its mission was ambitious: The Civil War in 1861 put an end to its cross-country journeys.

In addition to typical campsites, Devil's Den offers a walk-in, tents-only area for those who prefer a quieter, peaceful setting. The park's most popular accommodations, though, are its rock-and-log cabins, built by the Civilian Conservation Corps; updated to modern standards, these historic structures offer an appealing blend of comfort and rusticity.

To further experience the Ozarks more intimately, walk the park's 15-mile **Butterfield Hiking Trail,** which offers fine scenic views as it loops south of the park. The truly energetic could make the journey in a long day, but it's much better to take it more slowly and camp overnight at one of the designated sites along the way. *(The park has backpacking equipment for rent.)* You'll likely be alone for hours at a time as you hike, giving a hint of what the land was like when the only footprints here were those of Osage Indians.

Camping and Lodging

The park has 96 tent and RV sites, with showers, and 43 horse camp sites. Trailers longer than 24 feet have to enter at exit 53 of I-540. For reservable sites, call 479-761-3325. Camping fee. There are also 16 cabins, with kitchens and fireplaces. Reserve cabins well in advance; call 800-264-2417.

Devil's Den State Park, 11333 W. Ark. Hwy. 74, West Fork, AR 72774; 479-761-3325; www.arkansasstateparks.com/devilsden

Village Creek

13 miles north of Forrest City on Ark. 284

▪ 7,000 acres ▪ Year-round ▪ Unusual geology ▪ Hiking, swimming, fishing (license required), biking, horseback riding

Driving across the farmland of eastern Arkansas, mostly flat and featureless, you suddenly come upon a long ridge rising 200 feet above fields. Quite obviously, something extraordinary happened here. You can't help but wonder: What on Earth built this?

Geologists say that the precursor of the Mississippi River once flowed west

Horseback riding through Village Creek

of its current course, while the predecessor of the Ohio flowed where the Mississippi runs today. As these rivers meandered across the landscape, a strip of high ground between them was left relatively untouched. Later, during a dry period, windblown soil piled up against the elevated land, raising it higher. Today's 150-mile-long **Crowley's Ridge** is a region so different from the rest of Arkansas that biologists classify it as a separate natural division. Set in a lushly forested valley on the ridge's eastern slope lies Village Creek—Arkansas's second largest state park and, for naturalists, one of its most rewarding.

PARK TIP: *Discover the remnants of ancient oceans and swamps, Crowley's Ridge, in a valley of sugar maples and tulip trees at the bottom of the Austell Trail.*

What to See and Do

Stop at the **Visitor Center** for exhibits on local geology and history. You'll learn, for instance, that the higher, drier ground of Crowley's Ridge made it a natural choice for towns, such as Forrest City and Wynne, and that the first improved road between Memphis and Little Rock, authorized by Congress in 1821, passes through the park. Just steps away are two trails offering an introduction to area ecology. The easy **Arboretum Trail** identifies many of the park's trees, including sugar maple, beech, and butternut, all uncommon in most of Arkansas, and the magnificent tulip tree, a type of magnolia that grows naturally nowhere else west of the Mississippi. Other species found here include white oak, sweetgum, red oak, black hickory, and white ash.

Cross the road to the **Big Ben Nature Trail,** a pretty, 0.5-mile walk that runs alongside **Village Creek.** ("Big Ben" was a huge beech tree named for settler Benjamin Crowley. The venerable giant blew down several years ago, but left its name behind.) Here you'll get a close look at the wind-deposited soil, called loess, that caps Crowley's Ridge, sometimes to a depth of 50 feet. Fine as powder, it erodes easily when the protective forest cover is removed.

FOSSIL FINDS: Although a layer of loess—fine soil left by the wind— tops the crest of Crowley's Ridge, lower layers are made up of sediments left by an ancient sea that once covered the region. The sea receded 50 million years ago. Digging in the clay soil at the base of the ridge often turns up sharks' teeth and other marine fossils—reminders that, in the distant past, the land here would have been beachfront property.

If you'd like to walk in the footsteps of early pioneers, drive the short distance to **Lake Austell** and take the **Military Road Trail,** a 2.25-mile loop that follows part of the historic Old Military Road. In places, the path has been worn into the soft soil over the past 150 years by countless footsteps, hoofprints, and wagon wheels. If you're feeling energetic, you can continue east, where the Military Road Trail— now on the National Register of Historic Places for being part of the Trail of Tears—turns back; follow the path across a swinging bridge and hike to **Lake Dunn,** 3 miles north, before retracing your steps.

There are 23 miles of new multiuse horseback and biking trails, and new barns and a horse camp for riders. To cool off later, you can swim at both lakes *(The beach at Lake Dunn is for registered campers only.),* picnic near Lake Austell, or the marina at Lake Dunn offers boat rentals, if you'd like to try your fishing skills.

Camping and Lodging

The park has 96 tent and RV sites, with showers. For limited reservations, call the park. Camping fee. There are also 10 cabins, with kitchens and fireplaces. Call 800-264-2467 for reservations.

Village Creek State Park, 201 CR 754, Wynne, AR 72396; 870-238-9406; www.arkansasstateparks.com/villagecreek

Crater of Diamonds

2 miles southeast of Murfreesboro on Ark. 301

■ 911 acres ■ Year-round ■ Diamond hunting

When a park experience is described as rewarding, the meaning is not usually so literal as at this world-famous destination in southwestern Arkansas. The gems here are real, unearthed by an ancient volcanic eruption and exposed by millions of years of erosion.

For a small fee, you can join others scouring a 37.5-acre field of lamproite soil and keep any rocks or diamonds you find. Whoppers, such as the Uncle Sam (40.23 carats) and the Amarillo Starlight

(16.32 carats), are about as likely as a lottery win—but with more than 750 diamonds discovered in an average year, the odds are not bad that you'll come away with a souvenir. (Semiprecious stones such as jasper, garnet, and amethyst make pretty consolation prizes.)

Ask a park interpreter for tips on hunting diamonds, and look over the display samples before you start your search. You may see hopeful prospectors using everything from dowsing rods to "magic" glasses, but—as with many things in life—the best tools are persistence, patience, and hard work. And, of course, luck.

Camping

The park has 47 AAA-class campsites and 5 walk-in tent sites. For reservations, call the park. Camping fee.

Crater of Diamonds State Park, 209 State Park Rd., Murfreesboro, AR 71958; 870-285-3113; www.craterofdiamondsstatepark.com

Lake Chicot

8 miles northeast of Lake Village on Ark. 144

■ 132 acres ■ Year-round ■ Scenic lake ■ Bird-watching, fishing (license required) ■ Barge tours

This tiny park on the Mississippi River alluvial plain lies at the northern tip of picturesque **Lake Chicot**—America's largest natural oxbow lake. With its countless bald cypress trees, the lake is an evocative vision of the Deep South.

Rent a boat from the park marina to explore the lake or try your luck fishing for catfish, bass, bream, or crappie. In late spring or fall, join one of the park's celebrated barge tours *(870-265-5480. April–June, Aug.–Sept.; fare),* which provide close views of hundreds of egrets and herons. The endangered wood stork, an Arkansas rarity, is seen regularly here; in winter, bald eagles perch in lakeside cypress. Ask at the **Visitor Center** about a driving tour atop the nearby **Mississippi** and **Arkansas River levees**—an unconventional trip.

Camping and Lodging

The park has 122 tent and RV sites, with showers. For reservations, call the park. Camping fee. There are also 14 cabins. Call 800-264-2430 to reserve.

Lake Chicot State Park, 2542 Hwy. 257, Lake Village, AR 71653; 870-265-5480; www.arkansas stateparks.com/lakechicot

Pier fishing on Lake Chicot

Lake Fausse Pointe

18 miles southeast of St. Martinville via La. 96, La. 679, and La. 3083; 8 miles southeast along W. Atchafalaya Protection Levee Rd.

- 6,127 acres ▪ Year-round ▪ Entrance fee ▪ Atchafalaya Swamp
- Canoeing trails ▪ Hiking ▪ Boat rentals ▪ Conference Center

Sunset on Lake Fausse

Home of bald eagles, alligators, and otters, the Atchafalaya River easily deserves a place among the country's finest natural areas. The Atchafalaya (a Native American word meaning "long river") stretches about 140 miles northward from the Gulf of Mexico with a floodplain more than 20 miles wide in places. Few roads cross this wilderness, and access to the interior is hard for those without a boat and a guide to point the way amid trackless waterways.

PARK TIP: *Try dropping a fishing line from the cabin deck for spotted gar. They feed on the insects attracted by the lights around the bridges and docks.*

Lying just outside Atchafalaya's western levee, Lake Fausse Pointe offers a sampling of this environment but with the conveniences of a modern park. Visualize the scene by imagining yourself enjoying a cool drink on a cabin porch while an alligator glides across the bayou below.

What to See and Do

The most challenging part of a trip to Lake Fausse Pointe is simply getting here. Coming from St. Martinville, you'll change direction and roads several times as you wind east through the sugarcane fields and then south on the levee road for the final 8-mile stretch.

Although Lake Fausse Pointe encompasses extensive swamp, its developed area is compact. Bottomland woods line the roads and water is never far away. Local wildlife ranges from the tiny ruby-throated hummingbird to white-tailed deer and gators, and includes herons, egrets, armadillos, squirrels, and nutria—South American rodents introduced into Louisiana around the turn of the 20th century as a potential fur resource.

Cross the footbridge over **Old Bird Island Chute** to reach the hiking trails. Three paths—**A, B,** and **C**—a total of nearly 8 miles, loop through vine-tangled woods of bald cypress, oak, willow, sycamore, sugarberry, and hickory. The trailside can be alive with birds any time of year. Trail B passes an observation platform, overlooking the lake, from where you may see waterfowl, gulls, terns, or wading birds. Listen for the rattle of a belted kingfisher or the scream of a red-shouldered hawk.

The forests and waterways of southern Louisiana provide habitat for many reptiles—including snakes, the cause of much needless worry for some visitors. The reptiles you're most likely to see, though, are turtles: Variously called map turtles, painted turtles, cooters, and sliders, all can often be seen basking in the sun.

Three canoe trails, all of which are marked, lead through a canal system on the lake's east side; exploring these routes affords the best opportunity to experience the Atchafalaya ecosystem. Stick close to home by paddling the quiet Old Bird Island Chute, or venture farther away to see huge bald cypress trees around **Sandy Cove** (*Boat rentals at the entrance station. Fee*). Seek advice before heading out on your own.

> **CAJUN COUNTRY:** Lake Fausse Pointe lies in the heart of Cajun country, home to descendants of French-speaking Acadians—forced out of Canada by the British in the 1750s. Nearby Lafayette likes to call itself the "Cajun Capital"; its Acadian Cultural Center (*501 Fischer Rd., 337-232-0789. Adm. fee*) and the adjoining living history village of Vermilionville (*1600 Surrey St., 337-233-4077 or 800-992-2968. Closed Mon.; adm. fee*) are excellent places to discover that there's more to Cajun culture than spicy food and great dance music.

259

Camping and Lodging

The park has 50 tent and RV sites, with electricity and water; 1 primitive group, 5 primitive canoe, and 7 primitive backpack sites. Camping fee. There are also 18 waterfront cabins. For reservations call 877-226-7652.

Lake Fausse Pointe State Park, 5400 Levee Rd., St. Martinville, LA 70582; 337-229-4764; www.crt.state.la.us/parks

Alligators

Chicot

7 miles north of Ville Platte on La. 3042

▪ 6,400 acres ▪ Year-round ▪ Vehicle fee ▪ Hiking, fishing
(license required) ▪ Boat and canoe rentals

An appealingly varied forest surrounds 2,000-acre Lake Chicot,
where the pinewoods of northwestern Louisiana give way to the
swampy lowlands of the south. The lake is popular with locals fishing for largemouth bass and crappie (called *sac-à-lait* by Cajuns).
If you're not an angler, you'll enjoy hiking along the picturesque
lakeshore or exploring the arboretum.

For an introduction to the park's environment, drive the
4-mile road between the south and north landings. The route winds
through rolling terrain covered in pine, oak, sweetgum, palmetto,
and magnolia, dotted throughout with the straight gray trunks of
beech. Stop at the north landing, where a long fishing pier makes a
good lookout point. Winter is the best time to see waterfowl on the
bald cypress-ringed lake, and you may spot a bald eagle perched in
a tall tree nearby.

The **Walkers Branch Hiking Trail** circles the lake, passing areas
designated for primitive camping. Short sections of the trail allow
you to get away from cars and picnickers without having to carry
backpacking gear.

Be sure to visit the nearby **Louisiana State Arboretum** *(337-363-*
6289; off La. 3042), a mile north of the park entrance. The 2.5 miles
of trails here, traversing ridges and ravines amid lush woodland, are
among the state's prettiest. The type of beech-magnolia forest found
in the arboretum and the park was once widespread across the
South; today, mature examples are as exceptional and as treasured
as they are beautiful.

Camping and Lodging

There are 208 tent and RV sites, with showers; 20 cabins; and 2
lodges. For reservations, call 888-677-2442. Camping fee.

Chicot State Park, 3469 Chicot Park Rd., Ville Platte, LA 70586; 337-
363-2403; www.crt.state.la.us/parks/ichicot.aspx

Poverty Point

16 miles north of Delhi via La. 17, 134, and 577

▪ 402 acres ▪ Year-round ▪ Entrance fee ▪ No camping ▪ Museum
▪ Seasonal tram tours ▪ Self-guided trail

About the time Solomon was writing the Proverbs and tending to his
700 wives, a thriving community existed on the edge of a waterway
in what is now northeastern Louisiana. Expansive and orderly in
design, it seems to have been the region's dominant economic hub.

The community carried on trade and extended its influence over a wide area. They built near the Mississippi floodplain mammoth earthworks and erected grand ceremonial mounds—one of them in the form of a flying bird, nearly 100 feet high and more than 700 feet long.

Archaeologists call this place Poverty Point, a name that also has come to identify the principal culture of the lower Mississippi Valley from about 1600 to 1100 B.C. Today's Poverty Point State Historic Site rewards visitors with tantalizing glimpses of a long-vanished civilization, which left traces as haunting as a carved stone effigy, as substantial as the ground beneath your feet, and from as far away as the Ohio and Tennessee River Valleys.

261

Tree-studded Mound A

What to See and Do

Your experience at Poverty Point will probably begin before you even know it. As La. 577 approaches the park's **Visitor Center,** the road cuts across a series of low ridges so long and uniform in appearance that they seem at first to be naturally occurring geological features. In reality, though, you're crossing six concentric, semicircular earthworks stretching, from one extremity to the other, nearly three-quarters of a mile. Believed to have served as foundations for houses, these ridges originally stood 4 to 6 feet high, and their construction required a highly organized effort involving millions of hours of labor.

Poverty Point's Visitor Center is located in the 37-acre opening that was once the town's central plaza, alongside **Bayou Macon** (pronounced mason). A short video shown here explains the importance of the site and reviews its history. After watching it, take time to study the exhibits in the adjoining room, where some of the huge number of artifacts found in the area are displayed. Among them are beautiful little owls carved from red jasper; graceful plummets, which were probably used as weights for fishing nets; gorgets and beads; projectile

NAME GAME: What's in a name? Not much, really, at Poverty Point. Early settlers struggling to survive on America's frontier often gave their homesteads jokingly ironic epithets, such as "No Hope" or "Hard Times Farm." In the mid-19th century, a plantation on Bayou Macon was known as Poverty Point, and this traditional designation was eventually applied to the archaeological site. The cheerless name has nothing to do with the prehistoric inhabitants of the area, who, as far as we know, were a very prosperous and happy people.

points; and, especially, artificial cooking stones of fire-hardened silt that were heated and placed into earth ovens with food for cooking. These stones are identified so closely with the site and its culture that archaeologists call them "Poverty Point objects."

Climb to the top of **Mound A** to appreciate the enormity of the mound and surrounding earthworks. Shaped like a bird with its wings outstretched, this mound contains 300,000 cubic yards of earth and was built—probably for ceremonial purposes—one basket of dirt at a time, with material excavated from nearby "borrow pits."

From March through October, Poverty Point operates tram tours, which cross the ridges and visit Mound A (you'll be allowed time to climb to the top) and **Mound B.**

An alternative to the tram is a self-guided, 2.6-mile walking trail that winds alongside Bayou Macon, through the ridges, and back to the Visitor Center. *(Wear comfortable shoes if you plan to hike this trail, which can be wet in winter and spring.)*

As you can imagine, many mysteries remain about a place so far removed from our own time. Archaeological research continues here; if you come in summer, you may well get to watch scientists at work trying to resolve some of the countless questions still unanswered about Poverty Point and its industrious inhabitants.

Poverty Point State Historic Site, P.O. Box 276, Epps, LA 71237; 318-926-5492 or 888-926-5492; www.stateparks.com/poverty_point.html

Lake Bistineau

9 miles south of Doyline on La. 163

▪ 750 acres ▪ Year-round ▪ Vehicle fee ▪ 17,000-acre lake ▪ Boating, fishing (license required) ▪ Hiking, biking

Stand on the shore of Lake Bistineau, a large, shallow reservoir 30 miles east of Shreveport, and you find yourself at the meeting of two worlds. On one side is a swampy expanse of bald cypress and water tupelo, of wood ducks and catfish, muskrats and mud turtles. On the other is a segment of the great pine forest that stretches from the Atlantic to Texas. This conjunction makes the state park a place of diverse beauty—and an excellent base from which to explore the lake.

The entrance road to **Park Area 1,** where the office and cabins are located, passes through a forest dominated by loblolly pine, some of which have gained impressive size. Opportunities for dry-land recreation are limited at Bistineau, so check at the park office about renting a boat—by far the best way to enjoy a visit here.

You don't have to roam far to begin your discoveries. The shoreline near the park is a picturesque scene of bald cypress trees, their swollen trunks and protruding "knees" draped with Spanish moss. In spring and summer, you may see a brilliant golden-yellow prothonotary warbler, a sparrow-size bird that's something of a specialty in southern swamps. Pairs often nest in tree cavities over water. In fall, the needles of the bald cypress turn reddish brown, for this species is a deciduous conifer—that is, a cone-bearing tree, like pine and spruce, that loses its leaves annually, like an oak or a maple.

Low-flying great egret

PARK TIP: *For a comprehensive view of the park, play the 18-hole Frisbee golf course through the woodlands, along the lake's shoreline, and across the meadows.*

When you visit Bistineau, consider renting one of the cabins, attractively set on the lakeshore. Staying here, you'll have only to look out the window to appreciate this uniquely attractive park.

Camping and Lodging

There are 67 tent and RV sites, with showers, and 2 group camps. Camping fee. Also, 7 cabins. For reservations, call 888-677-2478.

Lake Bistineau State Park, P.O. Box 589, Doyline, LA 71023; 318-745-3503 or 888-677-2478; www.crt.state.la/us/parks/ibistino.aspx

Big Bend Ranch

3 miles southeast of Presidio on FM 170

- 300,000 acres ▪ Year-round ▪ Entrance fee ▪ Rugged wilderness
- Desert wildlife ▪ Barton Warnock Environmental Education
Center ▪ Rafting, hiking, backpacking, mountain biking

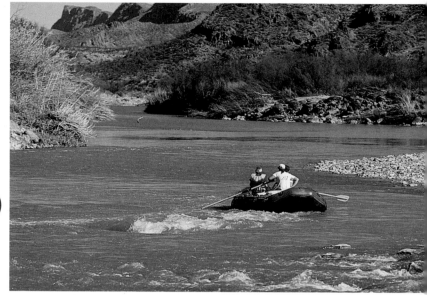

Rio Grande, Canyon Colorado

The Chihuahuan Desert stretches across an immense expanse of northern Mexico and the southwestern United States. To some, the terrain it encompasses is lonely and forbidding. To others, the wildlands here offer a renewing respite from civilization's demands.

Big Bend Ranch State Park sprawls northward from the Rio Grande, just west of Big Bend National Park. Its 467 square miles are composed mostly of desert grassland. The river acts as a long, narrow oasis, providing habitat for an incomparable variety of plants and animals (mountain lions still roam the rocky slopes, and golden eagles cruise the canyons) that otherwise would be absent from this parched land.

> **PARK TIP:** *Look for a campsite at the Grassy Banks primitive camp area, where the river rapids play their natural music while you sit, relax, and admire the sunset under the ramadas.*

Little development has taken place since the former cattle ranch was acquired by the state in 1988: FM 170 parallels the river, one gravel road penetrates the northern section, and a few hiking trails venture into the rugged backcountry, but access to most of the area is difficult.

What to See and Do

Your adventure begins as you drive southeast from Presidio on FM 170. Known as El Camino del Rio, or the **River Road,** it surely ranks among the most breathtakingly scenic drives in America. With the Rio Grande on one side and the Bofecillos Mountains on the other, the route twists and curls, climbs, and descends for 50 miles of ever changing views of a landscape shaped by ancient volcanoes, continental collision, and eroding rivers. Enjoy the surroundings, but drive with caution. Be especially careful at the road's many low-water crossings, and don't enter water that looks deep or fast-flowing and muddy.

En route to the park (just 3 miles from Presidio), you'll pass **Fort Leaton State Historical Site** (432-229-3613. *Adm. fee),* one of two places where you can pay fees and obtain information about Big Bend Ranch. If this is your first visit, though, continue on to the **Barton Warnock**

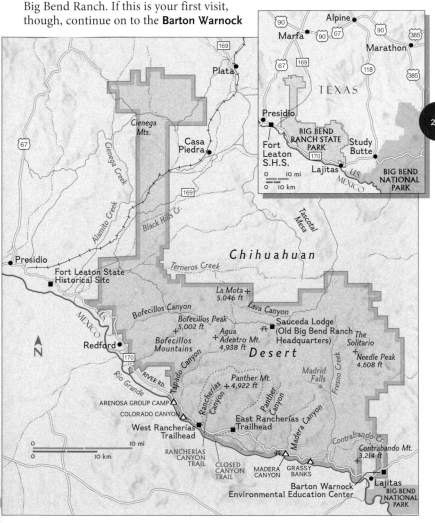

Environmental Education Center *(432-424-3327. Adm. fee)*, at the other side of the park in Lajitas, for your introduction to the area's natural history. Walk through the 2.5-acre botanical garden, which displays such typical regional plants as the lechuguilla, an agave that botanists call the Chihuahuan Desert's chief "indicator"—a species that grows naturally nowhere else.

Ask center personnel about current park trail and road conditions; also check on upcoming events such as photography workshops, longhorn cattle drives, or horseback rides.

Retrace your route for 20 miles to the trailhead for **Closed Canyon,** a short hike off FM 170. Here a tributary has carved a narrow, steep-sided gorge in welded tuff—rock that originated as fine volcanic ash. Not only is this an easy walk, but the high canyon sides keep much of it in shade, an important consideration in this sun-drenched climate.

Follow FM 170 northwest again toward Presidio; a few miles past the park's western border, turn right onto gravel Casa Piedra Road (FM 169), which runs for more than 30 miles into the mountains. *(Large motor homes may have difficulty on this road.)* Listen for desert birds, or at dusk, the eerie howling of coyotes. Mule deer and javelina (small piglike creatures) are seen often; a lucky traveler might catch a glimpse of a mountain lion.

The road leads to **Sauceda,** where lodging is available in the old ranch headquarters buildings. Beyond Sauceda, you'll find splendid views of the imposing laccocaldera formation called the **Solitario,** and a lookout point into Fresno Canyon.

Further Adventures

For hardy hikers, the **Rancherías Canyon Trail,** north of the River Road, leads up a canyon past ancient lava flows to a waterfall. Although the entire out-and-back distance is 9.6 miles, beautiful canyonland begins after just 2 miles or so, making shorter walks highly rewarding. The same trailhead serves the **Rancherías Loop Trail,** a 19-mile, two- or three-day wilderness trek that should be undertaken only by experienced backpackers.

RIVER RUNNING: River rafting and canoeing are popular activities at Big Bend Ranch, which borders the Rio Grande's majestic Canyon Colorado. With a permit, you can take your own craft downriver, but most travelers go through one of the outfitters in Lajitas or Terlingua; the park office can provide contacts. These companies can also organize a trip through Big Bend National Park's awesome Santa Elena, Mariscal, and Boquillas Canyons—one of the most spectacular river journeys on Earth.

Camping and Lodging

The park has 60 primitive campsites, including 7 group sites. In Sauceda, dormitory accommodations (30 bunk beds) are available, as well as lodging in a historic ranch house. For reservations, call 432-358-4444.

Big Bend Ranch State Park, P.O. Box 2319, Presidio, TX 79845; 432-229-3416; www.tpwd.state.tx.us/spdest

Enchanted Rock

17 miles north of Fredericksburg on Rte. 965

- 1,643 acres ▪ Year-round ▪ Entrance fee ▪ Visitor limits
- No vehicular camping ▪ Pink granite formations ▪ Rock climbing

The rugged countryside west of Austin, fondly called "Hill Country" by Texans, encompasses a variety of attractions, from scenic rivers to historic towns. For sheer visual impact, though, nothing can match the high dome of pink granite at the center of Enchanted Rock State Natural Area. Rising more than 425 feet above the surrounding terrain and covering some 640 acres with rock, it seems out of earthly scale, as if it had been transported from another world. Which, in effect, it was.

Eroded granite formations

Enchanted Rock is a batholith (rock from the deep)—a huge mass of molten material that rose from within the Earth and solidified as it neared the surface. In the billion years since the batholith's formation, the weaker overlying rock has eroded away, exposing its crown. The visible portion of Enchanted Rock is only a small fraction of the entire mass, which underlies almost 90 square miles of central Texas.

The descriptive name "enchanted" is said to have been passed down from Indians, who may have attributed the loud sounds of temperature-related rock expansion and contraction to spirits.

> **PARK TIP:** *The Echo Canyon Trail between Enchanted Rock and Little Rock provides quick access to numerous technical climbing routes.*

Archaeological evidence shows that Native Americans lived near the rock from at least 8,000 years ago until explorers displaced them in the mid-19th century.

What to See and Do

The foremost activity at Enchanted Rock is quite plainly to get to the top. While the **Summit Trail** is well-marked and requires no technical skill, an elevation gain of 425 feet in just over half a mile makes it more than a casual stroll.

Before you begin, stop at the **headquarters** to see displays on local geology. Enchanted Rock is part of Texas' Central Mineral Region, an area known for its geological diversity; an appreciation for what's below ground will enhance your experience here. You can

LITTLE GERMANY: Fredericks-burg, just south of Enchanted Rock, is one of the best-known ethnic communities in Texas. Founded by a German immigrants' society in 1846, it retains a strong Old World flavor, from its Fachwerk (half-timbered) buildings to bakeries specializing in German-style breads and pastries. The Pioneer Museum Complex (309 W. Main St. 830-990-8441, adm. fee) and the Vereins Kirche (people's church) Museum (Center of Markt Platz. 830-997-7832, adm. fee) vividly recount local history.

also pick up information on archaeology, birdlife, or rock climbing.

Among the plants along the Summit Trail are mesquite, several types of oak, black hickory, prickly pear cactus, elm, hackberry, and Texas persimmon, a smaller relative of the common persimmon found in the East. Bluebonnet and Indian paintbrush are seen in spring. Park animals, like the plants, constitute an intriguing blend of eastern and western species: You may see both foxes and rock squirrels at Enchanted Rock, just as you'll find both pecan and catclaw acacia.

As you climb higher onto the rock itself, look for the small depressions known as **vernal pools,** a remarkable ecological feature. Vegetation in these basins slowly progresses from lichens to grasses to live oaks, creating islands of life in a sea of bare granite. Tiny invertebrates called fairy shrimp inhabit this fragile environment, enduring drought as eggs, and hatching when it rains.

You'll discover a splendid panorama of the Hill Country at Enchanted Rock's broad summit. The high points surrounding you, similar to but smaller than the one you're standing on, represent other outcrops of the same mammoth granite batholith. Plan on taking plenty of time here to enjoy the views—and to celebrate your success at reaching the top.

After you've made your way back down, walk the 4-mile **Loop Trail,** which circles Enchanted Rock and provides a good look at the park's varied habitats, including oak woodland, mesquite grassland, and the floodplain of Sandy Creek. The trail leads to three designated primitive-camping areas.

Rock climbing is popular on the mountain's steep, northwest-facing cliffs, but it's not for the inexperienced. Climbers must check in at headquarters for rules before beginning; no pitons, bolts, or other devices that might damage the rock are permitted. Ask, too, about exploring the 1,000-foot-long **Enchanted Rock Fissure,** which runs beneath huge sections of fallen granite. This can be an exciting adventure, but you must have sturdy footwear, carry a flashlight, and be mindful of your physical limitations.

To protect the environment, the park limits the number of daily visitors; call in advance on weekends and holidays.

Camping

The park has 46 walk-in and 60 primitive tent sites, with shower facilities. Call 512-389-8900 to reserve. Camping fee.

Enchanted Rock State Natural Area, 16710 Ranch Rd. 965, Fredericks-burg, TX 78624; 325-247-3903; www.tpwd.state.tx.us/spdest

Brazos Bend

35 miles southwest of Houston

▪ 4,975 acres ▪ Year-round ▪ Entrance fee ▪ Excellent wildlife viewing
▪ Hiking, biking

269

Field of spider lilies

Named for its location on a broad curve of the Brazos River, Brazos Bend is one of Texas' prettiest and most popular parks. The greatest rewards await those who thrill to the insistent hoot of a great horned owl at dusk, the cold gaze of an alligator, or the graceful ballet of an egret searching for prey.

Much of the park is bottomland-hardwood forest of almost tropical lushness. Wispy strands of Spanish moss hang from the gnarled limbs of live oak; cottonwood and sycamore line the banks of the Brazos and the lakes that dot the flat floodplain. Marshes draw alligators, waterfowl, wading birds, otters, and nutria, while restored upland prairie sparkles with wildflowers. All such wonders can now be seen on the more than 35 miles of hiking and biking trails.

What to See and Do

Although you'll be tempted to get out of your car and begin exploring the park's trails immediately, your first stop will depend on whether it's the weekend, when the **Nature Center** is open all day and offers at least six nature programs *(Mon.–Fri., 11 a.m.–3 p.m.; weekends 9 a.m.–5 p.m.).* If so, continue past the entrance for 2.6 miles to the building on your left, where you'll learn about Brazos Bend's three ecological zones (forest, wetland, and prairie), and about the park's most popular resident, the American alligator. The **Creekfield Lake Nature Trail** continues your orientation. The paved 0.5-mile loop is completely handicapped accessible.

Next, return to the parking lot at **40-Acre Lake,** near the park entrance, where a fishing pier makes an excellent viewing platform. Depending on the time of year, you may see ducks, herons, egrets, coots, or grebes. Wood ducks, which many consider America's most beautiful waterfowl, are among the 70 or so bird species that nest in the park.

Before you walk the 1.2-mile trail that circles the lake, read (and heed) posted warnings about safety around alligators. Seeing these big reptiles is always a thrill, but don't be fooled by their sluggish demeanor: Gators can move with shocking speed when they want to. Never feed an alligator, and absolutely do not approach a nest or a female with young.

Along the trail you may also see white-tailed deer, bobcat, yellow-crowned night heron, swamp rabbit (closely related to the cottontail), or one of the several kinds of snakes found here. On the far side of the lake, climb the four-story observation tower for a view over extensive wetlands, where patient watching will reveal a variety of wading birds. A side trail leads to **Elm Lake;** following this route, circling Elm Lake, and returning to the 40-Acre Lake parking lot comprises a 4.1-mile hike, nearly guaranteed to reveal a variety of wildlife.

If you have more time, explore the trails that lead from **Hale Lake** down to the Brazos River. Intersecting loops make possible hikes of from less than a mile to several miles. The 2-mile **Red Buckeye Trail,** which loops down to **Big Creek,** takes its name from a shrub whose bright-red blossoms brighten the woods in spring.

On Saturday nights, the **George Observatory** *(979-553-3400),* operated by the Houston Museum of Natural Science and located at Creekfield Lake near the Visitor Center, offers public viewing through its 36-inch **telescope** *(tickets sold on a first-come, first-served basis; fee)* and a variety of smaller instruments.

Camping

Brazos Bend has 130 tent and RV sites, with showers. Reservations advised; call 512-389-8900. Camping fee.

Brazos Bend State Park, 21901 FM 762, Needville, TX 77461; 979-553-5101; www.tpwd.state.tx.us/spdest

ARMADILLO LAND: While at Brazos Bend, you may well come upon a nine-banded armadillo snuffling through the underbrush for beetles and other food. Though its armor plating makes it look something like a reptile, this intriguing and harmless little animal is a mammal; females give birth in spring to four, genetically identical young—all always of the same sex. The armadillo has poor eyesight, so if you approach quietly from downwind, you often can come quite close to it as it goes about its business.

Caddo Lake

15 miles northeast of Marshall via Tex. 43, Tex. 2198, and Tex. 2

- 8,489 acres ▪ Year-round
- Entrance fee ▪ Nature and hiking trails ▪ Picturesque lake
- Canoeing ▪ Recreation Hall

Bald cypress in autumn

Heading east from Caddo Lake State Park/Wildlife Management Area, a motivated crow could be in Louisiana in just a few minutes: The state line is only 8 miles away. This proximity is reflected in the park's environment—the swampy bottomland is more Mississippi Delta bayou than the pinewoods and prairies of East Texas.

For the adventurous, canoeing ranks as the most rewarding activity at this park bordering **Big Cypress Bayou.** Glide silently beneath moss-draped bald cypress, and feel the solitude, getting close-up looks at a barred owl or an occasional alligator. Enjoy it with this warning: Once you've left the immediate vicinity of the park and paddled downstream, take care not to get lost in the maze of channels on 27,000-acre **Caddo Lake.**

You can rent canoes at a small store *(903-679-3073 or 903-930-0075. Closed Tues.–Wed.; fee)* on **Saw Mill Pond.** Ask advice about the safest areas to explore and buy a map of the lake's "boat roads." If you don't trust your navigational skills, take a guided tour on a pontoon barge *(closed Mon.–Tues.).*

PARK TIP: *Book one of the 1930s log cabins; built by the CCC, they provide a sense of history with present-day comfort.*

Don't neglect the park's nature and hiking trails, which link to form a 2.5-mile loop. The paths meander over ridges and down into ravines, through a mixed forest of oak, sweetgum, hickory, elm, and pine. Bird-watching can be excellent here. At dawn in late April and early May, the woods ring with the songs of dozens of species, from the impressive red-shouldered hawk to diminutive warblers.

Camping and Lodging

Caddo Lake has 46 campsites (20 tent-only sites, 18 tent and RV sites with water, and 8 RV full hook-ups), 9 cabins, and 7 screened shelters. Camping fee. For reservations call 512-389-8900.

Caddo Lake State Park, 245 Park Rd. 2, Karnack, TX 75661; 903-679-3351; www.tpwd.state.tx.us/spdest

SOUTHWEST

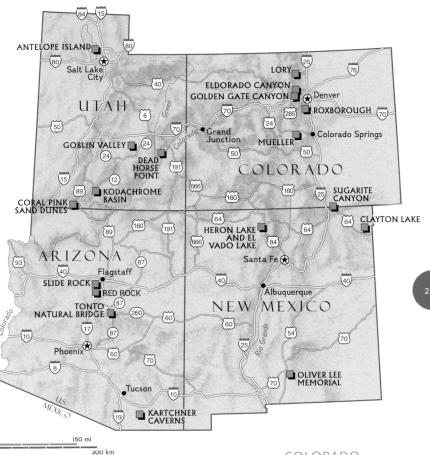

ANTELOPE ISLAND

Salt Lake City

UTAH

GOBLIN VALLEY

DEAD HORSE POINT

KODACHROME BASIN

CORAL PINK SAND DUNES

LORY

ELDORADO CANYON
GOLDEN GATE CANYON

Denver

ROXBOROUGH

Grand Junction

MUELLER

Colorado Springs

COLORADO

SUGARITE CANYON

CLAYTON LAKE

HERON LAKE AND EL VADO LAKE

ARIZONA

Flagstaff

SLIDE ROCK

RED ROCK

TONTO NATURAL BRIDGE

Phoenix

Santa Fe

Albuquerque

NEW MEXICO

Tucson

OLIVER LEE MEMORIAL

KARTCHNER CAVERNS

150 mi

300 km

273

UTAH

Antelope Island
Coral Pink Sand Dunes
Dead Horse Point
Goblin Valley
Kodachrome Basin

ARIZONA

Slide Rock
Red Rock
Tonto Natural Bridge
Kartchner Caverns

COLORADO

Mueller
Roxborough
Golden Gate Canyon
Eldorado Canyon
Lory

NEW MEXICO

Sugarite Canyon
Clayton Lake
Heron Lake and
 El Vado Lake
Oliver Lee Memorial

Goblin formation, Goblin Valley State Park, Utah

Mueller

3.5 miles south of Divide on Colo. 67

■ 5,121 acres ■ Year-round ■ Entrance fee ■ Panoramic views of the Rockies ■ Hiking, mountain biking, horseback riding ■ Wildlife viewing ■ Cross-country skiing

Near Outlook Ridge

Mueller State Park has retained much of the natural character of the Rocky Mountain ecology. Located on the west side of Pikes Peak, Mueller is punctuated by granite outcrops, timbered hills dominated by spruce–fir forest, aspen, and open grasslands. Throughout the park, overlooks take in this spectacular setting, along with offering long views of the surrounding Sawatch and Sangre de Cristo mountain ranges.

Among the park's diversity of wildlife is a herd of 250 elk. In fall, bulls in rut bellow across the landscape. Residents include mule deer, rabbits, mountain lions, black bears, bobcats, and Merriam wild turkeys.

PARK TIP: *Picnic at the staff's favorite spot—Bootlegger Picnic Area—scattered amid rocky outcroppings.*

Once the hunting grounds of the Ute, the region was settled by pioneers in the 1860s. The Mueller family owned a cattle ranch here in the late 1960s and later designated their property a wildlife preserve.

What to See and Do

Your first stop should be the **Visitor Center.** From the parking area, look out on the distant valleys and mountains. An open gazebo has plaques identifying the prominent features, including 14,110-foot

Pikes Peak. The Visitor Center provides a park overview and describes its importance as a wildlife habitat.

The developed areas of the park are concentrated on only 400 acres; the best way to visit the remaining 4,721 acres is on foot, mountain bike, horseback, or in the winter on cross-country skis or snowshoes along the nearly 50 miles of trails. If you're on a short visit, the 0.8-mile **Wapiti Self-Guided Nature Trail** (trailhead at Rock Pond) offers a quick primer on the region's diverse ecosystems. The 1.8-mile **Outlook Ridge Trail** (from Outlook Ridge trailhead) winds past several panoramic over-looks, including Raven Ridge, where you can look down into the beginning of the canyon formed by Fourmile Creek. The trail continues on to Lost Pond in the shade of aspen and conifer.

Camping

The park has 132 tent or RV sites, including 22 walk-in tent sites, with showers late-May through early Oct. Some sites open through winter. Reservations advised June through Sept.; call 303-470-1144 or 800-678-2267. Camping fee.

Nearby Sights

Abutting the park is the **Dome Rock State Wildlife Area.** While here, consider the 9.6-mile round-trip trail to **Dome Rock,** a popular trek into rugged Fourmile Canyon. You will pass the remains of Jack Cabin Lodge, built in the early 1900s to show cattle to prospective buyers. Farther ahead, you come to Dome Rock, rising 800 feet above the canyon floor. The trail fords Fourmile Creek nine times, so be prepared to get your feet wet. Along the way be on the lookout for the occasional bighorn sheep. *(For information on trail openings and closings to protect the bighorn population, call 719-227-5200.)*

Don't miss the mostly unpaved, 19-mile drive up nearby **Pikes Peak** *(719-684-9383. Toll),* which ascends 6,310 feet through forest and wildflower-sprinkled meadows to tundra—the highest vertical rise of any Colorado mountain that you can drive. The historic gold rush towns of Cripple Creek and Victor *(visitor information 719-689-2169 or 877-858-4653),* bustling with mine tours, gold panning, restored saloons, and gambling, lie 15 miles south of the park via Colo. 67.

275

MOUNTAIN LION ENCOUNTERS: Puma, cougar, ghost cat, mountain lion—by any name these big cats flourish in such wildlife-rich land-scapes as Mueller State Park, where they have an array of elk and deer to choose from for dinner. Numbering some 3,000 in Colorado, mountain lions are powerful but secretive; human attacks are extremely rare, and usually come from inexperienced adolescents. If you meet a mountain lion, stay calm and try to back away. If the lion behaves aggressively, throw stones, branches, or anything else handy. Stand up straight, wave your arms, and make a lot of noise. Most mountain lions will be deterred.

Mueller State Park and Wildlife Area, P.O. Box 39, Divide, CO 80814; 719-687-2366; www.parks.state.co.us/parks/mueller

Roxborough

Just south of Littleton, off Colo. 121 (Wadsworth Blvd.)

- 3,329 acres ▪ Year-round ▪ Entrance fee ▪ No pets ▪ No camping
▪ No bikes ▪ Red-rock formations ▪ Unusual mix of wildlife and
plant life ▪ Hiking

You enter Roxborough State Park through a cleft canyon that looks like it was cleaved by a giant ax—providing a taste of the terrain that lies beyond. Roxborough with its tilted layers of red sandstone embraces more than 1.2 billion years of geologic history.

TALES OF THE PAST: Until the early 1900s, Roxborough was known as Washington Park, for a sandstone formation that resembles the profile of the first president. In 1902, Henry Persse, then the owner of the property, changed the name to Roxborough, after the Persse family estate in Ireland. The 1903 Persse House, now found along the Fountain Valley Trail, was the first installment of a grand plan to turn Roxborough into a major tourist destination, much like the Broadmoor in Colorado Springs, complete with golf course and luxury amenities. Unfortunately, one day Henry chased his windblown hat into a Denver street, stepped in front of an oncoming streetcar, and was killed. This effectively scotched his development plans.

The park's showpiece is the Fountain Formation, made of debris eroded from the ancestral Rockies about 300 million years ago; the formation's striking red is caused by iron oxide minerals. The Lyons Formation, which overlies the Fountain, is composed of beach sands deposited about 250 million years ago, after the ancestral Rockies were eroded away.

On the park's eastern edge, the Dakota Formation forms a long ridge, known locally as the Dakota Hogback for its resemblance to a hog's spine. The tan sandstones and gray mudstones were deposited along a swampy coastal area about 100 to 125 million years ago, during the age of the dinosaurs. Paleontologists have found footprints and bones of several dinosaur species here. Examples of these prints are on display in the Visitor Center.

The park lies in a transitional zone, where eastern plains meet the Front Range. Seven plant communities are found here, ranging from riparian to prairie to a forest of ponderosa pine and Douglas-fir atop Carpenter Peak. It's not unusual to spot yucca and prickly pear thriving steps away from wild roses and aspen. Wildlife includes deer, coyotes, bears, fox, mountain lions, and the occasional bobcat or elk. Golden eagles and prairie falcons nest on the ridges.

The park's unusual topology and hydrology encourage the growth of aspens at elevations 1,000 feet lower than their usual range. Gambel oak, usually a shrub-size species, grows to a height of 40 feet in some park locations.

What to See and Do

Stop first at the **George O'Malley Visitor Center** to examine the displays on park geology and wildlife, and to pick up maps. If you're

Red-rock Fountain Formation

only going to do one hike, take the **Fountain Valley Trail** (trailhead at Visitor Center), a 2.2-mile loop through the Fountain and Lyons formations, past the stone Persse House. Short detours to Fountain Valley and Lyons Overlooks provide panoramas. Another excellent hike from the Visitor Center is the easy 1.4-mile **Willow Creek Loop**. Strolling along the gentle creek beneath cottonwoods and willows, listen for the cheerful tunes of canyon wrens and spotted towhees.

For a more difficult hike, take the 6.4-mile, out-and-back trek to 7,200-foot **Carpenter Peak** (trailhead at the Visitor Center), which includes an elevation gain of 1,000 feet. Along the way, look for signs of mountain lions and black bears. The very ambitious can continue from here along the famous 470-mile-long **Colorado Trail.**

PARK TIP: *Visit Lyons Overlook for views of Fountain Valley and the Denver skyline; linger and watch turkey vultures and prairie falcons soar above deer and bobcats.*

Roxborough State Park, 4751 N. Roxborough Dr., Littleton, CO 80125; 303-973-3959; www.parks.state.co.us/parks/roxborough

Golden Gate Canyon

14 miles west of Golden Gate Canyon Rd.

■ 12,000 acres ■ Year-round ■ Entrance fee ■ Hiking, mountain biking, horseback riding

Forgotten Valley

Just an hour's drive from Denver, Golden Gate Canyon shows you a classic, unspoiled Rocky Mountain environment, flanked by a rugged canyon. Gentle hiking trails explore lichen-covered granite outcrops, sunny meadows dotted with butterflies, lodgepole pine forests, and the arroyos of intermittent streams.

Roaming these lands is a representative sampling of Rockies wildlife—mule deer, cottontail rabbit, coyote, beaver, and elk. Encounters with mountain lions and black bears are rare, but backcountry users are advised about the possibility.

More than a half million people flock to the park annually, mostly on summer and fall weekends. If you can hike the timbered trails during the week or in the off-season, you will have the park much to yourself, even during the busy summer.

What to See and Do

Stop first at the **Visitor Center** for an orientation to this large park, and to take in the exhibits about the ecology, wildlife, and history. Outside, the handicapped-accessible **Wilbur and Nellie Larkin Memorial Nature Trail** winds around a pond filled with rainbow trout.

278

From here, head immediately to the park's northwest corner to **Panorama Point,** where an overlook offers spectacular views of the soaring granite peaks of the Rocky Mountain Front Range, topped in eternal snows. A plaque at the overlook helps you pick out Longs Peak, Mount Evans, and the Indian Peaks area, and the views invite you to linger.

PARK TIP: *Hike, bike, horseback ride, ski, or snowshoe to the front porch of the historic Talman Ranch House for a peaceful lunch or to try your luck fishing in the pond.*

Next, it's best to get out of the car and into your hiking boots. The park features 35 miles of multiple-use and hiking trails, and you can't go wrong on any of them. Remember that you are more than a mile and a half above sea level, so start out easy. The park recommends that you carry water, as water from park streams should be treated and purified before drinking.

If you would like a relatively short, easy, and interesting hike, take the 1.8-mile **Horseshoe Trail,** beginning just down the road from the Visitor Center. You ascend through a forested drainage to grassy **Frazer Meadow,** in the shadow of craggy Tremont Mountain. Dotted with harebells and brown-eyed Susans, Frazer Meadow entertains a variety of butterflies, including tiger swallowtail and the increasingly rare clodius parnassian. Here, too, you can view the remains of the Frazer homestead.

If you have more time, try the **Mountain Lion Trail** in the eastern portion of the park, a 6.7-mile loop to Windy Peak and a spectacular view of the plains to the east. City Lights Ridge along this trail looks out on Denver's lights (at night) and skyline on the plains below.

For those who want more of an adventure, the park's most difficult trail is the 2.8-mile (one way) **Black Bear Trail,** which begins from the Ralston Roost picnic area and trailhead near the Visitor Center and ascends to Frazer Meadow.

RICH HISTORY: First visited by Native Americans seeking game and berries, then by trappers looking for beaver in the early 19th century, the Golden Gate Canyon area first boomed with the gold discovery of 1859. No gold was ever found in the park itself; timber proved the treasure here, which built the gold camps of nearby Central City and Black Hawk. Golden Gate Canyon Road, which now brings visitors to the park, originally was a toll road for shipping gold out of and supplies into the gold fields. Eventually, when the gold petered out, ranching homesteads cropped up and the area became semiquiet—that is, except for its flourishing moonshine and bootleg operations during Prohibition.

Camping

Golden Gate Canyon has 97 tent and RV sites (some open year-round), with showers, and 35 tent-only sites; 27 backcountry sites, including 4 Appalachian-style wood huts; and 5 cabins and 2 yurts. Reservations advised in season; call 303-470-1144 or 800-678-2267. Camping fee. Backcountry sites are issued on a first-come, first-served basis at the Visitor Center.

Golden Gate Canyon State Park, 92 Crawford Gulch Rd., Golden, CO 80403; 303-582-3707; www.parks.state.co.us/parks/goldengatecanyon

279

Eldorado Canyon

Just west of Eldorado Springs via Colo. 170

- 885 acres in two units ▪ Year-round ▪ Entrance fee ▪ No camping
- Wild canyon ▪ Rock climbing, hiking, mountain biking

A spectacular, narrow canyon rising 800 feet from South Boulder Creek forms the core of Eldorado Canyon State Park. Speckled with vivid multicolored lichen, its sunlit red rock seems to glitter, recalling the fabled city of El Dorado—"the Gilded One." Long a shelter for Native Americans, it became a popular destination in the early 1900s for its scenery and artesian warm springs. Dwight and Mamie Eisenhower honeymooned here in 1916. One of the highlights then was the high-wire act of Ivy Baldwin, who walked a 400-foot-long wire strung 500 feet up. The canyon was preserved as a state park in 1978.

Eldorado Canyon is a well-known rock-climbing site, with more than 500 designated routes. **Bastille Crack** is perhaps the region's most popular 5.8 climb (a climber's degree of difficulty, with 5.14 the hardest), and the **Naked Edge,** at 5.11, was for a time considered the world's most difficult free climb. Even if you don't climb, watching the climbers attack the walls is entertainment in itself.

Mountain lion

Begin at the **Visitor Center,** where exhibits detail the natural history. If time is short, hike the 1.4-mile round-trip **Fowler Trail** (trailhead 0.5 mile east of the Visitor Center), which offers spectacular views of the plains beyond; on the canyon's opposite side, watch climbers advancing up Redgarden Wall.

If you have more time, take the moderately steep, 3.4-mile round-trip **Rattle-snake Gulch Trail** (from Fowler Trailhead) for views of the canyon and plains, up to the Crags Hotel ruin. The hotel burned down in 1913. The trail leads a little farther to an overlook of the Continental Divide, 1,200 breathtaking feet above the trailhead.

The **Crescent Meadows** portion of the park—featuring hiking and mountain-biking trails that wind through high, rolling meadows—is detached from the main canyon section and is most easily reached by car. However, there is a hiking connection via the **Eldorado Canyon Trail,** a difficult 7-mile out-and-back trek that gains more than 1,000 feet in elevation in less than 5 miles. Ask for directions at the Visitor Center.

Eldorado Canyon State Park, P.O. Box B, Eldorado Springs, CO 80025; 303-494-3943; www.parks.state.co.us/parks/eldoradocanyon

Lory
7 miles northwest of Fort Collins via US 287

■ 2,479 acres ■ Year-round ■ Entrance fee ■ Hiking, mountain biking, horseback riding ■ Wildlife viewing ■ Backcountry camping

Lory State Park sits in the Rocky Mountain foothills outside Fort Collins, where the grassy plains make an abrupt transition to a lower montane forest of ponderosa pine, Douglas fir, and aspen. The park fills a long valley that tips toward Horsetooth Reservoir, whose shimmering blue waters peek through low, red-rock canyon walls. Once ranchland, this area was acquired by the state in 1967 and named for Dr. Charles A. Lory, former president of Colorado State University.

Lory's chief attraction is its 25 miles of hiking trails. The park's marquee trail is the 1.7-mile trip up **Arthur's Rock.** Beginning at the end of the park road in a narrow granite canyon, the moderate-to-difficult trail switchbacks up the granite outcrop. Here, you find a panoramic view to the east, taking in most of Fort Collins and Loveland below. If you are short on time but still want a flavor of the park, take the **Well Gulch Nature Trail,** an easy 1.5-mile self-guided tour of the area's vegetation and ecology. It ends at the **Timber Trail,** providing the option of continuing on through thick forest. The new **Howard Trail** offers a chance to challenge yourself on a 6.2-mile loop connecting with the Timber Trail. The **Waterfall Trail,** located just inside the park entrance, offers a short (only one-tenth of a mile), pleasant stroll beside a series of small waterfalls (spring and early summer).

For mountain bikers, the new **Corral Center Mountain Bike Park** offers 69,000 square feet of riding excitement for all skill levels. Dirt jumps, a pump track, and a skills area are available for those wishing to hone their off-road riding skills.

One of Lory's attractions is its wildflowers. With the bloom season lasting 6 to 8 months it is a popular place for nature photography.

Camping
There are 6 backcountry sites; permits are required and are available at the park entrance on a first-come, first-served basis. Camping fee.

Lory State Park, 708 Lodgepole Dr., Bellvue, CO 80512; 970-493-1623; www.parks.state.co.us/parks/lory

281

Sugarite Canyon

6 miles east of Raton via N. Mex. 72 and N. Mex. 526

■ 3,420 acres ■ Year-round ■ 1,200-foot-deep canyon ■ Wildflowers ■ Boating, hiking, fishing (license required) ■ Cross-country skiing, ice skating

One of New Mexico's prettiest parks, Sugarite Canyon abuts Colorado's mountainous high country, where abundant water creates a lush mix of ecosystems. There are stands of fir and aspen on north-facing slopes; riparian grasslands on the meadowlike canyon floor; and scrub oak and ponderosa pine on sunnier, drier south slopes. The terrain is colorfully stippled by exuberant wildflower blooms in spring and summer.

The 1,200-foot-deep canyon was once hunted by the Ute and Apache, who came for its wild turkey (still abundant), deer, and beaver. From 1910 to 1941, mining sustained the Sugarite Coal Camp, swelling its population to a peak of 1,000 and bequeathing to the park an evocative collection of tumbledown stone buildings and foundations.

PITTSBURGH OF NEW MEXICO: Raton—Spanish for mouse—was a sleepy stopover on the Santa Fe Trail until 1879, when the new Atchison, Topeka & Santa Fe Railroad established a repair station there. Within a year the town claimed 3,000 citizens. Proximity to rails made for easy shipment of traditional building materials rare in the Southwest. Raton soon possessed so many Eastern-style structures that boosters proclaimed it the "Pittsburgh of New Mexico." Leaner decades followed, saving Raton's antique architecture from the demolition ball. The result is a downtown historic district of unusual authenticity.

What to See and Do

Take N. Mex. 72 east and north from Raton, bearing left after 4.8 miles onto N. Mex. 526. You'll soon reach the **Visitor Center,** where superb exhibits showcase Sugarite's natural and human history and its plant and animal life.

The historical accounts deepen your appreciation of the polyglot culture that briefly flourished in the coal-mining camp whose ruins adjoin. Take the 1-mile **Coal Camp Trail** (summer) from the Visitor Center along rattling Chicorica Creek. Crossing it, you'll find what remains of the camp, once populated mainly by laborers from the Far East and Europe. The path soon forks: The Coal Camp Trail continues to an abandoned mine, then loops back to the parking area.

Back in your car, continue north along the Chicorica past tiny **Lake Alice,** whose serenity is preserved by a boating restriction. Gasoline motors are banned on larger **Lake Maloya,** farther north. Both lakes are stocked with rainbow trout, and Lake Maloya has a fishing pier specially designed for flycasters in wheelchairs.

About a mile north of Lake Alice, a turnoff leads to **Soda Pocket Campground.** The new 1-mile **Deer Run Trail** *(foot traffic only)* connects Lake Alice and Soda Pocket Campground and provides stunning views of Lake Alice. At Soda Pocket, 25 sites stretch over a half mile of oaks, ponderosa pines, and meadows, with pleasing views of volcanic cones and hills to the south. Take time to walk the easy 0.25-mile **Vista Grande Nature Trail** looping away from the southwest corner. Self-guiding pamphlets keyed to markers reveal why Sugarite has such a diversity of wildlife—including cougar, bear, and elk. The trail ends on a knoll where you can sit on a bench and savor a grand view of the canyon. It's a bit arduous, but the nearby 0.25-mile **Little Horse Mesa Trail** to the 8,300-foot-high caprock of Little Horse Mesa ends with vistas extending north into Colorado.

Consider the moderately strenuous **Ponderosa Ridge/Opportunity Trail,** a 6-mile circle that leaves Soda Pocket's north end and passes through a succession of environments to panoramic canyon views from 8,100 feet. (In winter, the Opportunity Trail segment of the loop, which begins at Lake Maloya, is an excellent route for cross-country skiing and snowshoeing.)

Bull elk

283

Camping

There are 41 tent and RV sites, with nearby showers. Reservations advised in season; call 877-664-7787. Camping fee.

Sugarite Canyon State Park, HCR 63, P.O. Box 386, Raton, NM 87740; 575-445-5607; www.nmparks.com

Clayton Lake

12 miles northwest of Clayton via N. Mex. 370 and N. Mex. 455

▪ 570 acres ▪ Year-round ▪ Dinosaur tracks ▪ Rock garden ▪ Fishing (March–Oct., license required) ▪ Bird-watching ▪ Boating (March–Oct.)

A remarkably well-preserved dinosaur trackway with more than 500 footprints left in mud some 100 million years ago (one of the most extensive in North America) distinguish this out-of-the-way fishing spot and migratory bird refuge. Set on the mile-high western edge of the Great Plains among rolling grasslands, volcanic rocks, and sandstone bluffs, the park embraces a 170-acre lake noted for trout, catfish, bass, and walleye fishing from April through October. (New Mexico's record walleye, a giant of 16 pounds 9 ounces, was

Dinosaur tracks

hooked here in 1989.) A dam across Seneca Creek started the reservoir in 1955, creating a stopover for mallards, Canada geese, bald eagles, pintails, teals, and other waterfowl. Protective hillsides provide a windbreak, and rocky beaches notch the lake's rocky shoreline.

Heading toward the park from Clayton, the two-lane road wiggles through terrain that's scenic in a wide-open-spaces way, evoking the isolation 19th-century travelers must have felt as they traversed these lonely grasslands on the Santa Fe Trail's Cimarron Cutoff.

Inside the entrance gate, the new **Visitor Center** displays casts and exhibits focusing on the 100-million-year-old tracks. Walk the 0.25-mile trail across the dam to the **Dinosaur Pavilion interpretive center.** An adjoining boardwalk affords a close look at the tracks, impressions from the Mesozoic era, in the age of the dinosaurs. The best times for viewing the tracks are early morning and late afternoon on sunny days, when shadows darken their depressions. The awesome footprints are preserved in stone that was once the muddy shoreline of a primordial seaway running north from the Gulf of Mexico to what is now Canada. At least eight species planted their three-toed feet here. Some were plant eaters, some preyed on their cousins, and at least one, the giant sea crocodile, approached from below. Back at the parking lot is the boat launching ramp. *(Sailboats, canoes, and fishing scows are permitted, but motorized craft are restricted to trolling speeds.)*

PARK TIP: *Look among the beautiful rock formations along the Nature Trail for the buried petroglyphs.*

Camping

The park has 42 tent and RV sites, with showers. Reservations in season; call 877-664-7787. Camping fee.

Clayton Lake State Park, 141 Clayton Lake Rd., Clayton, NM 88415; 575-374-8808; www.nmparks.com

Heron Lake and El Vado Lake

Heron Lake: 5 miles southwest of Los Ojos via US 84 and N. Mex. 95.
El Vado Lake: 21 miles southwest of Tierra Amarilla via N. Mex. 531
and N. Mex. 112

- Heron Lake: 10,012 acres; El Vado Lake: 4,948 acres ▪ Year-round
- Two scenic lakes ▪ Hiking ▪ Swimming, sailing, boating, windsurfing, fishing (license required), Jet skiing ▪ Bird-watching ▪ Biking, snow-shoeing, cross-country skiing

A scenic day hike links the adjoining lakes of Heron and El Vado in northern New Mexico's forested mountain country, each surrounded by its own state park. On Heron Lake, a "no wake" speed limit makes the 5,900-acre reservoir especially popular with flycasters, sailors, windsurfers, swimmers, and campers who value tranquility. There are no speed limits on 3,200-acre El Vado Lake, where motorboaters, water-skiers, and Jet skiers roil the water from spring through autumn. Come winter, cross-country skiers, snowshoers, and dogsledders mush into the parks' snowbound timberlands.

Both lakes serve as important wintering grounds for bald eagles, which you may see perched on snags along the water's edge or floating by overhead. Preying on other birds, snakes, small animals, and fish, these majestic predators boast a wingspan up to 8 feet. Other birds to watch for include red-tailed hawks, white-throated swifts, ospreys, common mergansers, and western flycatchers.

What to See and Do

Primitive backcountry roads and the Rio Chama canyon make it difficult to access one park from the other. It's quicker and easier to backtrack to US 84 and loop around.

For peace, solitude, and a wider selection of campsites, make **Heron Lake** your destination. Southbound from Los Ojos on N. Mex. 95, watch for signs indicating the turnoff into **Willow Creek Recreation Area,** the reservoir's prime camping spot. There is a paved boat ramp here, and another just past the dam near the Ridge Rock campground. If you brought a boat, both lakes have serpentine shorelines with many sheltered coves, where fishing for trout and salmon is good. On Heron, windsurfers usually first check the breezes off the Island View, Brushy Point, and Salmon Run camping areas east of the dam.

You can rent a canoe or boat in Rutheron from the rustic Stone House Lodge near **El Vado Lake's** north end

---

YOU SAY YOU HATE CAMPING?
You say you had a miserable camping experience years ago? It's time to try again. Improved equipment has greatly reduced the labor associated with outdoor adventure. Forget the unwieldy canvas tents and heavy sleeping bags you shivered in at camp. Today's tents set up as easily as folding tables, and modern sleeping bags are as toasty as comforters. Forget leaky air mattresses that seldom made it through the night; newfangled sleeping pads inflate themselves. And for the ultimate luxury, fill a plastic-bag "solar shower" with water, leave it in the sun, and count on a hot shower at night.

Heron Lake's south shore

off N. Mex. 95. Built in 1935 by the Santa Fe Elks Club, the lodge is now privately operated, and a pleasant place to dine. In winter it's a bustling base camp for parties of cross-country skiers.

El Vado Lake's waterskiing season lasts from May through September, with skiers generally favoring the lake's northeastern arm. Conventional wisdom among flycasters is that the odds are best at the dam and just below it, where the Rio Chama runs free again. (A 20-pound 4-ounce brown trout reeled in here in 1946 still holds the state record for the species.)

If you're in good shape (remember that Heron has a 6,900-foot elevation) and have a day, walk the 5.5-mile **Rio Chama Trail** from the southwest corner of Heron Lake to El Vado Lake. Rated highly by naturalists, the trail explores the river canyon—crossing the Rio Chama on a suspended bridge—then winds overland past lofty viewpoints and meadows where quaking aspen flutter in the breeze. The trail is fairly strenuous, with occasionally slippery footing across rocky terrain. Sturdy hiking shoes are a must.

Camping

Heron Lake has 200 tent and RV sites (54 with electric and water), with showers. Another 100 primitive sites are situated west of the spillway. At El Vado Lake there are 60 tent and 20 RV sites (19 with electric and water), with showers. Reservations advised in season; contact both parks at 877-664-7787. Camping fee.

El Vado Lake State Park, P.O. Box 367, Tierra Amarilla, NM 87575; Heron Lake State Park, P.O. Box 159, Los Ojos, NM 87551; 575-588-7470 (Heron Lake) and 505-588-7247 (El Vado Lake); www.nmparks .com

Oliver Lee Memorial

8 miles south of Alamogordo via US 54, then 4 miles east on Dog Canyon Rd.

- 640 acres ▪ Year-round ▪ Vehicle fee ▪ Desert canyon oasis ▪ Hiking
- Bird-watching ▪ Nature trail

A west-trending cut in the massive 35-mile-long Sacramento Mountain Escarpment, Dog Canyon—Cañon del Perro—alerts the instincts at first sight: From the Tularosa Basin's sweep of yucca, mesquite, and prickly pear cactus, you sense a natural stronghold. Entering the canyon, you find an attenuated oasis between steep cliffs, watered by seeps and springs, and a rocky stairway into the piney Sacramento and Guadalupe Mountain uplands 3,000 feet above. The water and lush growth attracted both Native Americans and European settlers. Preserved here are rock walls and an irrigation system built by an immigrant French homesteader in the 1890s.

PARK TIP: *Relax and enjoy the succession of seasonal wildflowers and cactus blooms in the Chihuahuan desert garden.*

287

Start your visit at the **Visitor Center** beside the canyon mouth, where a 0.5-mile **Nature Trail** showcases native plants. Follow the creek through willows, cottonwoods, and ashes past wild orchids and ferns that grow on the steep faces. Birds and wildlife thrive here in this verdant canyon, which is highly unusual in this parched region.

Exhibits inside explain the chasm's geology, identify its abundant wildlife, and sketch its most significant historical events. Archaeological artifacts date from prehistoric human settlement through the late 19th-century homesteading era.

Wear sturdy shoes, take plenty of water with you, and plan on devoting an entire day to walk the strenuous 5.5-mile **Dog Canyon National Recreational Trail,** which climbs 3,100 feet from the Visitor Center to the trail's end on Joplin Ridge. This trail traces the route used by Native Americans for at least 4,000 years; during the 19th century, the canyon was an impregnable Apache enclave. Do not be daunted by this rigorous trail because even the first half-mile brings rewards—spectacular views of the White Sands and Tularosa Basin.

Ask about weekend tours of the reconstructed Oliver Lee **ranch house,** home of a controversial cattle baron and state lawmaker, who made the Dog Canyon area his headquarters in 1893 and figured large in New Mexico affairs until his death in 1941.

Camping

The park has 44 tent and RV sites, with showers. Reservations advised Feb.–April; call 877-664-7787. Camping fee.

Oliver Lee Memorial State Park, 409 Dog Canyon Rd., Alamogordo, NM 88310; 575-437-8284; www.nmparks.com

Slide Rock

7 miles north of Sedona, off US 89A

- 43 acres ▪ Year-round ▪ Parking fee ▪ No pets ▪ No camping
- Red-rock canyon ▪ Natural water slide ▪ Apple orchard ▪ Nature
walks ▪ Trout fishing (license required), hiking, bird-watching

People who urge you to visit Sedona often cite the scenic drive through the piney corridor of 12-mile-long **Oak Creek Canyon** as the primary reason. US 89A follows the stream's 2,000-foot-deep cut into the Colorado Plateau's rock shelf, skirting sheer-sided white, yellow, and red sandstone and limestone cliffs representing some three million years of erosion. About halfway through the gorge, the highway passes **Slide Rock,** one of Arizona's most popular natural playgrounds, best known for an 80-foot-long water chute worn by eons of water coursing over sandstone. Come autumn at Slide Rock, nearby Hospital Canyon's dense groves of Douglas fir, Gambel oak, bigtooth maple, sycamore, and Arizona walnut burst into vivid colors with the cymbal-clashing bombast of an orchestra.

Sliding down Slide Rock

Traffic through Oak Creek Canyon is often heavy from spring through fall, making it difficult to savor the wooded beauty and vertical drama of the enclosing cliffs. Take your camera and a pair of old jeans and shoes if you want to try the chilly water and the not-very-smooth ride down the slide. The park only has several short walks, but it is adjacent to the Secret Mountain Wilderness Area.

Early 20th-century homesteader Frank Pendley's legacy to Slide Rock is an **apple orchard,** still producing more than a dozen varieties harvested in autumn and sold at the park's snack bar. If it is a good apple year, visitors can pick and buy their own apples.

The park is a day-use area only; however, there are several campgrounds in the surrounding **Coconino National Forest** *(982-282-4119).*

Slide Rock State Park, P.O. Box 10358, Sedona, AZ 86339; 928-282-3034; www.azstateparks.com; www.fs.fed.us/r3/coconino

Red Rock

5 miles west of Sedona, off US 89A via Lower Red Rock Loop Rd.

- 286 acres - Entrance fee - No pets - No camping - Nature preserve
- Environmental Center - Hiking - Wildlife viewing, bird-watching

289

After a visit to Red Rock, a recreation spot on Oak Creek only 16 miles from Slide Rock, you might call it an outdoor living museum or think of it as one big interpretive nature trail. Biologists classify it as a diverse riparian habitat, rich as Eden in plant life and wildlife, and once a hunting ground of the Sinagua, Hohokom, and Yavapai peoples. Park literature dubs Red Rock a center for environmental education. In fact it is all of these, in a setting that begs to have its picture taken.

As its name implies, the park is framed by sheer cliffs of rust-red Hermit Formation sandstone that distinguishes the Sedona region, the product of iron oxide–rich silt deposited some 270 million years ago at the bottom of a primordial sea.

The park has ten nature trails, each exploring a distinctive life zone. Ranger-guided nature walks leave from the Visitor Center daily. Call ahead to ask about these times and about their year-round sunset walks and moonlight hikes, offered May through Oct.

EARLY FARMERS: Planting seeds in holes dug with sticks, the Southwest's early farming tribes grew varieties of corn, beans, squash, sunflowers, gourds, amaranth, and devil's claw. They used sunflower oil for cooking, and hollow gourds for bowls, scoops, cups, canteens, and other containers. Amaranth seeds mixed with other seeds thickened stews and soups, and were ground for flour. Black devil's claw fibers were woven into baskets for decoration. When boiled, they produced a deep black dye. Every March during Arizona's Archaeology Month, the park hosts various demonstrations including atlatl throwing, arrowhead making, and the how-to's of primitive firemaking.

Kingfisher Bridge over Oak Creek

For a sampler self-guided walk of Red Rock's diverse environments, take the 0.5-mile **Smoke Trail.** You wander past Bonpland willow and Arizona alder, ascending from one life zone to another. Drier, higher zones bring netleaf hackberry, whose leaves and branches local tribes boiled to produce dyes. Then comes the region's trademark red-earth, dusky-green pinyon-juniper, and scrub oak habitat. Rock faces near the trail's end bear petroglyphs, art probably the work of Sinagua people who, it's believed, camped here seasonally to hunt, fish, and perhaps farm between A.D. 600 and 1200.

Throughout the year, **Oak Creek** creates a natural refuge noisily abounding with birdlife, the variety of which is especially apparent to those with binoculars and a field guide. Arrive early on Wednesday and Saturday mornings throughout the year for ranger-guided bird walks, which leave the Visitor Center area at 7 a.m. in summer and 8 a.m. in winter.

Red Rock is a day-use area only; however, nearby campgrounds in the **Coconino National Forest** *(928-282-4119)* offer similar terrain.

Red Rock State Park, 4050 Lower Red Rock Loop Rd., Sedona, AZ 86336; 928-282-6907; www.azstateparks.com

Tonto Natural Bridge

13 miles northwest of Payson, off Ariz. 87

■ 160 acres ■ Year-round ■ Parking fee ■ No camping ■ Natural rock bridge ■ Nature trails ■ Swimming, wading ■ Historic building

Whether or not it truly is the world's largest natural travertine span, Tonto Natural Bridge's massive 183-foot-high arch over a 400-foot-long tunnel cut by spring-fed Pine Creek could hardly be more impressive. Nor could the park's setting, in a small, steep, forested valley notched by the stream's narrow canyon, create a more appealing, hidden-away-from-the-world feeling.

The Tonto Apache had used the site as a seasonal farming and hunting camp for nearly four centuries when, in 1877, a nomadic Scottish gold prospector named David Gowan escaped attacking warriors by darting into the dark passage and hiding on a ledge inside. Venturing out three days later, he found the all-but-inaccessible valley, with its dripping grotto, grassy meadows, and cool forest so inviting that he returned in 1882 to settle on the land. In 1898, kinfolk named Goodfellow emigrated from Scotland to join him and file a homestead claim. Their pack burros could barely negotiate the narrow, 3-mile-long trail into the valley; most of their possessions had to be lowered down the 500-foot slope with rope.

The bridge's fame spread, attracting visitors, and by 1908, the Goodfellow clan had carved out a cliff-hanging entrance road and built a guest lodge on the meadow below. Goodfellow completed the lodge in 1927, and it now serves as a small museum, displaying antiques and Gowan-Goodfellow family heirlooms; it's listed on the National Register of Historic Places.

> **BRIDGE-BUILDING: Tonto Natural Bridge is actually a part of the floor of the valley that surrounds it. Long ago, spring water high in concentrations of calcium carbonate laid down the bowl's flat travertine floor, across which primordial Pine Creek flowed. Some creek water seeped down through the rock, eventually opening up a small subterranean fissure. Erosion continued below as more travertine was deposited above, eventually channeling the stream's entire flow beneath the slowly thickening bridge. Geologists trace the beginning of this bridge-building activity back 1.7 billion years.**

291

What to See and Do

A day-use area only, the park is probably the most appealing public picnic spot in central Arizona's forested high country. (The elevation here is about 4,500 feet.) Leave your car in a parking area and walk to the renovated inn for a glimpse of the genteel styles of old-time "guest ranching" and an historical overview. If possible, include an alfresco lunch on the meadow flanking the inn.

Park trails are short, but steep and rough in places. Don sturdy shoes before you embark on the 0.5-mile **Gowan Trail,** which winds down from the roof of the bridge into **Pine Creek Canyon,** where an observation deck permits a dramatic view upstream through the passage, yawning 150 feet at its widest. From creekside you're look-ing up nearly 200 feet to the top of the bridge. You may explore the drippy tunnel, but rangers advise using caution, as the passage is dim and the footing slippery.

The 300-foot-long **Waterfall Trail** from the picnic area adjoin-ing the lodge stops short of the stream beside a small cascade and a cave similar to the one inside the tunnel where Gowan hid. For a leafy creek bank idyll, walk the 0.5-mile **Pine Creek Trail** beginning northeast of the waterfall parking lot. You'll quickly descend into a cool, dim, and peaceful fairyland of overhanging ferns and trickling springs. The new **Anna Mae Trail** descends 500 feet and offers more views of the canyon.

The park is a day-use facility only. The nearby Houston Mesa Campground in **Tonto National Forest** (*at junction of north Ariz. 87 and Houston Mesa Rd.*) has 75 tent and RV sites and a horse camp with 30 sites. For reservations and information call 877-444-6777. Camping fee.

Tonto Natural Bridge State Park, P.O. Box 1245, Payson, AZ 85547; 928-476-4202; www.azstateparks.com

Kartchner Caverns

Near Benson, off Ariz. 90, 8 miles south of I-10 exit 302

■ 550 acres ■ Year-round ■ Cavern tours, camping, hiking ■ Fee

In 1974, when cave explorers Randy Tufts and Gary Tenen discov-ered this beautiful limestone cave on the east side of the Whetstone Mountains, they dared not publicize their find until the site's protec-tion could be guaranteed. Preparing for visitor access meant elaborate planning and meticulous construction aimed at preserving this "liv-ing" cave.

During construction, workers found a number of fossils, the most impressive of which were the bones of a giant Shasta ground sloth estimated to have lived 80,000 years ago. Paleontologists also identified the bones of an ancient horse and a bear.

Start at the **Visitor Center,** where impressive displays provide an introduction to cave formation and ecology. A multimedia show in the Discovery Center recounts how the explorers found and entered the cave. Exhibits illustrate the formation of the cave and its features. A copy of the Throne Room's 21-foot soda straw stalac-tite hangs inside.

The park offers two tours, each a half-mile loop on paved trails (no steps); both are very popular and advance reservations are highly recommended. The Rotunda/Throne Room Tour goes year-round, but the Big Room Tour closes mid-April–mid-October to protect the myotis bats inside. A tram takes you up a hill to the cave entrance, where you pass through an air lock that maintains the 99 percent humidity needed for growth of the cave formations. Temperatures average a comfortable 68°F. Your guide will identify the many types of cave features seen on the 1.5- to 1.75-hour tours. The rich colors of the features come from hematite, manganese, and organic matter that have seeped in through the ceiling.

Above ground, you can wander in the hummingbird garden, hike the 2.4-mile **Foothills Loop Trail,** or head out on the 4.2-mile **Guindani Trail Loop** in adjacent Coronado National Forest.

Camping

The park has 62 campsites, all with electrical hookups. Available on a first-come, first-served basis. Camping fee.

Kartchner Caverns State Park, P.O. Box 1849, Benson, AZ 85602; 520-586-4100 (information), 520-586-2283 (tour reservations); www.azstateparks.com

The Kubla Kahn Formation, Kartchner Caverns

Antelope Island

35 miles north of Salt Lake City, off Utah 127

- 28,022 acres ▪ Year-round ▪ Entrance fee ▪ Buffalo ranch
- Scenic loop drive ▪ Saltwater bathing ▪ Boating, bird-watching, hiking, biking, horseback riding ▪ Wildlife viewing

The biggest of the Great Salt Lake's ten isles, with an area roughly twice that of Manhattan Island, Utah's largest state park rises nearly 2,400 feet above the saline sea, its treeless tan rumple of rocky ridges, hilly grasslands, and flat sagebrush prairie tethered to the mainland by a 7.2-mile causeway. For urbanites escaping the Ogden–Salt Lake City sprawl, the 8-mile paved scenic loop through the park is a popular day trip. The lake's extreme salinity (six to eight times that of the sea) makes for unusually buoyant floating.

Playa patterns, left by receding lake waters

Members of the Great Salt Lake band of Utah's prehistoric Fremont people living in the Wasatch foothills probably hunted the island's mule deer, waterfowl, and game birds: Described in the 1820s by trapper Jim Bridger and French explorer Étienne Provot, Antelope Island went unnamed by newcomers until the 1840s, when low water permitted frontiersman John C. Frémont and his guide, Kit Carson, to spur horses across what is usually briny shallows. Spotting pronghorn antelope (reintroduced to the island a few years ago), they christened it accordingly.

They might have called it Bobcat Island, or Coyote Island, for these creatures also roam its north-south trending ridgelines and slopes, along with myriad other small animals. Though not native to the isle, American bison were introduced in 1893, and about 600 graze here. In March 1997, a small herd of bighorn sheep was placed on the island.

Ranching began in 1848, when Mormon pioneers drove cattle out to the island and settler Fielding Garr claimed a knoll overlooking the southeastern shore and built an adobe ranch house. The following year, he led his wife and six children across the threshold, creating a monument to Utah's strong family tradition. Occupied until about a decade ago, the stolid residence became the state's oldest continually inhabited pioneer-built house.

What to See and Do

From I-15, take the Syracuse exit west to the 7.2-mile Davis County Causeway, which has extra-wide bike lanes for pedaling or roller-blading from the "mainland." (If you don't have a bicycle, check phone listings for bike rentals in the Clearfield/Syracuse area east of the causeway.)

In recent years, parts of the island's more mountainous, ecologically fragile southern reach have been opened to visitors. Plans call for increased access and an enlarged trail system. Today, about 36 miles of trails cross over into the limited-use area, permitting hikers, horseback riders, and bicyclists to venture south.

The causeway road passes the **marina** and follows the island's northern shoreline. Watch for signs to the **Visitor Center,** which has

Map labels: 127 · Marina · Egg Island Overlook · Visitor Center · Bridger Bay · Buffalo Bay · Ladyfinger Springs · Buffalo Point · 4,785 ft · Buffalo Corral · Intermittent Shallow Water · Great Salt Lake · 2 mi · 2 km · Camera Flats · White Rock Bay · Elephant Head 5,126 ft · Dairy Springs · Intermittent Shallow Water · ANTELOPE · N · Stringham Peak 6,374 ft · ISLAND · Cambria Point · Red Rocks 6,198 ft · Bamberger Hill · Garr Ranch House · Sea Gull Point · Cedar Spring · Great Salt Lake · Mushroom Springs · Blackburn Spring · Porcupine Spring · Westside Spring · Dooly Spring · Freds Spring · Mollys Nipple 5,387 ft · McIntyre Spring · Salt Flat

Inset map: 84 · 15 · 91 · 89 · Tremonton · Logan · 91 · 83 · Brigham City · 89 · Great Salt Lake · 15 · Promontory Point · 84 · 39 · 108 · Ogden · CAUSEWAY · Clearfield · 89 · 84 · 127 · ANTELOPE ISLAND STATE PARK · Salt Lake City · 80 · 215 · 15 · N · 20 mi · 30 km · 80

295

STILL UNTAMED: Though Great Salt Lake averages only 14 feet deep (its greatest known depth is 40 feet), fluctuating water levels have played havoc with park access. The lake's surface normally stands at 4,200 feet and covers an area roughly 75 by 30 miles, about 1,500 square miles of brine. In 1983, however, record Wasatch Range runoff flooded the causeway, closing Antelope Island for a decade. (Levels peaked 12 feet above normal in 1987, claiming an additional 1,000 square miles of shoreline.) A massive pumping program diverted water to an adjoining evaporation basin, and all's well again—for now.

an excellent little historical and natural history museum. Here you'll find maps of the park's roads and trails, and current information about access to the island's southern reach. The **Garr Ranch House,** located 11 miles south of the Visitor Center, is open on a daily basis. Horse-and-buggy rides are available from the ranch *(801-782-4946. Fee).*

Continue on to **Egg Island Overlook,** where an easy 0.25-mile trail leads to a promontory with a view of **Egg Island,** a seagull and migratory bird rookery in Bridger Bay. Picnic tables here make the overlook an appealing place to linger and scout the long white beach fronting Bridger Bay. (It's not sand you'll see, but tiny rock pellets called oolites, deposited by brine shrimp and encrusted with calcium carbonate crystals to form their distinctive oval shape.)

Coming off the hill, you'll pass a succession of picnic areas along the Bridger Bay strand, Antelope's most popular swimming and sunbathing spot. Don't miss the café and its house specialty, broiled buffalo burgers. A spur road leads to Bridger Bay Campground. From here, a 3-mile trail winds south along the lakeshore to a group camping ground at **White Rock Bay.**

PARK TIP: *Try the new 6-mile loop Sentry Trail originating at Garr Ranch; it provides spectacular views of the island and the Great Salt Lake.*

Be sure to drive up to **Buffalo Point Overlook.** You can walk the short but steep 0.25-mile trail up to 4,785-foot-high **Buffalo Point,** a lookout with a 360-degree panorama.

Most of the park's bison range freely in the island's southern section, keeping their distance from visitors. Several of the shaggy brown beasts are kept ready for close-ups in the **Buffalo Corral,** where they graze with a ponderous dignity. If you're in the market for your own bison, plan to attend the annual fall bison roundup, where the herd is thinned and extra animals sold to the public.

Camping

The park has 2 campgrounds, one at Bridger Bay with 26 primitive tent and RV sites, and the other on White Rock Bay with 12 large group sites (801-773-2941). For camping reservations call 801-322-3770. Camping fee.

Antelope Island State Park, 4528 West 1700 South, Syracuse, UT 84075; 801-773-2941; www.stateparks.utah.gov

Coral Pink Sand Dunes

11 miles off US 89, northwest of Kanab

■ 3,730 acres ■ Year-round ■ Entrance fee ■ Hiking, biking, horseback riding, photography ■ OHVs

Notice the namesake dunes as you near Coral Pink Sand Dunes State Park, and you will attest that they are pink (up close more red or orange). The dune field located 35 miles from Zion National Park is optically a world away. Composed of 10,000- to 15,000-year-old iron-oxide crystals, the dunes were formed by wind funneling through a crack in the Navajo sandstone rock between the Moccasin and Moquith Mountains—known as the Venturi effect.

The place to start, once in the park (mountain bikers may decide the roads outside the park are the most fun), is with the 0.5-mile nature trail and accessible concrete walkway, which provide an orientation to the dunes. Then it's off to the dunes. The object is to enjoy them—run, jump, roll, or just walk. Although you will be sharing the dunes, including two high ones—110 feet and 90 feet—with off-highway vehicles (OHV), there is plenty of room for both the hiker and 4-wheeler to coexist. *(OHVs are required to stay 100 feet from pedestrians, 265 acres are off-limits at all times, and all vehicles are prohibited from 10 p.m. to 9 a.m., so enjoy the dunes during the quiet hours.)* Despite the struggle to climb to the top of the larger dunes, the view is worth it. On a perfect day you might get a glimpse of the North Rim of the Grand Canyon.

On a sweltering day, it's understandable if you assume that nothing lives here, but you couldn't be further from the truth. Look at the sand and note the prints of the creatures that survive here, among them the threatened Coral Pink Sand Dunes tiger beetle *(Cicindela limbata albissima),* about the size of a thumbnail. Other wildlife includes lizards and beetles, deer and fox. *Do be aware that it is easy to become disoriented among the dunes, so always carry water and a map!*

Camping

The park has 22 tent and RV sites, with showers. Reservations recommended; call 800-322-3770. Camping fee.

Coral Pink Sand Dunes State Park, P.O. Box 95, Kanab, UT 84741; 435-648-2800; www.stateparks .utah.gov

Spring in Coral Pink Sand Dunes

297

Dead Horse Point

31 miles from Moab via Utah 191 and Utah 313

- 5,362 acres ▪ Year-round ▪ Entrance fee ▪ Interpretive museum
- Hiking ▪ Limited water available

Dead Horse Point

Carved mainly by the Colorado and Green Rivers, the vast, labyrinthine wilderness of southeast Utah's canyonlands is so impressive, so provocative, and so enticing that it's no wonder the panoramas from 5,900-foot-high Dead Horse Point are often praised as the most spectacular of any Beehive State park. Add a scenic drive from Moab through sand and sagebrush canyons, past cliffs and spires of liver-hued Kayenta sandstone, and you have one of Utah's most memorable day trips—ending with long views sweeping some 50 miles south across Canyonlands National Park to a horizon steepled by the Henry, La Sal, and Abajo Mountains. Easy walking trails along the mesa flirt with the edge of the 2,000-foot-deep gorge, leading to a half dozen overlooks of some of the Southwest's least-accessible public land.

Wranglers once corralled wild mustangs on the long, narrow rimrock promontory for which the park is named. Local lore holds that culls, or "broomtails," left there unfenced failed to move to nearby water-filled slickrock potholes and died of thirst. Nothing else here conjures dark thoughts, however; the scenery is simply too grand.

If time is limited, drive to Dead Horse Point, leave your car, and walk to **Dead Horse Point Overlook,** the park's signature panorama. You can savor the experience of this exhilarating overlook by parking at the **Visitor Center,** letting its historical and geological exhibits deepen your appreciation, then strolling the 1.5-mile **Main Trail,** skirting the mesa's southeast precipice to the 90-foot-wide "neck" of the promontory (where the wranglers placed their fence). From here, stroll the half mile to the Dead Horse Point Overlook and the Observation Shelter in the day-use area, whose picnic tables are arguably the best situated in Canyonlands.

From here, the main trail loops back along the mesa's western edge to the **Meander Overlook.** Less well-marked and with trickier footing, this footpath looks down on an exceptionally complex landscape—spires, pinnacles, buttes, and convoluted benchlands and wriggly canyons notorious for disorienting wilderness hikers. Keep walking north and you'll come to the **Rim Overlook,** and then the **Big Horn Overlook,** each claiming a section of the Canyonlands panorama. Along the way you'll encounter shallow slickrock concavities called potholes, some supporting tiny fairy shrimp and tadpoles.

Check at the Visitor Center for ranger-led activities, particularly the evening talks offered from late spring through early autumn.

> **FLOATING CANYONLANDS:**
> The Green River's gorge holds magnificent, ever changing rock formations. Outfitters in Moab rent fully equipped canoes at modest prices, drop you off near Canyonlands National Park's northern boundary, and pick you up 3 to 6 days and some 60 placid river miles south at The Confluence, where the olive-drab stream joins the Colorado. In between are ancient Indian ruins and petroglyphs; The Maze, a vast puzzle of dry canyons; and silence so pure you'll hear things you might not have heard before, like the feathery whistle of bird wings and the beating of your wonderstruck heart.

Camping

The park has 21 tent and RV sites (electric available, no water). Reservations advised in season; call 800-322-3770. Camping fee.

Dead Horse Point State Park, P.O. Box 609, Moab, UT 84532; 435-259-2614; www.stateparks.utah.gov

Goblin Valley

47 miles southwest of Green River, off Utah 24

■ 3,014 acres ■ Year-round ■ Vehicle fee ■ Hiking ■ Interactive displays

Its wind and water-worn formations make some people laugh. Others shake their heads in wonder at the spires, balanced boulders, and pedestals. For few places exhibit the appealingly mixed-up topography of Goblin Valley, an out-of-step cut-up at the remote south end of the geologic chorus line known as the San Rafael Reef. Massive upheavals pushed up the reef's jagged ridge, a great rock spine running north from the park to I-70 and beyond. Goblin Valley's bowl, however, is an ancient tidal flat whose layers of silt, mud, and sand formed this region's rusty red-brown, gray-green, and dark brown bands of sedimentary rock. Softer in some places than others, it erodes unevenly—after the rare cloudburst you'll see runoff reshaping before your eyes the vast basin of improbable shapes adults liken to sculptures and young children treat as cartoon creatures come to life.

Remote to begin with, these sunbaked badlands, cliffs, and myriad eroded oddities, surrounded by imposing buttes, impart to hikers, campers, and day-tripping strollers a delightful sense of escape and discovery. If you visit in summer, be prepared for blistering heat. The park is nearly treeless, and the stone formations radiate warmth.

What to See and Do

As you enter the park, look for the **Observation Shelter** overlooking Goblin Valley. There's interesting geologic information here about the unusual shapes before you, and a useful brochure of trail routes will help you choose a walk. Short, easy footpaths wander down to the Goblins ranging in height from around 10 feet to 20 times that.

Two trails offer rewarding hikes. The 1.5-mile **Carmel Canyon Loop** leaves the parking lot, drops into a canyon, and wanders among cliffs and badlands of red siltstone and sandstone in the direction of **Molly's Castle,** a towering, magnificent butte with striations of greenish gray Curtis Formation sediments on top. The **Curtis Bench Trail** from the campground is a bit longer at 2 miles, and though its landscapes are similar to the Carmel Canyon trail, its rumpled up-and-down route is considered by some a more entertaining stroll. One spur leads into Goblin Valley; another winds up to a view of the north-south–trending **Henry Mountains,** rising above 11,000 feet some 15 miles south, and a panorama of the **San Rafael Plain.**

Only hardy desert plants, which have learned to survive fiery temperatures and constantly blowing sand, grow in this environment. As you hike, look for Mormon tea, Russian thistle or rabbitbrush, and various cactuses. Higher elevations outside the park sustain juniper and pinyon pine. You probably won't see any resident wildlife during the day; pronghorn, desert spiny lizards, kangaroo rats, kit foxes, and coyotes usually wait for the cooler evening temperatures to venture into the open.

> **CALL 'EM AS YOU SEE 'EM:** In the early 1900s, when cowboys were still fetching stray cattle from what is now called Goblin Valley, the sandy basin had no name. A Colorado River ferry operator scouting roads through it in the late 1920s proposed Mushroom Valley. The fanciful shapes of the fairy-tale landscape inspired the whimsy of locals and visitors alike, who dubbed them Utah's "Parade of the Elephants," a "Dance of the Dolls" where "Skulls in the Sky" grinned among "hoodoos, stone babies, toadstools, ghosts, knobs, gnomes"—and, of course, "goblins."

Camping

The park has 24 tent and RV sites, with showers, and a group campsite. Reservations advised in season; call 800-322-3770. Camping fee.

Goblin Valley State Park, P.O. Box 637, Green River, UT 84525; 435-564-3633; www.stateparks .utah.gov

Goblin Valley moonscape

Kodachrome Basin

*9 miles southeast of Cannonville via Utah 12
and Cottonwood Canyon Rd.*

■ 4,000 acres ■ Year-round ■ Entrance fee ■ Unusual geology ■ Hiking
■ General store ■ Photography

A pleasing sense of remote-ness and desert solitude attracts visitors to 5,800-foot-high Kodachrome Basin's peculiar geology, a meringue of red-rock spires that changes its hues as the sun moves across Utah's arid "color country." Geologists speculate that the park's tow-ers formed when liquid sand intrusions rose to the surface after earthquake activity and subsequently hardened. (The tallest rises 156 feet.)

Thunderstorm over Kodachrome Basin

Struck by the park's photogenic character and vivid palette, National Geographic Society visitors in 1948 suggested it be named in honor of the pioneering color film.

If your itinerary doesn't permit an overnight stay amid juniper and red-rock spires, be sure to treat yourself to a walk on at least one of the park's trails. Take your camera. *(A park trail map, available at the information kiosks throughout the park, is a must.)* The 0.5-mile self-guided **Nature Trail** leaves the campground for a tour of desert plants and Kodachrome's trademark for-mations. The **Panorama Trail** is an easy 3- or 6-mile trail leading to unusual for-mations, including the graceful Ballerina Slipper spire, wide-brimmed pedestals in Hat Shop, and the intriguing Secret

PARK TIP: *Follow the Angel's Palace Trail, a 1.5-mile loop 150 feet above the basin floor, for an amazing sunset.*

Passage, a narrow corridor squeezed between high red-rock walls. The main trail continues on to **Panorama Point,** an overlook with sweeping views of the multihued landscape.

Camping

The park has 27 tent and RV sites, with shower facilities. Reservations advised; call 800-322-3770. Camping fee.

Kodachrome Basin State Park, P.O. Box 180069, Cannonville, UT 84718; 435-679-8562; www.stateparks.utah.gov

THE ROCKIES

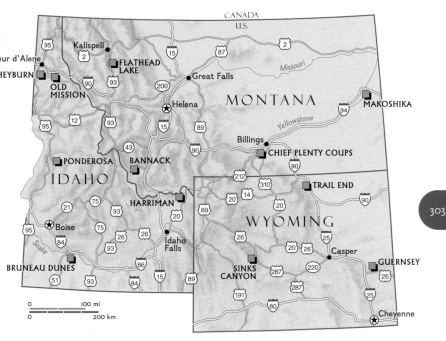

IDAHO
Ponderosa
Harriman
Bruneau Dunes
Old Mission
Heyburn

MONTANA
Flathead Lake
Bannack
Chief Plenty Coups
Makoshika

WYOMING
Sinks Canyon
Guernsey
Trail End

Savoring the solitude of Sinks Canyon State Park, Wyoming

Flathead Lake

Between Kalispell and Polson via US 93 and Mont. 35

■ 2,607 acres ■ Year-round ■ Day-use fee ■ West's largest natural freshwater lake ■ Hiking ■ Abundant wildlife ■ Boating, swimming, fishing (state or Salish/Kootenai license required)

Mountain-ringed Flathead Lake

Flathead Lake—the largest natural freshwater lake west of the Mississippi—stretches for 28 miles along the steep, darkly wooded base of northwest Montana's awesome Mission Range. Among the bays, coves, points, and peninsulas that make up the lake's irregular shoreline, Flathead Lake State Park lies scattered in six separate units that offer a sample of the area's varying terrain, vistas, and wildlife.

PARK TIP: *Try snorkeling amid the large boulders and rock slabs in the West Shore Unit's crystal clear waters or along the east shore of Wild Horse Island.*

Clean, deep, irresistible on a hot August day, Flathead is one of just a handful of large Rocky Mountain lakes warm enough for swimming most of the summer. Push off from shore and, as you float along on your back, a bald eagle or an osprey may glide out over the water, plunge for a trout, then return with its catch to a roost in the pines. Large sailboats angle silently across the bays, and thundering speedboats make a racket throughout the day.

The lake was formed during the last Ice Age, when large glaciers scoured much of the surrounding terrain. As the glaciers retreated, they left behind an enormous block of ice at the foot of the Mission Range. Mud, sand, stones, and gravel were washed down from the highlands and filled in around the block. When the ice melted, it left the depression now occupied by Flathead Lake.

The bulk of the state park consists of one large unit, Wild Horse Island, an enticing, largely undeveloped place where bighorn sheep, deer, coyotes, and a few wild horses live amid knobby upland prairies and mature Douglas fir and ponderosa pine forests. Accessible only by private boat, the island rises roughly 800 feet from the water and offers grand vistas of the lake, the Missions, and two other mountain ranges.

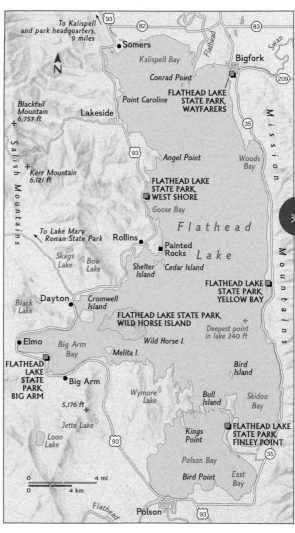

The other units are compact, shaded tracts for campground space, picnic area, boat ramp, beach, and perhaps some casual walking trails. Along the west shore, Big Arm lies beneath a canopy of ponderosa pine and offers a narrow, pebbly beach frequented by Canada geese. It also makes a convenient launching point to Wild Horse Island, standing 3 miles offshore. Farther north, the larch-fir forest at West Shore park ends abruptly along a set of glacially carved cliffs facing the Mission and Swan Ranges. It's a particularly appealing spot at sunset, with the breadth of the lake in shadow and the mountains bathed in yellow light.

Three more units dot the eastern shore. The southernmost, Finley Point, lies along a narrow peninsula shaped a bit like a fishhook. Though the campground caters to RV owners with large boats,

305

DON'T MESS WITH MOTHER NATURE: During the 1980s, an attempt to increase the average size of kokanee salmon led to the dramatic collapse of kokanee populations throughout the Flathead drainage. Taking a tip from Canadian biologists, who had fattened up kokanee in British Columbia's Kootenay Lakes, Montana's Department of Fish, Wildlife, and Parks introduced as a food source a half-inch crustacean called the opossum shrimp. Unfortunately, the shrimp competed directly for the kokanee's main food source, zooplankton. Worse, they failed to serve as prey because they settled to the bottom of the lake at night, when the fish rose to feed. In Canada, the approach worked because lake bed springs forced the shrimp to spend the night near the surface.

the point offers good views of the lake and a string of islands that stretch across the mouth of Polson Bay like stepping-stones. Sweet cherry orchards abound near Yellow Bay, a tiny park unit tucked into the shoreline beside a small creek and a broad gravel beach. Finally, Wayfarers lies within a mature evergreen forest near the town of Big Fork and offers lovely vistas of the gently rolling Salish Mountains across the lake. It has a good beach, but strong swimmers may prefer the low cliffs and rocks that also line the shore.

What to See and Do

Though it requires some planning, a trip to **Wild Horse Island** combines some of the best experiences Flathead has to offer: a nautical jaunt, an invigorating hike, opportunities for spotting wildlife, stirring vistas of mountain and lake, secluded swimming holes, peace and quiet. (No camping or pets.)

The park publishes a pamphlet (available at campgrounds) with a topographical map and logistical advice. There is one compost toilet and no drinking water on the island, so go prepared. If you don't have a boat, you can rent one at any of the private marinas that dot Big Arm Bay. Once equipped and afloat, plot a course for **Little Skeeko Bay** on the island's northwest side, where a loop trail climbs into the highlands. There are five other landings, and you're free to roam the island as long as you keep clear of several dozen private cottages.

For a more casual outing, head for any of the other units for a picnic, a swim, some bird-watching, or fishing. (One caution about swimming in Flathead Lake: The "swimmer's itch" parasite is common in shallow water, so towel off immediately or take a shower.) Along the way, you might pick up a sack of sweet cherries at one of the orchards or a bottle of sparkling wine at the **Mission Mountain Winery** (406-849-5524. May–Oct.) in Dayton. Take the opportunity to hike the overlook trails at West Shore and Big Arm to catch a spectacular sunrise. Sea kayaking from Finley Point State Park to the Bird Islands is also a Flathead Lake highlight. Excursion vessels ply the waters from Polson, Somers, and Big Fork. Most are large, motorized craft, but Big Fork's Questa Sailing Charters (406-837-5569) glides across the lake in a restored 1929 Q-class sloop.

Camping

The park's Big Arm unit (406-849-5255) has 37 RV sites and 3 tent sites, with showers; 1 group site and 3 yurts. The West Shore unit

(406-844-3066) has 26 RV sites, 12 with electric. Finley Point (406-887-2715) has 16 RV sites, with accompanying boat slips, no showers. Yellow Bay (406-752-5501) has 5 sites, including 4 walk-in tent sites. Wayfarers (406-837-4196) has 25 tent and RV sites, with showers. To make reservations for group or yurt sites, call 406-751-4577. No camping permitted on Wild Horse Island. Camping fee.

Nearby Sights

In late summer, you can pick huckleberries—a tiny type of blueberry—at the higher levels in the Salish Mountains surrounding **Lake Mary Ronan State Park** (*7 miles NW of Dayton. 406-849-5082*). It's a pleasant spot, shaded by Douglas fir and larch, and the lake offers good fishing for trout and bass. Camping is also available.

The southern half of Flathead Lake, as well as much of the land extending nearly to Missoula, lies within the Flathead Indian Reservation. For a Native American view of the area, visit **The People's Center** (*53253 Mont. 93 W, N of Pablo. 406-675-0160. Adm. fee*), which examines the lives of the Kootenai and Salish, past and present.

Farther south, at the **National Bison Range** (*35 miles S of Polson, near Moiese. 406-644-2211*), a herd of 300 to 400 bison amble among rolling palouse prairie grasslands. A 19-mile loop gravel road (*no trailers*) winds through the refuge and climbs 2,000 feet to panoramic vistas. The drive offers excellent chances for seeing bison as well as elk, deer, pronghorn, bighorn sheep, and many different birds.

For a pleasant day in the high country, head for the **Jewel Basin Hiking Area** (*NE of Flathead Lake. Maps available in Big Fork and at forest stations*), a 15,000-acre tract set aside in the Swan Range for the exclusive use of foot travelers. The network of short trails explores forests, alpine lakes, streams, snowfields, and wildflower meadows.

Flathead Lake State Park, 490 N. Meridian Rd., Kalispell, MT 59901; 406-752-5501; www.fwp.mt.us/parks

Flathead country

307

Bannack

25 miles southwest of Dillon via I-15 and Mont. 278

■ 1,600 acres ■ Year-round, Visitor Center closed Oct. through April
■ Entrance fee ■ Gold rush ghost town

Hotel Meade

Gold is the story of Bannack—gold in the ground, but mostly gold in the dreams of people drawn to this quiet corner of Montana. In 1862, a group of prospectors made the first significant gold discovery in Montana when they sank their shovels into the bed of Grasshopper Creek. Within a year, a new town of more than 3,000 people mushroomed into existence. In 1864, Bannack was declared the territorial capital and seemed to be headed for bigger things. But the fortunes of gold towns are by nature ephemeral. Bigger discoveries soon drew attention elsewhere. The fabulous placer strike at Alder Gulch gave rise to Virginia City. To the north, a vast copper lode built the brick mansions of Butte, while gold from Last Chance Gulch supported Helena and its claim as the permanent state capital.

Meanwhile, Bannack survived for nearly a century and produced millions in gold by various techniques. The hand-operated pans and sluices of the original miners gave way to hydraulic jets and great dredges that scoured the gravel to bedrock. Other efforts focused on quartz veins and tunnels blasted beneath the hills. Built in 1919, the Apex Mill still stands, though its hammers ceased their thunder in 1976.

Today, with its more than 50 original buildings, Bannack reveals much about frontier mining town life. The bawdy houses, saloons, and tumbledown shacks were built at a time when the sheriff himself led a gang of murderous road agents called The Innocents. Bannack also reveals the gentler side of human nature—the desire to establish home, church, school, and community.

What to See and Do

Exhibits at the **Visitor Center** describe Bannack's role in Montana's gold rush. Sign up for a tour or strike off at your own pace with a self-guiding brochure. Highlights include the redbrick **Hotel Meade,** originally the courthouse. Next door, **Skinner's Saloon** was home base for Henry Plummer's gang of road agents (see sidebar this page). The first electric dredge in North America, the **Fielding L. Graves** floated in a pond of its own making; its generator was powered by water brought 30 miles in a hand-dug ditch. Some of the buildings are empty, but others—notably the **Masonic Temple** and school—have been restored and retain some original furnishings.

What is a ghost town without ghosts? It is said that crying babies can be heard in **Amede Bessette's house,** where a number of infants died of diphtheria, and that the Hotel Meade houses the apparition of a young girl who died in Grasshopper Creek.

> **PARK TIP:** *Take the trail to the old barn and lean-to filled with a trove of horse-drawn equipment, plows, and wagon and buggy wheels.*

Camping

Bannack has 2 campgrounds with 24 primitive tent and RV sites. First come, first served. Camping fee.

Nearby Sights

An undeveloped site along the Beaverhead River commemorates the passing of Meriwether Lewis and William Clark on their way to the Pacific. South of Twin Bridges along Mont. 41, **Beaverhead Rock** was a landmark recognized by Sacagawea. Seeing the rock, she knew they were close to her people's summer hunting camps and soon located her brother, Chief Cameawhait.

Not far upstream, Clark scrambled to the top of a limestone outcrop above the river to take compass bearings and sketch a map. The spot, now called **Clark's Lookout State Park,** stands a mile south of Dillon on old US 191. Stand here and imagine how the country looked in 1805.

Bannack State Park, 4200 Bannack Rd., Dillon, MT 59725; 406-834-3413; www.bannack.org

LADIES' MAN, HIGHWAYMAN: When Henry Plummer drifted into Bannack in the winter of 1862–63, he was already an outlaw. Smooth-talking, gray-eyed, and mean, he had left a trail of broken hearts and dead men in mining camps from California to Idaho. But he was no miner. He wanted gold without digging, so he organized a gang of highwaymen. Bannack's Sheriff Crawford ambushed Plummer but failed to kill him; so it was Crawford, intimidated by Plummer's gang, who fled the scene in the middle of the night. The wounded Plummer got himself elected sheriff. While pretending to protect gold shipments, he orchestrated robberies, and did well until January 10, 1864, when members of the Montana Vigilante Committee overrode his silver star and hanged him with two of his deputies.

Chief Plenty Coups

35 miles south of Billings, 1 mile west of Pryor

■ 195 acres ■ May through Sept. ■ Vehicle fee ■ No camping
■ Historic buildings

Born in 1848, Alech-chea-hoos (Plenty Coups) was the last head chief of the Crow Tribe. A dedicated peacemaker, he strove to help his people through the difficult transition from nomadic freedom to government-imposed confinement on a reservation. In the 1880s, he built a log house and store beside a sacred medicine spring to set an example of a new, more settled way of life. Before his death in 1932, he wanted his homestead as "a park for all people." The gift was eventually accepted by Montana and in 1965 became a state park.

PARK TIP: *Start your day on the bench at Eyeful Vista. With expansive views of the badlands, watch as the rising sun illuminates the land's contrasts.*

Go first to the **Chief Plenty Coups Museum,** which tells the story of Plenty Coups. His life bridged two centuries, two cultures, and a broad sweep of history. It began as a traditional Crow boyhood and grew in scope to include friendships with such men as Theodore Roosevelt. Primarily, however, the museum focuses on the culture and history of the chief's people, the Apsaalooke, or Crow.

Outside, stroll around and visit the **medicine spring,** a spiritual place shaded by cottonwood, where people leave offerings, sample the water, and whisper prayers. Walk on to the grave of Plenty Coups and ponder the stormy confluence of cultures that he tried to understand.

If you visit at the right time, don't miss the Crow Fair *(406-638-3793; www.crowfair.com),* held annually in August at Crow Agency. This cultural celebration is a major Native American powwow, a vibrant display of color, dancing, and drumming. For a glimpse into prehistory, visit **Pictograph Cave State Park** *(7 miles SE of Billings via I-90. 406-247-2970).* A self-guided interpretive trail leads along the base of an overhanging sandstone cliff covered with prehistoric rock paintings.

Chief Plenty Coups State Park, Box 100A, Pryor, MT 59066; 406-252-1289; www.fwp.mt.us/parks

Makoshika

Just east of Glendive on Snyder Ave.

■ 11,531 acres ■ Year-round ■ Entrance fee ■ Scenic badlands
■ Fossils ■ Hiking

The Makoshika badlands reveal a significant transition in the Earth's history. Their buff-colored sediments were laid down 65 million years ago, when eastern Montana lay flat and swampy on the edge of a shallow sea. Tyrannosaurs, triceratops, and others roamed the plain, but this was near the end of their era. They would fall and new species would rise in their place. At Makoshika, the lower levels contain heavy dinosaur bones, the upper levels, the delicate skeletons of early mammals.

Makoshika's scenic drive climbs to the rim of a pine-studded mesa, where viewpoints overlook the canyons. The **Visitor Center,** near the entrance, is at the bottom of **Cains Coulee.** Stop for a look at fossils, prehistoric stone tools, and the enormous skull of a triceratops, and to pick up a park road guide.

Don't pass up **Cap Rock Nature Trail,** a mile-long trail through a sculpture garden of erosional features. Mud, stone, and weather combine to create the wonderfully eccentric forms—rain pillars, baked potatoes, toadstools, and popcorn. There are sinkholes, a natural bridge, and a black coal seam. *Be careful: Exposed wet clay is more slippery than ice.*

311

Continue past Radio Hill Junction, where an unimproved road turns off to **Artists Vista** and **Sand Creek Overlook.** In wet weather this road can be difficult to navigate; if in doubt, stay on the all-weather main road, which leads to more views of the badlands.

Badlands rock formations

For a boots-on experience, try the **Kinney Coulee Trail.** From the trailhead along the drive, the rugged marked trail descends 300 feet to the base of the badlands. Look for fossils. The triceratops skull at the Visitor Center was discovered when a worker nearly sat on the brow tine sticking out of the dirt. If you do find something interesting, leave it alone and notify a park employee. The 1-mile **Diane Gabriel Trail** introduces hikers to badlands features—grassy "tabletops" that escaped erosional forces and caves with sediment resistant to wear—and the exposed hadrosaur vertebrae.

Camping

The park has 16 tent and RV sites, plus additional primitive tent sites. Group reservations only. Camping fee.

Makoshika State Park, P.O. Box 1242, Glendive, MT 59330; (406)))-6256; www.fwp.state.mt.us/parks

Sinks Canyon

6 miles southwest of Lander on Wyo. 131

- 600 acres ▪ Year-round ▪ Scenic canyon with disappearing river
- ▪ Hiking, wildlife viewing, fishing (license required)

The Rise, fed by glacier melt

High in the Wind River Range, the Middle Fork Popo Agie River begins among glaciers, rock, and alpine meadows. It is a lovely river, but only one of many streams pouring out of these well-watered mountains. What sets this one apart is an unexpected trick. Having entered a narrow canyon on the east side of the range, the river turns suddenly to the right and dives into a yawning cavern called The Sinks. Half a mile away, it quietly returns to the surface in a deep green pool called The Rise.

It seems obvious that The Sinks and The Rise would be connected, yet it took years and several attempts to prove the case. Even now the underground picture remains a matter of conjecture. Tracer dye poured into the river above The Sinks turns up in The Rise as expected, but it takes two hours to get there, and the water comes out warmer than it went in. There is also more water coming out than entering, suggesting additional underground sources and a complicated network of passages—perhaps a large subterranean reservoir.

Even without its centerpiece geologic stunt, Sinks Canyon would make a worthy state park. Stretched out for more than 2 miles along the river, it lies sheltered beneath high buff-colored walls of sandstone and limestone. Its sunny, south-facing side has elements of a desert environment, with juniper, limber pine, and sagebrush. The shady, north-facing slope, being cooler and wetter, supports

HIGHER AND DEEPER: The road that climbs Sinks Canyon provides an overview of Wind River Range geology. From Lander to Switchback Overlook is nearly 4,000 feet of different rock layers. The mountains were formed by uplifting of a block of old granite tilting through younger sediments that now dip basinward on the flanks of the range, so hiking the canyon takes you to older rocks as you climb higher. The trip begins with brilliant red Triassic shale and sandstone, yielding to Tensleep sandstone at the canyon entrance. The Sinks are formed in Madison limestone, while farther up-canyon, the road switchbacks through Devonian and Cambrian sediments before emerging at the overlook among Precambrian granite and spectacular views of the Wind River Range.

Douglas fir, cottonwood, aspen, and willow. These, together with the riparian zone, provide a wide range of wildlife habitat. Elk, moose, deer, and bighorn sheep live in the canyon's narrow confines, along with mink and muskrats, rainbow and cutthroat trout, prairie rattlers, and 94 species of birds.

What to See and Do

Start at the **Visitor Center** *(Mem. Day–Labor Day)*, but first walk the short distance to **The Sinks.** At its normal summer level, the river is much smaller than the cavern, and it's hard not to feel a little spooky shiver as you stand watching the water disappear into that yawning darkness. The Visitor Center's excellent displays interpret the underground story in addition to the natural history of the area.

Next stop is **The Rise,** located a half-mile drive down the canyon. A platform provides a good view of the pool. Huge rainbow and brown trout drift like happy whales in the spring water. No fishing is allowed in this stretch of the river, but food pellets are available for tossing, and the trout enjoy them.

In spring, the river floods The Sinks and fills an overflow channel. You can see this along the 0.25-mile **Sinks to Rise Trail,** and learn about native vegetation in the process. For a longer self-guided walk (just under a mile), head for the **Popo Agie Nature Trail** near the upper campground. Interpretive signs describe many aspects of the canyon's natural history.

Treks of greater length begin with the **Middle Fork Trail,** which begins at Bruces Camp parking lot, outside the park, and leads into the Popo Agie Wilderness and beyond. Just 1.5 miles up the trail, **Popo Agie Falls** marks the head of the canyon. Connecting the Popo Agie and Middle Fork Trails is the 4-mile **Canyon Trail** loop.

Throughout the park, watch for bighorn sheep. The canyon should be an ideal wintering ground for them; its south-facing slope stays relatively warm and free of snow, while the rocks and lack of forest provide the sort of open, rugged country in which they feel secure. However, sheep have not had an easy time here. The original population died out many years ago. In the 1980s, a new herd of 54 animals was brought here from the north end of the Wind River Range. Yet they have not thrived and currently

PARK TIP: *Try boulder-hopping along the seldom visited overflow channel between The Sinks and The Rise.*

number only about a dozen animals. One problem is their failure to discover migration routes to summer grazing in the high mountains. As a result, they stay year-round on range that cannot provide sufficient forage.

Contributing to their decline are the recent increase in human contact and an outbreak of pneumonia, which killed a third of the population in 1992.

Camping

Sinks Canyon has 30 tent and RV sites in two campgrounds. May–mid-Oct., with limited sites open through winter. Available on a first-come, first-served basis. Camping fee.

Overlooking the canyon

Nearby Sights

Above The Sinks, Wyo. 131 gives way to a seasonal forest road that climbs to the head of the canyon. The road wanders through rolling country of forest and meadow, past several alpine lakes, campgrounds, and trailheads to Wyo. 28 near **South Pass,** an important landmark in Western history. Here, emigrants on the Oregon, California, and Mormon Trails crossed the Continental Divide. Despite the considerable difficulties still facing them, they must have been encouraged to know they had topped the ridgeline of the continent.

In 1867, prospectors found gold near South Pass. The discovery set off a gold rush that, at its peak, involved thousands of miners, a dozen stamp mills, two stage lines, and the usual assortment of saloons, hotels, promoters, lawyers, and grocers. The only thing lacking was enough gold to support expectations, and by 1875, fewer than 100 people clung to diminished hopes. Despite several attempts at revival, including one energetic fraud, South Pass never hit the big time. Today, the **South Pass City State Historic Site** *(42 miles S via Wyo. 131 and US 28. 307-332-3684. Mid-May–Sept.; adm. fee)* protects 27 original, restored, or reconstructed buildings crammed with artifacts. Check in at the Visitor Center, a former store and warehouse, before exploring the buildings and history of South Pass Avenue.

Ask park staff about other historical landmarks in the area, including **Pony Express stations,** visible **ruts of the Oregon Trail,** further mining relics, and **Willie's Handcart Site,** where Mormon emigrants pulling handcarts to Salt Lake City were caught—and many killed—by early winter storms in October 1856.

Sinks Canyon State Park, 3079 Sinks Canyon Rd., Rte. 63, Lander, WY 82520; 307-332-6333; http://wyoparks.state.wy.us

315

Guernsey

1.5 miles north of Guernsey, off Wyo. 26

- 8,602 acres ▪ Year-round ▪ Entrance fee (spring through fall)
- Historic buildings ▪ Oregon Trail ▪ Hiking, swimming, boating

Located near the main route of the Oregon Trail, Guernsey State Park takes in a pleasant, serpentine canyon rimmed with sandstone cliffs and shaded by stands of ponderosa pine and juniper. The North Platte River, impounded as a reservoir here, laps placidly at the base of the cliffs and offers an inviting respite from the heat of the Wyoming plains.

During the 1930s, the Civilian Conservation Corps (CCC) built trails, roads, bridges, and rustic buildings throughout the park. Much of the CCC's work survives, including the lovely stone-and-timber Visitor Center overlooking the reservoir.

Starting in the 1840s, waves of Oregon Trail emigrants traveled this way as they followed the North Platte River through southeastern Wyoming. Just a few miles south of the park,

A LIGHTER YOKE TO BEAR: When traffic along the Oregon Trail was at its height in the 1840s and '50s, emigrants jettisoned a large variety of high-quality trash between Fort Laramie and modern Glenrock. The route was strewn with bar-iron and steel, anvils, bellows, crowbars, drills, augers, gold-washers, chisels, axes, trunks, grindstones, plows, ovens, cookstoves, kegs, barrels, clothing, books, and food. Why did people with overloaded wagons wait until this point to reduce their burden? With the mountains looming ahead, the trail became steeper—and the trash piles rose.

they left two vivid records of their passage—deep wagon ruts carved across a stony bluff and hundreds of names etched onto the face of Register Cliff.

What to See and Do

The park's **Visitor Center** is worth a stop just to admire the handiwork of the CCC and to gaze across the rock-rimmed canyon. Exhibits touch on Native American culture, but focus more on 1880s cattle ranching and the activities of the CCC.

Commanding officer's restored office, Fort Laramie

The 1.5-mile **Evergreen Glade Nature Trail** departs from the Visitor Center and wanders among grassy rolling hills dotted with ponderosa pine, juniper, and cedar. Plaques and a self-guiding brochure help identify various wildflowers, trees, and animals and their tracks.

To get to the **Oregon Trail ruts,** drive south on Wyo. 26 through the town of Guernsey and follow the signs across the North Platte River. From the well-marked parking area, a short trail climbs to the top of a ridge of sandstone, where you'll find unmistakable wagon ruts cut deeply into the rock. Forced by a topographical bottleneck to come this way, hundreds of thousands of emigrants guided their creaking loads over this beautiful prairie highland. Their wagon wheels soon cut through the thin soil and eventually left ruts in the stone as deep as 5 feet.

Many of the emigrants who struggled over this ridge spent the previous evening just a few miles downriver scratching their names into **Register Cliff,** a 60-foot bluff of tan sandstone. Visible names date back to the 1840s and '50s, but legions of modern vandals have desecrated the site by adding their own names.

Camping

The park has 225 tent and RV sites (no hook-ups) in 7 separate campgrounds. Open year-round; no water from Oct.–April. Available first come, first served. Camping fee.

Nearby Sights

It would be a shame to come this close and not visit **Fort Laramie National Historic Site** *(13 miles E of Guernsey on US 26. 307-837-2221),* one of the West's finest living history museums with more than a dozen fully restored military buildings and a large cast of costumed guides. Founded in 1834 by fur-trappers, it became an important stopover on the Oregon Trail and a major military outpost.

Guernsey State Park, P.O. Box 429, Guernsey, WY 82214; 307-836-2334; http://wyoparks.state.wy.us

Trail End

400 Clarendon Ave., Sheridan

▪ 3.8 acres ▪ April to mid-Dec. ▪ No camping ▪ Restored 1913 mansion ▪ Carriage house ▪ Landscaped grounds ▪ Picnic area

A posh, 1913 Flemish Revival mansion, **Trail End** overlooks Sheridan from landscaped grounds offering views of the Bighorn Mountains. Built for John B. Kendrick—cattle baron, governor, and three-term U.S. senator—the 21-room house portrays early 20th-century Wyoming life. The polished mahogany woodwork, Italian marble fireplaces, stained-glass windows, and hand-painted ceilings all speak of a life far removed from the sweat and dust that built the Kendrick fortune.

As you approach Trail End's red-tile roofs, balconies, and neoclassic porticos, it's interesting to note that Kendrick started out as a Texas orphan who drifted north as a common cowpoke. He began building a 210,000-acre cattle ranch that sprawled across northern Wyoming and southern Montana, and in 1891 married into an influential ranch family.

Most visitors simply wander though the mansion at their own pace, but guided tours are available by appointment. While in the drawing room, you might pause over the Kurdistan rug, which served as a touchstone for decorating much of the home's interior. Virtually all of the furnishings you see throughout the house—from beds and bureaus to dolls and golf clubs—belonged to the Kendricks.

The **Carriage House** finished in 1910 served as the Kendricks' home during mansion construction. In 1979, it was converted into an 88-seat community theater.

Finish up with a stroll on the mansion's shaded grounds, which include a sunken rose garden, lawn tennis court, and apple orchard.

Trail End State Historic Site, 400 Clarendon Ave., Sheridan, WY 82801; 307-674-4589; www.trailend.org

Ponderosa

1 mile northeast of McCall, follow signs

■ 1,450 acres ■ Year-round ■ Vehicle fee, winter trail fee ■ Old-growth forest ■ High cliffs ■ Lake ■ Boating, fishing (license required) ■ Biking, hiking, cross-country skiing

Cross-country skiing along Payette Lake

High in the gently rolling mountains of west-central Idaho, Ponderosa State Park occupies a narrow, wooded peninsula that stretches across the crystalline waters of Payette Lake. This relatively small finger of land rises through groves of immense fir, larch, and ponderosa and lodgepole pine to an airy bluff of basalt lava overlooking the lake. Here and there, grassy meadows, bug-rich marshes, and even vest-pocket sagebrush flats press back the trees and provide an abundance of habitats for wildlife. Mule deer nibble shrubs along the forest edge. Hawks and owls hunt for mice and other rodents in the meadows, while beavers, muskrats, salamanders, and frogs muck about in the spongy ooze of the marshes.

Footpaths and bike trails skirt the shoreline, climb the bluffs, and loop through forest, marshes, and meadows. Most are suitable for casual strolls or, during winter, for cross-country skiing. There is a paved 0.25-mile path along the lakeshore that is wheelchair accessible.

You'll find sand beaches on the peninsula, but the most inviting tracts of warm sand lies across the water at Ponderosa's North Beach

Area. There, the North Fork Payette River lazily enters the lake after meandering through a forest of mature evergreens and gliding past a marsh full of ducks and songbirds.

What to See and Do

First of all, stop at the **Visitor Center** to pick up a park map and to review the schedule of ranger-led activities *(mid-June–Labor Day)*. These include guided nature walks, campfire chats, and special programs for children that cover geology, plants, animals, local history, and archaeology. Sometimes, a naturalist from the nearby Snowdon Wildlife Sanctuary drops by with a fox, a hawk, an owl, or some other injured animal the sanctuary has rehabilitated.

For a quick overview of the park, drive the length of the peninsula (about 3 miles) and follow the short footpaths to **Osprey Cliff Overlook** and the **Narrows Overlook,** where a terrific vista of Payette Lake opens from the top of the lava cliffs. The rock here was deposited as part of the Columbia Plateau, a vast accumulation of lava that spread over much of the Northwest about 16 million years ago. Later, glaciers covered this area, smoothing the mountains and scooping out the lake bed to a maximum depth of 304 feet.

On the return trip, take some time to watch for ducks and other waterfowl dabbling on **Lily Marsh,** or park in the shade by the picnic area and take a quick dip in **Payette Lake.** The water, enticingly clear, is bracing but swimmable most of the summer.

319

PONDEROSA PINES: Area vegetation has evolved with frequent fires, which create scattered, old-growth ponderosa pines widely spaced in pleasant open groves, where little more than mountain grasses, shrubs, and wildflowers form the understory. This is not true at Ponderosa State Park, where a century of fire suppression and no logging have permitted the growth of a rather lush understory and shade-tolerant evergreens such as firs.

To admire the most impressive examples of the park's namesake tree, the ponderosa pine, stroll through the Peninsula Campground. Some of the trees tower 150 feet high and were seedlings when the Spanish Armada set sail for England.

Next, slather on some bug repellent and follow the 1.4-mile **Meadow Marsh Trail** through the forest around Meadow Marsh, a spongy wetland gradually evolving into a meadow. You'll find the trailhead at a parking area just north of the Activity Center. A pamphlet *(available at the Visitor Center)* identifies various shrubs and trees throughout the park and points out likely areas for spotting animals and rare wildflowers.

Designated mountain-biking trails cover most of the park's important landscapes and extend from Meadow Marsh to Osprey Cliff Overlook. By combining the trails with stretches of the main park road, bikers can stitch together several casual loop tours of the peninsula. If you don't have a bike, you can rent one in McCall.

If time permits, enjoy a drive around the lake to the **North Beach Area** and spread your towel on the large sand beach that

River otter

faces due south and offers fine views of the entire lake. From the parking area, an interpretive boardwalk wanders over the marsh to the beach.

One of the most inviting ways to visit the North Beach Area is to float to it on the **North Fork Payette River,** a gentle stream appropriate for novice paddlers. As it switchbacks through forest and marsh, the river offers good chances for seeing deer, moose, ducks, herons, beavers, otters, and other animals. For a leisurely half-day trip, start a few miles north of the lake at the Fisher Creek bridge. Local outfitters rent canoes and provide shuttle service.

In the winter, the park grooms 13 miles of cross-country skiing trails that loop through rolling forested hills and climb to some of the ridgetops overlooking Payette Lake.

Camping

Ponderosa has 163 tent and RV sites (mid-May–mid-Oct.), with shower facilities. Reservations advised Mem. Day to Labor Day; call 888-922-6743. There are also 22 tent sites at the Northwest Passage unit and 5 cabins at Payette Lake. Camping fee.

Nearby Sights

In McCall, an old timber and resort town, you can tour the **McCall Smokejumper Base** *(Mission St. 208-634-0390),* where skydiving firefighters train for their mission of suppressing remote forest fires. Also in town, you can wander through the **McCall Summer Chinook Fish Hatchery** *(300 Mather Rd. 208-634-2690),* where thousands of small summer chinook salmon teem in narrow raceways and larger rainbow trout pump their gills in a nearby pond.

Ponderosa State Park, P.O. Box 89, McCall, ID 83638; 208-634-2164; www.parksandrecreation.idaho.gov

Harriman

18 miles north of Ashton on US 20

- 11,000 acres ▪ Year-round ▪ Entrance fee ▪ No pets ▪ No camping
- Historic buildings ▪ Wildlife viewing ▪ Hiking, mountain biking, horseback riding, cross-country skiing, snowshoeing ▪ Fishing (license required)

Perched on the edge of the rugged Yellowstone Plateau and sur-rounding mountainous terrain, Harriman is a peaceful place with a violent past. Roughly 1.3 million years ago a volcanic eruption blew everything sky high—even the underlying rock—leaving behind a collapsed volcanic crater some 20 miles across. What was a steaming gaseous ruin is now a haven for wildlife, a placid terrain of mead-ows, marshes, lakes, and streams. The only visible remnant of the rim is a line of hills to the northwest, but these are enough to give a sense of scale. Skirting their eastern corner, the trout-filled Henrys Fork slips gently through lodgepole pine into the meadows before plunging into a canyon and over two impressive waterfalls.

At the park's center stand 27 original buildings of the Railroad Ranch, founded in 1902 as a working cattle company and retreat for wealthy Eastern families, notably the Harrimans (of the Union Pacific Railroad) and Guggenheims. In 1977, the land was donated by its owners to Idaho. Together with adjoining national forest land, the park is the heart of the 16,000-acre **Harriman Wildlife Refuge.**

What to See and Do

Begin at the **Visitor Center** for a map and information. Then venture to the Jones House, which features history and wildlife displays, and join a guided tour through historic ranch buildings. Cottages for rent are set on a low rise overlooking the **Henrys Fork** and, in the distance, the distinctive crags of the Teton Range. The **Harriman**

Island Park, Harriman

Cottage is kept in its 1970s condition, as it was when the family turned it over to the state. Other structures belonged to the working ranch of the time.

The Harrimans came here for wildlife and the natural setting, and these remain the best features of the park. You might do nothing more than sit by the ranch buildings and scan the river meadows for trumpeter swans, sandhill cranes, moose, or elk. Beyond that, 20 miles of trails are open to hiking, mountain biking, and horseback riding. First choice is the mile-long **Ranch Loop,** which visits **Silver Lake** and the Henrys Fork, as well as the historic buildings. Fly fishermen will head straight for the meadow trails for access to some of the best fly-fishing waters in the West (flies only, catch-and-release). A rewarding longer hike is the 4.5-mile **Golden Lake Loop,** which, if connected to the **Ridge Loop** (5.5 more miles and 400 vertical feet of climbing), takes in the whole range of park habitats.

On winter weekends, the Visitor Center and Jones House are open for cross-country skiers and snowshoers. Being mostly spring water, the river almost never freezes, making this an important wintering area for trumpeter swans, bald eagles, and other wildlife.

Lodging

There is no campground, but groups can reserve 2 fully furnished historic cabins, 2 yurts, or 2 dorm facilities. Call 888-922-6743 or visit the park's website. Several hotels, national forest campgrounds, and Henry's Lake State Park are located nearby.

Nearby Sights

Follow the Henrys Fork downstream to **Mesa Falls Scenic Area** *(14 miles S of Harriman on Idaho 47/Mesa Falls Scenic Byway).* Boardwalks lead to views of two impressive waterfalls.

Henrys Fork originates with a small stream flowing out of Henrys Lake, but most of its water comes from **Big Springs** *(4.5 miles E of Mack's Inn),* whose crystalline water forms a small pond filled with protected fish: cutthroat, brook, and rainbow trout. There is no fishing, but you can stand on footbridges and watch trout and salmon forage among gently waving aquatic plants.

Harriman State Park, 3489 Green Canyon Rd., Island Park, ID 83429; 208-558-7368; www.parksandrecreation .idaho.gov

GRAND CATASTROPHE: The volcanic explosion that created Harriman's landscape was one in a long chain of such eruptions that moved across southern Idaho over a period of some 17 million years. The eruptions seem to have moved from Oregon to Yellowstone, but in fact the continent has done the moving, sliding across the top of a stationary hot spot that periodically blows up. Almost 2 million years ago, it was the Huckleberry Ridge Caldera on Yellowstone's southwest corner. The most recent, the Yellowstone Caldera, took out the center of the park 600,000 years ago. In a matter of hours it spewed hundreds of cubic miles of molten rock. By comparison, the famous eruptions of Krakatau and Pompeii fade to insignificance. The hot spot still broods beneath Yellowstone. Geologists predict it will erupt again, in what we must hope is the very distant future.

Bruneau Dunes

20 miles south of Mountain Home via Idaho 51 and Idaho 78

■ 4,800 acres ■ Year-round ■ Entrance fee ■ Dune field ■ Lake, marsh, and desert ■ Swimming, hiking, fishing (license required) ■ Observatory ■ Wildlife museum

Rippled Bruneau Dunes

Bruneau Dunes is the sort of place children might build if they could design their own landscape. With mountains of clean, sifted sand rising above a cluster of lakes and marshes, there are bluegills to catch, lizards to chase, and clear water for swimming. The dunes are an unearthly terrain where the lead-footed sensation of going up combines with the thrill of leaping or rolling down. For those who make the hike, a wind-carved crater sets into the crest of the dunes.

The dunes have been here for some 15,000 years, thanks to an abandoned meander of the Bonneville Flood called Eagle Cove, which serves as a trap for windblown sand. Because countervailing winds blow just about equally from the northwest and the southeast, the dunes remain stationary. A relatively small dune field, it boasts the highest single-structured dune in North America—470 feet high. The lakes clustered at its base are a much more recent development, having appeared after 1950 as a result of flood irrigation in the surrounding Snake River Plain. The water table came up, and the lakes rose among the dunes. The result is a happy coincidence of dunes, prairie, desert, lake, marsh, and a rich variety of flora and fauna, all in one compact area.

What to See and Do

Start at the **Visitor Center**. Among its natural history displays are fossils collected from the sediments of prehistoric lakes within a few miles of the park. They call to mind an era when camels and giant ground sloths wandered the area. The mammoth femur, turtle shells, and the skull and jawbone from 6-foot minnow are highlights.

Bruneau's little lake is more peaceful, and attracts swimmers, boaters *(electric motors only)*, and bird-watchers. Dune hikers can choose from several routes. Start at the boat launch and climb the western ramp to the dune, or pick up the trail at the picnic area and approach from the east.

For an ambitious walk that takes in most of the park's varied landscape, consider the **Sand Dunes Hiking Trail**, a 5-mile loop that begins and ends at the Visitor Center. It can be a hot trek in summer. Much of the trail is in desert country, where jackrabbits run from coyotes, and lizards zip beneath rocks. After climbing the high dunes, the path descends to the lakeshore and circles around.

For stargazers, the **Bruneau Dunes Observatory** *(Fri.–Sat. March–Nov.; fee)* opens the skies to study. The hit of an evening presentation is the Obsession Telescope, a custom-made 25-inch reflector.

WIND SHAPES: Sand dunes reflect the winds that built them. A single grain moves up the windward, gentler side of the dune and tumbles into the calm space on the steep lee side. Where prevailing winds blow in one direction, dunes form crescents called barchans, their horns pointing downwind. In exposed desert landscapes, barchans themselves are in constant motion, migrating gently downwind. However, if the winds are variable, dune shapes become more complicated. The sinuous crest of Bruneau's main dune is caused by opposing winds that push it first one way, then the other. The big dune, in turn, alters wind patterns in the immediate vicinity, as reflected by the fields of smaller dunes on either side.

Camping

There are 98 tent and RV sites, with showers. Reservations advised in season; 866-343-3246 or go to the park's website. Camping fee.

Nearby Sights

In the area, **C.J. Strike Reservoir** *(Idaho 78. 208-845-2324)* is a popular fishing lake and wintering ground for waterbirds. If the high desert sounds appealing, drive southeast from Bruneau on Hot Springs Road for 20 miles (12 of which are unpaved) to an overlook of the spectacular Bruneau River Canyon. A map is available at the park.

History adds interest to the landscape at **Three Island Crossing State Park** *(1 mile W of Glenns Ferry. 208-366-2394)*. Here on their long journey, Oregon-bound emigrants had a difficult choice. Should they continue along the harder, drier southern route, or brave a river crossing to reach the easier northern trail? Visitor Center displays and interpretive programs recount the dramatic story.

Bruneau Dunes State Park, 27608 Sand Dunes Rd., Mountain Home, ID 83647; 208-366-7919; www.parksandrecreation.idaho.gov

324

Old Mission

24 miles east of Coeur d'Alene on I-90

■ 100 acres ■ Year-round ■ Vehicle fee ■ No camping ■ 1850 church

Anchoring this small park, the ivory-colored **Old Mission** was built in 1850 by Coeur d'Alene Indians and Catholic missionaries. Using the simplest of tools, they erected the elegant timber-frame marvel of rustic ingenuity overlooking the Coeur d'Alene River. The Indians worshiped in its sanctuary until 1877, when they were forced onto a reservation. The church is the oldest building in Idaho.

Old Mission, Cataldo

Start at the **Visitor Center** *(March–mid-Nov.)*, where a slide show traces the history of the Coeur d'Alene and explains how the Jesuits and Indians built the church. Then visit the structure to admire the hand-carved altar, the chandeliers fashioned from tin cans, and the sky-blue ceiling painted with berry juice.

Old Mission State Park, P.O. Box 30, Cataldo, ID 83810; 208-682-3814; www.parksandrecreation.idaho.gov

325

Heyburn

34 miles south of Coeur d'Alene on US 95, then 5 miles east on Idaho 5

■ 7,835 acres ■ Year-round ■ Canoeing, hiking, mountain biking, fishing

Located at the marshy southern end of **Coeur d'Alene Lake,** Heyburn combines the serenity of deep, old-growth forest with the bird-busy clamor of extensive wetlands that harbor ducks, songbirds, herons, frogs, and salamanders. Trails trace the shoreline, explore portions of the marsh, and climb through lush cedar-and-hemlock forest to open stands of immense ponderosa pine overlooking the lake.

Drop by the new **Welcome Center** then head for **Plummer Creek Marsh,** where you can bird-watch or paddle your canoe among the bulrushes. Or bike the spectacular **Trail of the Coeur d'Alenes,** which passes through the park. If a forest hike appeals, consider the **Indian Cliffs Trail,** a 3-mile loop offering excellent views of the St. Joe River.

Camping

The park has 72 tent sites and 57 RV sites (April–Oct.), with showers. Limited reservations (nine months in advance). Camping fee.

Heyburn State Park, 57 Chatcholet Rd., Plummer, ID 83851; 208-686-1308; www.parksandrecreation.idaho.gov

NORTHWEST

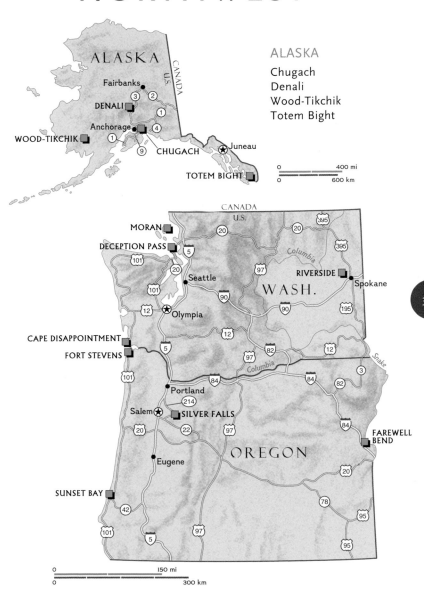

ALASKA

ALASKA

Chugach
Denali
Wood-Tikchik
Totem Bight

Fairbanks

3 2

DENALI

1

Anchorage

4

WOOD-TIKCHIK

1

9 CHUGACH

Juneau

TOTEM BIGHT

CANADA
U.S.

0   400 mi

0   600 km

CANADA
U.S.

MORAN

20

395

DECEPTION PASS

5

395

Columbia

101

20

Seattle

97

RIVERSIDE

Spokane

101

WASH.

12

90

Olympia

90

195

CAPE DISAPPOINTMENT

5

12

FORT STEVENS

82

12

101

84

Columbia

84

82

3

Portland

214

Salem SILVER FALLS

84

FAREWELL
BEND

20

22

97

OREGON

Eugene

20

SUNSET BAY

42

78

95

101

97

5

95

327

0   150 mi

0   300 km

WASHINGTON

Deception Pass
Moran
Cape Disappointment
Riverside

OREGON

Fort Stevens
Silver Falls
Sunset Bay
Farewell Bend

Denali, or Mount McKinley, Denali State Park, Alaska

Fort Stevens

10 miles west of Astoria via US 101 and Fort Stevens Hwy.

- 4,200 acres ▪ Year-round ▪ Vehicle fee ▪ Military museum
- Historic artillery emplacements ▪ *Peter Iredale* shipwreck
- Hiking, biking ▪ Beach

Since the early years of the republic, the nation's military has been prepared for attacks from foreign adversaries. From the Civil War until shortly after World War II, Fort Stevens helped defend our borders; along with Forts Canby and Columbia in Washington (see pp. 337–339), the artillery of Fort Stevens guarded the mouth of the Columbia River.

And it was right here at Fort Stevens that the continental U.S. came under fire during World War II. In 1942 a Japanese submarine shelled the fort, making it the only military installation in the lower 48 states to be fired upon by a foreign power since the War of 1812 (see sidebar this page).

Though the big guns are gone, the massive concrete bunkers remain atop the bluffs. Logically enough, the emplacements command a sweeping view of the Columbia's mouth, which visitors today can enjoy without the added burden of scanning for enemy warships. The park also includes natural areas, such as a long beach that extends to the extreme northwestern tip of Oregon.

JAPANESE ATTACK: One Saturday in June 1942, an intruder came down from the north. It was a Japanese submarine. Discovering a fishing fleet in the area, it stayed submerged until Sunday night, June 21, when it surfaced and its deck gun opened fire on Fort Stevens. Of 17 shots, most landed on the beach or in a swamp. The worst damage occurred when a shell blew up the backstop of a baseball diamond. The men of Fort Stevens were ordered to hold their fire, since the sub was out of range. However, recent studies have indicated that, indeed, the sub was probably within reach after all.

What to See and Do

It's fitting to begin your tour at the **Military Museum** *(503-861-2000. Parking fee),* which also serves as a Visitor Center. The museum exhibits weapons, uniforms, photos, and other artifacts from the installation's 100-plus years as an active fort, along with much illuminating information. For example, you can learn why the United States decided to build a fort way out here during the Civil War, when virtually all the action was taking place far to the east: The Union feared that the Confederacy would ally with Britain and that both Confederate and British sea raiders would come sailing up the Columbia.

Before heading out the door, pick up a walking tour map and, during the summer, sign up for a guided tour of the fortifications in a two-ton Army truck.

Outside the museum, you can explore the extensive network of gun emplacements. One is a restored earthworks artillery site that dates back to the Civil War, but most are massive concrete structures constructed at the turn of the 20th century. In summer you also can

PARK TIP: *Like to fish? Rainbow trout, perch, bass, catfish, and steelhead trout can be found in Coffenbury Lake.*

visit an underground gun battery that served as a command center during World War II. From atop the batteries awaits an exhilarating panorama of the mouth of the Columbia River and the Oregon and Washington coasts.

Aside from the artillery batteries, only a few buildings remain at the fort. But if you use the walking tour map and your imagination, or take the guided tour, these few structures and the bits and pieces of foundations come together to create an accurate picture of Fort Stevens during its active days. The **Guardhouse,** built in 1908, still stands and can be visited on a limited schedule during the summer. Its main function was to corral disorderly soldiers on payday. Other sites run the gamut from the mundane (laundry, bakery) to the flashy (buildings far from the heart of the post, where torpedoes and sea mines were stored and tested).

From the museum, a 0.5-mile trail leads to a wildlife-viewing platform above **Swash Lake,** where you might spot waterfowl, wading birds, or even a herd of Roosevelt elk. Another mile west through the trees and undergrowth will land you on the beach. Or you can head south half a mile to the campground and gain access to several other trails.

You can hike, bike, or drive to the *Peter Iredale,* once a sleek British barque. Part of the skeleton of this 1906 shipwreck protrudes from the sandy beach at the park's southwest corner. Go to **Clatsop Spit,** the most northwestern point in Oregon, where there is a wildlife-viewing bunker on **Trestle Bay** and a platform on the ocean side from which you can watch ships crossing the dangerous Columbia River bar.

Wreck of *Peter Iredale*

Camping

Fort Stevens offers 19 tent sites with water nearby, 174 full hook-up sites, 302 electrical sites with water, and 15 yurts (circular domed tents with wood floors), all with showers nearby. Reservations advised in season; call 800-452-5687. Camping fee.

Fort Stevens State Park, 100 Peter Iredale Rd., Hammond, OR 97121; 503-861-1671; www.oregonstateparks.org/park_179.php

329

Silver Falls

26 miles east of Salem on Oreg. 214

- 9,064 acres ▪ Year-round ▪ Day-use fee ▪ Waterfalls
- Historic lodge ▪ Wildflowers ▪ Hiking, biking, horseback riding ▪ Wildlife viewing

Silver Falls

330

Waterfalls are some of nature's most charming extravagances: that graceful arc as gravity and the forward rush of the stream combine to curve the water down through the air; that fine mist that dampens your face and creates rainbows; that refreshing rush of water-cooled air; that surflike sound of water splashing on water. Flamboyant displays, waterfalls simultaneously exhilarate and calm our souls. And ten waterfalls—four of which you can walk behind —lie at the heart of Silver Falls State Park.

These ten falls range in height from 27 feet to 178 feet, but numbers hardly capture their beauty. Festooned with ferns and surrounded by vine maples, Douglas firs, and western hemlocks, they tumble over old lava flows—left over from volcanic activity some 16 million years ago. In spring, violets and trilliums brighten the already bright sights, and in autumn, the vine maples burn with color, while winter ice frames the falls, forming silvery sculptures.

Something you won't see is a logger riding a canoe over the falls. Nor will you see old cars being pushed over the edge. These stunts went on in the 1920s, when one D. E. Geiser owned the property; he even charged a dime to look at the falls, when nothing else but water

WHY THE FALLS FALL: The park's falls came to be because Yakima basalt is hard. This rock underlies much of the park, and it strongly resists erosion. But below the Yakima basalt lie layers of softer material, which erodes lower and lower beneath the pounding water while the basalt stands tall. The falls also migrate upstream when winter winds blow tumbling water back into cracks in the basalt cliffs, where it freezes, expands, and splits the rock.

was spilling over them. The falls became a state park in 1933.

Although the Trail of Ten Falls serves as the park's centerpiece, the park offers other attractions. Equestrians can explore the forested hills along 20 miles of multiuse trails in the southern portion of the park. There's a man-made natural swimming pond that bulges out from the South Fork Silver Creek, near the main parking area.

What to See and Do

Heed the siren call of those waterfalls and head right for the main parking area, at the South Falls Day Use Area. Here, drop by the historic **South Falls Lodge,** built by the Civilian Conservation Corps (CCC) in the 1930s, and take a look at the interpretive panels on the park's history, wildlife, and geology, or visit the log cabin Nature Store. A short walk brings you to a viewpoint overlooking 177-foot-high **South Falls.**

From here try the **Trail of Ten Falls** (Silver Creek Canyon Trail), which follows the South Fork Silver Creek to the north, swings east along the North Fork Silver Creek, then strikes out through the forest back to the South Falls area. The full, ten-falls loop is 7 miles, but cutoffs allow less ambitious hikers round-trips of either 2 or 5 miles.

Hugging the creek, the trail winds a mile or so to **Lower South Falls,** where you stroll behind the curtain of cascading water; the trail then curves over to **Lower North Falls** and the North Fork Silver Creek. Seven more cascades await as you continue up this creek branch. Don't forget to appreciate some of the sights beyond the falling water: lush hemlocks, wood violets, browsing deer, and a profusion of ferns. Under North Falls, also note the holes, or tree casts, formed when lava flowed and cooled around standing trees, which later decomposed and left the huge shafts. People unable or unwilling to take the trail can view North Falls from an overlook along Oreg. 214.

PARK TIP: *Look for the plaque at the North Falls Group Area that pays tribute to the men who were stationed here with the CCC.*

Camping and Lodging

The park offers 45 tent sites and 49 RV sites, 14 rustic cabins, 3 group tent sites, 2 group RV sites, and 2 ranch bunkhouses accommodating 75 guests each. Reservations advised in season; call 800-452-5687. Camping fee. The Silver Falls Conference Center has 4 lodges; call 503-873-8875 for reservations.

Silver Falls State Park, 20024 Silver Falls Highway SE, Sublimity, OR 97385; 503-873-8681 ext. 31; www.oregonstateparks.org/park_211.php

Sunset Bay

12 miles southwest of Coos Bay on Cape Arago Hwy.

▪ 1,286 acres ▪ Year-round ▪ Vehicle permit fee for Shore Acres
State Park only; day-use for others ▪ Rocky coastline ▪ Sandy beach
▪ Seal and sea lion colonies ▪ Historic garden ▪ Hiking, tide pooling,
whale-watching,

Oregon's wild coast, at Sunset Bay

Embraced by sandstone bluffs, half-moon **Sunset Bay** showcases the Oregon coast perfectly. Here you can hike atop 100-foot-high cliffs and watch burly Pacific waves burst against massive rocks; lounge on a sandy beach backed by a verdant conifer forest; or poke through tide pools filled with tiny crabs, sea anemones, and purple sea urchins. Low tide exposes a tide-pooling area on the beach's north end.

Sunset Bay is one of three adjacent state parks overlooking the Pacific Ocean. You can drive from one to the next, or hike a 4-mile section of the **Oregon Coast Trail.** Passing through lush coastal forest, the narrow trail winds atop sandstone bluffs that yield fine ocean views.

Neighboring **Shore Acres State Park** *(541-888-3732)* invites you to walk along seaside cliffs; there's an enclosed gazebo for watching the crashing surf of winter storms. But the heart of Shore Acres—the former estate of pioneer shipbuilder and lumberman Louis J. Simpson—lies a few hundred feet inland, amid the tulips, elegant roses, azaleas, and other seasonal flowers that fill the elaborate formal gardens.

Of the three state parks, **Cape Arago** *(541-888-3778),* located just south of Shore Acres, possesses the most dramatic bluff views, taking in Simpson Reef and Shell Island. From this high perch you can watch sea lions and elephant seals cavort offshore, plus gray whales migrating south from March to June. For a closer look, take the trail that leads down to a sandy beach.

PARK TIP: *Wander down to the often empty Simpson Beach, a secluded beach with "sand" of small seashell particles ground and worn by the surf.*

Camping

Sunset Bay has 66 tent sites, 29 RV sites with full hook-ups, 36 sites with electricity; 8 yurts, group tent camp (2 areas); and 1 hiker/biker camp. Showers. Reservations advised in season; call 800-452-5687. Camping fee.

Sunset Bay State Park, 89814 Cape Arago Hwy., Coos Bay, OR 97420; 541-888-4902 ext. 25; www.oregonstateparks.org/park_100.php

Farewell Bend

25 miles northwest of Ontario, off I-84

■ 70 acres ■ Year-round ■ Oregon Trail history ■ Snake River fishing (license required) ■ Camping

More than 150 years ago, pioneers used Farewell Bend as a rest stop for the final leg of the Oregon Trail. After following the Snake River for 320 miles, they left the river here to avoid the forbidding Hells Canyon area—hence, "Farewell Bend." If those pioneers were traveling through today, they still would recognize the rolling sagebrush grasslands harboring deer, pronghorn, partridge, chukar, and, in season, a profusion of high-desert wild-flowers. But they would also find a popular site for camping, hiking, and fishing. And the Snake River—since impoundment—they wouldn't know at all.

To get your historical bearings, start at the **kiosk,** which provides the basics about the Oregon Trail. Knowing that the pioneers began their trek in Missouri, hundreds of grueling miles away, helps you comprehend the bone-weary fatigue that must have plagued them at this point in their journey.

Now drive north from the park on US 30, toward Huntington. After a mile or two, pull over and look for the **wagon wheel ruts** on either side of the road, made by bulky Conestoga wagons loaded with the lifelong possessions of pioneers.

About 2 miles from the park, you'll spot a small iron cross. It marks the site of an 1860 conflict between pioneers and Snake River Shoshone Indians, in which eight settlers were killed and two small children were carried away.

Back at the park, appreciate the ease of your life as you fish, picnic, or hike the hills watching for wildlife. Come nightfall, you can taste a bit of the frontier experience by staying in one of the rustic cabins.

Camping and Lodging

The park has 132 tent and RV sites, with showers; 1 hiker/biker camp; 1 group site; and 2 rustic cabins. Reservations advised in season; call 800-452-5687. Camping fee.

Farewell Bend Recreation Area, 23751 Old Hwy. 30, Huntington, OR 97907; 541-869-2365; www.oregonstateparks.org/park_7.php

Deception Pass

North end of Whidbey Island and south end of Fidalgo Island, on Wash. 20

- 4,200 acres - Year-round - Beaches - Forest and wetlands
- Interpretive Center - Tide pooling - Wildlife viewing, hiking, swimming - Boating, fishing (license required)

Lighthouse Point and Deception Pass

Most people who daydream of island vacations envision tropical isles, but a visit to Deception Pass can make contenders of the islands off Washington's coast. Evergreens instead of palm trees, rocky shores instead of sugar-sand beaches—it's like comparing apples and oranges when both taste great. Small wonder that this is Washington's most popular state park, with nearly three million visitors a year.

The park straddles Fidalgo and Whidbey Islands—two of the largest islands that sprinkle the Strait of Juan de Fuca and Rosario Strait. The soaring bridge that connects the two islands is in itself a prime attraction, affording views of the islands, Rosario Strait, and the narrow channel below. On either side of the bridge, visitors enjoy hiking trails, forested hills, bird-rich marshes, freshwater lakes, quiet coves, striking seaside bluffs, and even a few sandy beaches.

Capt. George Vancouver, the 18th-century British explorer, gave the park its name. In fact, he named it twice. In 1792, when he first sailed through the area, he dubbed the inlet near today's bridge "Port Gardner." He later discovered that it wasn't an inlet, but a channel between the two islands; feeling deceived, he came up with "Deception Pass."

PARK TIP: *Make a reservation for your own island hideaway. Just a short way across Cornet Bay is Ben Ure Island, with a small but classy cabin and views of Mount Baker.*

What to See and Do

Start at the **Deception Pass Bridge.** For the full, vertiginous effect, park in the lot at the south end, on Whidbey Island, and walk to the center of the 1,000-foot-long, 186-foot-high span. Gazing over the railing, most people step gingerly and parents clutch children's arms. You'll enjoy maximum spine tingles and knee weakness if the tide is running. Deception Pass is the only channel for many miles north and south, so a huge volume of water funnels through this narrow opening between Rosario Strait and Skagit Bay, at times resembling a white-water river.

Next, follow Wash. 20 south about a mile to the **park office,** where you can get maps and information. From the office, drive along the north shore of **Cranberry Lake** to **West Beach.** The park's longest sandy shore, West Beach is strewn with shells and driftwood, making it a favorite among beachcombers. It also features picnic sites, seasonal concessionaires, and, across the parking lot on the

335

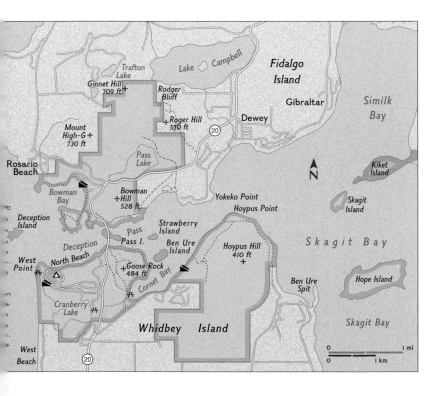

northern tip of Cranberry Lake, a cordoned-off swimming area. Here, too, is the trailhead for the 0.8-mile **Sand Dune Trail,** a paved loop through low beach dunes and along Cranberry Lake's western shore. Linger at the **Marshland Environmental Overlook** and scan the reeds and grasses for loons, thrushes, wrens, beavers, muskrats, and mink.

To explore the Fidalgo side of the park, drive over the bridge and take the turnoff to **Bowman Bay.** The handsome stone picnic shelters and restrooms you soon pass by, along with trails throughout the park, were built by the Civilian Conservation Corps (CCC) in 1934–35. During the summer, a small but informative **Interpretive Center** displays artifacts and photographs of everyday life in the CCC camp.

The nearby **Bowman Bay/Rosario Beach Trail** heads north and west half a mile to Rosario Bay. Don't let the steep stretch near the trailhead discourage you; most of the trail is gentle. Passing through a forest, you occasionally glimpse the rocky bayshore. At trail's end, branch onto the 0.25-mile **Rosario Head Vista Point Trail,** looping out to Rosario Head Vista Point and back. From atop the 100-foot bluffs you'll have grand views of the straits and of the San Juans. If it's low tide, investigate the fecund tide pools along the way.

Further Adventures

People with more time and stamina can try any of eight other trails. The longest is the 1.5-mile **Lighthouse Point Trail,** which begins at the lower parking lot at Bowman Bay and skirts a peninsula thrusting into the sea. Hikers savor skyscraping groves of Douglas fir and western red cedar, a lively marsh, expansive ocean views, and a trek along the beach when the tide allows. *(Note that it's dangerous and prohibited to climb up to the lighthouse.)* Near the beginning, branch onto the 0.5-mile **Canoe Pass Vista Trail,** which provides a splendid view of Canoe Pass, as well as a look at numerous secluded coves.

The steepest trail, which leads to the highest point in the park, is the **Goose Rock Summit Trail,** a 0.3-mile ascent yielding a vast panorama of the straits.

A very different view of the straits awaits below sea level. Off Rosario Head, a designated underwater park gives scuba divers a look at life in these rich coastal waters. Visitors with the proper experience and gear—a thick wet suit—can get close-up and personal with sea cucumbers, ling cod, purple sea urchins, and perhaps a stingray.

Camping

Deception Pass has 320 tent and RV sites (hook-ups) and a cabin, with showers; 5 walk-in sites; 3 group camps; and a retreat center for 186. Reservations required; call 888-226-7688. Camping fee.

Deception Pass State Park, 41020 State Rte. 20, Oak Harbor, WA 98277; 360-675-3767; www.parks.wa.gov

Moran

6 miles southeast of Eastsound on Orcas Island, in the San Juan Islands

▪ 5,252 acres ▪ Year-round ▪ Mount Constitution ▪ Hiking, wildlife viewing ▪ Boating, swimming, fishing (license required)

Drive (or hike) to the summit of Mount Constitution; at 2,409 feet, it's the highest mountain in the San Juan Islands. Ascend the historic stone tower and imbibe the nearly 360-degree views of Orcas Island, the rest of the San Juans, Vancouver Island, the Gulf Islands, and the Washington and Canadian mainlands. Don't overlook the tower itself. Patterned after the 12th-century watchtowers of the Caucasus, it was built by Civilian Conservation Corps artisans in the 1930s.

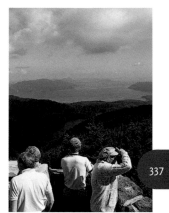

The forests and lakes visible from the tower can be explored via some 38 miles of hiking trails. A 4-mile path circles **Mountain Lake,** providing views of Mount Constitution and of bald eagles, ospreys, kingfishers, and other birds. Another trail rich with wildlife, the 2.7-mile **Cascade Loop,** passes through a conifer forest. Watch for river otters, deer, muskrats, and an abundance of birds.

Mount Constitution, Orcas Island

Camping

The park has 129 campsites, with showers; a 7-site group camp; and 15 primitive sites. Reservations recommended mid-May–mid-Sept.; call 888-226-7688. Camping fee.

Moran State Park, 3572 Olga Rd., Olga, WA 98279; 360-376-2326; www.parks.wa.gov

Cape Disappointment

2 miles southwest of Ilwaco off US 101, on Wash. 100

▪ 1,882 acres ▪ Year-round ▪ Lewis and Clark Interpretive Center ▪ Historic lighthouses ▪ Overlook of Columbia River mouth ▪ Benson Beach ▪ Hiking, biking, surf fishing (license required), clamming

British fur trader John Meares first called this headland Cape Disappointment in 1788. Following a search for a way across the breaking waves and around the sand bars clogging the opening to the coast before him, he named the opening Deception Bay.

For millennia this junction of the Columbia with the Pacific Ocean was a focal point for Native Americans. In more recent times, this crossroads drew the ships of 18th-century explorers, including

Cape Disappointment Light

Robert Gray, the American captain who in 1792 gave the river its name after making the first successful crossing of the bar.

The Corps of Discovery first encountered the Pacific at this site in 1805, inspiring Capt. William Clark to write in his journal: "men appear much satisfied with their trip beholding with astonishment the high waves dashing against the rock and this 'emence Ocian.'" Today, Cape Disappointment State Park, formerly known as Fort Canby, is part of the Lewis and Clark National and State Historical Parks *(www.nps.gov/lewi).*

FORT COLUMBIA: East of Fort Canby lies another historic military site, Fort Columbia State Park *(360-777-8221. Interpretive Center: May–Sept. daily, grounds: year-round).* Like its neighbor, Fort Columbia was built to protect the entrance to the Columbia. Here buildings, bunkers, and artillery remain from its active days. An Interpretive Center reveals much about life at the fort, including old letters written by soldiers stationed here. One, penned in 1917 to "My dearest girl Rose," says in part: ". . . never until Uncle Sam called me from you did I fully realize what life would be like without you. . . ." The lovesick GI goes on to propose.

What to See and Do

Drive directly to the newly renovated **Lewis and Clark Interpretive Center** and savor its richly detailed exhibits. The bulk of the story of Meriwether Lewis and William Clark and their exploration of the West is told via a "trail." The artifacts and information follow the expedition from its beginning in 1803 to the return in 1806. Take the time to read some of the colorful journal entries.

At the end of the Lewis and Clark path you'll emerge into a viewing room. Walk over to the huge windows and look upon the broad mouth of the mighty Columbia—as Lewis and Clark did more than 200 years ago.

Exhibits here tell why the mouth of the Columbia is known as the "graveyard of the Pacific"—these treacherous waters have claimed nearly 2,000 vessels. That's the reason for the large **Coast Guard station** just below the Interpretive

Center. It's also the reason for the **Cape Disappointment Lighthouse** *(closed)*; reached via a short trail from the Interpretive Center. Built in 1856, it's the oldest operating lighthouse on the West Coast.

Drive out to the **North Jetty,** and you may see the Coast Guard doing drills at their National Motor Lifeboat Training School. From the jetty, stroll along **Benson Beach** or hike along 9 miles of trails through the forests. Near the other end of the park you can visit the 1898 **North Head Lighthouse** *(360-642-3078. Daily June–Aug., weekends April–May & Sept.–Oct.; fee).*

> **PARK TIP:** *Check out the Confluence Project, where crushed oyster shell paths weave through native plant restoration sites.*

Camping and Lodging

Cape Disappointment offers 234 tent and RV sites, with showers. Camping fee. Also 14 yurts and 3 cabins. The North Head Lighthouse keeper's complex offers historic vacation rentals. For reservations, call 888-226-7688.

Cape Disappointment State Park, P.O. Box 488, Ilwaco, WA 98624; 360-642-3078; www.parks.wa.gov

Riverside

Northwest edge of Spokane, off Wash. 291

- 10,000 acres ▪ Year-round ▪ Spokane House Interpretive Center
- Riverside trails ▪ Wetlands ▪ Off-road vehicle park

Riverside State Park consists of several areas. The main parcel winds for several miles along a pretty, wooded stretch of the Spokane River. Aubrey L. White Parkway provides motorists with a scenic river overlook, taking in striking "bowl and pitcher" rock formations rising from the water. Hiking trails range from the 1-mile ADA trail to the 37-mile **Centennial Trail** that runs to the Idaho state line.

A little farther north, at the confluence of the Little Spokane River, lies the **Spokane House Interpretive Center** *(509-466-4747. Mem. Day–Labor Day),* which recalls the history of a fur-trading post built on that site in 1810. Just east of the center awaits the **Little Spokane Natural Area,** comprising about 1,300 acres of wetlands and woods. Much of the natural area is a freshwater marsh favored by wildlife, including a great blue heron rookery. Nearby are **Indian Rock Paintings,** a 1-acre parcel containing a large rock covered with Indian pictographs.

Camping

The park has 57 tent and RV sites, with 38 hook-ups; 2 group campgrounds. Reservations accepted, call 888-226-7688. Camping fee.

Riverside State Park, 9711 W. Charles Rd., Nine Mile Falls, WA 99026; 509-465-5064; www.parks.wa.gov

Chugach

Eagle River Nature Center: 26 miles east of Anchorage via Glenn Hwy. (Alas. 1) and Eagle River Rd.; Park Headquarters: 12 miles south of Anchorage via Seward Hwy. (Alas. 1)

■ 495,204 acres ■ Year-round ■ Hiking, backpacking, mountaineering, mountain biking, rock and ice climbing, horseback riding ■ Skiing, snowmobiling ■ Whitewater rafting, ATVing ■ Fishing and hunting (license required for both) ■ Historic railroad section house

What Central Park is to Manhattan, Chugach is to Anchorage: Here locals relax, play with their kids, read a book under a tree, bird-watch, picnic, take a stroll, row a boat—even cross-country ski in winter—except that Anchorage's "backyard wilderness" is about 37 times the area of Manhattan, and its animals are not in a zoo.

Chugach also has several dozen glaciers and 70 peaks. Part of the northern terminus of the 300-mile-long towering Chugach range, the dark, jagged

> **PARK TIP:** *Backpackers can experience a portion of the Iditarod National Historic Trail on the Crow Pass Trail section (23 miles, one way).*

mountains are the wreckage of ancient sea-bottom sediments lifted by colliding continental plates, then crushed by Ice Age glaciers so heavy the region rose in elevation as they melted. White dots on the rock faces might be climbers, but more likely they are Dall sheep, some 2,000 of which live here along with hundreds of mountain goats, black bears, lynx, and moose. Fewer in number are wolves and perhaps five dozen Alaskan brown bears—the fabled humpbacked grizzly—citizens of a park whose main Visitor Center is barely a half-hour drive from Anchorage.

What to See and Do

Chugach State Park is situated on the doorstep of a growing metropolis that harbors half the population of Alaska. The park provides

Ice floes drifting in Turnagain Arm

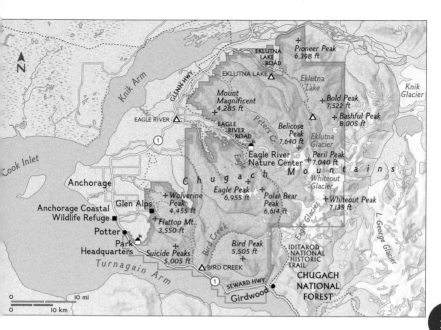

easy access to diverse recreational opportunities that capitalize on Alaska's wilderness characteristics. The nearby urban areas have not compromised the park's wildness; the quality of wilderness here, with 300 miles of trails, rivals that of remote roadless destinations.

If you have only half a day, drive east from Anchorage on the Glenn Highway (Alas. 1), taking Eagle River Road from Milepost 19 to the **Eagle River Nature Center,** where interpretive exhibits survey park wildlife and geology. Pick up a copy of the park's brochure, which provides a great introduction to the park. Stroll along the glacier-fed **Eagle River,** which crosses a tundralike basin between the

timbered foothills of the forbidding Chugach Mountains. For an introduction to Alaskan wilderness, walk the **Albert Loop Trail,** a level 3-mile loop through mixed forest to the river, where silt-laden snowmelt rushes over braided gravel bars. Picnic tables in the **Eagle River Campground** offer an excellent place to relax a bit on your return.

Another half-day option is to take the Seward Highway *(Alas. 1)* south from Anchorage. Near MM 116, the reedy **Potter Marsh** wetlands, part of the **Anchorage Coastal Wildlife Refuge** *(907-267-2556),* hide limpid trout and salmon streams where migratory waterbirds nest. A boardwalk across the marsh is posted with interpretive information on the fish and wildlife at your feet.

> **ENCOUNTERS WITH *URSIDAE*:** The principle for dealing with bears is brains versus brawn. If you spot one, backtrack. If it sees you, retreat slowly and diagonally. If it approaches, stop. If it charges (usually a bluff), don't run. (You can't outrun it.) Stand tall, wave your arms, and speak loudly in a deep voice. Charging bears usually veer off at the last moment. If attacked, play dead—curl up in a ball with your hands behind your neck. The bear might nudge you, but will typically stop attacking. If not, fight back ferociously: Aggressive bears are often young and can be intimidated.

Continue south 1 mile to **Park Headquarters** at the **Potter Section House State Historic Site,** once an important Alaska Railroad worker camp. Numerous waysides and turnouts along scenic Seward Highway afford a spot for picnicking and sweeping views of **Turnagain Arm,** an extension of Cook Inlet dug by glaciers and swept by dangerous tides. (The **Turnagain Arm Trail** parallels the shoreline, highway, and railroad south for 9.4 miles, and a popular 13-mile **national recreation trail** paved bicycle pathway winds from Indian to Girwood, also affording spectacular views.)

For an easy but rewarding quarter-mile walk to dramatic views across Anchorage and Cook Inlet to the Alaska Range 80 miles distant, backtrack toward Anchorage on Alas. 1, turning right (east) onto De Armoun Road. Continue east via Hillside, Upper Huffman, and Toilsome Roads to the head of the **Glen Alps Trailhead.** A wheelchair-accessible path leads to a sitting area and viewing deck.

If your schedule permits a day-long visit, and you have a mountain bike, pedal the 12.7-mile **Lakeside Trail** from **Eklutna Lake** to the **Eklutna Glacier.** (Access the lake from Glenn Highway, Eklutna Lake Road exit.) The trail skirts the lake, then follows vast gravel bars to a final mile-long walk over glacial detritus to the foot of the mammoth blue ice river. The easy trail climbs only 300 feet, but it ends with a face-to-face meeting with the Alaskan wilds.

Camping

The park has 3 campgrounds with 147 tent and RV sites (May–Sept.), no showers. Camping fee.

Chugach State Park, Headquarters, 18620 Seward Hwy., Anchorage, AK 99561; 907-345-5014; www.dnr.state.ak.us/parks

Denali

132 miles north of Anchorage, on the George Parks Hwy. (Alas. 3)

■ 324,240 acres ■ Year-round, but facilities closed mid-Oct. to mid-May ■ Mount McKinley viewpoints ■ Backcountry hiking, white-water kayaking, fishing (license required)

In the sunset shadow of Mount McKinley and its mammoth, glacier-collared companions in the Alaska Range, this unsung neighbor of Denali National Park and Preserve is much less visited, yet, unlike its neighbor, traversed with an extensive trail system. Alaska's own Denali requires no backcountry permits and is designed for avid hikers and campers seeking deep solitude amid wilderness terrain rising from lowland river basins and glacier-gouged valleys to alpine tundra and barren peaks.

343

Fleet-footed Dall sheep

The park is bisected by the braided gravel channels of the Chulitna River and an adjoining, 37-mile stretch of the George Parks Highway. River and road are paralleled on the east by the imposing Curry and Kesugi Ridges, their slopes etched by six trails ranging in length from a well-maintained and easy 1.2 miles to a difficult 36.2-mile trek requiring first-rate map-reading skills.

PARK TIP: *Camp at the small Beyer's Lakeshore site, where each tent platform has a view of Denali and you can dine on fresh-caught fish for breakfast.*

What to See and Do

If you're just driving through, stop at Milepost 135.2 along the George Parks Highway for what is considered the finest roadside view of the **Alaska Range.** There's an interpretive display that explains the geology of the panorama and identifies the mountains, but you'll need no prompting to appreciate the mountains' grandeur. (Other viewpoints are located at MM 147.1, 158.1, and 162.3.)

Park information is available at the **Visitor Contact Station,** adjoining the Alaska Veterans Memorial at MM 147.1. There are forested picnic sites at nearby **Byers Lake Campground,** a roadside haven at MM 147. If you have two hours and comfortable walking shoes, consider strolling the easy, well-maintained 4.8-mile **Byers Lake Loop Trail** from here around tree-ringed Byers Lake. There are picnic sites

THE HIGH ONE: Long before William McKinley became 25th President of the U.S. in 1897, Athapaskan-speaking Alaska natives knew Denali—"the high one"—as the 20,320-foot mountain that would eventually commemorate him. High indeed. Driving from Anchorage you'll first see the eternally snow-mantled massif, North America's tallest peak, around Milepost 69.1, weather permitting—though you are still 95 miles from the mountain. And no wonder: McKinley towers 18,000 feet above the surrounding terrain, a vertical rise surpassing Mount Everest's.

there as well, and three rental cabins. The lake's serenity is preserved by a ban against gasoline-powered boats.

If you're prepared to hike difficult terrain and have a day to do it, consider trekking a portion of the **Kesugi Ridge Trail,** which you can access from Byers Lake Campground, the Ermine Hill trailhead at MM 156.9, or roadside trailhead at Little Coal Creek at MM 163.9.

As you drive through the park, you'll skirt the churning gray flow of the **Chulitna River.** The milky soup is laden with "glacial flour," rock pulverized by glaciers rasping the Alaska Range to the west. From the Lower Troublesome Creek Campground Trailhead at MM 137.2, it's an easy, 1.2-mile stroll to the river on the **Chulitna Confluence Trail.**

If you're prepared for extended backcountry sojourning, consider exploring the rugged **Peters Hills** in the park's western reach, where the absence of trails rewards hikers with a splendid isolation watched over by Mount McKinley.

Camping and Lodging

The park has 4 campgrounds with 114 tent and RV sites. Backcountry camping permitted throughout the park. Available on a first-come, first-served basis. Camping fee. Byers Lake cabins available by reservation year-round; call the park or 907-269-8400.

Denali State Park, Division of Parks & Outdoor Recreation, HC 32 Box 6706, Wasilla, AK 99654; 907-745-3975; www.dnr.state.ak.us/parks

Wood-Tikchik

350 miles west of Anchorage, access by plane

■ 1,600,000 acres ■ Year-round ■ Wilderness camping ■ Hiking, river running/float trips ■ Hunting, fishing (license required for both)

A sampler of Alaskan terrain, the Delaware-size preserve is not only the nation's largest state park but also its most remote. Wood-Tikchik takes its name from two separate systems of river-connected lakes. Deep, crystal-clear, and teeming with trout and other sport fish, the 14 lakes range in length from 7 to 45 miles, lapping gravel shores in marshy lowland tundra on the east and mirroring the dark spires of the Wood River Mountains in fjordlike arms on the west.

Heather tundra and spruce-birch forest green the lower elevations. Climbing, hikers pass through coniferous forest into alder-choked foothills, then alpine meadows giving way to treeless mountains of glacier-polished rock. They also find beavers, moose, bears, marmots, otters, caribou, wolverines, mink, foxes, and bald eagles in an utterly wild kingdom.

Daily airline service links Anchorage and Dillingham; however, the park's isolation makes it best suited for experienced campers well-equipped for self-reliant backcountry fishing, boating, and hiking sojourns. Access to the Wood River lakes is possible by jet boat from Dillingham or Aleknagik, 24 road miles north. Most visitors fly in and out *(expect air taxis to charge at least $750 per hour)*. Ask park personnel to suggest destinations appropriate to your interests, abilities, equipment, as well as commercially available guide services.

Camping

The park is very primitive, with few designated camping sites.

Wood-Tikchik State Park, P.O. Box 1822, Dillingham, AK 99576; 907-842-2641; www.dnr.state.ak.us/parks

Totem Bight

10 miles north of Ketchikan on North Tongass Hwy.

▪ 11 acres ▪ Daily May–Sept., Mon.–Fri. rest of year ▪ No camping
▪ Interpretive trail ▪ Native Alaskan totem art and architecture

Native American culture found extraordinary expression among southeast Alaska's Tlingit and Haida people, who were skilled hunters and fishermen in the Inside Passage region, as well as refined artists of carving and painting totem poles. By the early 20th century, many of the villages were unoccupied, and houses and totems fell into decay. A program of reconstruction using tribal artists and traditional methods and materials commenced in the 1930s. Its crowning achievement is Totem Bight, where a re-created

Detail of reconstructed Clan House

19th-century clan house and 14 totem poles are arranged along a self-guided **interpretive trail.**

Don't walk the forested trail without the keyed brochure. It's essential for appreciating the totems' storytelling symbolism and understanding family life in the clan house.

Totem Bight State Historical Park, 9883 N. Tongass Hwy. Ketchikan, AK 99901; 907-247-8574; www.dnr.state.ak.us/parks

FAR WEST

LAKE TAHOE NEVADA

NEVADA

Carson City

BERLIN-ICHTHYOSAUR

Sacramento

CATHEDRAL GORGE

MOUNT TAMALPAIS

San Francisco

AÑO NUEVO

CALIF.

PFEIFFER BIG SUR

VALLEY OF FIRE

Las Vegas

AHJUMAWI LAVA SPRINGS

HUMBOLDT REDWOODS

Los Angeles

ANZA-BORREGO DESERT

San Diego

100 mi
200 km

Colorado

NA PALI COAST

KOKEE

KAUAI

NI'IHAU

WAIMEA CANYON

IOLANI PALACE

Honolulu

OAHU

MOLOKAI

LANAI

MAUI

KAHOOLAWE

IAO VALLEY

HAWAII

100 mi
200 km

KEALAKEKUA BAY

HAWAII

NEVADA

Lake Tahoe Nevada
Valley of Fire
Cathedral Gorge
Berlin-Ichthyosaur

CALIFORNIA

Anza-Borrego Desert
Humboldt Redwoods
Ahjumawi Lava Springs
Mount Tamalpais
Pfeiffer Big Sur
Año Nuevo

HAWAII

Na Pali Coast
Waimea Canyon and Kokee
Kealakekua
Iao Valley
Iolani Palace

Anza-Borrego Desert State Park, California

Lake Tahoe Nevada

15 miles west of Carson City on Nev. 28

■ 14,242 acres ■ Year-round ■ Day-use fee ■ Snow closes some trails in winter ■ Lakeside beaches ■ Mountain backcountry ■ Fishing (license required), hiking, mountain biking, cross-country skiing

Lake Tahoe

The most popular state park in Nevada reaches toward the sky among the granite peaks and pine trees of the Carson Range, and also sprawls along the undeveloped northeastern shore of Lake Tahoe, the second largest alpine lake in North America after Crater Lake. From 6,225 feet at the lakeshore, the terrain rises to 9,214 feet at Snow Valley Peak.

Tahoe, in the language of the Washo Indians, probably means "edge of the lake." The lake, filling a basin between the Sierra Nevada mountains and the Carson Range, measures 22 miles long, 12 miles wide, and 1,645 feet deep. It holds more than 39.8 trillion gallons of water and is clear enough in places to see to a depth of 65 feet. Its vibrant colors range through prismatic spectrums of blue and green.

After the 1850s, loggers came to Tahoe, then settlers. Tourism and summer houses began before the turn of the 20th century and boomed after World War II. Today, the park has five visitor areas along Nev. 28 and US 50 that offer resources, from white-sand beaches and swimming spots to 13,000 acres of wooded backcountry laced with trails and small lakes.

What to See and Do

Many travelers set off for the park from the casinos of South Lake Tahoe. Leaving behind the temples of temptation, drive north on US 50 to the park's first section at **Cave Rock.** Here take in gorgeous views of the lake, with the mighty Sierra Nevada as a backdrop. Cave Rock is a popular spot to launch boats and catch fish; it also has picnic sites and a small beach.

The entrance to the next section, **Spooner Lake,** is on Nev. 28 just north of the junction with US 50. Visitors can enjoy fishing for trout, as well as picnicking, mountain biking, and hiking. Along the lakeside nature trail, you'll likely see herons; if you're lucky, you may even spy an American bald eagle.

Spooner Lake is also a backcountry trailhead. The **North Canyon Trail** leads 5 miles to **Marlette Lake,** while a scenic trail follows the western shore. This connects with the historic **Flume Trail,** which mountain bikers rate among the top in the nation; the terrain is

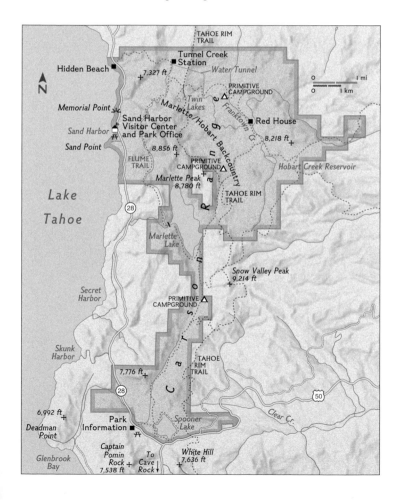

TAHOE RIM TRAIL

Tunnel Creek Station

Hidden Beach

7,327 ft

Water Tunnel

PRIMITIVE CAMPGROUND

N

Memorial Point

Marlette

Twin Lakes

Frankton

0   1 mi
0   1 km

Sand Harbor Visitor Center and Park Office

Red House

Marlette/Hobart Backcountry

Sand Harbor

Sand Point

8,856 ft

8,218 ft

FLUME TRAIL

PRIMITIVE CAMPGROUND

Hobart Creek Reservoir

Marlette Peak 8,780 ft

Lake

TAHOE RIM TRAIL

Tahoe

28

Marlette Lake

Snow Valley Peak 9,214 ft

Secret Harbor

PRIMITIVE CAMPGROUND

Skunk Harbor

7,776 ft

TAHOE RIM TRAIL

28

50

Clear Cr.

6,992 ft

Park Information

Spooner Lake

Deadman Point

Captain Pomin Rock 7,538 ft

To Cave Rock

White Hill 7,636 ft

Glenbrook Bay

challenging, the views of Lake Tahoe unforgettable. North of Marlette Lake, above **Little Valley,** stands an old-growth forest saved because 19th-century lumbermen found the trees too difficult to clear. Or take the new alternative **Marlette Lake Trail** *(4 miles, hikers and equestrians only)* up North Canyon.

For an alternative route from Spooner Lake, hike the **Tahoe Rim Trail** along the crest of the Carson Range. From this angle, you see Lake Tahoe as it can't be viewed from water level. Look for glacier-gouged **Emerald Bay** on the far shore. Or gaze east at the Carson Valley, the Stillwater Range, and the Shoshone Mountains.

In winter, Spooner Lake maintains 60 miles of groomed cross-country ski trails *(775-749-5349. Trail pass required; equipment rentals and ski lessons offered).*

Back on Nev. 28, head north about 8 miles to **Sand Harbor,** where beaches edge a point of land marked by boulders and pines. The warm, sun-drenched sand is a welcome relief if you've waded into the lake, whose high temperature in midsummer is only 68°F. Snorkelers and scuba divers often plunge into the water north of the point, where conditions are calm; there's also a boat launch here. You can explore the point itself along the **Sand Point Nature Trail,** then have lunch in the shade of Jeffrey pines in a designated picnic area equipped with barbecue grills. At the end of the 19th century, a Comstock mining mogul named Walter Hobart threw spectacular parties at his Sand Harbor summer home. Nowadays the community hosts a summer festival of music and Shakespeare at an outdoor theater *(800-747-4697. Adm. fee)* by the lake.

A mile north of Sand Harbor, you reach the park's final section, alongside Nev. 28. Stop first at **Memorial Point** overlook, which offers a broad view of Lake Tahoe (photographers take note); a trail here leads down to the rocky shoreline. Drive another mile toward Incline Village to a spot known mostly to locals, **Hidden Beach.** *(Note: There's no parking here; leave your car along the highway and walk in.)* The beach is popular with sunbathers (who aren't always wearing clothes).

Also in this area is the **Tunnel Creek Trailhead,** another way into the Carson Range backcountry. The trail climbs steeply to link with the Flume Trail, the Tahoe Rim Trail, and **Hobart Creek Reservoir.**

Camping

The park has 15 primitive tent sites. Available on a first-come, first-served basis. Camping fee.

Lake Tahoe Nevada State Park, P.O. Box 6116, Incline, NV 89452; 775-831-0494; www.parks.nv.gov/lt.htm

TAHOE'S TREES: During the latter part of the 19th century, Nevada's Comstock Lode and booming Virginia City created a ravenous market for mine timbers, building materials, and firewood. Most of the centuries-old pine trees around Lake Tahoe fell to the woodsman's ax. Thickets of fir trees replaced pine forests, but unfortunately, firs aren't well adapted to Tahoe's periodic droughts. Today, visitors see many large, dead, second-growth firs, weakened by drought and attacked by bark beetles.

Valley of Fire

55 miles northeast of Las Vegas on Nev.169

■ 35,500 acres ■ Year-round ■ Entrance fee ■ Summer temperatures reach well above 100°F ■ Colorful rock formations ■ Prehistoric rock art ■ Petrified wood ■ Hiking

The Valley of Fire seems otherworldly, a surreal realm of stone formations with evocative names like Cobra Rock, Indian Marbles, and Grand Piano. Indeed, the area is named for a phenomenon of cosmic scale: In the morning and the evening, the low slanting sun touches the ancient red sandstone like a torch, setting it ablaze.

351

Here the past is laid bare. You have entered a basin of Aztec sandstone that formed during the age of dinosaurs (about 200 million years ago) from vast dunes of sand. In this stone, water carved canyons, spires, domes, and spiny ridges. Wind scoured the exposed walls of buttes and canyons, gouging them into odd textures and shapes, including arches and balancing rocks. Upon these sculptures, chemical reactions created tints across the entire warm spectrum: ruby, rosé wine, terra-cotta, apricot, copper, gold.

On some of the sandstone walls, prehistoric Indians left petroglyphs depicting lizards, eagles, moun-

Hiker on sandstone slickrock

tain sheep, snakes, and other symbols of life in the desert. The park still offers a habitat for these creatures, as well as for the gila monster and desert tortoise, two rare reptiles that visitors must avoid disturbing. The Valley of Fire State Park, the oldest in Nevada, was established in 1935 to protect this fragile and beautiful desert environment.

What to See and Do

If you've driven east from Las Vegas on I-15 and Nev. 169, you'll enter the park through the west gate into a classic scene of the Wild West, where red rocks are set off by skies as blue as Navajo turquoise. In the jumbled stone formations you might see sphinxes, whales, or anything else your imagination can conjure out of all these oddities of rock. Just ahead, for instance, lie the **Beehives,** sandstone deposits that were shaped in a swirling pattern by the desert's relentless onslaught of heat, cold, rain, and wind.

Beyond the Beehives on the right, a **loop trail** leads to a deposit of petrified wood, solid evidence of a forest that thrived here 225 million years ago. You'll see some whole logs, but mostly fragments.

A spur road on the opposite side of Nev. 169 leads to **Atlatl Rock.** Here you climb iron stairs up a sheer wall of rock to see a panel of Indian petroglyphs. This register of ancient life was left by the valley's earliest visitors, the ancestral Puebloans who, from around 300 B.C. to A.D. 1150, occupied the Lost City, located just east of the park along the floodplain of the Muddy River (see sidebar p. 353). These prehistoric people came to the Valley of Fire to hunt game and gather seeds.

The designs were carved through desert varnish, a dark coating created when leaching water draws minerals from the rock. Outstanding among the depictions is an atlatl, a notched wooden stick used by prehistoric hunters to throw darts faster and farther. You'll also see concentric circles and bounding mountain sheep. The designs' meanings are not known, but some may have had ceremonial significance or represented social clans.

Atlatl Rock petroglyphs

Driving again on Nev. 169, stop at the **Visitor Center** to study fine exhibits on the valley's human and natural history. You'll learn that the dominant plants here are creosote bushes, and beavertail and cholla cactuses, all of which have adapted to living on sparse, irregular rainfall. Spring wildflowers include marigolds and desert mallow, which bloom along the park roads.

From the Visitor Center, a spur road leads to the **Petroglyph Canyon Trail,** a 0.5-mile, round-trip walk on the sandy floor of a canyon. On the vertical walls look for more prehistoric Indian rock art. In this canyon you'll also experience the park's immense silence; the only sounds are the crunching of your shoes in the sandy wash and your breath huffing into the empty skies.

The trail leads to **Mouse's Tank,** named for a renegade Paiute Indian of the 1890s, who reportedly murdered two prospectors and then fled to the Valley of Fire. This rugged spot offered a perfect hideout—but how could anyone live here without water? Mouse stumbled upon a natural water-collection basin, a depression in the rocks that could hold rainwater for months, known today as Mouse's Tank.

Continue along the spur road *(closed at sunset)* to **Rainbow Vista,** where you can look out over rock formations tinged in a dramatic splash of reds. Across from Rainbow Vista catch a roller-coaster of a gravel road to an overlook on **Fire Canyon,** a 600-foot-deep gorge. Also here is **Silica Dome,** whose whiteness contrasts starkly with the underlying red rock, separated by a line as straight as a yardstick. Back on the spur road, continue north about 3 miles. You will come to a closed dirt road used as a hiking and mountain-biking trail to **Duck Rock** (which looks vaguely like a duck, or perhaps a baseball hat). At road's end stand the **White Domes,** two formations of white silica melting together with red sandstone to create tints of pink and lavender.

Upon returning to Nev. 169 east, you pass the **Seven Sisters,** a gaggle of towering monoliths on the south side of the road. Ahead you'll see the stone cabins built by the Civilian Conservation Corps in the 1930s, later used to accommodate overnight travelers. Then comes the much-photographed **Elephant Rock,** reached via a short trail; the chunky rock indeed looks as wrinkled as an elephant's hide.

Camping

The park has 51 tent and RV sites, with showers. Available first come, first served. Camping fee.

Valley of Fire State Park, P.O. Box 515, Overton, NV 89040; 702-397-2088; www.parks.nv.gov/vf.htm

353

LOST CITY: An exhibit in nearby Overton commemorates the vanished culture of the ancestral Puebloans, also known as the Anasazi ("Ancient Ones"), who hunted and gathered in the Valley of Fire. They lived in the Pueblo Grande de Nevada, an area where pit houses and pueblo apartments once were clustered in sites stretching over some 30 miles. The Lost City Museum *(721 Moapa Valley Blvd. 702-397-2193. Adm. fee)* stands on part of this old pueblo, now referred to as the Lost City. Exhibits include a replicated dwelling of wattle and daub, as well as tools, jewelry, and pots made before the Anasazi disappeared mysteriously around A.D. 1150.

Cathedral Gorge

2 miles northwest of Panaca on US 93

- 1,633 acres ▪ Year-round ▪ Entrance fee ▪ Dogs must be leashed
- Slot canyons ▪ Horseback riding, hiking, biking

Bentonite cliffs and canyon

354

At first the park's main feature—bentonite clay formations—sounds like something only a geologist could love. But you soon adopt a geologist's appreciative eye as you see the ragged remnant of a Pliocene lake bed. If you were standing here three million years ago, you'd be under water and mud 1,000 feet deep. Over time the lake drained; sediments dried and hardened into siltstone, which was eroded by the elements forming the badland landscape.

After Mormon settlers founded nearby Panaca in 1864, ranchers used the chasm as a garbage dump. In the 1890s, a local woman, upon viewing the delicately eroded spires, was reminded of European cathedrals—thus Cathedral Gorge. Later, two Panaca teenagers built a series of ladders through the maze of canyons and crawl ways. By the 1920s, families came to picnic, and open-air pageants were staged at the gorge. It became a state park in 1935.

The **Regional Visitor Center** *(closed Oct.–Feb.)* exhibits regional geology and wildlife, including coyotes, bobcats, lizards, and snakes. A 0.5-mile loop trail links the campground and the **"caves,"** actually narrow canyon sections also accessible by car. A 4-mile trail leads from the campground through the remote **upper gorge.** The **Miller Point** and **Juniper Draw Trails** pass between 100-foot-high walls. Off US 93, 2 miles north of the entrance, **Miller Point Overlook** offers views into two side canyons. A nature loop along the access road reveals the upper gorge.

Camping

The park has 22 tent and RV sites, with showers, 2 handicapped-accessible campsites, and 2 group sites. Available first come, first served (group sites require reservations). Camping fee.

Cathedral Gorge State Park, P.O. Box 176, Panaca, NV 89042; 775-728-4460; www.parks.nv.gov/cg.htm

Berlin-Ichthyosaur

22 miles east of Gabbs, off Nev. 844

- 1,132 acres ▪ Year-round ▪ Marine fossils ▪ Ghost town ▪ Old mine
- Seasonal tours

For more than a century, men have dug here on the slope of the Shoshone Range seeking two things: precious metals and fossils. Not surprisingly, this park has two main attractions. The first is **Berlin,** a turn-of-the-20th-century mining town set among pinyon pines and junipers; its mine produced about 850,000 dollars worth of silver and gold, which supported a community of 250 people, including a doctor and a prostitute. The other attraction is a display of fossil ichthyosaurs, ancient marine reptiles that swam in warm seas covering central Nevada perhaps 225 million years ago.

Stop at the **park office** at the town entrance for an informational brochure. From here a trail leads among a dozen wood-frame buildings, many containing artifacts from the early 1900s. You may also want to tour the **Diana Mine** *(May–Sept., reservations recommended);* examine the walls for quartz deposits veined with real gold.

From Berlin head to the adjacent settlement of **Union,** or what's left of it: a ghost town with one adobe building and traces of a mill along an interpretive trail.

Then drive (or walk the 0.5-mile nature trail from the campground) to the **Fossil Shelter** *(tours daily Mem. Day–Labor Day, Sat.–Sun. mid-March–Mem. Day & Labor Day–mid-Nov.).* The A-frame structure stands above a deposit of fossil ichthyosaurs, or "fish lizards," which grew up to 50 feet long and had eyes as big as dinner plates. They gave birth to live young, making them unique among reptiles.

The Berlin site was first excavated in 1928 by S. W. Muller. Later, archaeological teams from the University of California at Berkeley uncovered about 40 ichthyosaur fossils here, including the largest specimens in the world.

355

Camping

The park has 14 tent and RV sites. First come, first served. Camping fee.

Berlin-Ichthyosaur State Park, HC 61 Box 61200, Austin, NV 89310; 775-964-2440; www.parks.nv .gov/bi.htm

Berlin mining camp

Anza-Borrego Desert

85 miles northeast of San Diego on Calif. 78

■ 600,000 acres ■ Year-round ■ Entrance fee in developed camp-grounds only ■ Summer temperatures exceed 100°F ■ Desert flora and fauna ■ Historic trails ■ Indian rock art ■ Hiking

New to the desert? At first you may be dismayed by the seeming emptiness of Anza-Borrego. The park sprawls across more than 900 square miles of rock and grit, and hundreds of washes and canyons. But soon the vast space, the pure light, and the silence flood your soul—healing antidotes to the noise of civilization.

The "empty" park turns out to contain riches—oases of palm trees, bighorn sheep, and eroded badlands. Paradoxically much of the terrain was shaped by the one element of nature conspicuous by its absence: water. A desert cloudburst can deepen a canyon by a few feet in just a few hours.

PARK TIP: *Explore fascinating Split Mountain, where the 400-foot red walls reveal millions of years of geologic history.*

Mammoth fossils have been uncovered here, and humans have dwelled in this desert for more than 5,000 years. Native Americans left mysterious petroglyphs and pictographs on rock walls. Some of the first outsiders to see the region were a party of Spanish led by Juan Bautista de Anza in 1774. You can see traces of his overland route, as well as the later Southern Overland Trail that brought gold seekers and others to California. The park takes its name from Anza and from the Spanish word for lamb, *borrego,* referring to desert bighorn sheep.

Yaqui Flat

What to See and Do

Approach the **Visitor Center** *(2 miles W of Borrego Springs on Palm Canyon Dr.)* from any of several scenic routes: Montezuma Valley Road (Cty. Rd. S22) from the west, Borrego-Salton Seaway (Cty. Rd. S22) from the east, or County Road S2 from the southeast.

The underground center presents four high-definition videos and information on the park's 60 species of mammals, 225 birds, and 60 reptiles and amphibians. In the gardens outside grow native shrubs and trees, and a pond contains endangered desert pupfish, Ice Age holdovers that can live in both fresh and salty water, at temperatures from near freezing to 108°F.

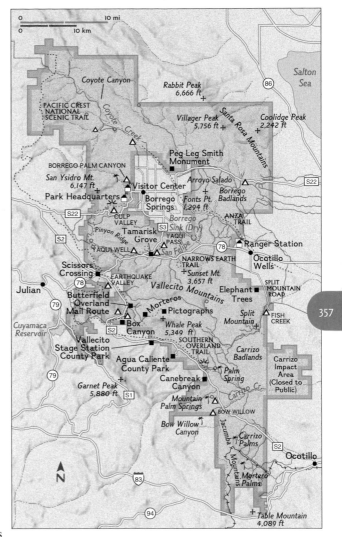

The pupfish pond is at the **Borrego Palm Canyon** trailhead *(west end of Borrego Palm Canyon campground)*. The first mile of this trail is a self-guided walk that introduces the park's notable features—alluvial fans, ocotillos, dry washes, Cahuilla *morteros* (holes in boulders where Indians ground seeds), and scurrying lizards. Another half mile brings you to a grove of native California fan palms, whose trunks are sheathed in skirts of dead leaves that evoke Hawaiian hula dancers. Indians once ate the fruits and used the frond fibers for sandals and baskets.

357

To explore more of the park, head east on County Road S22. After a couple of miles you can turn north on Di Giorgio Road for a side trip to **Coyote Canyon.** *(The route is suitable only for hikers, bicyclists, horseback riders, and four-wheel-drive vehicles.)* You'll find here a stream, surprisingly lush vegetation, and part of the historic Anza Trail.

358

California fan palms

Ahead on County Road S22 stands a pile of rocks called the **Peg Leg Smith Monument,** honoring a colorful, 19th-century prospector who claimed to have found a gold mine—and then lost it in the rugged terrain. The faker inspired the annual Peg Leg Liar's Contest *(held on the Sat. closest to April 1);* anyone is invited to tell a tale, as long as none of it is true. Behind the monument rises Coyote Mountain, whose metamorphic rocks hold deep-red garnets.

Continue to Font's Point Road for a 4-mile side trip to view the gullies and ragged ridges of the **Borrego Badlands,** which were carved by countless thunderstorms. **Font's Point** itself is being eroded by rain and faulting.

North of County Road S22 lies **Clark Dry Lake,** the desiccated basin of a lake that existed 20,000 years ago. Its clay bottom conceals the eggs of fairy shrimp that hatch when floodwaters penetrate the soil. Ahead rise the **Santa Rosa Mountains,** where rain has washed rocks and sand down from the slopes, forming classic alluvial fans. These ragged mountains are so young that they are still rising. The Santa Rosas lie along the active San Jacinto Fault.

To visit the park's center, known as the **Yaqui Pass Triangle,** take County Road S3 south from Borrego Springs toward Calif. 78. Take the Kenyon Overlook Trail from the top of Yaqui Pass and the **Mescal Bajada Overlook,** which shows off a *bajada* (ba-HA-da), a sloping plain created when a series of alluvial fans blend together at the base of desert mountains. Just ahead, the **Cactus Loop Trail** leads you among hundreds of teddybear cholla, beavertail, and hedgehog cactuses.

At Calif. 78, turn east to the **Narrows Earth Trail,** where a short walk reveals how mighty mountains are reduced to grains of sand. In this small canyon you'll view a fault line and rocks 100 million years old. Look also for the chuparosa plant, whose red flowers draw hummingbirds.

If time permits, continue on Calif. 78 to Ocotillo Wells, then turn south on Split Mountain Road to the **Elephant Trees Nature Trail,** named for a small herd of chubby-trunked trees with wrinkly bark. Other plants include smoke trees and barrel cactuses, whose ribs expand like an accordion to hold water.

Another major park route is the old **Southern Overland Trail,** which you pick up where County Road S2 joins Calif. 78 at Scissors Crossing. Over this trail have passed Spanish explorers, frontier scout Kit Carson, and passengers on the Butterfield Overland stage. After driving through Shelter Valley, turn east on the marked dirt road for a side trip to the **Butterfield Overland Mail Route Historical Monument.** You'll come to **Foot and Walker Pass,** where you can walk in wheel ruts dating from the 1850s. Farther along lies a short trail to Indian morteros and a rutted spur road leading to a 1-mile trail to Indian pictographs.

Back on County Road S2, proceed to **Box Canyon.** During the Mexican War in 1847, the Mormon Battalion conquered this dead-end canyon, using only axes and a pry bar to hack out a wagon trail. After that, thousands of soldiers, travelers, and gold-crazed emigrants poured across California on the two rough trails below you.

Continue to the **Vallecito Stage Station,** originally built in 1857 and authentically reconstructed. Ahead, take a side trip on the bumpy road to **Palm Spring,** where trails lead to oases shaded by California fan palms. Take a moment to rest here, as stagecoach travelers did more than 130 years ago.

One more route is the Monte-zuma Valley Road *(County Rd. S22, SW of Visitor Center);* turn north on the dirt road to the Culp Valley primi-tive camp area. A trail leads west of the campground about three-quarters of a mile to **Peña Spring,** whose waters lure deer, coyotes, and many birds, includ-ing quail. Another short, marked trail leads to a lookout on the **Borrego Valley** and the Santa Rosa Mountains. At 3,400 feet, this spot offers a retreat from the hot desert floor.

DESERT BLOOM: After a wet win-ter, it appears that a passing god-dess has strewn blossoms across Anza-Borrego—creamy dune prim-roses, purple sand verbena, and bright red flowers on the twiggy ocotillo. Blooming season runs from late February into April, usually peak-ing in early March. Tip: Write a self-addressed postcard saying, "The flowers are blooming," stamp it, and mail it in an envelope to Anza-Borrego Desert State Park, 200 Palm Canyon Dr., Borrego Springs, CA 92004. The staff will mail back the card two weeks before the expected peak. *(For recorded wildflower infor-mation, call 760-767-4684.)*

Camping

The park has 118 tent/RV and 52 RV sites, some with showers; 8 primi-tive camping areas; and 5 group camps. Reservations advised Feb. through April; call 800-444-7275. Camping fee.

Anza-Borrego Desert State Park, 200 Palm Canyon Dr., Borrego Springs, CA 92004; 760-767-5311; www.parks.ca.gov

359

Humboldt Redwoods

45 miles south of Eureka on US 101

- 53,000 acres ▪ Year-round ▪ Day-use fees for Williams Grove
- Old-growth redwoods ▪ Hiking, biking, horseback riding, swimming, canoeing ▪ Summer interpretive programs

When early morning fog drapes the giant coast redwoods, you can almost peer into the past, when ancestors of these magnificent trees flourished across the Northern Hemisphere. Climatic changes over time altered the lush, moist growing conditions, reducing the number of coast redwoods to a narrow strip running 450 miles from southern Oregon to central California. In the heart of this unique world lies Humboldt Redwoods State Park—53,000 glorious acres of redwoods, plus cool mountain streams, brilliant spring wildflowers, chaparral-clad hills, steep ridges, and prairies.

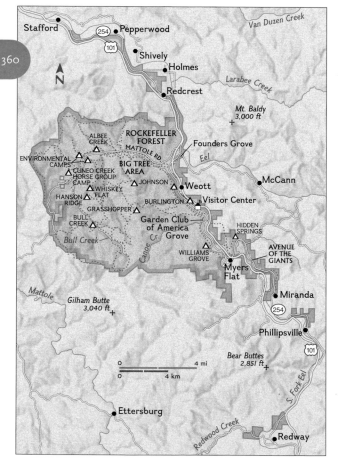

Take a moment to ponder the greatness of the redwoods: So immense are they—many standing more than 300 feet tall—that they occupy three different climatic zones: semishade at the base, cool and moist at the midriff, and dry and windy at the crown. So high up is the canopy that such creatures as marbled murrelets and flying squirrels never touch the ground.

These trees are tolerant of fire, thanks to a thick bark and lack of resin, and only the greatest of

360

conflagrations can bring them down. Indeed, their scientific name, *Sequoia sempervirens,* roughly translates as "ever living." Appropriate, since many you see are 600 to 1,200 years old—some more than 2,000.

What these trees can't survive is the lumberman's ax. In the late 1800s and early 1900s, the lumber companies started bringing these giants down. Fearful that the trees would be lost forever, a group of citizens formed the Save-the-Redwoods League in 1918. In 1921, the league made its first purchase in what would become this state park. Since then, more than 100 memorial groves have been established with the league's help. Humboldt is California's third largest park, and it continues to grow.

361

Coast redwoods

What to See and Do

Most of the state park can be seen along the 32-mile **Avenue of the Giants** *(driving-tour guide available at the Phillipsville and Jordan Rd. entrances),* a curving, slow-moving route paralleling US 101. Winding along the **Eel River,** it passes turnouts, hiking trails, picnic areas, and campgrounds. While the sunny southern and the dark, moody northern portions each have their charms, it's the central section that epitomizes the redwood experience. Begin at the **Visitor Center,** midway along the drive. Exhibits here detail life in the redwood forest, spotlighting such denizens as the mountain lion and black bear. Pick up brochures and maps and watch the slide show; then be off.

The most popular hiking trail, starting about 4 miles north at **Founders Grove,** provides a short, interpretive foray into the forest of monarchs. Right off you're greeted by the 346-foot **Founders Tree,** believed to be 1,600 years old. Delving deeper, you can't help but be amazed by the girths of the ruddy barked trunks that tower above lush ferns and oxalis. Midway lies a veritable graveyard of fallen giants, the most venerable the **Dyerville Giant.** Before toppling in a rainstorm some years back, this tree stood at least 362 feet tall—57 feet higher than the Statue of Liberty.

Ranking in spectacular scenery is nearby **Rockefeller Forest** *(along Bull Creek via Mattole Rd.)*—the largest, undisturbed, contiguous tract of old-growth coast redwoods in existence. A half mile long, the **Rockefeller Forest Loop Trail** gives a sense of what the north coast looked like centuries ago.

For a longer hike, follow the **Bull Creek Flats Trail** through the forest to the **Big Tree Area,** where reside three world-class specimens, including the Giant Tree, which has replaced the Dyerville Giant as the champion redwood. The 8.8-mile round-trip trail returns to Rockefeller Forest on the opposite side of Bull Creek. You can also reach the Big Tree Area by driving west on scenic Mattole Road, a narrow, winding route fringed with redwoods so close you can lean out the window and touch them.

Further Adventures

Laced with footpaths and fire roads, Humboldt's backcountry promises all kinds of adventures for backpackers, mountain bikers, and horseback riders alike. While the redwoods congregate along stream valleys, the backcountry mostly embraces prairies, sunny uplands, and steep ridges covered with madrone, chaparral, and Douglas fir. Trails wind past pioneer cemeteries, homestead ruins, and old moonshine locations, dating back to the area's first settlers.

For an overnight, you have a choice of five trail camps. All trails begin at Bull Creek Flats Road; distances from the trailheads aren't far, but can be steep. The two closest camps are also the most appealing: At **Johnson Trail Camp,** you can stay in a rustic cabin used by tie hacks from the 1920s to 1950s. At the **Whiskey Flat Trail Camp**—named for a moonshine operation run here during Prohibition—you can sleep beneath old-growth redwoods.

"COAST" REDWOODS: You won't find coast redwoods near the ocean—the salt air is too drying and the ocean winds too rough for their shallow root systems. Instead, these magnificent giants prefer foggy stream courses that wind through inland canyons. One reason is that this location supplies life-giving water. A mature redwood can lose 500 gallons of moisture a day; thick fog helps condense this lost water into a rainlike drip, which is then recycled back into the redwood's environment. Secondly, the streams bring rich alluvial silts and gravels from farther upstream, compacting them in benches and flats—ideal places for nurturing big trees. So where are the biggest trees? Founders Grove and Rockefeller Forest, of course, where the air is the foggiest and the soil the richest.

Camping

The park has 250 tent and RV sites (some open year-round), with shower facilities. There are also 2 environmental (primitive) campgrounds, 5 trail camps (permits required); and two group camps. A horse camp can accommodate up to 75 people with horses. Reservations advised in season; call 800-444-7275. Camping fee.

Humboldt Redwoods State Park, P.O. Box 100, Weott, CA 95571; 707-946-2409; www.humboldtredwoods.org

Ahjumawi Lava Springs

62 miles east of Redding off Calif. 299

■ 6,000 acres ■ Year-round (best season summer) ■ Undeveloped, access by boat only ■ Primitive camping, hiking, boating, fishing, bird-watching

Ahjuwami, an Indian word for the "coming together of waters," describes the merging of Big Lake, Tule River, Ja-She Creek, Lava Creek, and Fall River into one of the largest freshwater spring systems in the country. Brilliant aqua bays and tree-studded islets dot the shorelines of the pristine and largely untouched acreage preserved in Ahjumawi Lava Springs State Park.

> PARK TIP: *Don't forget the mosquito repellent, as the park has a reputation for having some of the country's finest.*

More than two thirds of the area is covered by recent (3,000 to 5,000 years) lava flows, which represent only a small portion of the extensive volcanic activity that pushed up the peaks of the Cascade Range over the past 20 million years. The result is an expanse of lava tubes and jagged black basalt—not easy to walk on—interspersed with freshwater springs that gush through faults and cracks in the volcanic rock.

363

What to See and Do

More than 20 miles of park trails allow visitors to explore this

Paddling across Horr Pond

primeval landscape, beautifully preserved by the absence of roads and automotive traffic. The undisturbed crowd-free environment harbors a thriving migratory wildlife population, with bird species ranging from western grebe, marsh hawk, quail, and osprey to bald eagle and great blue heron, usually spotted near Crystal Lake.

To explore the cobalt waters, plan to bring your own canoe, kayak, or small powerboat, as there are no rentals in the area. Fly-fishers delight in the park on the north bank of **Horr Pond**—named for the Horr family, who donated the land to the state in 1975. The best fishing holes are only a short northwest paddle from the public launching area **Rat Farm,** where muskrats were raised in the 1920s. Remnants of the stone wing-dam fish traps used by Pit River Indians inspire fishers along the way, hinting at the abundance of suckers and rainbow trout just beneath the water's crystal surface.

McARTHUR-BURNEY FALLS: Southwest of Ahjuwami on Calif. 299 is McArthur-Burney Falls Memorial State Park. Located within the Cascade Range, it is home to the majestic McArthur-Burney Falls. The falls drops 129 feet over a basalt shelf into a mist-filled basin created by the upsurge of fresh springwater. A steady 100 million gallons of springwater flows through the cascade each day, providing shelter for various birds nesting in the greenery behind, including the Black Swift. The 800 acres of parkland surrounding the falls offer hiking trails amid breathtaking backdrops.

Those visiting on foot should prepare adequately. While there are several trails traversing the park, note that going off-trail requires preparation and equipment and is not generally advised. Enjoy the 1-mile walk from **Crystal Springs** to Horr Pond, taking in the magnificent vistas of 14,163-foot Mount Shasta, 10,456-foot Lassen Peak, and other nearby Cascade peaks. From here, you can head north on the 3-mile **Spatter Cone Loop Trail** for views of lava tubes, lava flows, and the trail's namesake, a volcanic formation similar to a plug dome.

Despite the dominance of rugged lava rock, pockets of sagebrush and grass fields; oak, pine, and juniper forests; and wetlands provide a habitat for mule deer, black bears, mountain lions, and yellow-bellied marmots. The abundant wildlife population and rich ecosystem are evident in all seasons, but the color ranges of the oak, redbud, and mountain mahogany make fall prime visiting time.

Camping

There are nine primitive, or "environmental," campsites in the park, centered around Crystal Springs and Ja-She Creek. Though these are the most popular spots in the park, campsites are often empty, with spots vacant even on big vacation days.

California State Parks, Hwy. 89, Burney, CA 96013; 530-335-2777; www.parks.ca.gov/?page_id=464

Mount Tamalpais

10 miles north of San Francisco, off Calif. 1

▪ 6,400 acres ▪ Year-round ▪ Parking fee ▪ Mountain wilderness
▪ Panoramic views ▪ Spring wildflowers ▪ Mountain Theatre ▪ Hiking,
horseback riding

Bolinas Ridge

Standing sentinel over Marin County, Mount Tamalpais is the
dream-come-true of every nature lover. Trails wind through shady
redwood groves and lupine-covered meadows, across sunny, chaparral hillsides, and to dramatic East Peak, where a heart-stopping view
takes in the entire San Francisco bay area.

As mountains go, Mount Tam, as known locally, isn't so big—just
2,571 feet above sea level. But its slopes plunge to the San Francisco
Bay on one side and to the Pacific Ocean on the other, making it seem
mightier. The Coast Miwok Indians were among the first people to
sense its mystique; they believed its peak was inhabited by evil spirits.
Legend likens the mountain's silhouette to a sleeping maiden.

In the 1890s, the local gentry rode a creaking train to the mountaintop, where they danced and dined at the Tamalpais Tavern (only
the view platform remains). Back then, elk, grizzlies, and mountain
lions roamed the wilds, before the mountain was designated a game
refuge and their populations reduced. Mount Tam owes much to the
Tamalpais Conservation Club, which as early as 1912 began fighting
to save the land for hikers. In 1928, 692 acres were set aside for the
fledgling state park. Today the park, Muir Woods National Monument, Golden Gate National Recreation Area, and Marin Municipal
Water District preserve the whole mountain.

What to See and Do

Head up Pantoll Road *(off Panoramic Hwy.)* to E. Ridgecrest
Boulevard toward East Peak and hit the 0.5-mile **Plank Trail** to

the fire tower, where there's a 360-degree view of the bay, the buildings of San Francisco, acres of chaparral-covered slopes, and the Pacific. Like many people, you may be content to just sit on this magical mountaintop. However, you won't regret strolling along the easy, 0.75-mile **Verna Dunshee Trail,** which circles the peak.

Next, you're ready to explore the mountain, laced with 50 miles of marked trails (offering access to an additional 200-plus miles of trails contained in adjoining Muir Woods and Golden Gate NRA). Stop by the **Pantoll Park Headquarters** for a trail map. Popular among families is the 6.8-mile **Matt Davis Trail,** which descends to Stinson Beach. Visit the **Mountain Home Inn** *(415-381-9000. Reservations suggested),* since 1912 a hikers' rendezvous still offering cocktails, meals—and stunning sunsets.

The perennial favorite is the **Redwood Creek Trail,** a 2.5-mile hike through majestic redwood groves. Begin near the **Muir Woods park headquarters** (preferably in early morning or late afternoon to avoid the crowds), and become entranced by the ruddy barked giants that tower hundreds of feet above the lush, fern-carpeted earth. Only the brave (and the fit) should undertake the spectacular 7.2-mile (one way) **Dipsea Trail,** the scene of an excruciating footrace every June. Beginning in Mill Valley, just east of the park, with a steep ascent of 671 steps, the trail climbs over the mountain, crosses Suicide and Cardiac Hills and finally drops through redwoods to **Stinson Beach,** popular with surfers and sunbathers.

After a day of hiking, sit back and enjoy a musical at the **Mountain Theater** *(reached by shuttle or on foot; May–June, 415-383-0155. Adm. fee),* set in a natural bowl above the bay.

BIKE FEVER: Back in the 1970s, daredevil cyclists would truck their balloon-tired, beach-cruiser bicycles to the top of Mount Tam, then whiz downhill. In order to climb back up the mountain, bike techies Joe Breeze, Gary Fisher, and Tom Ritchey fashioned multigear components that could better negotiate rapid changes in slope and terrain. The trend caught on: In 1981 the first mass-produced mountain bike, called the Stump Jumper, entered the marketplace. By 1990 some 15 million mountain bikes had hit the trails; that same year the number of mountain bikes sold surpassed that of road bikes. Today, mountain bikers flock to the Old Railroad Grade, a smooth and easy doubletrack trail that begins opposite the Pantoll Park Headquarters and follows a former railbed. Those up for a more thrilling ride start atop East Peak.

PARK TIP: *The Mountain Theater was built in the 1930s. Also known as The Cushing Memorial Theater, it features the Mountain Play each spring.*

Camping and Lodging

The park has 16 walk-in tent sites; all first come, first served. There are also 10 cabins, 7 campsites, 2 group sites, and one equestrian site. Reservations required; call 800-444-7275. Camping fee.

Mount Tamalpais State Park, 801 Panoramic Hwy., Mill Valley, CA 94941; 415-388-2070; www.parks.ca.gov

Pfeiffer Big Sur

30 miles south of Monterey on Calif. 1

- 1,345 acres ▪ Year-round ▪ Day-use fee ▪ Redwood groves ▪ Big Sur
River ▪ Hiking, swimming ▪ Summer interpretive programs

Flowing through the rugged Santa Lucia Mountains, the clear-running
Big Sur River has carved a small, flat-bottomed valley—the site of
Pfeiffer Big Sur State Park. Tiny by most park standards, Pfeiffer Big
Sur contains a grand share of stunning scenery: Chaparral- and oak-
covered slopes plunge to the valley floor, adorned with a regal stand of
coast redwoods, the planet's tallest living organisms. Located near the
dramatic Big Sur coast, this shady sanctuary annually draws thousands
of hikers and campers.

Named for the Pfeiffer family, who settled here in the 1860s and
later sold its land to the state, the park flanks the river. Trails trace
the river, winding up ridges into the splendid backcountry of the
Ventana Wilderness, a glorious realm of sharp-crested ridges and
V-shaped valleys.

What to See and Do

At the heart of the park sits the **Big Sur Lodge,** with its cozy restaurant overlooking the Big Sur River. The nearby **Nature Center** *(June–
Aug.)* offers an introduction to the area's natural features.

Short and easy Pfeiffer Falls Trail *(temporarily closed)* makes
for a pleasant, brookside stroll through lush redwoods to **Pfeiffer
Falls,** which flows into Pfeiffer Redwood Creek. Return the
way you came or make a loop via the 0.7-mile **Valley View Trail,**
which climbs among oak, madrone, and coastal scrub to a scenic

367

Big Sur coastline from Ventana Wilderness

McWay Cove, Julia Pfeiffer Burns State Park

overlook of the Santa Lucia Mountains and distant Point Sur. During your walk, you may spot black-tailed deer, gray squirrels, raccoons, wild turkeys, foxes, or opossums. There are also mountain lions, coyotes, and boars in the region, but they are more elusive.

Next, return to the lodge and walk south on the park road to pick up the 0.3-mile **Nature Trail,** which interprets the area's diverse plant life. The woodland here is dominated by California bays (whose crushed leaves evoke the aroma of Italian cuisine), western sycamores, live and tan oaks, and stately redwoods. In spring, Douglas iris, hedge nettle, and globe lilies brighten the forest floor.

To see one of Big Sur's largest redwoods, drive to the group picnic area, where the **Colonial Tree** (27 feet in circumference) towers. If it's a hot summer day, follow the nearby **Gorge Trail,** an unofficial but well-traveled path to the cooling Big Sur River. A few boulder hops away you'll find one of the area's best swimming holes.

Camping and Lodging

The park has 200 tent and RV sites, with showers; two hike-in group camps (Mem. Day–mid-Sept.); a bike-in camp; and 61 cottages. For reservations, call 800-444-7275; for reservations at Big Sur Lodge call 800-442-4787. Camping fee.

Nearby Sights

Head south about a mile on Calif. 1 to **Pfeiffer Beach** *(via unmarked Sycamore Canyon Rd. Adm. fee),* a beautiful crescent of purple and white sands under craggy cliffs. It's a fine spot for picnicking, sunbathing, and watching sunsets, but think twice about swimming here: The water is cold and the surf rough.

Pfeiffer Big Sur State Park, Big Sur, CA 93920; 831-667-2315; www .parks.ca.gov/pbssp

368

BY THE WAY: Just 12 miles south of Pfeiffer Big Sur, Julia Pfeiffer Burns State Park *(831-667-2315. Adm. fee)* is not to be bypassed. While you are here, hike McWay Creek Trail to McWay Cove. Surrounded by high, rugged cliffs, this pretty cove showcases an 80-foot waterfall that plummets directly onto the beach. Look for sea otters and migrating gray whales. The park also features a 1,680-acre underwater park (for experienced divers only) and 1,800 acres of upland forest with trails. Tanbark Trail passes through several groves of redwood flourishing at their southernmost range.

Año Nuevo

On Calif. 1 between Santa Cruz and Half Moon Bay

▪ 4,000 acres ▪ Year-round ▪ Entrance fee ▪ No pets ▪ Breeding ground of northern elephant seals ▪ Rocky beaches ▪ Spring wildflowers ▪ Hiking, sunbathing, picnicking

The setting is rocky, windswept Point Año Nuevo, which juts into the crashing, blue Pacific. Here, coastal mountains, bluffs, dunes, and beaches mingle to create a breathtaking mosaic that looks much as it might have in January 1603, when Spanish explorer Sebastian Viscaino sailed by and named it to honor the new year.

With such diverse terrain, Año Nuevo not surprisingly harbors a great variety of wildlife, including some 300 species of birds, bobcats, black-tailed deer, sea lions, sea otters—and northern elephant seals.

Twice a year hundreds of elephant seals lumber ashore to mate, give birth, and molt (shed their pelts) in the dunes. The park's main draw, this biannual rite lures thousands, who come to watch one of nature's amazing displays.

From December to March (mating and pupping season), rangers offer 2.5-hour guided hikes *(reservations recommended, 800-444-4445; fee)* to this wildlife protection area. During the molting season, April through August, you must obtain a hiking permit from the entrance station to enter the protected area and use the designated trail.

If it's not seal season, sample one of the park's other trails: The short **Cove Beach Trail** leads to a beach sprinkled with rocks and fossils, while the **Atkinson Bluff Trail** meanders through acres of spring-blooming lupine and poppies.

Año Nuevo State Park, New Years Creek Rd., Pescadero, CA 94060; 650-879-0227; www.parks.ca.gov

ENDURANCE SWIM: Resembling beached whales, northern elephant seals lounge about the sand dunes, seemingly too lazy to blink an eye, much less eat. You'd lie about, too, if you knew that soon you'd be hauling out to sea, where you'll swim constantly—even while asleep. Indeed, over a period of 250 days, male elephant seals travel some 12,500 miles, swimming as far north as the Aleutian Islands, while the females are at sea 307 days a year, averaging 11,000 miles on their journeys west toward Japan. These marathon travels represent the longest known migration of any mammal. Returning twice a year to rookeries along the West Coast, these seals are also the only known animals to undertake an annual double migration.

369

Northern elephant seal

Na Pali Coast

8 miles west of Hanalei at end of Hawaii 560, Kauai

▪ 6,175 acres ▪ Year-round ▪ No pets ▪ Ocean conditions unpredictable; swimming not recommended ▪ Sea cliffs, river valleys, waterfalls ▪ Archaeological sites

Kalalau Beach

The name tells it all: Na Pali, "the cliffs." Here the volcanic island of Kauai plunges into the sea. Lush valleys open onto hidden beaches, and the famous Kalalau Trail lives up to its reputation as a pathway to paradise. The daunting terrain and sheer sea cliffs, which can drop more than 1,000 feet, have prevented roadbuilding, so the only way in to Na Pali is by foot trail or boat.

The ocean approach offers a broad perspective of sheer coastal palis and waterfalls cascading into the sea—a view that has awed visitors since a British fur trader named George Dixon first sailed along this coast in the late 1780s. The valleys of Na Pali, with their early agricultural terraces, still seem part of Old Hawaii.

What to See and Do

Suitable for fit hikers, the **Kalalau Trail** (which follows much of the same route trod by early Hawaiians) runs 11 miles, from Haena State Park to Kalalau Beach. It cuts above towering sea cliffs and winds through green valleys, dropping now and then to beaches. *(The trail can be precipitous, muddy, and rutted; in some spots along high cliffs it narrows to barely more than a foot wide. Be aware of the dangers of crossing rain-swollen streams and of swimming in the surf.)*

Day hikers can experience a bit of the Kalalau Trail, including fine views of the coast, on the 2-mile section from **Kee Beach** at Haena State Park to **Hanakapiai Beach.**

At Hanakapiai Beach, a maintained but sometimes rough side trail leads 2 miles up the **Hanakapiai Valley,** which receives 75 inches of rain a year—more than anywhere else along the Na Pali Coast. The water creates a paradisiacal forest of guava and *kukui,* with an understory of ferns and grasses. On the up-valley trail you pass bamboo, wild ginger, and mango trees, as well as rock-faced terraces where early Hawaiians grew taro, which they made into the starchy, pasty dish called poi. You also see traces of a coffee mill from the late 1800s. At the top is a waterfall about 300 feet high, with a pool for swimming—but not directly below the falls, since rocks and debris may be washed over. *(Hike the upper part of this trail only in good weather, as there is danger from flash floods and falling rocks.)*

If you choose to continue along the Kalalau Trail *(hiking and camping permit required beyond this point),* the hike becomes more strenuous in its next 4 miles, with steep switchbacks and two hanging valleys to cross. Climbing away from the sea, it reaches **Hanakoa,** a valley with agricultural terraces, where coffee plants now grow wild. Cool off in the pools of **Hanakoa Stream,** or hike a third of a mile up the east fork of the valley to **Hanakoa Falls.** *(Beware of eroded trail sections and treacherous footing.)*

Around the 7-mile point, the Kalalau Trail returns to the coast, crossing some dry terrain, formerly cattle country, where sisal and lantana grow. Ahead you see the ridges of Na Pali plunging toward the sea, then the **Kalalau Valley** appears, spreading 2 miles wide between fluted walls. Look for the sites of ancient houses and a *heiau* (temple) on the plateau above the shore. A lacework of creeks feeds into Kalalau Stream; you can take a 2-mile side trip up the valley to a natural water slide and pools at **Big Pond.** On the way you pass terraces covered with guava, Java plum, and mango trees. You'll spy goats around the cliffs.

371

The Kalalau Trail continues to **Kalalau Beach,** a 4,000-foot stretch of sand in the summer that extends to the small Hoolea waterfall. In early days the Hawaiian residents of the Kalalau Valley moved down to the beach in summer, living in sea caves and fishing from canoes. Today, campers frequent the beach in summer. Beware of falling rocks around cliff faces.

Further Adventures

Along the northwest coast is **Nualolo Kai,** a coastal flat accessible only by commercial boat *(for outfitters, contact the park);* it is isolated by cliffs nearly 2,000 feet high. More than six centuries ago, Hawaiians lived here, no doubt drawn by the coral reef where they caught rudderfish, tangs, parrot fish, and other sea creatures for food; now the reef draws snorkelers. In the 1820s, missionaries would stop here to rest as they canoed along the coast. And the cliff above Nualolo Kai was a prime spot for *oahi*—a display of early fireworks, created by throwing burning sticks off the cliff. It's said that, in the mid-1800s, King Kamehameha III stayed overnight at Nualolo just to see this spectacular light show. Today an **interpretive trail** guides you to early Hawaiian sites on the flat: mounds where sweet potatoes were grown, stone walls, house platforms, and an impressive ceremonial complex, evidence of its importance as a chiefly center.

Still farther along the coast lies **Milolii,** another coastal flat. Boats bring you through a fringed reef to a white-sand beach. About three-quarters of a mile up the **Milolii Valley Trail,** a waterfall tumbles, and you'll see old house sites and farming terraces.

GETTING AWAY FROM IT ALL: During the flower-power 1960s, young people drifted into the Eden of Kalalau Valley to mellow out and live on nature's bounty, such as the orange, papaya, and banana trees growing there. They weren't the first people to seek escape from the outside world: In 1893 a young Hawaiian named Koolau, who had contracted leprosy, hid here with his wife and small son, rather than be forced to leave them and live at the leper colony on Molokai. Neither sheriff nor soldiers could dislodge him from the valley—even with a cannon. The hippie residents of later years were evicted in 1974, when the area was established as a wilderness park.

Camping

The park has primitive camping areas (year-round) at Hanakoa and Kalalau, and at Milolii (mid-May–early Sept.). Permit required; available from park office in Lihue. Reservations advised in season; call 808-587-0300. In summer, only 60 campers total allowed per night. Each campsite is located near a stream; bring some means to purify water.

Division of State Parks, 3060 Eiwa St., Ste. 306, Lihue, Kauai, HI 96766; 808-587-0300; www.hawaiistateparks.org

Waimea Canyon and Kokee

8 miles north of Waimea on Hawaii 550, Kauai

- Waimea Canyon: 1,837 acres; Kokee: 4,345 acres ▪ Year-round
- Dirt roads very slick in wet weather ▪ Spectacular gorge ▪ Rain
forest ▪ Dramatic views ▪ Hiking

Mark Twain is believed to have dubbed the 3,600-foot-deep gorge at Waimea Canyon State Park the "Grand Canyon of the Pacific." It was once an active volcano, but part of its flank collapsed along a geological fault, creating a pathway for the Waimea River to cut the canyon.

For five million years water has sculptured the gorge. Erosion has exposed colorful layers of lava in the canyon walls, showing how many volcanic eruptions it took to build Kauai. The canyon has a red tinge because water has rusted the iron in the soil.

373

Adjacent Kokee State Park protects an island-top, native forest of koa and red-blossoming ohia lehua trees, and streams edged with ferns. Here you'll discover panoramic views of the remote Kalalau Valley, where green ridges plunge toward the blue sea at the Na Pali Coast. There is no foolproof method for avoiding the view-obscuring fogs that come and go. They do, however, come and go.

Waimea Canyon

What to See and Do

After driving up Hawaii 550 into Waimea, stop at the 0.25-mile **Iliau Nature Loop** (between Mileposts 8 and 9). Skirting the canyon rim, this trail offers dramatic views; it also introduces you to native plants, including *pukiawe*. In Old Hawaii, when high chiefs wanted to socialize with their people, they would walk through the smoke of burning pukiawe to temporarily nullify a taboo that required common folk

Wild ginger blossoms

to prostrate themselves. From here you can hike the steep, 2.5-mile **Kukui Trail,** which drops 2,000 feet to the Waimea River.

Continue driving up Hawaii 550 to the **Waimea Canyon Lookout** (between Miles 10 and 11). Along with the fantastic formations, spires, and amphitheaters of the gorge, you'll see three side canyons opening into the main chasm. At times mists drift across these canyons like wraiths.

Just ahead, stop at the railing at **Puu Ka Pele** to look across the canyon at **Waipoo Falls,** which makes an 800-foot plunge—if there's been any rain. Drive on to **Puu Hinahina Lookout** (between Miles 13 and 14), which offers two very different vistas: down 10-mile-long Waimea Canyon and toward the sea and Niihau Island. At the lookout, you'll spy white-tailed tropicbirds, which soar on updrafts in the canyon and nest on rocky perches.

Ahead on the left you can take a side trip on paved Makaha Road, a very steep route that leads to remote picnic areas and ends at a Navy radar station.

Or continue on the main road until you reach the **Kokee Natural History Museum** *(808-335-9975).* Tiptoe among the wild jungle chickens, called moa, to the door of this small institution that has been providing visitors with free information since 1953. (Ask the helpful museum staff for a trail map and the latest road conditions.) A three-dimensional model gives you a clear overview of Waimea Canyon, and an exhibit tells about hurricanes, which occasionally thrash Kauai; the most recent was Hurricane Iniki in 1992. Other displays look at island flora and fauna, including a humpback whale's vertebra and a Pacific green sea turtle, or *honu,* long valued for its shell and meat but now a threatened species. And those jungle chickens outside? You'll learn they're descended from escaped chickens from hurricanes and fowl brought by early Polynesian voyagers to Hawaii.

Near the museum the gentle, 0.1-mile **Nature Trail** takes you through a forest where plaques identify native plants, such as the *hahalua,* whose stalks rise as high as 40 feet. Another popular walking route is the 2.2-mile **Canyon Trail,** which crosses **Kokee Stream** and has awe-inspiring views of Waimea Canyon.

Continue on Kokee Road, perhaps stopping to hike the 3.25-mile **Awaawapuhi Trail,** which overlooks green valleys above the

Na Pali Coast. Next, the main road winds among ohia trees, begonias, and tree ferns to **Kalalau Lookout** (Mile 18). Don't be surprised if the view is blocked by clouds; you're at an elevation of 4,000 feet, where clouds form on Kauai. Wait a bit in case the mists clear, allowing you to see into the Kalalau Valley. The biggest valley along the Na Pali Coast, it was once the home of farmers and taro fields, but the last residents moved out in 1919. The ruins of rock-faced irrigation ditches and house foundations remain in the valley.

Drive on until the road ends at **Puu o Kila Lookout.** Below you the Kalalau Valley spreads 2 miles wide, between furrowed walls of green and brown—one of the finest views in the Hawaiian Islands. From here the 3.7-mile **Pihea Trail** leads along the valley's edge, among ohia trees and ferns, to the 3.5-mile **Alakai Swamp Trail.**

Alakai Swamp consists of 30 square miles of bogs and ridges. Why all this moisture? The swamp lies just below one of the world's wettest spots, Mount Waialeale (5,148 feet), which receives an average of 451 inches of rain annually. (One year 681 inches fell—more than 56 feet of water.) A wooden boardwalk along much of the trail saves you from bogging down on the muddy, often slippery ground. The trail brings you to the **Kilohana Lookout,** on the edge of a cliff. From here you can see the sweep of the Wainiha Valley, with lovely Hanalei Bay beckoning on the distant coastline.

> **LEGEND OF KOKEE MEADOW:** Why should there be an open meadow in front of the Kokee Natural History Museum, while dense forests grow all around? Legend tells us that the meadow was once filled with trees, where an unpleasant *akua* (spirit) lurked. He liked to bedevil fatigued travelers walking the trail to Kalalau Valley. Finally, in response to people's prayers, the god Kanaloa tore out all the trees. Now the evil akua had no place to hide. Today the only mischievous spirits you might see around the meadow are mynah birds.

375

Camping

Kokee State Park offers tent sites (permits required) for up to 15 campers per night. Reservations advised in season; call 808-274-3444.

Division of State Parks, 3060 Eiwa St., Ste. 306, Lihue, Kauai, HI 96766; 808-274-3444; www.hawaiistateparks.org

Kealakekua Bay

12 miles south of Kailua, off Napoopoo Rd., Hawaii

- Year-round ▪ No pets ▪ No camping ▪ Site of early foreign contact
- Temple ruins ▪ Captain Cook's Monument ▪ Snorkeling

In this picturesque bay, Hawaiians and Europeans had their first prolonged encounter when Capt. James Cook visited in 1779. Kealakekua was a Hawaiian political and religious center, and the chiefs and priests may have believed that Cook was the god Lono. (After all, Cook arrived under full sail, and legends foretold that Lono would appear on a "floating island" under streamers of white tapa cloth.)

During a monthlong stay, Cook's scientists and artists documented early Hawaiian villages, ceremonies, and crafts. But local hospitality ran out when Cook later had to return to Kealakekua to repair a broken mast. The Hawaiians took a small boat, and Cook, hoping to persuade them to return it, tried to take an important chief hostage. In the ensuing fight, Cook was killed on the shore.

Most visitors come simply to stand for a moment where these momentous historical events occurred. Motorists arrive at Napoopoo; the once sandy beach is now covered in basalt boulders and coral deposited by high surf during hurricanes. Near the parking area is the stone platform of **Hikiau Heiau,** a temple that was once the scene of human sacrifices.

Along the bay rises **Pali Kapu O Keoua,** a 600-foot-high sea cliff pocked with lava tubes where Hawaiian chiefs were buried. On the far side is **Kaawaloa,** a flat, lava peninsula home to high chiefs. Cook was killed here, and the white obelisk Captain Cook's Monument stands among kiawe trees. The best way to reach this side of the bay is by boat or kayak.

Calm **Kaawaloa Cove** is popular with snorkelers because its shallow coral reef harbors many species of colorful fish. A playful school of spinner dolphins also lives in the bay. Regulations prohibit anyone from approaching or bothering the dolphins. The bay's pristine waters and spectacular setting should be enough for anyone. Another alternative is the very challenging 2-mile (one way) **Kaawaloa Trail** to the cove.

Division of State Parks, P.O. Box 936, Hilo, HI 96721; 808-974-6200; www.hawaiistateparks.org

Iao Valley

5 miles west of Wailuku on Iao Valley Rd. (Hawaii 32), Maui

■ 6 acres ■ Year-round ■ Historic site ■ Lush valley ■ Rock spire

This green valley in the West Maui Mountains was named after the demigod Maui's daughter, Iao (Cloud Supreme). Long considered a spiritual place, it also makes an important claim on history: Here in 1790, during the Battle of Kepaniwai, the island's defenders under Kalanikupule were trapped by the invading forces of King Kamehameha I who sought to unite the Hawaiian Islands into a kingdom. So terrible was the slaughter that Iao Stream ran red with blood and bodies choked the water. (Kepaniwai means "damming of the waters.")

A 0.6-mile walkway offers vistas of the valley and velvet-green **Kukaemoku,** or **Iao Needle**—an eroded basalt spire that rises 1,200 feet from the valley floor. Stairs climb to a look-out shelter—welcome in case some of the valley's annual 150 inches of rain falls. The walkway also dips down to **Iao Stream,** where a dirt path leads among ginger plants to pretty pools.

Just below the bridge, a trail winds through a colorful **botanical garden** of native Hawaiian and Polynesian plants, including a demonstration taro patch.

Division of State Parks, 54 South High St. #101, Wailuku, HI 96793; 808-984-8109; www.hawaii stateparks.org

Iao Needle

Iolani Palace

King and Richards Sts., downtown Honolulu, Oahu

▪ 11 acres ▪ Year-round ▪ No camping ▪ Royal residence and grounds

The United States' only official state residence of royalty, this was the home of Hawaii's last monarchs. Island rulers lived here from 1882, when King Kalakaua moved in, until his sister and successor Liliuokalani was overthrown in 1893 by those who wanted Hawaii annexed to the United States. The palace's American Florentine architecture, borrowed from the Italian-Renaissance style, and eclectic furnishings are evidence of Kalakaua's love affair not only with Europe, but with the rest of the world. Thoroughly modern, he installed one of Hawaii's first telephones and wired the palace for electricity—even before the White House did. After 1893, the palace served as capitol of the Republic of Hawaii and later of the American territory and state.

Iolani Palace—the name means "royal or heavenly hawk"—stands on well-tended grounds, which are approached from any of the four major gates. The Kauikeaouli was the one used for state occasions and most popular with guests.

The guided tour *(fee, reservations suggested)* starts on the rear lanai and takes in the **Grand Hall,** with its gleaming native woods and royal portraits; the **Throne Room;** and the **State Dining Room.** On the second floor are royal bedrooms, the King's library, and the family music room.

Also on the property are the copper-domed **Coronation Pavilion** built for the coronation ceremonies of King Kalakaua and Queen Kapiolani, and the **Iolani Barracks** home to the royal guard. Also in a corner of the grounds is a **fenced mound** that once was the royal tomb. The Royal Hawaiian Band *(808-922-5331)* gives concerts most Fridays at noon.

The Friends of Iolani Palace, P.O. Box 2259, Honolulu, HI 96804; 808-522-0832; www.iolanipalace.org

377

Canadian
PROVINCIAL PARKS

CANADA

0   200 mi
0   400 km

U.S.
CANADA

YUKON

NORTHWEST
TERRITORIES

N U N

C   A   N   A

LIARD RIVER
HOTSPRINGS
MUNCHO LAKE

BRITISH

COLUMBIA

ALBERTA

MANITOBA

BOWRON LAKE

WELLS GRAY

LAC LA RONGE

PAINT LAKE &
PISEW FALLS

STRATHCONA   GARIBALDI

SASKATCHEWAN

GRASS
RIVER

E.C. MANNING   CATHEDRAL   DINOSAUR

DUCK
MOUNTAIN

WOODLAND
CARIBOU

CYPRESS HILLS

NOPIMING

O N

CANADA
U.S.

SPRUCE
WOODS

WHITESHELL

NEWFOUNDLAND
Barachois Pond

NOVA SCOTIA
Whycocomagh

PRINCE EDWARD ISLAND
Northumberland

NEW BRUNSWICK
Hopewell Rocks
Mount Carleton

QUÉBEC
Mont-Tremblant
Gatineau

ONTARIO
Bon Echo
Algonquin
Killarney
Lake Superior
Woodland Caribou
Polar Bear

MANITOBA
Whiteshell
Nopiming
Grass River
Spruce Woods
Duck Mountain
Paint Lake &
    Pisew Falls

SASKATCHEWAN
Lac La Ronge
Cypress Hills

ALBERTA
Dinosaur

BRITISH COLUMBIA
Liard River Hot
    Springs
Muncho Lake
Bowron Lake
Cathedral
Wells Gray
E.C. Manning
Garibaldi
Strathcona

U   T

A

LAR BEAR

QUEBEC

NEWFOUNDLAND AND LABRADOR

BARACHOIS POND

PRINCE EDWARD I.

MOUNT CARLETON

WHYCOCOMAGH
NORTHUMBERLAND
HOPEWELL ROCKS

NOVA SCOTIA

LAKE SUPERIOR
MONT-TREMBLANT

KILLARNEY
GATINEAU

NEW BRUNSWICK

ALGONQUIN   BON ECHO

Barachois Pond Provincial Park

Southwest Newfoundland, 12 miles (19 km) east of Stephenville off Trans-Canada 1

- 8,648 acres ▪ Year-round ▪ Hiking, sailing, canoeing, swimming
- Fishing, ice fishing

Swimming at Barachois Pond

A wild and lonely landscape, this provincial park—the largest in western Newfoundland—is perhaps the most accessible and family friendly of all the island's nature areas. Balsam fir and stands of birch, maple, and rare black ash blanket U-shaped glacial valleys, while bogs pockmark the higher elevations. Tuckamore—a nearly impenetrable, stunted thicket of entwined fir and spruce—grows upon the ridges.

What to See and Do

Boardwalk trails traverse mountain streams and forest. For the more adventurous hiker, **Erin Mountain Trail** climbs 2 miles (3.2 km) through the forest to the mountain's barren, 1,115-foot-high (340 m) summit. The views over the Long Range Mountains to the east and of St. George's Bay and the Gulf of St. Lawrence to the west are splendid. You can overnight at the summit's primitive campsite. The trail leaves from the end of the loop road around campsites 1 to 44 on the peninsula and crosses a bridge over the narrows of Barachois Pond. A freshwater beach lines each side of the peninsula.

Camping

The park has 150 tent and RV campsites, with one shower facility. Call 709-649-0048 for reservations. Camping fee.

Barachois Pond Provincial Park, Newfoundland and Labrador Department of Tourism, Culture and Recreation, P.O. Box 8700, St. John's, NF A1B 4J6; 709-729-0862; www.env.gov.nl.ca/env/parks/parks/p_bp

Whycocomagh Provincial Park

Northeast Nova Scotia on Cape Breton, 0.2 mile (0.4 km) east of Whycocomagh on Hwy. 105

■ 12 acres ■ June–Oct. ■ Hiking, boating ■ Bald eagles, wildlife

It's said that Alexander Graham Bell dubbed the town of Whycocomagh the "Rio de Janeiro of North America." Though Bell was most likely referring to the picturesque island just south of town and analogous inlet geography, these days, the parallel is less obvious. Located on the southern end of Cape Breton, the town of Whycocomagh is a small, isolated community of 450 people.

In Whycocomagh Provincial Park, a stunning 12 acres sprawled up a steep hillside overlooking the Bras d'Or Lake, you may spot as many bald eagles as people. Cape Breton Island holds the largest concentration of bald eagle nests in northeastern North America, and Whycocomagh's rural location and dramatic vistas make it easy to spot one of these soaring birds, often riding the thermals around Salt Mountain.

What to See and Do

The park's three marked hiking trails begin at the park's lakefront campground and end at the summit of Salt Mountain, where you'll enjoy a panorama of the Skye River Valley and the meanderings of Bras d'Or Lake. But, you've got to earn the spectacular view— all three trails ascend 800 feet (240 m) to the summit in less than 1.5 miles (2.4 km).

Beginning at site #27, the **Scout Trail** (1.2 miles/2 km) traverses the valley and climbs a rocky ascent before it joins the **Salt Mountain Trail** (trailhead at site #49, 0.8 mile/1.3 km) for the final stretch. The **Highlander Trail** begins at the parking lot near the administration

THE CABOT TRAIL: Just 17 miles (27 km) from the park, you can hop on one of the most stunning scenic drives in North America: The Cabot Trail. This 185-mile (298 km) road loops around most of Cape Breton, winding along costal cliffs and through seaside hamlets. Pause for a breathtaking, wind-swept view over these towering cliffs, hike through rugged wilderness, play 18 holes of golf with the ocean at your back, or try fresh-caught Atlantic lobster. At its northern-most tip, the trail passes through Cape Breton Highlands National Park, a tangle of wilderness with some 25 hiking trails and 8 campgrounds to choose from.

Named after explorer John Cabot, the trail was completed in 1932 to connect previously isolated fishing villages. Today, it connects eight major communities of Cape Breton, showcasing the thriving Gaelic and Acadian cultures of northern Nova Scotia. From Whycocomagh, head north on Hwy. 105 to the town of Buckwheat Corner, 17 miles (27 km) away. The Cabot Trail joins the highway at exit 11. From here, you can take the loop in either direction, cutting west across the cape or heading north toward Cape Breton National Park. Visit www.cabottrail.travel for maps and more information.

building and swings south for a steep half-mile (0.8 km) ascent before it joins the Salt Mountain trail.

The town of Whycocomagh is a traditional center for Nova Scotia's native Mi'kmaq people, and the nearby town of Waycobah also hosts a thriving community of Mi'kmaq, who often hold cultural events like powwows and sell a variety of handicrafts.

The campground at Whycocomagh—which means "head of the waters" in Mi'kmaq—is literally at the head of the waters on Bras d'Or Lake. Known internationally for its boating, Bras d'Or Lake is not actually a lake, but rather an inland arm of the Atlantic Ocean. The unique tidal waters of the lake support a diverse array of wildlife, both in and out of the water. There's a boat put-in at the park's campground, but the nearest canoe and kayak rentals are in Baddeck, 25 miles (40 km) up Hwy. 105. The **Bras d'Or Lakes Scenic Drive** *(800-565-0000)* passes through Wycocomagh from Baddeck on its loop around the lake. Stop at any of the towns along the way for bird-watching tours, sailboat rentals, or boat cruises.

Secluded picnic spot

Camping

There are 62 tent campsites in the park (open mid-June–mid-Oct.), with showers. Group camping available. Camping fee.

Whycocomagh Provincial Park, 960 Hampton Mountain Rd.; Department of Natural Resources, P.O. Box 130, Whycocomagh, Nova Scotia, B0E 3M0; 902-756-2448 or 888-544-3434 for reservations; www.novascotiaparks.ca

Northumberland Provincial Park

Southeast Prince Edward Island, 1.8 miles (2.9 km) east of Wood Islands ferry terminal

- 76 acres ▪ Year-round ▪ Family-friendly ▪ Beaches ▪ Nature trail
- Bird-watching

Head east after driving off the ferry that carried you across Northumberland Strait to Prince Edward Island from Caribou, Nova Scotia, and within a few short miles you'll discover a park that is deservedly popular with families. They are drawn to Northumberland Provincial Park by its safe, supervised beach *(on Rte. 4, behind visitor center)* and by its warm (70°F/21°C) ocean water. Armed with small shovels and pails, dozens of family groups can be seen working their way along the shoreline in summer, digging up fresh clams for that night's dinner. Indeed, with laundry facilities, hot showers, restrooms, playground, kitchen shelter, dump station, and camp store *(902-962-7418)* all nearby, this park is probably about as far as you can get from Outward Bound.

What to See and Do

From the park office, an interpretive nature trail meanders 1 mile (1.6 km) through a mix of forests and meadows that display the flora and fauna native to Prince Edward Island. A spectrum of shorebirds and waterfowl will have birders scrambling for their life lists. Cliff swallows are a frequent sight; they nest in burrows along the shore.

At the ferry docks, another small picnic park, **Wood Islands,** offers a beach, changing facilities, a playground, and restrooms for campers.

Camping

There are 46 tent and RV sites, with showers. Open late May–mid-Sept.; services limited June and Sept. There are also 7 cabins with electricity. For reservations, visit http://search.tourismpei.com/accommodations.

Northumberland Provincial Park, Parks Division East, Box 370, Montague, PEI C0A 1R0; 902-962-7418 or 800-463-4734; www .tourismpei.com/provincial-park/northumberland

Hopewell Rocks Provincial Park

Southeast New Brunswick in Shepody Bay, 20 miles (32 km) southeast of Moncton on Hwy. 114

- 45 acres ▪ Year-round ▪ Stone formations ▪ Bird-watching, tide-watching ▪ No camping

Head for Hopewell Cape to see what people look like when turned to stone by an angry whale. That's how Mi'kmaq legend explains the existence of the Hopewell Rocks—curious flowerpot stone formations, erosional pillars, and freestanding sea stacks eaten away by the voracious tides in the nearby Bay of Fundy. At high tide, the Hopewell Rocks appear to be unexceptional small islands, each capped by dwarf spruce and fir. By low tide, however, when the water has dropped away—as it does here at an extraordinary 6–8 vertical feet (1.8–2.4 m) per hour—the true shape and scope of the rocks are exposed: They tower as tall as five-story buildings sitting on the ocean floor.

Hopewell Rocks, billed as an Ocean Tidal Exploration Site, has interpretive guides available to lead ocean-floor walks from May to

Sunset at Hopewell Rocks

early October, but you are free to explore on your own—at low tide, naturally. Tide tables are posted in the reception center. The beach, reached via a staircase from the reception center's observation deck, is accessible for a few hours on either side of low tide.

As at so many other spots along the Bay of Fundy shore, the Hopewell Rocks area is a critical stop for millions of migrating birds, which pause here each spring and fall to feast on mud clams, periwinkles, and marine worms. Any time from July to October is optimum for spotting a variety of shorebirds, including plover, sandpipers, curlews, and godwits. Low tide is the best time to spy them feeding; at high tide they tend to roost in the cliffs, out of sight of the visitor center and its deck.

Hopewell Rocks Ocean Tidal Exploration Site, 131 Discovery Rd., Hopewell Cape, Albert County, NB E4H 4Z5; 506-734-3534 or 877-734-3429; www.thehopewellrocks.ca

Mount Carleton Provincial Park

Northern New Brunswick, 50 miles (80 km) west of Bathurst via Hwy. 180 west and Hwy. 385 south

- 43,000 acres ▪ Year-round ▪ Trans-Canada trail ▪ Hiking, backpacking, mountain climbing, boating, canoeing ▪ Cross-country skiing

A hard scramble after an unhurried hike, the last few hundred yards of the trail to Mount Carleton's 2,690-foot (820 m) summit—the highest point in the Maritimes—are well worth the effort. From the viewing platform of the fire tower you'll find clinging to the craggy peak, views extend in every direction over the park. You can take in the Nepisiguit Lakes to the east, Mount Head and Sagamook Mountain to the north, Mount Bailey to the northwest, and the Serpentine Mountains and Sisson Branch Reservoir to the southwest.

The park encompasses several of the highest mountains of northern New Brunswick's Appalachians. Seven lakes—and the headwaters of two river systems—lie in the valleys among them. The Tobique River rises in the northwest corner of the park and flows southwest to join the St. John, while the Nepisiguit River debouches from the Nepisiguit Lakes and eventually empties into Chaleur Bay. Forests of white birch, white and black spruce, and balsam fir are mixed with pockets of red maple at lower elevations, giving the mountain views a different texture in each season: green to black in summer, jeweled with red in fall, white on black in winter.

Equally startling are the views from the crest of 2,550-foot-high (777 m) Sagamook Mountain. Having slogged your way to the summit, you can rest on a rocky cliff and look down at Little Nictau Lake.

What to See and Do

One of the park's two easiest **hiking** paths is the half-mile (0.8 km/round-trip) **Williams Falls Trail,** a wheelchair-accessible stroll through old mixed forest to a pleasant view of the falls. The **Pine Point Trail,**

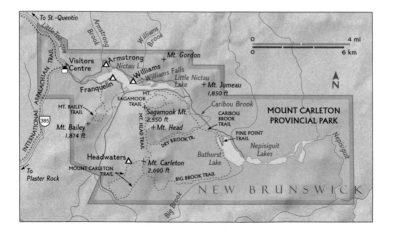

a 1.4-mile (2.3 km) loop, starts at the parking area west of Bathurst Lake and ambles along the lakeshore.

Another moderate path, the 4-mile (6.4 km) **Caribou Brook Trail** *(access via S shore of Little Nictau Lake),* follows the waterway of the same name as it flows from the south flank of Sagamook Mountain into Little Nictau Lake. Along the way you'll be using part of an aboriginal portage route between the Nictau and Nepisiguit Lake systems. No woodland caribou live in the region anymore, but moose and deer are plentiful, and the handiwork of beavers is everywhere.

More challenging are the trails to mountaintops. **Mount Carleton** itself occupies the junction of two such trails. The 3-mile (4.8 km/ one way) **Eastern Trail**—reached by driving south on the park road from Nictau Lake for 8 miles (12.9 km) to a parking lot on the mountain's south side—follows an old supply road culminating in a hard, 300-yard (275 m) scramble to the fire tower. The **Western Trail,** a bit longer, starts at the same parking lot and winds through the trees to reach a campground called Headwaters. The two ends of a loop trail lead from the campsite to the summit; a sheltered route climbs to the top. You can return to the campsite by descending along the loop's other branch, which is rockier and more exposed to the wind.

The **Mount Bailey Trail,** a 6-mile (9.7 km) round-trip beginning near the park headquarters at Nictau Lake, climbs steadily through sugar maples and beeches, which give way to white birch and mountain ash. About 2.5 miles (4 km) along the trail, a half-mile (0.8 km) side trail strikes off for **Mount Bailey.** The most difficult hike is the 5-mile (8 km/round-trip) slog to the summit of **Sagamook Mountain** from Little Nictau Lake. Spectacular views of the Nictau lakes await you en route, but the path can be treacherous on rainy days.

Winter comes early to the mountains of New Brunswick. Snow falls in October and lingers on the slopes until June, when spring is in full swing in the valleys. In fact, the area is free of frost only 60 days a year. The best cross-country skiing is in March, when fresh snow forms a carpet 6 feet (1.8 m) deep on slopes and trails and the lake ice is still a yard thick.

Several easy groomed trails start at park headquarters *(W end of Big Nictau Lake).* One is a 4.5-mile (7.2 km) loop that begins and ends at a heated cabin; shortcuts allow you to cinch the loop to 3 miles (4.8 km) or just 1 (1.6 km). All three circuits yield splendid views of Franquelin Hill and Mount Bailey. Experienced skiers will want to test themselves on the 10-mile (16 km) swing around **Nictau Lake,** or the 19-mile (31 km) round-trip to the top of Mount Carleton. The park roads, unplowed in winter, must be shared with snowmobiles.

Camping

The park campground has 88 wilderness sites, with showers; 506-235-0793. Camping fee.

Mount Carleton Provincial Park, 7612 Rte. 385 Saint-Quentin, NB; 506-235-0793 or 800-561-0123 for reservations; www.tourism newbrunswick.ca/Home/Destinations/Parks/ProvincialParks.aspx

Mont-Tremblant National Park

Southern Québec, 87 miles (140 km) north of Montréal via Hwys. 15 and 117

- 375,000 acres ▪ Year-round ▪ Downhill skiing, cross-country skiing, snowshoeing ▪ Lakes, hardwood forest ▪ Canoeing, canoe camping ▪ Hiking, mountain biking ▪ Three zones

389

Eastern cougar

Mont-Tremblant National Park is located on the other side of the mountain from the famous ski area with 92 ski runs and 46 miles (74 km) of trails of the same name. This is a gateway to true wilderness, set in lovely rolling countryside an easy morning's drive from Montréal. Québec's largest provincial park affords nature lovers a quiet and tranquil experience. Within the park's borders lie some 400 lakes, six rivers, and the endless roll of the Laurentides Mountains, most of them covered in maple and yellow birch—gloriously scarlet and gold in fall, often blanketed in a 40-inch (1 m) mantle of snow in winter.

The Laurentides harbor a host of wild creatures, including black bears, foxes, and moose, as well as wolverines and fishers. White-tailed deer roam the park's southern reaches and rumors of cougar sightings have begun to circulate once more (see sidebar p. 391).

The park has three developed zones: La Diable in the west, closest to Mont Tremblant and Montréal; La Pimbina in the center; and L'Assomption in the east. The roads connecting the three are unpaved but easily negotiated, and all three zones have visitor centers and reception stations that furnish maps.

What to See and Do

The 51-mile (82 km) **Grande Randonné Trail** winds from east to west across the park through hardwood maple and birch forests, traversing the softly modeled mountains of the Laurentides profile. Beginning at the Lac-Monroe Service Center, the trail includes an 8.7-mile (14 km) loop to the Croches Falls, followed by a long trek to the Saint-Donat Reception Station. For this section of the trail, you may want to overnight in one of the four shelters that are located along the route.

Of several short hiking trails in La Diable sector (most can be accessed at or near the Lac-Monroe Service Center), the easy **Chute du Diable Trail** (less than 1 mile/1.6 km) holds the greatest appeal. Water tumbles beside it through a heavily wooded ravine that is ideal for picnicking. Also less than a mile long, **Les Chutes Croches Trail** begins 3.5 miles (5.6 km) north of the service center and provides a relaxing stroll to a small bridge that affords a mesmerizing view of the falls. **La Roche Trail** winds for 3.1 miles (5 km) through mixed forest and along a small brook, culminating in a startling panorama of the Lac Monroe glacial valley and the spine of Mont Tremblant. Depart from Le Chevreuil campsite for a day's outing along the manageable 10.6-mile (17 km) **L'Ours Trail** with its fine views of the surrounding landscape. The slightly more difficult **Le Centenaire Trail** (5.7 miles/9.2 km) reveals splendid vistas of the River of the Devil and the Boulé Forest.

In La Pimbina, an inviting 6.2-mile (10 km) trail follows the shores of Lakes Provost and Lajoie until it heads inland to the Chute aux Rats. Here Pimbina Creek somersaults 56 feet (17 m) into a gorge set amid dense forest. Six miles (9.6 km) north of the

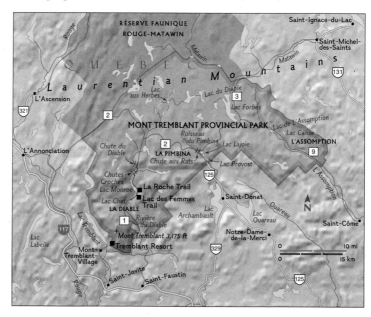

reception station in L'Assomption sector, the 2.7-mile (4.3 km) round-trip **Grandes-Vallées Trail** yields views of two picture-perfect valleys with azure lakes nestled in their centers.

For the remote tranquility of the deep woods, there's nothing quite like backcountry canoeing. For the most part, La Diable River charms rather than bedevils canoeists; the **Diable canoe route** covers 29 miles (47 km) through rapids that range from Class I to Class IV, with a 4-mile (6.4 km) portage, halfway through, around a series of waterfalls. *(To arrange for a shuttle, call 819-688-2281.)*

Less developed La Pimbina promises fewer people and ideal paddling. Canoes may be rented at Lac Provost beach, where you can also cool off in the lake's cold, invigorating waters *(lifeguards on duty in summer).*

EASTERN COUGAR: For decades, the harsh screams of mating cougars have been absent from the eastern Canadian wilderness. Many believed the great cats were extinct here though only endangered elsewhere in eastern North America. In the 1990s, however, sightings in New Brunswick and in the Abitibi and Bas-St. Laurent areas suggested that cougars may still make their homes in the more remote mountains of Mont-Tremblant park. Second in size only to the jaguar, the eastern cougar is one of the largest of America's great cats. The best way to guarantee its return is to set aside large tracts of undisturbed habitat.

The canoeing in L'Assomption ranges from a peaceful drift down the sector's namesake river *(put-in at Lac de L'Assomption; some rapids follow)* to the spectacular **Six Lakes canoe route** *(put-in at Lac Crapaud).*

For mountain biking enthusiasts, choose from more than 35 miles (56 km) of park trails—a mix of dirt roads and jeep tracks—the majority located in **La Diable's Lac Monroe area.**

More than 53 miles (85 km) of patrolled and groomed cross-country skiing trails—marked with a recommended skill level—lace the park. Warming huts along several trails sleep eight people *(reservations required).* Skiers, bundle up! Temperatures can plummet to minus 40°F (–40°C) or lower. For backcountry skiing, the main trail covers around 71 miles (114 km).

La Diable's snowshoe trails start at Lac Monroe and include **La Roche Trail,** which skirts Lac Monroe and Lac Chat on a 3.1-mile (5 km) round-trip. In La Pimbina, try the 3.1-mile (5 km) loop trail from the Saint-Donat Reception Station.

Camping and Lodging

There are 629 campsites and 178 canoe-camping sites in La Diable. Eight lakeside cottages in L'Assomption, with showers and hot water, hold 2 to 18 people (mid-May–mid-Oct.). L'Assomption has 86 campsites and 29 canoe-camping sites. La Pimbina has 265 campsites. Camping fee.

Mont-Tremblant National Park, Chemin du Lac-Supérieur, Lac-Supérieur, QC J0T 1P0; 819-688-2281 or 819-688-2336; www.sepaq.com/pq/mot/index.dot

Gatineau Park

*Southeast Ontario, 7.5 miles (12 km) northeast of Ottawa's
Parliament Hill*

- 89,661 acres ■ Year-round ■ Hiking ■ Lakes, fishing ■ Beavers
- Cross-country skiing, snowshoeing

Autumn waterfall

Straddling the edge of the Canadian Shield between the Ottawa and
Gatineau Rivers, Gatineau Park comprises a triangle of forested hills
and limpid lakes within sight of the confines of Ottawa. The impressive Eardley Escarpment, a 1,000-foot-high (305 m) cliff that delin-
eates the edge of the Canadian Shield, gives extensive views of the
Ottawa River Valley along its 18-mile (29 km) length.

Some 50 lakes are found in the park, home to 40 species of fish,
especially bass, yellow perch, and trout. Substantial populations of
beaver (the national emblem) and of white-tailed deer live in the
park as well. Gatineau's black bears tend to shy away from people
and rarely create a problem.

Because of the park's proximity to Ottawa, sections have
been preempted for government service including Mousseau Lake
(formerly Harrington Lake), the summer home of the prime minister—something like a Canadian Camp David. However, open to
the public is the Mackenzie King Estate on Kingsmere Lake, which
served as the summer residence of Canada's prime minister during
World War II *(819-827-3405. May–Oct.; fee).*

Gatineau counts almost 7.5 million visitors annually. Most people come in summer, but Gatineau's crisp, cold winters bring reliable snowfall and many sunny days, making for superb cross-country skiing and snowshoeing. As the first autumn frosts settle upon hillsides blanketed in mixed deciduous forest, blinding scarlets and brilliant golds sear the park. In spring, which arrives in late April or early May, the park comes alive with the calls of migrating birds and other animals raising their young (the resident baby porcupines are particularly enchanting). In spring and early summer, carry insect repellent to ward off the black flies; they won't relent until the heat of summer descends.

What to See and Do

The park's 77 miles (124 km) of hiking trails include **Pink Lake Trail,** a leisurely 1.5-mile (2.4 km) amble around the lake's perimeter, from the parking lot off Gatineau Parkway. The mile-long (1.6 km) **King Mountain Trail** begins at the parking lot near Black Lake and leads past lovely views of the broad Ottawa River Valley. Follow mile-long **Champlain Trail** to the top of the **Eardley Escarpment,** where informative panels explain the cliff's unique geology. A 3-mile (4.8 km) hike along the **Luskville Falls Trail** begins at the village of Luskville's picnic grounds and likewise leads you up the escarpment. Detailed maps of park trails are for sale at the visitor center in Chelsea, off Hwy. 5.

Gatineau's **ski-trail network**—one of the finest in Canada— includes easy and difficult sections. Close to 125 miles (200 km) of graded trails wind through deciduous forests and gentle meadows. Some 90 miles (145 km) of trail are groomed for classic Nordic skiing, while about 50 miles (80 km) of these allow for skate skiing—a kind of energetic skating on skis that requires more room than the push-and-glide style of traditional skiing. Another 35 miles (56 km) are designed for snowshoers and winter hikers.

You'll find heated shelters at intervals along many trails. Some are patrolled by park staff watching for skiers in trouble (temperatures may fall to minus 30°F/−34°C, in winter). The 20-mile (32 km) **Highway 1 Trail** starts near the park's Chelsea entrance and runs deep into the interior. Contact the visitor center *(819-827-2020)* for trail maps, passes, and information about ski conditions.

Camping

Three campgrounds operate in summer (mid-May–mid-Oct.): Philippe Lake with 246 campsites; Taylor Lake (semi-wilderness family camping) with 33; and La Pêche Lake (canoe camping) with 35 campsites among 12 locations. Reservations accepted from mid-May to mid-Oct.; call 819-456-3016. There are five winter campsites in the northern Philippe Lake sector of the park, a 2-mile (3.2 km) ski or snowshoe trek from the nearest parking lot (reservations required). Camping fee.

Gatineau Park, 33 Scott Rd., Chelsea, QC J9B 1A1, 819-827-2020; National Capital Commission, 800-465-1867; www.capcan.ca/gatineau

Bon Echo Provincial Park

Southeast Ontario, between Renfrew and Belleville on Hwy. 41

- 16,408 acres ▪ Year-round ▪ Pictographs ▪ Hiking, rock climbing
- Boating, canoeing, swimming, fishing

Bon Echo's massive rock—dubbed the Canadian Gibraltar—is a sheer cliff that rises more than 330 feet (100 m) out of Mazinaw Lake. Stunted cedars, some nearly 900 years old, cling to the rock face. But

Mazinaw Lake

what draws most visitors is the remarkable concentration of **Ojibwa pictographs** that stretch for a mile (1.6 km) along the cliff face. More than 260 images have been cataloged—the biggest collection in the Canadian Shield. Public boat launches pepper Bon Echo's 13 small lakes, and a ferry crosses the waters of **Mazinaw Lake** to visit several of the pictographs.

There are 17 miles (27.3 km) of hiking trails winding through forest habitats and along the shores of the lakes. The most popular is the mile-long (1.6 km) **Cliff Top Trail,** which runs from the Mazinaw lakefront—accessible by ferry—to the top of the rock.

The **Abes and Essens Trail** is made up of three interconnecting loops offering a choice of 2.5-mile (4 km), 5.6-mile (9 km), or 10.6-mile (17 km) hikes. The trailhead is located at the parking lot about 3 miles (4.8 km) along the road to Hardwood Hill Campground. It takes 90 minutes or so to hike the first loop around Clutes Lake; four hours to hike the first two loops around **Essens Lake** and back; and seven hours to complete all three loops.

Starting and ending in Mazinaw Lake, the leisurely 13-mile (21 km) **Kishkebus Canoe Trail** treats you to the pictographs.

Camping and Lodging

Bon Echo has 528 campsites. Sites at Mazinaw Lake and Hardwood Hill campgrounds are vehicle-accessible, with showers. There are 24 canoe-in sites at Joeperry and Pearson Lakes, and wilderness sites on Little Rock, Abes, Essens, and Clutes Lakes (reservations required). Camping fee. There are also two yurts and one rustic cabin.

Bon Echo Provincial Park, R.R. 1, Cloyne, ON K0H 1K0; 613-336-2228; www.ontarioparks.com/english/bone.html

394

Algonquin Provincial Park

Central Ontario, 160 miles (257 km) north of Toronto

- 1.9 million acres ▪ Year-round ▪ Maple forest, autumn foliage
- Hiking, backpacking, biking ▪ Boating, canoeing, swimming,
fishing ▪ Bird-watching, wildlife, wildflowers ▪ Cross-country
skiing, snowshoeing, dogsledding

Established in 1893 to protect the headwaters of the five major rivers that originate here—the Petawawa, Bonnechere, Oxtongue, Madawaska, and Amable du Fond—this is Ontario's best known and most beloved park. It rewards all sorts of visitors, from the long-distance paddler to the gregarious camper.

Three separate Algonquins make this possible. First is the vast **"interior,"** as the backcountry is referred to here, and the only way to see it is on foot, by canoe, or through a combination of both. The second and less demanding Algonquin is the **Parkway Corridor,** a 34-mile (55 km) section of Hwy. 60 that cuts through the park's southwest corner. The third Algonquin is what's becoming known as **Algonquin South,** a tongue of park adjacent to the Haliburton Highlands with hiking and camping facilities.

395

Although the park had been heavily logged early in the 20th century, considerable numbers of mature old-growth trees still stand, especially red and white pine up to 350 years old, a few hemlock groves, and some maple woods. Logging still persists in the northern reaches of the park.

Most central Ontario mammal species are found in Algonquin: moose and white-tailed deer, black bear, marten and

Portage trail

fishers, porcupines and beavers. The park is also famous for its wolf packs.

More than 250 bird species have been recorded in the park, including the spruce grouse and the gray jay. Warblers, thrushes, finches, and waterfowl join this avian chorus, but the most famous soloist is the common loon; it nests on virtually every lake, where its soul-stirring cry can be heard at dusk in spring, summer, and fall.

What to See and Do

Most of the interior is a connected network of lakes, and there are more than 1,300 miles (2,100 km) of canoe routes. Many, such as **Lake Lavieille, Dickson Lake,** and **Lake Opeongo,** are appropriate for beginners; others, such as the **Nipissing, Petawawa,** and **Tim Rivers,** involve long portages that make them more demanding.

There are three major canoe routes in Algonquin South: a day trip to **Upper** and **Lower Minnow Lakes,** a day trip to **Big Rock Lake,** and a three-day trip to **Scorch Lake.** Access is through the Kingscote Lake Campground, 36 miles (58 km) northwest of Bancroft.

The **Scorch Lake Lookout Trail** is the reward for getting to the lake. Steep but short, it rises in less than a mile (1.6 km) through hardwood forest to spectacular views over the lake and the woods beyond. Most of the routes in this area are designed for canoeists who want a slightly easier wilderness experience than the deep interior of the park proper.

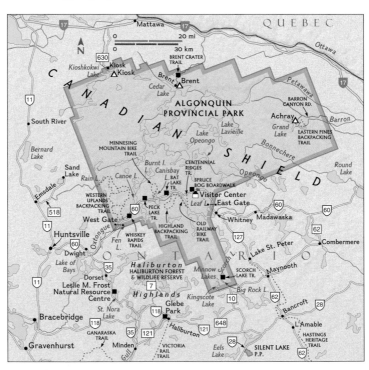

Most of the 16 hiking trails of varying length and challenge are accessible from the Parkway Corridor. (Detailed hiking guides are usually tucked inside boxes at the trailheads.)

Among them, the **Whiskey Rapids Trail** is a 1.3-mile (2.1 km) hike along the Oxtongue River; the 1.1-mile (1.8 km) **Peck Lake Trail** circumnavigates Peck Lake; the 3.4-mile (5.5 km) **Bat Lake Trail** passes through hardwood and coniferous forests and visits a substantial hemlock grove; the 6.2-mile (10 km) **Centennial Ridges Trail** offers spectacular views over the forests; and the 1-mile (1.6 km) **Spruce Bog Boardwalk** loop passes through typical spruce bog. The 1.2-mile (1.9 km) **Brent Crater Trail** *(accessible from Hwy. 17 on Brent Rd.)* offers a view of a meteorite crater from an observation tower. Additionally there are backpacking trails, with loops ranging from 3.7 to 55 miles (6 to 89 km).

Two trails have been laid out for cyclists, both of them along the Parkway Corridor. The **Minnesing Mountain Bike Trail** is moderately difficult, with four loops ranging from 2.9 miles to 14.5 miles (4.7 to 23.3 km). The **Old Railway Bike Trail** is a 6.2-mile trail (10 km/one way) that is suitable for families. Ask at the park about places to rent bikes.

Algonquin has some of the best trout fishing in Canada. More than 230 lakes contain brook trout (**Welcome** and **Dickson Lakes** are particularly good) and 149 have lake trout (**Lake Louisa** and **Hogan Lake** are recommended). Many lakes are also stocked with splake, a hybrid of these two types of trout. Spring is the best season for trout, summer for bass. Purchase a fishing license at the park's information offices at the east and west gates.

All 50 miles (80.5 km) of groomed cross-country skiing trails in the park are along the Parkway Corridor, but possibilities for snowshoeing exist almost everywhere. Ski loops range from 3 to 18 miles (4.8 to 29 km). **Pine Tree Loop** at Leaf Lake and **Minnesing Trail** are the most challenging. Dogsledding excursions are also available, two along the corridor and one in the northwest sector.

Camping and Lodging

There are approximately 1,200 campsites in 8 campgrounds along the Parkway Corridor, while an additional 1,900 primitive campsites are scattered throughout the interior. The corridor sites have a range of amenities, including electrical hookups, flush toilets, and laundry facilities. There are a few paddle-in campsites on **Canisbay Lake,** as well as four primitive, vehicle-accessible campgrounds located on Kioshkokwi, Cedar, Grand, and Kingscote Lakes. Winter wilderness camping is allowed, with some restrictions.

The Algonquin Nordic Wilderness Lodge (905-471-9453; www .algonquinecolodge.com) sits by a secluded lake on the park's borders in nearby Cavan, Ontario, and requires a 1.6-mile (2.6 km) ski-in from its parking lot.

Algonquin Provincial Park, P.O. Box 219, Whitney, ON K0J 2M0; 705-633-5572; www.algonquinpark.on.ca

397

Killarney Provincial Park

Southeast Ontario, north shore of Georgian Bay, northeast of Manitoulin Island

- 119,842 acres ▪ Year-round ▪ Scenic landscape ▪ Wildflowers, fall foliage ▪ Hiking, canoeing ▪ Cross-country skiing, snowshoeing

Canoe and kayaks on Chikanishing River

Established at the urgings of prominent landscape painters, not at the behest of naturalists, Killarney's many beauty marks include the startling ivory-white quartzite ridges and striated red granites of La Cloche and Killarney ranges, as well as the park's string of lakes—many of them brilliantly azure and crystal clear—set in forested valleys. These attractions have lured artists here since the early days of the 20th century.

No fewer than four members of Canada's so-called Group of Seven landscape painters painted in the Killarney area. It was one of that quartet, A. Y. Jackson, who pushed the Ontario government to establish Killarney as a reserve. Eventually, in 1964, a formal park was created. Lakes in the park are named after Jackson and two other members of the Group of Seven, Franklin Carmichael and A. J. Casson.

What to See and Do

Starting at the George Lake Campground, **La Cloche Silhouette Trail** is a 62-mile (99.8 km) loop that traverses much of the park. Along the way, it passes by lakes and secluded forests, as well as occasional lookout points that give spectacular views and much needed rest stops. The trail is strenuous; for the experienced backpacker, this seven- to ten-day hike should provide all the challenge you need. A number of shorter trails also start and end at the campground, and sections of the main trail can be used as day hikes.

If you head northwest from George Lake along **La Cloche,** for example, you'll end up at Artist Lake, Bay Finn, and Threenarrows Lake, a day hike covering 8 miles (12.9 km). A day hike to the northeast along La Cloche takes you up to Killarney Ridge and to the **Crack,** where the ridge has shattered and oddly square quartzite boulders have split off. A more ambitious, five-day backpacking trip leads beyond the Crack to **Silver Peak,** which, at 1,781 feet (543 m), is the highest point in the park. From here you can see a dozen small lakes ensconced in their forests and the shores of Georgian Bay itself. Simpler and shorter trails include **Chikanishing Trail,** a moderate 1.8-mile (2.9 km) loop that travels over pink granite outcroppings and through dense forest. Another is the **Granite Ridge Trail,** an easy 1.5-mile (2.4 km) hike with interpretive signs and interesting looks at the park's varied geology. Fall hiking is becoming increasingly popular, as the spectacular autumn colors, set against the white pines and the dazzling white hills, make for an exhilarating visual display.

KILLARNEY'S CLEAR LAKES: The brilliant clarity of Killarney's lakes is a sign not of their health, but of their frailty. In the 1950s and 1960s, the lakes became increasingly acidic due to their proximity to the massive metal smelters in Sudbury and within a zone of high acid deposits, much of it generated in the United States. By the late 1970s, the fish, algae, and plankton populations had gone into a steep decline, as had the waterfowl that depended on them for food. By 1997, however, a species biodiversity survey showed that matters had improved. Plants and animals were beginning to return as emissions from most of the offending sources had been reduced. Even so, the survey also concluded that as many as 95,000 of Ontario's 250,000 lakes still suffer from some degree of over-acidification.

399

A network of lakes, rivers, and short portages makes Killarney a paradise for **canoeing.** The campground at **George Lake** is the launching point for most of the one-day and longer trips, but other parts of the park are worth trying, too. Nellie Lake, in the northwest, has the park's clearest water, with visibility of about 90 feet (27 m). A popular weekend trip is the one from George Lake through **Freeland** and **Killarney Lakes** and on to O.S.A. Dozens of longer routes take you deep into the park's interior. Most start either from George Lake or **Johnnie Lake** to the southeast, or from **Bell Lake** to the east.

Reservations for backcountry canoeing are a must. Detailed maps for routes and portages are available from the camp office. You can rent canoes and equipment from Killarney Kanoes *(888-461-4446)* or Killarney Outfitters *(800-461-1117).* Both keep canoes at the George Lake Campground.

Camping

George Lake Campground has 126 tent and RV sites, with showers; open year-round. Camping fee. There are also six yurts; call 888-668-7275 to reserve.

Killarney Provincial Park, ON P0M 2A0; 705-287-2900; www.ontarioparks.com/english/kill.html

Lake Superior Provincial Park

Southeast Ontario, lakeshore between Sault Ste. Marie and Wawa

- 384,628 acres ▪ Park facilities close in winter but visitors allowed ▪ Scenic highway ▪ Bird-watching ▪ Pictographs ▪ Lakes ▪ Hiking, kayaking, canoeing, fishing ▪ Snowmobiling, snowshoeing

Gargantua Harbour

A good way to get a feel for the topography of this park is to take Scenic Highway 17—the famous Trans-Canada Highway. The highway takes you the full length of the park, from the Lake Superior shore inland past rivers and interior lakes. Lookout points and rest stops provide a chance to get out of the car, stretch your legs, and take in the views along the way. Several gravel roads provide access to backcountry hiking trails and canoe routes, including Mijinemungshing, Gargantua, and Frater Roads.

What to See and Do

The best way to see Lake Superior Provincial Park is by canoe or on foot. Approximately 75 miles (121 km) of hiking trails are maintained, in varying lengths and degrees of difficulty. The **Coastal Trail** is 40 miles (64 km) one way—from Chalfant Cove in the north to Agawa Bay in the south. The northern section from Gargantua to Warp Bay is an easy-to-moderate one-day hike over relatively flat terrain. The southerly section from Gargantua to Agawa Bay (34 miles/54.7 km) is tougher, taking four to seven days.

For those with a lower tolerance for strenuous effort—or less time—a variety of trails are available. **Agawa Rock** is a 15- to 30-minute hike from the highway to the giant rock overhanging

Lake Superior (see sidebar below). The **Orphan Lake Trail** (5 miles/8 km) offers a boreal forest, a lovely pebble beach, Baldhead Falls, and splendid views over Orphan Lake and Lake Superior. **Trapper's Trail,** only a mile (1.6 km) long, features a floating boardwalk; keep your eyes peeled for moose, beavers, and wading great blue herons.

More challenging trails include **Towab** (15 miles/24 km round-trip), which is best as a two-day hike in autumn—with its scarlet and crimson sugar maples; you'll find a campsite below **Agawa Falls,** an 82-foot (25 m) cascade on the Agawa River. The 7-mile (11.3 km) **Peat Mountain Trail** includes a steady climb of 500 feet (152 m), but the reward is a panoramic view.

Eight maintained **canoe routes** cut through the park, some easy day trips, others longer affairs with frequent portaging; at least four may require shuttle services for boat pickup at the end.

The **Fenton-Treeby route** (*access via Trans-Canada Hwy.*) is a 10-mile (16 km) loop, good for a day trip with 11 portages, most short. **Belanger Lake** (*access via Gargantua Rd.*) is an 8-mile (12.9 km) return day trip with four portages. This is a nice overnight trip, with good brook and lake trout fishing.

The **Sand River** (*access via Algoma Central Railway*) runs from the northeast corner of the park and, with 29 portages, can take four to five days to cover. The scenery changes dramatically along the way, from lowland wetlands and woods to high cliffs and hardwood forests. The river drops about 600 feet (183 m) over its 35-mile (56 km) length from Sand Lake to Lake Superior.

You can also canoe or kayak the shores of Lake Superior itself, but this is not recommended for the beginner. Though there are many fine beaches, you'll also encounter sheer cliffs and rock shorelines—spectacular to look at but inhospitable in case you have to put in.

For information about canoe rentals and routes, contact the Agawa Bay visitor center, open May to October and located at the entrance to the Agawa Bay Campground (*705-882-2026*).

Camping

There are campgrounds at Rabbit Blanket Lake and Agawa Bay, with showers, and Crescent Lake, with a total of 249 tent and RV sites. There are an additional 174 backcountry sites scattered through the park interior. Camping fee.

Lake Superior Provincial Park, P.O. Box 267, Wawa, ON P0S 1K0; 705-856-2284 (information), 888-668-7275 (reservations); www.ontarioparks.com/english/lakes.html

STORIES IN STONE: Animals. Canoeists. Warriors. The horned lynx and other mythical creatures. These are just some of the subjects painted by the Ojibwa Indians on Agawa Rock. To view the pictographs, visitors must walk along a rock ledge next to the lake. Extreme caution is necessary, and the site is accessible only when lake conditions are calm. No one knows the age of the pictographs, but they were probably created over the course of many centuries. The only image that gives us a clue is the horse: It must have been painted within the last 400 years, after horses arrived with the Europeans.

Woodland Caribou Provincial Park

North of Lake Superior on the Manitoba border, 370 miles (595 km) west of Thunder Bay

- 1.2 million acres ▪ Year-round ▪ Canoeing (park accessible by water only) ▪ Pictographs ▪ Caribou ▪ Sportfishing, bird-watching ▪ Primitive camping

402

Woodland caribou

If you want to walk in woods that have never been logged or paddle across lakes that have never been named, this park is the place for you. Even the creatures for which the park is named are secretive, adding to the park's sense of solitude. There are about 130 in all, and most are seen in or near lakes and rivers. They share the park with moose, black bears, wolverines, river otters, great blue herons, and bald eagles.

Getting There

With no roads leading into Woodland Caribou Provincial Park, reaching the site can be an adventure in itself. All access points, even those by road, take you only to places where you can canoe into the park proper. Most visitors arrive through the western Ontario towns of Ear Falls and Red Lake. At Red Lake the highway ends and the wilderness takes over.

Canoeists can reach five of the six entry points by driving along a forest access (logging) road from either Red Lake or Ear Falls. Visitors should be cautious because they will be sharing the road with long-haul trucks.

The sixth entry point is located north of Red Lake on the Upper Chukuni River. This option takes paddlers through crown land wilderness (state-owned) for three days before reaching the park boundary and the headwaters of the **Bloodvein River,** a Canadian heritage river. The river's 190-mile (306 km) water trail conveys canoers on a 15- to 20-day journey through the heart of the land, eventually depositing them at the community of Bloodvein on the east shore of Lake Winnipeg.

The park can also be accessed by canoe from the Manitoba side at Oiseau Creek, Garner Lake, Wanipigow River, and Carroll Lake. Reaching the park from any of these places entails a paddle of one to three days. Paddlers should ask an outfitter or the park offices about water levels before they venture out.

What to See and Do

403

Paddlers have the freedom to venture out on side trips from the Bloodvein. One such trip is from Bigshell, where you can veer off onto unbeaten paths and aim for Burntwood Lake; from there a series of short portages lead to the Dutch River. The Dutch, in turn, makes its way to **Thicketwood Lake,** a long and eye-pleasing body of water that pours out through the Sabourin River into **Sabourin Lake.** Here you'll find an attractive main base lodge. From Sabourin Lake the route joins the Bloodvein, which meanders placidly through wetlands and into Barclay Lake, Mary's Lake, and then Artery Lake on the western border of the park.

The second large river system, the **Gammon,** cuts the park roughly in two halves, eventually emptying into the Bloodvein River inside Manitoba. The Gammon also enables you to wander across large lakes with sharp drops in elevation between bodies of water.

Five canoe outfitters operate from Red Lake: Woodland Caribou Outfitters *(807-727-9943),* Goldseekers Outfitting *(807-727-2353 or 800-591-9282),* Woodland Caribou Canoe Outfitters *(807-727-2262),* Atikaki Canoe Outfitters *(807-727-2797 or 651-483-1920 before May),* and Caribou Country Eco-Tours and Bow Narrows Camp *(winter, 801-836-1519; summer, 807-475-7246).* Each offers similar packages and can help you plot out a route, select and rent equipment, and coordinate flight and shuttle services into the park.

In country as wild as this, good maps are essential. For a detailed map of the canoe routes and large-scale topographic maps of the park, contact Northern Sporting Supplies *(807-727-2302)* or Four Seasons Sport Shop *(807-222-2200).* The canoe outfitters listed above may also have these maps on hand. The park publishes a canoe route map; call 807-727-1336 or 807-727-1388 for a copy.

Further Adventures

Spectacular sportfishing awaits anglers on almost any foray into the park, which supports a plentiful supply of eagerly sought-after freshwater game fish species—walleye, northern pike, and lake trout. Fish are caught easily on lures; no bait is required. Indeed, park personnel prefer that no live bait be brought into the park lest it introduce new species into the water ecosystem.

Woodland Caribou has some of the largest and best preserved Native American **pictographs** in the Canadian Shield. Customarily drawn or painted on the base of a cliff, pictographs are an eloquent reminder of the Ojibwa peoples who have lived, fished, and hunted in this wilderness for millennia. Many Ojibwa still consider the pictographs to possess spiritual significance. Be on the lookout for offerings of tobacco, cedar, or coins tucked into cracks in the rock.

Mushrooms

Along the stretch of the Bloodvein River within Woodland Caribou are six pictograph sites. This river, steeped in history, was long used as a major traveling corridor by the first inhabitants of this continent, then later as a secondary fur trade route. The pictographs at **Artery Lake** may date back 900 to 1,200 years. Other pictograph sites can be found near **Bigshell** and on **Beamish, Aegean, Musclow, Hansen,** and **Hjalmar Lakes.** Ask a park staffer for locations.

Camping and Lodging

There are 1,000 backcountry sites in the park. To lessen visitor impact, site occupancy is limited to nine campers. A number of lodges and outpost camps are located on lakes along the Bloodvein and Gammon Rivers. The largest lodge sits on Sabourin Lake, with others on Douglas Lake and Carroll Lake. Gammon and Donald Lakes are home to a pair of private lodges. There are also 15 outpost camps, with room for four to ten people, and a handful of private cottages. Access to all sites is by aircraft or canoe only. Contact the park for a list of commercial accommodations and phone numbers.

Woodland Caribou Provincial Park, P.O. Box 5003, Red Lake, ON P0V 2M0; 807-727-1329; www.ontarioparks.com/english/wood.html

Polar Bear Provincial Park

Northeast Ontario, on shores of James and Hudson Bays

- 6 million acres ▪ Year-round ▪ Bird-watching, geese ▪ Polar bears
- Muskeg ▪ Kayaking, canoeing, fishing ▪ No facilities ▪ Wilderness camping only ▪ Access by chartered aircraft from Hearst, Cochrane, or Moosonee, Ontario

Polar bears

Flying north toward this remote park, you'll spy terrain that appears to be flat, monochromatic, and waterlogged—something like an unsqueezed sponge. At lower altitudes, however, it resolves into a subtle and beautiful palette of pinks, browns, mauves, and greens so intense they look black, an intricate mosaic of rivers, shallow lakes, and fens. This is the Great Muskeg country, the world's largest continuous peat bogs, also known as the Hudson Bay lowlands.

In Ontario alone, the muskeg (a ground layer of organic material, or peat, 25 to 30 inches/0.6 to 0.7 m thick) covers almost 380,000 square miles (611,550 sq km), spreading into Manitoba to the west and Québec to the east. The park itself is but a fraction of this immensity, a section of muskeg selected for formal protection along James and Hudson Bays (see sidebar p. 406).

Although winter turns the lowlands into millions of tiny frozen peat plateaus, in summer the bogs and fens burst into exquisite bloom—a wondrous rainbow of colors from pale yellows and greens through ochers, umbers, purples, and browns. Prominent blossoms include flame-colored lousewort, purple lousewort, bunchberry, and chickweed.

MUSKEG MUCK: The James and Hudson Bays, together with the Hudson Bay lowlands, are the remnants of the ancient Tyrrell Sea, created by the meltwaters of the Pleistocene epoch. As this sea slowly disappeared, it left behind clay layers up to 10 feet (3 m) thick, which provided poor drainage. The resulting sodden land, paired with the cool climate, retarded the decay of dead plants. Each year's growth therefore left behind a waterlogged muck that slowly morphed into peat. In many places, the peat reached a thickness of 13 feet (4 m); this base became the "soil" in which new plants took root, but it also meant those roots lost contact with the actual soil beneath. As a result, rainwater was the sole source of moisture and nutrients. This in turn encouraged the formation of bogs, in which flourished such typically acid-resistant flora as gnarly dwarf spruces, sphagnum mosses, bog laurel, and Labrador tea laurel.

What to See and Do

Averaging only 600 visitors per year, Polar Bear Provincial Park offers no campsites, shelters, boat landings, supplies, or staff. The weather is harsh and unpredictable; in summer it may swing from almost 80°F (27°C) to not much above freezing in a matter of hours. Visitors must bring tents with a low profile lest they be torn away by the frequent gales. Why, then, do people visit?

Mainly for the birds. The spongy muskeg and endless marsh support dozens of bird species—some common, some exotic—in astonishing numbers. These include the willow ptarmigan, tundra swan, snowy owl, bald eagle, the ungainly godwit, and a long list of others: red-throated loons, king eiders, rough-legged hawks, stilt and pectoral sandpipers, plovers and jaegers, greater and lesser yellowlegs, dowitchers, sandhill cranes, and huge flocks of Canada geese from the Mississippi Flyway.

The **lowlands** are generally an important part of the yearly migration cycle for large numbers of birds—almost one million Canada geese and upward of 50,000 Atlantic brant. The spring goose migration is eagerly anticipated by the local Cree, who retain unlimited duck hunting rights in the area.

The jewel in this avian crown is the world's southernmost colony of lesser snow geese. During the spring breeding season, the **snow goose "homestead"** can be heard—and sometimes smelled—miles away as the ganders honk and squawk to protect their nests. This extraordinary gathering place was discovered in 1944, when it was estimated at 100 nesting pairs. (Such early counts were based on anecdotal tallies, whereas today's populations are gauged by aerial survey.) By 1973, the count had reached 30,000 pairs. There are now more than 60,000.

A canoe affords the best way to scope out all this birdlife. Short hikes on land are possible, but the sopping ground makes walking a challenge at best: When the muskeg is not sucking at your boots, mosquitoes are sucking your blood. Thanks to the region's flattened topography, wilderness canoe trips here tend to be blessedly free of both white water and portages, making for some pleasantly undemanding paddling. Many rivers offer excellent canoe routes; particularly good are the **Brant, Kinushseo, Lakitusaki, Shagamu, Sutton,** and **Winisk.**

Even if most people come for the birds, the place lives up to its name with a polar bear population estimated at 400. When the bears return to the water with their cubs after a hungry summer ashore, the coast may be populated by 200 of the huge white beasts, virtually guaranteeing a sighting. Keep in mind that a distant polar bear is a safe one.

Myriad other mammals live around Polar Bear Provincial Park. Atlantic walrus can frequently be seen loafing offshore. Beluga whales and bearded seals are also common. In the muskeg you might spot beaver, otter, gray wolf, arctic fox, red fox and marten, moose, woodland caribou, or black bear.

Getting There

Charter services usually cost about $2,000 per person, including air transport and canoe or kayak rental. Only four landing sites are allowed within the park: Brant River, Shagamu River, Sutton River, and a place simply called Site 415. Scheduled flights *(Air Creebec, 819-825-8375; www.aircreebec.ca)* operate twice weekly from Moosonee to Peawanuck, the Cree enclave in the park's north-central coastal area. You'll need the services of an outfitter if you plan to fish.

Camping

Visitors should bring everything they will need, plus a week's extra rations to accommodate the inevitable delays involved in being extracted. Survival camping—living off the land—is not permitted. In summer the mosquitoes, deerflies, and horseflies are relentless and maddening.

Polar Bear Provincial Park, c/o Northeast Zone Office, P.O. Box 7302 Third Ave., Cochrane, ON PoL 1Co; 705-272-7139; www.ontario parks.com/english/pola .html

Sik sik, or ground squirrel

Whiteshell Provincial Park

Southeast Manitoba, 80 miles (129 km) east of Winnipeg

- 672,371 acres ■ Year-round ■ Waterfalls, lakes ■ Wildflowers
■ Goose sanctuary ■ Scenic drives ■ Hiking, rock climbing,
mountain biking, boating, canoeing, swimming, fishing ■ Snowmobiling, cross-country skiing

For an introduction to Canadian Shield country and a lesson in its
virtues, Whiteshell Provincial Park is the place to go. On Whiteshell's
numerous trails, you'll walk across low domes of ancient stone and
wander through a forest of white spruce, jack pine, and balsam fir,
with a sprinkling of aspen, balsam poplar, and birch. In many places
you will encounter bogs and fens where black spruce and tamarack
are the only trees that can survive. Other bodies of water abound,
including wetlands, ponds, and more than 200 lakes.

Big and beautiful and only a 90-minute drive from Winnipeg,
the park attracts well over a million visitors a year. Within Whiteshell's boundaries you will find 11 campgrounds and about 3,300
cottages. There are resorts, tennis courts, marinas, riding stables,
and a golf course. Even in the heavily developed areas, you'll see
river otters sliding through the water and hear loons calling. Most of
the park is wilderness, so if you want to escape the crowds, you can
go backpacking or take one of the backcountry canoe routes to find
abundant wildlife, unspoiled nature, and solitude.

What to See and Do

There are four park offices scattered about Whiteshell. The office at
Falcon Lake, in the far south of the park, is off Trans-Canada 1 from

Bannock Point petroforms

Winnipeg. The Falcon Lake town site is one of the most developed places in the park. Cottages line the shore of this 8-mile-long (13 km) lake, but roads on the north and south shores yield pleasant scenery and occasional sightings of river otters, mergansers, red foxes, loons, and other wildlife.

West Hawk Lake is located on Hwy. 44 half a mile (0.8 km) north of the Trans-Canada and a couple of miles north of Falcon Lake. At 377 feet (115 m), West Hawk is Manitoba's deepest lake. It is almost completely undeveloped on its east side, where the only land access is via the fairly demanding 7.8-mile (12.6 km) out-and-back **Hunt Lake Trail.**

Some 6 miles (9.7 km) north of West Hawk on Hwy. 44, the **McGillivray Falls Trail** explores a drainage system, typical of Whiteshell, in which water flows every way but uphill. You can make this easy-to-moderate trail into a 1.7-mile (2.7 km) or 2.8-mile (4.5 km) loop.

McGillivray Falls is more a tumbling rapid than a true waterfall, but it tumbles through a lovely wooded glade. Near the far end of the trail's oval loop lies McGillivray Lake. Characteristic of Canadian Shield lakes, it is shallow—about 10 feet (3 m) maximum—and tea colored, thanks to its load of nutrients, algae, and humic acid.

A couple of miles past McGillivray, on Hwy. 44, stop at the **Lily Pond pullout.** About a quarter mile (0.4 km) long, the pond is underlain and walled in by cliffs of 2.5-billion-year-old Canadian Shield rock. Both yellow and white lilies grow here. The yellow species blooms in May, the white in June, and both blossom into September.

Further Adventures

Located beside Hwy. 44 on the park's western edge, the **Alfred Hole Goose Sanctuary** is home to about 100 geese in the summer, among them five or six nesting pairs at the main pond. From the **visitor center,** where you can observe the geese through floor-to-ceiling windows and a spotting scope, a 1.6-mile (2.6 km) trail follows the pond's north and west banks. Along the trail you'll find other wildlife, such as beavers, snapping turtles (known to eat goslings at times), hybrid mallard, and many duck species.

Off Rte. 309, the north shore of **Big Whiteshell Lake** offers hiking, a bike trail, two public beaches, and some developed amenities, but it's also one of the best jump-off points to explore the backcountry. For many visitors a canoe is the vehicle of choice in this watery world. Whiteshell boasts some 200 miles (322 km) of connected rivers, lakes, and streams and routes that will suit everyone from novice to rabid adventurer. From the marina on the north or south shores of Big Whiteshell Lake, you can paddle deep into the park to the north or south.

If you prefer terra firma, at the north shore of Big Whiteshell Lake you'll find the northern trailhead for the **Mantario Trail.** At 37 miles (60 km) one way, it is the longest trail in the park. Mantario Trail is difficult and remote, so make sure you're prepared before tackling this three- to six-day wilderness trek. Try the hike between late August and late September, when the ground is dry, the horseflies and mosquitoes have abated, and the temperatures are cool enough to make backpacking comfortable.

Returning on Rte. 309 from Big Whiteshell Lake, continue north on Rte. 307, heading northwest out of the park. Stop just north of Betula Lake and stroll the **Pine Point Rapids Trail,** Whiteshell's most scenic day hike. The route consists of two joined loops, so you can go 3.2 miles (5 km) or 4.9 miles (7.9 km).

Camping and Lodging

There are 11 campgrounds at Whiteshell, with a total of 890 sites, ranging from rustic to full-service. Call 888-482-2267 for reservations or 800-214-6497 for information. Camping fee. Rental cabins and lodges also available.

Whiteshell Provincial Park, Manitoba Conservation, Box 22, 200 Saulteaux Crescent, Winnipeg, MB R3J 3W3; 204-945-6784 or 800-214-6497; www.gov.mb.ca/conservation/parks/popular_parks/ eastern/whiteshell.html

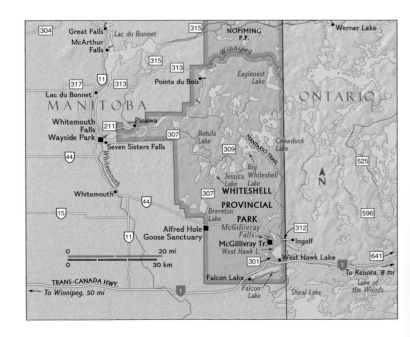

Nopiming Provincial Park

Southeast Manitoba, 90 miles (145 km) northeast of Winnipeg

▪ 353,112 acres ▪ Year-round ▪ Canadian Shield ▪ Hiking, mountain biking, canoeing, fishing ▪ Skiing ▪ Birds, bats

Living up to its name ("nopiming" is Anishinabe for "entrance to the wilderness"), Nopiming Provincial Park serves as a transition between the settled country to the south and the trackless wilderness to the north. A mix of civilization and nature, the park is home to wolves, bears, and lynx.

Nopiming is classic shield country: ancient rock mixed with boreal forest and bodies of water. For a closer look, hike the **Ancient Mountains Trail,** just off Rte. 314, east of Tooth Lake. This moderately difficult 1.1-mile (1.8 km) round-trip walk passes through an area swept by a fire in 1983 that exposed the bedrock.

The **Fire of 'Eighty-Three Trail** also enters an area hit by fire that year. Short but fairly strenuous, the trail starts from Rte. 314 at the park's northern end. Get the interpretive brochure at the trailhead or the campground office, which explains how the forest is recovering and the vital role played by the burned landscape.

You'll also see many snags—dead trees that are still standing. These charred skeletons are essential to life here. Insects prosper in snags, and other wildlife, such as three-toed woodpeckers, in turn jackhammer into the snags and feed on the insects. Tall snags also make good nesting sites and perches for birds such as northern hawk owls (which hunt during the day, so watch for them), ospreys, and bald eagles.

Birds of all sorts flock here, yet the most popular flier is a bat. At dusk these famously nocturnal feeders pour out in a fluttering stream. To witness this phenomenon, go to the **Tulabi Falls Campground,** located off Rte. 315 in the southern part of the park.

A map of distances, portages, and backcountry camping for canoeists is available at the district offices in Lac du Bonnet *(204-345-1431)* and Bissett *(204-277-5212).* The popular **Manigotagan Canoe Route** has rapids from Class II to Class V. For a seven-day trip, access the Manigotagan River at Long Lake via Rte. 304. For a four-day trip, reach Quesnel Lake via the road south to Caribou Lake Landing from Rte. 304 just west of Bissett.

Camping and Lodging

Nopiming Park has four campgrounds with a total of 155 tent sites; limited services. Call 888-482-2267 for reservations or 800-214-6497 for information. Seasonal camping at Beresford Lake and Black Lake Campgrounds. There are also three lodges in the park.

Nopiming Provincial Park, Manitoba Conservation, Box 22, 200 Saulteaux Crescent, Winnipeg, MB R3J 3W3; 800-214-6497; www.gov.mb.ca/conservation/parks/popular_parks/eastern/ nopiming.html

411

Grass River Provincial Park

Central Manitoba, 35 miles (56 km) southeast of Flin Flon

- 563,133 acres ▪ Year-round ▪ Lakes, wetlands ▪ Woodland caribou
- Canadian Shield ▪ Boating, canoeing, fishing

Water covers about 35 percent of Grass River Provincial Park. Everywhere you turn there's a lake, a marsh, a river, a fen, or some other body of water. Though you can glimpse the area's scenic beauty from land, in order to experience the park's essence you must venture into those liquid realms. The park's name conjures an image of a channel of water, but as the Grass River snakes through the park it repeatedly balloons to form lakes. If you take the 80-mile (129 km) canoe route that follows the river the length of the park, you'll be paddling across lakes most of the time.

Whether lake or river, the water is remarkably clear and clean; in fact, this area was designated a park, in part, to protect the superb water quality. The largely undeveloped park also protects an ark of wildlife, notably a population of rare woodland caribou. The woodlands in which these caribou prosper consist of black spruce, jack pine, assorted hardwoods, and other boreal forest trees underlain by the granite of the Canadian Shield, which characterizes the majority of the park.

However, the southern portion lies in the boggy Manitoba lowlands, whose fens and bogs contain only stunted spruce and tamarack trees. Well-drained glacial features, such as moraines, and limestone outcrops support lush pine and white spruce forests. This geologic divide between north and south clearly reveals itself to visitors passing through the park on Hwy. 39.

Autumn colors of red osier dogwood, Four Mile Island

What to See and Do

There are two ways to see Grass River Provincial Park: by water or on land. Hiking the trails requires less in the way of preparation and equipment, but exploring the park by boat can be worth all the effort. If you decide on water travel, contact the park or the tourism association for advice on routes and safety precautions. You might hire a guide for canoe trips or motorboat tours. If you go on your own, be cautious if you're a novice, as some of the lakes are large enough to whip up 5-foot (1.5 m) waves during a big blow, and you'll want to stay away from the rapids.

An easy day trip is the 3-mile (4.8 km) one-way section of the **trans-park canoe route** that begins at Iskwasum Campground and ends at Loucks Falls. Keep an eye on the forest of 50-foot (15 m) spruce and pine, as you may spot a moose plunging its face into the shallows to feed on vegetation or a river otter sliding down the well-worn runways that stripe the north bank not far from the campground. And, if you're really fortunate, you may even spy a caribou. Hundreds occupy the park, yet people so seldom see these elusive beasts that they've been nicknamed "gray ghosts." Your best chance of being one of the lucky few is during May and June, when the females retreat to the islands in the lakes to calve. The many islands dotted throughout the lake make for great picnic sites, as does **Loucks Falls,** the turnaround point for this day trip.

Hwy. 39 traverses the southern portion of the park; though motorists are faced mostly with a wall of trees on either side, you will see the occasional black bear or deer by the road. Road cuts reveal pancaked slabs of dolomite, a sedimentary rock that lets you know you're in the Manitoba lowlands.

The **Karst Spring Trail**—an easy, 2-mile (3.2 km) loop that starts from the northwest end of the Iskwasum Campground off Hwy. 39— is the park's only established path. The trail starts amid forest carpeted by moss, and then pulls alongside a narrow channel of the Grass River. After bridging a creek near the trail's confluence with the Grass River, the path turns upslope and follows the tumbling water about 100 yards (91 m) to its source: a hillside of sedimentary rock—hence "karst" (an area filled with sinkholes, caverns, and subterranean flowing water) "spring" trail.

Camping

There are three campgrounds off Hwy. 39—Gyles Lake, Iskwasum Landing, and Reed Lake—with a total of 143 sites, with showers. Call 888-482-2267 for reservations or 800-214-6497 for information. Camping fee. There are also dozens of backcountry campgrounds designed for canoeists, as well as three backcountry lodges.

Manitoba Conservation, Box 130, Cranberry Portage, MB R0B 0H0; 204-472-3331; www.gov.mb.ca/conservation/parks/popular_parks/ northwest/grass.html ▪ Grass River Corridor Tourism Assn., 228–35 Main St., Flin Flon, MB R8A 1J7; 204-687-6967; www.grassriver .mb.ca

413

Spruce Woods Provincial Park

Southern Manitoba, 40 miles (64 km) southeast of Brandon

■ 66,593 acres ■ Year-round ■ Spirit Sands ■ Hiking, mountain biking, horseback riding, canoeing, fishing

Children playing in sand dunes at Spirit Sands

There are indeed spruce woods in this lovely provincial park, as well as river bottom forest along the Assiniboine River, mixed-grass prairie, and upland deciduous forest. But despite its name, Spruce Woods Provincial Park is best known as the home of the Spirit Sands. Named for their religious significance to local aboriginal people, these expansive and largely un-vegetated dune fields are absent in the rest of Manitoba and rare throughout Canada.

The dunes formed at the end of the last ice age. Today the Assiniboine River is a meandering waterway narrow enough to throw a rock across, but 12,000 years ago it was a mile-wide (1.6 km) rush of glacial meltwater pouring into ancient glacial Lake Agassiz. When this vast lake dried up, a 1.6-million-acre (65,000 sq km) delta of sand and other sediments was revealed. Of this, only the 1,000 acres (400 ha) of the Spirit Sands remain as living dunes that shift with the prevailing winds; the rest has been blown away or overrun by vegetation.

Spruce Woods is located in the Canadian prairie, part of the Great Plains of North America. Strongly influenced by distance from the Pacific Ocean, the prairie shifts from fescue in the west to mixed grass in the middle to tallgrass in the east.

What to See and Do

The eastern three-quarters of the park is somewhat inaccessible backcountry, but the western swath along Hwy. 5 can easily be explored via a few gravel roads, several established hiking (and some biking) trails, and the **Assiniboine River canoe route** *(rentals available in season; call Up the Creek Outfitters, 204-526-7145).*

Most of the easily accessible features of Spruce Woods, including the interpretive center and the Kiche Manitou Campground, lie in the southwest corner of the park, just off Hwy. 5. Bird-watchers can indulge themselves by walking around the edge of this wetland—great blue herons, belted kingfishers, Canada geese, and myriad ducks abound. Just east of the campground you can walk the 0.9-mile (1.4 km) **Isputinaw Trail,** an interpretive loop that passes through a surprising number of habitats in such a short distance.

The **Spirit Sands** to the northwest of Kiche Manitou Campground can be explored on numerous trails that begin at the interpretive kiosk in the parking area off Hwy. 5; look at the map and devise a loop of your own. You'll begin in dunes overgrown by a verdant blend of white spruce, ground juniper, grasses, aspen, oak, and other greenery. Near the heart of the Spirit Sands the vegetation thins and you finally emerge onto the open dunes, a sea of sand in which the waves move very slowly—the dunes travel southeast by about 10 inches (25.4 cm) a year.

415

In the far southwest sits the **Devil's Punch Bowl,** a depression where subterranean streams undercut the sand hills and caused a collapse. This sunken oasis features beaver ponds inhabited by muskrat, weasels, and painted turtles. If slogging through the soft sand sounds unappealing, consider a covered wagon tour run by a private operator *(Spirit Sands Wagon Outfitters, 204-827-2800).*

Five miles (8 km) north of Marshs Lake, take a short road east to the parking lot for the **Epinette Creek Trails.** This extensive network of trails leads deep into the park and draws overnight backcountry hikers, as well as mountain bikers looking for challenging rides. If you lack the time or inclination for exploring the trails, you can experience the variety and beauty of Epinette Creek in a half-day out-and-back walk. In just the first few miles you'll see a meandering creek interrupted by beaver dams; open grasslands favored by hawks; a dense forest of maple, ash, balsam poplar, and elm; and a 1997 burn site where blackened trees contrast with the lush fireweed and young aspens that are starting the next forest.

Camping

Kiche Manitou Campground has 197 tent and RV sites, with showers; an area for group camping; and ten yurts. Open May–Oct., 204-827-8851; out of season, call 888-482-2267. Camping fee.

Spruce Woods Provincial Park, Manitoba Conservation, Box 900, Carberry, MB R0K 0H0; 204-834-8800 or 800-214-6497; www.gov .mb.ca/conservation/parks/popular_parks/western/spruce.html

Duck Mountain Provincial Park

Southwest Manitoba, 40 miles (64 km) northwest of Dauphin, on the Manitoba–Saskatchewan border

■ 351,945 acres ■ Year-round ■ Boreal forest ■ Elk, wildlife ■ Hiking, canoeing

Poised atop a high plateau at the northern edge of the prairie, a southern thrust of the boreal forest—white spruce, jack pine, and balsam fir—cloaks the higher portions of this park. The lower portions feature aspen, birch, and willow, species typical of the park's prairie lands. Mostly undeveloped, the park is a scenic sanctuary for black bear, red fox, coyote, bald eagle, wood duck, wolf, white-tailed deer, and moose.

You can explore Duck Mountain via a couple of easy canoe routes or three roads cut through the park, but the best way is to hike some of the many trails. In the extreme southeast corner you

416

Wellman Lake

can start hiking at Manitoba's highest point, **Baldy Mountain.** Drive to the summit, at 2,727 feet (831 m), then climb an additional 40 feet (12 m) up a tower, from which you can see south all the way to Riding Mountain. The viewing tower stands along the sometimes steep 1.9-mile (3 km) **Baldy Mountain Trail.**

About 10 miles (16 km) northwest of Baldy Mountain on PR 366, just before it intersects PR 367, lies the **Wapiti Trail** (2.8-mile/4.5-km loop). "Wapiti" is the proper name for elk, and nearly 1,500 of these regal creatures call Duck Mountain home. You'll often see some at dawn or dusk, especially in the meadows close to the trailhead.

Another path, the 2.8-mile (4.5 km) **Shell River Valley Trail,** loops through mixed forest and a meadow, past the Shell River, and through a calcium bog. Finish your visit to the park with a flourish: Hike the 0.7-mile (1.1 km) loop to the top of **Copernicus Hill.** There's a plaque honoring the Polish astronomer near the summit, but the sights from the 30-foot (9 m) viewing tower are the real prize.

Camping

There are four campgrounds in the park with 177 tent and RV sites, with showers, and group-use sites at Blue and Childs Lake campgrounds. Reservations advised in season; call 888-482-2267 or 800-214-6497 for information. Camping fee. Rental cabins and full-service lodges also available.

Duck Mountain Provincial Park, Manitoba Conservation, Box 640, Swan River, MB R0L 1Z0; 204-734-3429 or 800-214-6497; www.gov .mb.ca/conservation/parks/popular_parks/western/duck.html

Paint Lake & Pisew Falls Provincial Parks

Northern Manitoba: Paint Lake, 20 miles (32 km) south of Thompson; Pisew Falls, 50 miles (80.5 km) south of Thompson

▪ 56,091 acres ▪ Year-round ▪ Grass River ▪ Hiking, boating, canoeing, swimming, fishing ▪ Bird-watching

Paint Lake and Pisew Falls Provincial Parks generally are lumped together because they're close to each other and share an intimate connection—the Grass River. However, though the river anchors both parks, its nature differs radically from one to the other.

At **Paint Lake,** the Grass River widens into a maze of lakes, channels, and islands nearly 10 miles (16 km) across. You can find some hikes, but try to get out in a canoe or boat and meander among the islands and along the rugged shoreline. Take in the ancient bedrock, the boreal forest of spruce and pine, and sightings of black bear, river otter, and moose.

At **Pisew Falls,** the Grass River narrows to 200 feet (61 m) and drops more than 40 feet (12 m) over a fault in the Thompson Nickel Belt. Then it changes direction and thrashes down a stony gorge. **Observation platforms** by the falls and a suspension bridge just downriver provide fantastic views. Across the bridge, one trail leads to the top of the cascades; another, the **Upper Track Hiking Trail,** ranges downriver 6.8 miles (11 km) one way to **Kwasitchewan Falls—** at 46 feet (14 m), Manitoba's highest.

417

Camping

There are 190 tent and RV sites in Paint Lake and Lakeview Campgrounds, with showers. Seasonal and group-use sites available. Call 888-482-2267 for reservations or 800-214-6497 for information. Camping fee.

Paint Lake & Pisew Falls Provincial Parks, Manitoba Conservation, Box 22, 200 Saulteaux Crescent, Winnipeg, MB R3J 3W3; 800-214-6497; www.gov.mb.ca/conservation/parks/popular_parks/northeast/paint .html and www.gov.mb.ca/conservation/parks/popular_parks/north east/pisew.html

Lac La Ronge Provincial Park

Northern Saskatchewan, 100 miles (161 km) north of Prince Albert National Park

■ 830,731 acres ■ Year-round ■ Boreal forest, lakes ■ Hiking, boating, canoeing, swimming, fishing ■ Light-seeing ■ Prepare for summer insects

Horsetail ferns along the Nemeiben Lake Trail

The largest provincial park in Saskatchewan, Lac La Ronge is a world of lakes, boreal forest, and the rugged granite of the Canadian Shield. Water defines the park, as its name suggests. The lake is enormous, covering hundreds of square miles and containing some 1,300 islands. More than 100 smaller lakes hydrate the area, and the Churchill River marks the park's northern boundary.

What to See and Do

Like other parks in the area, Lac La Ronge can be explored via hiking trails or waterways. First stop, however, should be at the Saskatchewan Environment and Resource Management office in La Ronge *(306-425-4234)* or at the tourism booth (sporadically staffed) along Hwy. 2 in Air Ronge for help in developing a plan.

At the north end of Nut Point Campground, you'll find the trailhead for the **Nut Point Hiking Trail.** This hike offers some fine views of the surrounding waterscape. At several points, you can take side trails to the lake to swim or fish. On boardwalks the path passes through numerous muskegs (boggy depressions that are underlain by decaying plant matter). The trail runs 9.3 miles (15 km) and takes about eight hours one way, so if you plan to traverse the entire trail, take camping gear or arrange for a boat to drop you off at Nut Point (trail's end) so you can walk to the campground.

To see more of the park, head north from La Ronge on Hwy. 102. At Nemeiben Lake Campground, you'll find the trailhead for the 0.9-mile (1.4 km) **Nemeiben Lake Trail,** which meanders through a forest of pine and spruce and past outcroppings of Precambrian rock and muskegs (see sidebar p. 406).

The hub for exploring the **Churchill River** wilderness is the village of **Missinipe,** 50 miles (80 km) north of La Ronge on Hwy. 102 (the last 30 miles/48 km are on gravel). The village sits on the banks of Otter Lake, part of the river system. For an overview of this area, take a sightseeing flight in a floatplane. You'll observe how the Churchill broadens into lakes, then contracts into narrow whitewater channels as it flows toward Hudson Bay.

For a look around from the water, Thompson's Camps *(800-667-5554)* runs a 30- to 45-minute jet boat tour. Horizon Unlimited/ Churchill River Canoe Outfitters *(877-511-2726)* offers a slower, more intimate experience on canoe trips that last from a few hours to a few weeks. If you want to head out on your own, they'll outfit you with a canoe and arm you with maps and information. Unless you're a savvy veteran, though, it's best to go with a guide.

419

Within hours of paddling away from the dock in Missinipe, you'll be deep into **Otter Lake.** Watch for bald eagles circling overhead or American white pelicans swimming across the water as they sway and dip in search of fish. If you head north, you'll come to **Otter Rapids,** a quarter-mile (0.4 km) stretch of white water where the Churchill funnels into a narrow channel. Experienced canoeists and kayakers come from all over to play in this white water, but novices can portage around it. Beyond Otter Rapids lie more islands and lakes, coves and waterfalls.

Camping and Lodging

There are five campgrounds in the park with 256 tent and RV sites. Availability limited; reservations required after May 20. Nut Point, Nemeiben, Wadin Bay, and Missinipe Campgrounds have service centers with hot showers. Camping fee. Eagle Point Resort, located on McGibbon Bay, also rents houseboats; call 888-332-4536.

WINTER LODGING: The only place you'll see a beaver in a northern winter is on the Canadian nickel. But beavers don't hibernate. So how do they survive when their ponds freeze over?

Their lodges are the key. From the outside, a beaver lodge resembles a heap of sticks. Inside it's a tidy, cozy haven that shelters a family of beavers in comfort (interior temperatures can hit 60°F/15°C even when it's zero outside). Tunnels leading beneath the pond ice allow the beavers to reach their submerged stashes of food.

Lac La Ronge Provincial Park, Box 5000, La Ronge, SK S0J 1L0; 306-425-4234; www.tpcs.gov.sk.ca/LacLaRonge

Cypress Hills Interprovincial Park

*Southwest Saskatchewan and southeast Alberta, 40 miles (64 km)
southeast of Medicine Hat*

- 89,771 acres ▪ Year-round ▪ Auto tours ▪ Lodgepole pines, beavers
▪ Hiking, biking, canoeing, fishing ▪ Downhill skiing, cross-country
skiing, snowshoeing

Deer on frozen Elkwater Lake

The Cypress Hills were once part of a much larger plateau, but the
preglacial ancestors of the Milk and South Saskatchewan Rivers
eroded away most of it. They left only the part in the middle that
lay beyond the reach of either river, the Cypress Hills. At 4,810 feet
(1,466 m) above sea level, the highest point between Labrador and the
Rockies, the Cypress Hills get more precipitation and less heat, so the
vegetation differs from that of the prairie below. In addition to lodgepole pines, you'll find white spruce, aspen, buffaloberry, twinflower,
and other plants characteristic of the Rocky Mountain foothills. But
you'll also find some grasses and shrubs typical of the prairie. The
fauna is diverse as well, though less so than it was before the area's
bison, wolves, grizzlies, and black bears were hunted out.

What to See and Do

Once two parks, the interprovincial park was created in 1989. The
Saskatchewan portion is made up of two areas—the Centre Block and
the West Block (there is no East Block)—separated by a 10-mile-wide

(16 km) tract of private land known as the Gap. The West Block adjoins the Alberta Block.

The park's busiest hub lies in the **Centre Block.** During the summer this 17-square-mile (27 sq km) piece of plateau teems with visitors, who stay at more than a dozen campgrounds and lodges and throng the pool, the golf course, the ball fields, and the café. Wilderness this is not, but you can still see some of the Cypress Hills as nature made them.

Begin with the **Centre Block Auto Tour,** a 15-mile (24 km) drive that covers many features of this tract of the park. Start at the nature center and proceed to **Loch** (as in "lake") **Leven,** popular with anglers and canoeists. You might see American white pelicans sweeping their bills through the water in hopes of netting some fish. These huge birds (5 feet/1.5 m tall with a wingspan of 9 feet/2.7 m) nest in the Cypress Hills and visit many of the park's waters to feed.

After you leave Loch Leven, you ascend into some hills covered by a longpole pine forest, the only place in Saskatchewan where these tall, straight trees grow. A little farther up, the road pulls alongside the upper reach of **Boiler Creek,** which beavers have transformed into a series of ponds much favored by wildlife—from white-tailed deer to chickadees and great blue heron. Continue up to **Lookout Point,** where you can see the Great Sand Hills to the north.

If you want to explore the Centre Block on foot, you can follow 15 miles (24 km) of cross-country ski routes that double as hiking paths. In addition, two interpretive trails offer pleasant walking.

To visit the **West Block,** pick up a guide to the 50-mile (80 km) round-trip **West Block Auto Tour** at the Centre Block's nature center. From the Centre Block Auto Tour, turn west and drive across

421

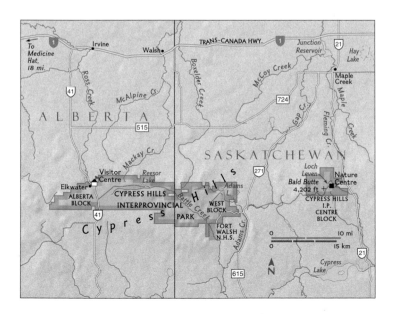

the **Gap.** Note the "knob and kettle" topography of the Gap. The kettles are depressions created from the weight of great blocks of ice left behind by retreating glaciers. Watch for pronghorn, North America's swiftest land mammal, in this open sagebrush country.

The West Block's most famed attraction is the **Conglomerate Cliffs.** They were formed by water passing through the thick layers of sand, gravel, and cobblestone that cap the Cypress Hills uplands. When the water evaporated, it left a residue of calcium carbonate that cemented the rocks together. The cliffs' edge offers a big, 180-degree view to the east and drops steeply to **Adams Lake.**

Bumping along gravel roads, you can cross from the West Block into the **Alberta Block.** The countryside is a scenic blend of conifer forest, aspen grove, and grassy meadows as you proceed to **Reesor Lake,** where the road is paved. Here the route traces the north shore and climbs to a high plateau that was never glaciated. Keep an eye out for coyotes, elk, and, more commonly, 13-lined ground squirrels as you drive to the town of Elkwater.

At the Elkwater Lake Visitor Centre *(mid-May–early Sept.)* ask about the several gravel roads and 11 established hiking trails that make it easy to explore the Alberta Block. The 1.8-mile (2.9 km) **Shoreline Trail,** and the 0.6-mile (1 km) loop **Soggy Bottom Trail** at its end, is a boardwalk and asphalt path that takes walkers, cyclists, and bladers along the lake's scenic south shore. The wilder 0.6-mile (1 km) **Sunset Trail** begins across the road from the east side of Soggy Bottom.

Starting from Beaver Creek Campground, at the southwest edge of town, the easy 1.8-mile (2.9 km) **Beaver Creek Trail** emerges into the open at a series of about half a dozen beaver ponds, where you might see beavers hauling aspen limbs through the water or slapping mud onto their lodges.

Camping and Lodging

On the Alberta side, there are 12 campgrounds with 400 sites, ranging from full-service with showers to basic, walk-in tent sites; and three group campsites. Reservations accepted at Elkwater townsite area beginning May 1; call 403-893-3782. Campgrounds outside of the Elkwater townsite are available on a first-come, first-served basis. For group reservations or park information, call 403-893-3835.

There are seven campgrounds on the Saskatchewan side of the park, most in the lodgepole pine forest, with 650 sites, ranging from full-service with showers to basic, walk-in tent sites; and seven group campsites. Reservations accepted; call 306-662-5484. Camping fee.

The Elkwater Lake Lodge & Resort has 48 suites, 6 cabins, and 11 condominiums for rent (888-893-3811). The Cypress Park Resort Inn (306-662-4477) offers cabins, condominiums, and hotel rooms. There are also several bed-and-breakfasts and guest ranches.

Cypress Hills Interprovincial Park, Saskatchewan, P.O. Box 850, Maple Creek, SK S0N 1N0; 306-662-5411; or Alberta, P.O. Box 12, Elkwater, AB T0J 1C0; 403-893-3777; www.cypresshills.com

Dinosaur Provincial Park

Southeast Alberta, 88 miles (142 km) southeast of Drumheller

■ 18,039 acres ■ Best months, late May–early Oct. ■ Camping, hiking, scenic drive, interpretive tours, fossils, badlands

Eroded badlands, Coulee Viewpoint Trail

If you love dinosaurs—real dinosaurs—head for Dinosaur Provincial Park in southeast Alberta's badlands, one of the richest dinosaur fossil reservoirs in the world. Some 75 million years ago, during the late Cretaceous period, this parched, rocky, eroded land looked dramatically different: It was a coastal plain covered by a lush subtropical forest peppered with swamps and rivers—excellent dinosaur habitat.

When the dinosaurs died, their bodies became encased in layers of mud, silt, and sand, which built up and eventually turned into sedimentary rock. Subsequently, more layers of sediment buried the layers entombing the dinosaurs. But ice age glaciers stripped away much of the overlying sediments, and rushing meltwater at the end of the last ice age gouged deep into the landscape. Erosion hasn't stopped since then. Fossilized dinosaur bones now lie just beneath the surface in many places; sometimes they even can be found lying in the open on dry streambeds or sticking out of the wall of a ravine.

Dinosaur Provincial Park's badlands are visually stunning as erosive forces have carved hoodoos (rock pillars), sinkholes, narrow gullies, and multicolored, deeply grooved hillsides. In addition, a green strip—the riparian corridor created by the Red Deer River—runs through the park. This elongated oasis of life is rare in the prairie badlands, as are its old cottonwoods and many of the plant and animal species found within. For this reason, as well as the exceptional fossil beds and the park's location in Canada's most extensive tract of badlands, the United Nations bestowed upon Dinosaur the much coveted designation of World Heritage site.

What to See and Do

On your own, you can wander down one of the park's five established hiking trails (found in three habitats) and take a scenic drive through the badlands on the Public Loop Road. Just as you enter the park, stop to stroll the easy **Prairie Trail.** This 300-yard (274 m) path circles through a sample of the grasslands that characterize the fringe of the park. Most compelling, the trail leads to viewpoints from which you can look across the badlands that constitute the heart of Dinosaur.

Then continue half a mile (0.8 km) to the field station of the **Royal Tyrrell Museum**—considered by many to be one of the finest paleontology museums in the world (see sidebar p. 425). Displays at the field station include fossils of species that aren't the usual suspects, such as the *Quetzalcoatlus,* a flying reptile with a 40-foot (12 m) wingspan.

Take advantage of one of the tours available here (reservations suggested). Better yet, go on two or three. Try to get tickets for a 30- to 45-minute talk in the field station's **Prep Lab.** Inside the wonderfully disheveled, warehouselike lab, its shelves heaped with fossils in plaster jackets, technicians labor at long tables, brushing and picking at discovered specimens.

For an easy, general overview of the park, with an emphasis on dinosaurs, take the **Badlands Bus Tour.** This two-hour trip *(fee)* takes you onto a gravel road that winds through the natural preserve. The bus stops at several intervals so you can get off for a closer look.

Styracosaurus model, outside the Royal Tyrrell Museum

Two guided hikes, each 2.5 hours long, take you to fossil sites. On the easy-to-moderately strenuous **Fossil Safari** you'll head to a known fossil site in the natural preserve, where you'll see fossils and learn about the creatures that once fleshed out those bones. **The Centrosaurus Bone Bed Hike** (1.5 mile/2.4 km round-trip) leads to one of the world's most renowned dinosaur excavations, though it's now inactive. In the 1980s, this bone bed—the size of two tennis courts—yielded a tremendous number of fossils and extensive knowledge about the way the *Centrosaurus* dinosaurs lived.

To sample the badlands scenery, drive the 2.25-mile (3.6 km) **Public Loop Road.** Although the gravel road is only a couple of miles long, it curves along the perimeter of the natural preserve, showcasing some of the badlands' beautiful erosion patterns and formations. Three trails branch off the road. The 0.8-mile (1.3 km) **Badlands**

ROYAL TYRRELL MUSEUM: The world-class Royal Tyrrell (*4 miles/6.4 km NW of Drumheller, in Midland Provincial Park; 888-440-4240; www.tyrrellmuseum .com; closed Mon. early Sept.–mid-May; adm. fee*) displays more than 35 dinosaur skeletons and hundreds of fossils, the most under one roof anywhere. Its imaginative presentations and interactive learning opportunities are a perfect blend of the engaging and the educational.

The museum covers the breadth of life on Earth, beginning with the first evidence of slimy life about 3.5 billion years ago up to the last ice age, some 12,000 years ago; however, the dinosaurs of the late Cretaceous occupy center stage. You'll see old favorites, such as *Triceratops* and *Stegosaurus*, as well as the less familiar, including a *Parasaurolophus*, a duckbill found in Dinosaur Provincial Park.

During summer and early autumn, the museum conducts a full menu of programs ranging from a 90-minute tour of a dig site to multiweek "field experience" opportunities, where volunteers shovel and sweat alongside crews digging for dinosaurs. A popular compromise is the day dig; participants work with excavators and even learn to map and jacket fossils.

Trail will take you through a slice of the badlands. Though this habitat is seemingly barren, tough animals and plants have adapted to its rigors. Sagebrush and cactuses manage to get by. Occasionally you'll spot a white-tailed deer nibbling at some grass. Watch overhead for golden eagles and prairie falcons. (The half-mile/0.8 km **Coulee Viewpoint Trail** beginning at the field station travels through similar landscape, but avoid it during wet weather because the rock surfaces get slippery.)

Follow the **Trail of the Fossil Hunters** half a mile (0.8 km) to a quarry marker. It is here that Barnum Brown—perhaps the greatest dinosaur hunter of the 20th century—conducted excavations for the American Museum of Natural History in New York.

The 1-mile (1.6 km) **Cottonwood Flats Trail** loops through the Red Deer River riparian zone—the hotbed for plant and animal life. Riparian woodland areas make up only about one percent of the Alberta prairie, so they provide a rare sanctuary for eastern kingbirds, orioles, mountain bluebirds, great blue herons, porcupines, bobcats, deer, and more. Above it all spread the big old cottonwood trees, some anchored by gnarly, deeply incised trunks a hefty 3 to 4 feet (0.9 to 1.2 m) in diameter. Sadly, the cottonwoods are not regenerating: Dams upriver have stopped the big floods that provide the conditions required by cottonwood seeds to germinate.

Camping

There are two campgrounds at Dinosaur Provincial Park with a total of 116 campsites and all levels of service, including a group camping site. Reservations suggested year-round. Call 877-537-2757 or visit www.reserve.albertaparks.ca.

Dinosaur Provincial Park, P.O. Box 60, Patricia, AB T0J 2K0; 403-378-4342; http://tpr.alberta.ca/parks/dinosaur

425

Liard River Hot Springs Provincial Park

North-central British Columbia

- 2,673 acres ▪ Year-round ▪ Bird-watching, diverse flora
- Hot springs (fee)

Filled with delightful hot springs, petite but exquisite Liard River Hot Springs Provincial Park is located in Canada's interior plateau, which spans British Columbia from the Coast Mountains in the west to the Rocky Mountains in the east. South to north, the plateau stretches from the U.S. border all the way up to the southwest corner of the Yukon.

Hot springs are one of nature's sweetest luxuries. But lolling in the 108°F to 126°F (42°C to 52°C) water is not the best part of the park. It's the surrounding natural community that steals the show.

Stroll the boardwalks and see familiar boreal plants, such as the gigantic cow parsnip, that grow exuberantly due to the thermal influence. You can also see plants that look tropical and out of place in this cold, northern land, like ostrich fern. Aquatic plants include sundews, bladderworts, and butterworts, all carnivorous species. From the boardwalk between the bathing pools you can look out on the **Hanging Gardens,** a luxuriant cascade of wildflowers and exotic greenery growing on terraces of tufa (calcium deposits precipitating from hot springs water).

The warm swamps that are created by the thermal springs harbor animals, too. Beneath the boardwalk to Alpha Pool swim small lake chub endemic to the park. On a larger scale, moose are frequently seen as they graze in the swamps. Above the pools fly kingfishers, gulls, nighthawks, bohemian waxwings, and many other birds.

Camping

The park has 53 tent and RV sites, with showers (full services May–Oct.; reservations accepted mid-May–early Sept.). Winter camping is also available. Camping fee.

Liard River Hot Springs Provincial Park, BC Parks, Peace-Liard District, Bag 1000, 4604 Sunset Dr., Fort Nelson, BC V0C 1R0; 250-774-7190; www.env .gov.bc.ca/bcparks/explore/parkpgs/ liard_rv_hs/

STONE MOUNTAIN PROVINCIAL PARK: When you reach kilometer marker 595 on the Alaska Hwy., you'll be in Stone Mountain Provincial Park (250-776-7190). But sometimes there's another way to tell you've entered this 63,000-acre (255 sq km) wilderness park—the roadside traffic jams of motorists watching Stone's sheep. A large population of these sheep (relatives of the bighorn) inhabit the park and display their climbing prowess on steep slopes.

To appreciate the park, get out of your vehicle; this is one of the north's easily accessible parks. Camp at Summit Lake, a deep blue beauty that lies along the Alaska Hwy. Day hikes lead to flower-fringed subalpine lakes and through grassy tundra, where you may see hoary marmots and golden eagles. West of Summit Pass, at the Rocky Crest picnic area, the short Erosion Pillars Trail provides views of the eroded rock pillars known as hoodoos.

Muncho Lake Provincial Park

North-central British Columbia, kilometer 681 of Alaska Hwy.

■ 218,397 acres ■ Year-round ■ Scenic drive ■ Folded limestone mountains ■ Moose, bears, mountain caribou ■ Hiking, boating, canoeing, fishing

Muncho Lake Provincial Park serves up a visual feast. For more than 55 miles (88 km) the Alaska Hwy. curves through the park, treating motorists to one of the most beautiful stretches of that long road north.

The park's rumpled mountains—the northern tip of the Rockies—rise 8,000 feet (2,438 m), their wrinkled look the result of tectonic deformations that have folded the limestone. In the southern part of the park along the highway, you'll see a fine example in the aptly named Folded Mountain. Clothed in pine and spruce, the slopes sliding by your car window sport patches of moss campion, lousewort, wintergreen, asters, and lupine. Around the lake, where creeks enter and bogs are created, look for lady's slipper, wild rose, and bog orchids.

What to See and Do

Muncho Lake is the park's scenic centerpiece: 7 miles (11.3 km) long, tinted green-blue by suspended minerals, framed by husky mountains, its cold water teeming with lake trout, Arctic grayling, bull trout, and whitefish. The lake is a great place to camp, hike, picnic, and fish. During the summer season, local operators run boat tours of the lake *(for recommendations call Tourism Northern Rockies, 250-774-2541).*

427

Mirror image of Muncho Lake

Wildlife seems to like the park as much as tourists do. Moose commonly are sighted in the marshy parts of the park. Bears ramble all over. Mountain caribou and Stone's sheep—a gray-to-almost-black version of the more familiar white Dall sheep—often come down to the road to lick the salt left from winter road maintenance.

Camping

The park has 30 first-come, first-served tent and RV sites, with showers (open May–mid-Sept.). Camping fee. Hike-in wilderness sites are also available.

Muncho Lake Provincial Park, BC Parks, Peace-Liard District, Bag 1000, 4604 Sunset Dr., Fort Nelson, BC V0C 1R0; 250-774-7190; www.env.gov.bc.ca/bcparks/explore/parkpgs/muncho_lk/

Bowron Lake Provincial Park

East-central British Columbia, 70 miles (115 km) east of Quesnel

■ 368,541 acres ■ Kayaking, canoeing, fishing ■ Daily quotas for canoe departures; reserve well ahead

Bowron Lake Provincial Park's 11 lakes are laid out end to end in an almost perfect rectangle. Rivers and creeks provide much of what little connection is needed between them; the whole 72-mile (116 km) route requires just 7 miles (11.25 km) of portaging.

These waterways pass through eye-catching wilderness—and only one short stretch on the **Cariboo River** where you're going against the current. You paddle in the shadows of the 8,000-foot-high (2,438 m), glacier-streaked Cariboo Mountains or canoe along banks overhung by big western red cedar and western hemlock. Hike the trail from **Unna Lake** to glimpse the 80-foot (24 m) **Cariboo River Falls.**

A common sight, especially in the morning, is moose high-stepping through the shallow water as they feed on tasty sedges or willows. Beavers are everywhere, as are beaver dams, which you have to crawl over in a few places. In the spring be on the lookout for grizzly bears digging out roots and bulbs; in early fall they gather to feast on the spawning sockeye salmon.

Register at the visitor center at Bowron Lake, where you can contract an outfitter or rent equipment. Your voyage will take six to ten days, depending on the weather. You should have some canoeing and wilderness skills, but the circuit is moderately easy and you needn't be an expert. Plenty of established campsites, excellent portage trails, and metal containers to store food so bears can't get it make the trip easier.

Along Bowron Lake

Camping

Bowron Lake Campground has 25 tent and RV sites; first come, first served, open mid-May–Oct. Camping fee. There are 54 wilderness sites on the canoe circuit, open mid-May–Oct.; reservations highly recommended. There are seven shared-use cabins on the circuit for emergency use or drying out.

Bowron Lake Provincial Park, BC Parks, Cariboo District, 281 First Ave. N., Williams Lake, BC V2G 1Y7; 778-373-6107 for park information; 800-689-9025 for required canoe circuit reservations; www.env.gov .bc.ca/bcparks/explore/parkpgs/bowron_lk/

Cathedral Provincial Park

South-central British Columbia, on Washington State border

■ 82,667 acres ■ Open April–Oct. ■ Mountain goats ■ Wildflowers, lakes ■ Hiking ■ No private vehicles, no bicycles

Cathedral Provincial Park may mark the northern end of the Cascade Range, but as might be expected, these grand mountains go out with a bang, not a whimper. In places, you'll encounter flora, fauna, and terrain typical of the drier transition landforms that lie between the Washington Cascades and the interior plateaus of British Columbia. But the bulk of the park features forests, stony pinnacles, meadows, lakes, and plenty of wildlife.

Note that you can't drive into the park on your own. Vehicles must be left in the secure parking lot at the base camp, from which you can hike into the park or pay to get a ride. It's a hard, all-day hike—some 10 miles (16 km), with a 4,200-foot (1,280 m) elevation gain—so many people opt for the shuttle service provided by the Cathedral Lakes Lodge *(888-255-4453)*. Reservations for transportation should be made in advance, and for the popular lodge even further in advance.

What to See and Do

You can grasp the essence of Cathedral Provincial Park by exploring the **Cathedral lakes area,** which is made up of six lakes—Quiniscoe, Ladyslipper, Scout, Pyramid, Glacier, and Lake of the Woods—in the center of the park.

Cupped by looming mountains, **Quiniscoe Lake** anchors the core area. You can savor views of the peaks as you stroll along the easy 1-mile (1.6 km) trail that circles Quiniscoe. Along the way look for bog orchids and marsh marigolds in the wetlands that edge the lake. Several trails fan out from the lake including the relatively flat, 1-mile (1.6 km) path that goes to **Lake of the Woods,** and an equally

Bighorn sheep

429

easy 2-mile (3.2 km, one way) trail leading through the forest to **Glacier Lake.** Hikers looking to get their blood pumping a little bit more should try the moderately up-and-down **Diamond Trail;** the 3-mile (5 km, one way) route rings **Scout Mountain** and takes hikers through some lovely subalpine meadows.

However, to take your exploration to a higher level, hike up into the alpine terrain—the tundra zone above timberline—along the **Rim Trail.** This is the park's showcase route, running along the edge of the wall of mountains that enfolds the Cathedral lakes. Three trails switchback up to the Rim Trail, making it possible to create a variety of loops, including a grand, daylong tour of the entire rim.

For the latter, head out on the **Diamond Trail** and turn north toward Red Mountain. You'll wind your way through fields purpled by a sea of lupine blooms and flecked with the reds, yellows, whites, and blues of other wildflower species. Scan the sloping rock piles for pikas. You'll probably also see hoary marmots on these rocky slopes, as well as deer and moose on the grassy areas.

The trail crests on **Red Mountain,** where it levels out and then proceeds south on a broad ridge above Quiniscoe Lake. You're in the alpine region now, where brutal winters force plants to hug the ground for dear life. The low-growing vegetation offers visitors one welcome advantage: Nothing gets in the way of the vistas. Glance to the west and you can see as far as Mount Baker, 100 miles (160 km) away in Washington.

Lowering your gaze you may find yourself staring into the eyes of a mountain goat. During the summer, males usually go their solitary way and females and their kids gather in groups of about ten. In mid-to-late August also look for bighorn sheep up here in the high country.

Close to the southern end of the Rim Trail loop, you pass the **Devil's Woodpile,** a formation of columnar-jointed basalt. Not much farther down the path stands **Stone City,** which consists of monumental boulders of quartz monzonite more than 200 million years old and eroded by the wind into bizarre shapes. See if you can find the Giant Hamburger or Smokey the Bear. Gaze south and deep into the Cascades.

At Stone City the loop turns east on the **Ladyslipper Trail** and descends to Ladyslipper Lake. **Giant Cleft,** a deep fissure in the granite face of a mountain, lies about a mile (1.6 km) to the south.

Camping

There are 10 vehicle-accessible, rustic tent sites, and 6 walk-in tent sites. No fee; first-come, first-served. There are also 3 backcountry campgrounds with 70 sites. Backcountry camping fee; first-come, first-served. Cathedral Lakes Lodge also has accommodations and provides transportation into the park. Open June–Oct.; call 888-255-4453, or visit www.cathedral-lakes-lodge.com.

Cathedral Provincial Park, Box 399, Summerland, BC V0H 1Z0; 250-494-6500; www.env.gov.bc.ca/bcparks/explore/parkpgs/cathedral

Wells Gray Provincial Park

East-central British Columbia, 100 miles (160 km) north of Kamloops

- 1.3 million acres - Year-round - Waterfalls - Wildlife - Wildflowers
- Hiking, horseback riding, boating, white-water rafting, kayaking, canoeing, fishing - High-clearance vehicles recommended for road to Trophy Meadows

431

Caribou Meadows from Green Mountain Viewing Tower

Some people refer to Wells Gray as the "waterfall park." But singling out this one—admittedly spectacular—aspect of this vast, multifaceted park does not do it justice. The park's 2,000 square miles (3,218 sq km) encompass the Clearwater River drainage in the Cariboo Mountains, part of the Columbia Mountains system. Wells Gray is a rugged park, a place shaped by rivers, glaciers, and volcanic activity. The varied terrain supports an equally varied mix of wildlife, including wolves, moose, grizzly bears, lynx, mountain goats, and the last remaining intact herd of woodland caribou in British Columbia. At lower elevations you'll find cathedral old-growth forests of western red cedar, Douglas fir, and hemlock, while in the alpine terrace visitors find hanging valleys and cirques.

Some 85 percent of this wilderness park is utterly undeveloped, accessible only to experienced backcountry travelers. The southern portion, though largely wild, has several access roads and a number of developed trails, campgrounds, and boat launches.

What to See and Do

The most popular area is known as the **Wells Gray Corridor.** Start at the visitor center *(250-674-2646)* in Clearwater, a town about 20 miles (32 km) south of the park. Drive north up paved Clearwater Valley Road, which turns to gravel shortly after entering the park. At kilometer marker 37.7, turn south on Green Mountain Road, a steep and narrow track that leads a couple of miles to the **Green Mountain Viewing Tower,** which provides a grand overview of the Battle, Flight, and 52 Ridge mountain ranges.

The **Helmcken Falls Rim Trail** begins at a parking lot at kilometer 42.2 on the main road. This strenuous 6.2-mile (10 km) round-trip hike follows the **Murtle River** west to the point at which the river takes a 466-foot (142 m) dive, creating **Helmcken Falls,** the most storied of the waterfalls. If you'd like an effortless way to see the falls, drive across the Murtle River to kilometer 47.3 and turn west on the access road to the **Helmcken Falls viewing platform.**

Just past the viewing platform turnoff, the main road heads north along the east bank of the lovely **Clearwater River.** For easy access to the river, try the very short **Bailey's Chute Trail loop** *(marker 59.3).* Here the chute forms a natural impasse to the spawning salmon. At kilometer 67.9, just a couple of miles (3.2 km) from the end of the road, you hit **Clearwater Lake.** This area brims with attractions, including two campgrounds, a boat launch onto the lake, the nice and easy **Lakeshore Trail,** and the harder but rewarding, 10.5-mile (17 km) **Chain Meadows Trail,** which leads to the Dragon's Tongue lava beds, Sticta Falls, and fine meadows.

To see what many consider the best wildflower meadows in the Cariboo Mountains, head for **Trophy Mountain,** just northeast of the town of Clearwater. Branch off the Clearwater Valley Road and follow signs for 7 miles (11.3 km) to the parking lot. Though Trophy Mountain is one of the park's backcountry areas, some of its most appealing places are easily reached by day hikers. A half-mile (0.8 km) hike takes you to fields abounding with glacier lilies in June and later awash with arnica, daisy, lupine, and monkey flower blossoms. It's grizzly habitat, though, so behave accordingly. If you're up for a vigorous, 7.4-mile (12 km) round-trip trek, labor up to **Skyline Ridge** for views as fine as the name suggests.

Camping

There are 130 tent and RV sites in the Corridor area and 34 at Mahood Lake (first come, first served; full-service mid-May–late Sept.). Camping fee. There are also walk-in wilderness campsites at Clearwater, Azure, Mahood, and Murtle Lakes (no facilities; fee).

Wells Gray Provincial Park, Thompson River District, 1210 McGill Rd., Kamloops, BC V2C 6N6; 250-674-2194; www.env.gov.bc.ca/bcparks/explore/parkpgs/wells_gry/

E. C. Manning Provincial Park

Southwest British Columbia, 100 miles east of Vancouver off Hwy. 3

■ 176,000 acres ■ Year-round ■ Wildflowers ■ Ecological divide, diverse flora and fauna ■ Hiking, mountain biking, horseback riding, boating, canoeing ■ Cross-country skiing

E. C. Manning Provincial Park forms the transitional zone between the Cascade mountains and flatlands of the Kamloops Plateau. Here, in the heart of Manning, grow Engelmann spruce, lodgepole pine, and Douglas fir—typical Cascades species. But toward the northeast boundary of the park, black cottonwood appears along the waterways and ponderosa pine occupies the slopes; these trees prefer drier climates and lower elevations. Tellingly, it is in Manning that the Pacific Crest Trail ends its 2,650-mile (4,265 km) run from the U.S.-Mexico border, presumably because this is the place where the crests begin to dwindle.

433

Hiking the Heather Trail

What to See and Do

The visitor center and nearby Manning Park Resort *(800-330-3321, www.manningpark .com),* off Hwy. 3 between Hope and Princeton, serve as the staging area for many park activities. From here the bulk of the park sprawls south and west toward North Cascades National Park in Washington.

Delve into this area by heading west on Gibson Pass Road. After about a mile (1.6 km), you'll come to the start of the 1.2-mile (1.9 km) **Canyon Nature Trail,** an interpretive loop that follows the west bank of the Similkameen River and comes back down the east bank.

Across the road is the horse corral, which offers guided rides *(fee)* along the park's equestrian trails. Another interpretive loop, the 0.3-mile (0.5 km) **Rein Orchid Trail,** starts a quarter mile farther down the road. Boardwalks circle through a bog, where beavers labor at dawn and dusk and you can see orchids blooming white in early summer.

About a mile (1.6 km) farther down the road lies **Lightning Lake,** a hot spot of outdoor recreation. You can rent canoes at the resort and paddle this 1.5-mile-long (2.4 km) lake or stroll around it on the 5.6-mile (9 km) **Lightning Lake Loop.** At the far end of the lake, you can hike up the **Lightning Lake Chain Trail** and continue southwest several miles to Flash, Strike, and Thunder Lakes. Whether canoeing or hiking, watch for ducks and loons. Around Rainbow Bridge at dusk you may glimpse beavers sculling across the water. Black bears sometimes use this trail, too, so stay alert and adhere to bear safety procedures.

One of the most popular hikes here grinds up to the summit of **Frosty Mountain;** at 7,900 feet (2,407 m) it's the highest point in the park. Two routes leaving from the Lightning Lake day-use area reach the top: one a 14-mile (22.5 km) route that simply goes up and back, the other a somewhat longer loop at 17 miles (27.3 km). It's an elevation gain of nearly 4,000 feet (1,219 m), but the views and flower-packed meadows will reward your effort.

The **Skyline I Trail** also originates at Lightning Lake. This moderately difficult hike leads through deep forest and along a high ridgeline that yields knockout views. The loop is 13 miles (21 km) long and gains 2,500 vertical feet (762 m). Park at Spruce Bay, near the campground, and go south on Lightning Lake Chain Trail to the start of the Skyline I Trail. Take it northwest up the heavily forested slope. Within a couple of miles, the grade steepens, and hairy

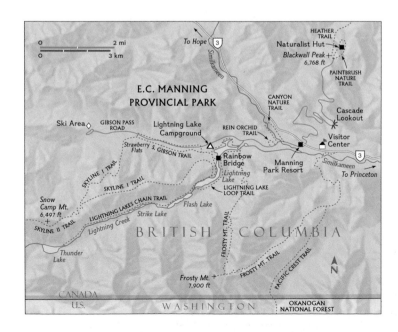

woodpeckers hammer away at the dead standing trees from a 1994 fire. Just above the burn, the skyline ridge begins. Here, look out over the glaciers, avalanche chutes, lakes, cirques, rivers, and hundreds of miles of the North Cascades wilderness. As the trail starts a gradual descent, it passes through sprawling meadows.

After about 6.5 miles (10.5 km), you'll intersect the Skyline II Trail. Stick with Skyline I, which makes a turn to the north and descends several miles through forest to the **South Gibson Trail** and **Strawberry Flats.** Located at the confluence of alpine, interior, and coastal plain zones, the flats contain more than 150 species of plants, about a quarter of all the floral species present in the park. From Strawberry Flats continue about 2 miles (3.2 km) east on the South Gibson Trail back to Spruce Bay.

To the north of the visitor center lies the subalpine wildflower meadows of the **Blackwell Peak** area. Across the highway from the resort, a paved road snakes 6 miles (10 km) up a steep grade to **Cascade Lookout.** From Cascade Lookout a gravel road leads 4.5 miles (7 km) up to Blackwell Peak, where wildflower havens extend north for about 15 miles (24 km). Several interpretive walks led by naturalists go through this area *(check the boards for announcements).* One of the favorite routes follows the 1-mile (1.6 km) loop of the **Paintbrush Nature Trail.** To see more wildflowers, hike a few miles north on the moderately difficult **Heather Trail,** which wanders for 13 miles (21 km) amid tens of thousands of acres of hillside.

Before you leave the park, make a stop in **Western Manning,** which consists of a long, narrow corridor along the **Sumallo** and **Skagit Rivers.** Near the rivers' confluence is **Sumallo Grove,** where visitors can take a half-mile (0.8 km) interpretive loop through a stand of gigantic western red cedar and Douglas fir. Western red cedar are characteristic of cool, moist climates, so their presence in this portion of the park indicates that this river valley is an oasis of coastal habitat.

Coastal flora also prevail in neighboring **Rhododendron Flats.** There's a half-mile (0.8 km) loop through the flats, best to walk in early to mid-June, when the flowers are at their peak. Several long trails leave from this area, including the 8-mile (12.9 km) **Skagit River Trail.** It starts in Sumallo Grove, crosses into the adjacent **Skagit Valley Provincial Park** *(604-924-2200),* and continues down the lush valley of the Skagit.

Camping

The park has 4 summer campgrounds with a total of 355 tent and RV sites, with showers, and 55 hike-in wilderness sites with limited facilities. Check website for full service dates. The 143 sites at Lightning Lake are reservation-only in season; the rest are first come, first served. Two areas are set aside for winter camping. Lone Duck offers group camping May–Oct.; call 250-840-8842. Camping fee.

E. C. Manning Provincial Park, Box 3, Manning Park, BC V0X 1R0; 250-840-8836; www.env.gov.bc.ca/bcparks/explore/parkpgs/ecmanning

Garibaldi Provincial Park

Southwest British Columbia, 40 miles (64 km) north of Vancouver

- 466,229 acres ▪ Year-round ▪ Wildflowers ▪ Hiking, backpacking, mountain climbing ▪ Skiing ▪ Access off five spur roads

Rafting on Green Lake

Garibaldi Provincial Park shows off waves of 8,000-foot (2,438 m) peaks, glaciers clinging to their flanks; high valleys in which the green of alpine meadows mixes with the blue-green of glacial lakes; low valleys bristling with thick forests of Douglas fir, western red cedar, and western hemlock. But the park's southwest corner comes within 5.6 miles (9 km) of salt water, and the nearby Pacific determines the park's climate, flora, and fauna.

The park was connected to the coast early on. In 1860, a naval captain surveying Howe Sound in the Strait of Georgia dubbed one of the area's tallest peaks, Mount Garibaldi, after the famous Italian patriot. The name stuck—and was recycled 67 years later, when the views from the 8,786-foot-high (2,678 m) summit spurred the creation of Garibaldi Provincial Park.

Visitors lacking advanced outdoor skills should approach Garibaldi from the west; trackless wilderness lies to the east. Starting in Vancouver, drive about 40 miles (64 km) north on Hwy. 99 and you'll arrive at the southwest corner of the park. From there the highway continues along Garibaldi's western border. In five places spur roads thrust east into the park, each leading to one of the five lightly developed areas within Garibaldi, with established trails and the occasional campground.

What to See and Do

The northernmost spur road leaves Hwy. 99 about 8 miles (13 km) north of Whistler, leads a few miles into the park, and ends at a trailhead. From there a 4-mile (6.5 km) trail ascends to the **Wedgemount Lake** area. This demanding trail gains about 4,000 vertical feet (1,219 m) and, near the end, traverses a treacherous, rock-strewn slope. The payoff: a 1,000-foot (305 m) waterfall, a chance to see mountain goats, and superb high-country views.

The next spur road to the south starts in the ski resort of **Whistler Village** and once led to the trailhead for the **Singing Pass** area. Part of the road is unstable, however, so it has been closed to vehicles. The hike to this celebrated alpine haven now includes several miles of the old road, making it a tough, 15-mile (24 km, round-trip) trek.

A couple of miles (3.2 km) south of Whistler, the third spur threads east 5 miles (8 km) from Hwy. 99, dead-ending at a parking lot from which you can walk into the **Cheakamus Lake** area. A pleasingly flat trail follows the **Cheakamus River** beneath a high canopy of old-growth western red cedar, Douglas fir, and western hemlock, and continues along the 4-mile-long (6.4 km) lake.

Seven miles (11 km) south of the Cheakamus turnoff, you'll arrive at the fourth of the spur roads into Garibaldi. This 1.5-mile (2.4 km) drive takes you to the trail that penetrates the heart of the park: the **Black Tusk/Garibaldi Lake** area. The trail to Garibaldi Lake, about 6 miles (9.7 km) with an elevation gain of 2,500 feet (762 m), climbs relentlessly for the first two-thirds. The grade is humane, though, as you travel through a forest of monumental old-growth western red cedar and Douglas fir. At the end of this push, you pass the **Barrier**, a wall of volcanic rock, and the trail levels out as it leads from Barrier Lake to Lesser Garibaldi Lake to the most storied place in the park: **Garibaldi Lake.**

On the lake's west bank is a ranger station and a big campsite. Glaciers and knife-point peaks encircle the 1,000-foot-deep (305 m), miles-long lake. From the Garibaldi Lake Campground you can walk a mile (1.6 km) northwest to **Taylor Meadows,** a painter's palette of colors when the wildflowers peak in mid-July and August; there's also a small camping area there.

Another fine hike—though a much harder one—takes you 3 miles (4.8 km) north from Garibaldi Lake to the base of the **Black Tusk,** a dramatically isolated volcanic tower that you can climb if you're so inclined—and suitably equipped. But you don't have to climb the Black Tusk to get fabulous views. About halfway up the Black

GRIZZLY BEAR RANGE: Garibaldi Provincial Park lies near the southern boundary of grizzly bear country. A few of these awesome carnivores inhabit the northern sections of Washington, Idaho, and Montana, and some live in isolated pockets farther south, notably in Yellowstone National Park. But almost the entire North American population of *Ursus arctos* resides in western Canada and Alaska. It wasn't always so. Grizzlies once ranged as far east as Manitoba and western Iowa—and as far south as Mexico.

Tusk Trail, branch off to the east and proceed about 1.5 miles (2.4 km) to the crest of **Panorama Ridge.** As wizened conifers give way to tree line, the trail winds through ground-hugging alpine plants; it then curves past **Mimulus, Black Tusk,** and **Helm Lakes.** As you approach the **Helm Glacier,** the trail turns south and starts its steep ascent toward the aptly named Panorama Ridge.

Mamquam Road, southernmost of the five spur roads into Garibaldi, cuts off Hwy. 99 about 2 miles (3.2 km) north of the town of Squamish. It meanders east 10 miles (16 km) to the **Diamond Head** area. From Hwy. 99 the road follows the Mamquam River and Ring Creek before crossing into the park and rising into the high country. The views en route are arresting, especially as you near the end-of-the-road parking lot, above 3,000 feet (914.4 m).

To truly see the Diamond Head area, hike northeast 3 miles (4.8 km) to **Red Heather Meadows,** an expanse of summer wildflowers and, as promised, red heather. Four miles (6.4 km) farther up Paul Ridge, the trail hits **Elfin Lakes.** Many people camp near Elfin Lakes and follow trails deeper into the park.

Camping and Lodging

There are nine walk-in, tent-only campgrounds throughout the park, with 160 non-reservable sites. Winter camping is also available. Elfin Lakes offers an overnight shelter equipped with bunks for 33 people; Wedgemont and Russet Lakes offer shelters that can accommodate six people. Camping fee.

Garibaldi Provincial Park, Squamish BC Parks Office, Box 220, Brackendale, BC V0N 1H0, 604-898-3678; www.env.gov.bc.ca/bcparks/explore/parkpgs/garibaldi/

Strathcona Provincial Park

Southwest British Columbia, central Vancouver Island, 25 miles (40 km) west of Courtenay

- 618,600 acres ▪ Year-round ▪ Canada's highest waterfall ▪ Boating, kayaking, canoeing, fishing ▪ Wildflowers

Unlike many places billed as the "Canadian Alps," Strathcona Provincial Park comes by the comparison honestly. Six of Vancouver Island's seven highest peaks—including the 7,201-foot-tall (2,195 m) **Golden Hinde**—rise from the park, while Canada's highest cascade, 1,443-foot (440 m) **Della Falls,** dives off a cliff here. Strathcona has alpine tundra, alpine lakes, and an ice field. The park's dense conifer forests, its flowered subalpine meadows, and its horned peaks crowned with snow all project the gestalt of the Swiss Alps.

The vast majority of the park is wilderness. For car camping and superb day hikes, Strathcona offers the Forbidden Plateau and the Buttle Lake area, both on the park's east side.

Paradise Meadows is the main gateway to the **Forbidden Plateau**—actually a gentle land known for its wildflower displays. The easy, 1.4-mile (2.3 km) **Paradise Meadows Loop** provides a lovely introduction to the meadows. It circles through a summer riot of pink heather, lupines, violets, and monkey flowers. Equally easy but longer is the **Lake Helen McKenzie Loop,** a jaunt of three or four hours. It splits from the Paradise Meadows Loop a few hundred yards from its start and curves south through meadows and forests to reach the lake.

On the summit of the Golden Hinde

Drive 30 miles (48 km) west from Campbell River on Hwy. 28 to reach the spur road skirting Buttle Lake's east bank. Along the lake's 15-mile (24 km) length are campgrounds, boat launches, picnic areas, and a number of good day hikes. A couple of miles (3.2 km) south of Hwy. 28, savor the cool mist of **Lupin Falls.** Easy trails of half an hour include the **Auger Point Trail,** which explores woods recovering from a 1984 fire, and the **Wild Ginger** and **Shepherd Creek** Loops, which slip through the forest along the Ralph River.

Camping and Lodging

There are 85 tent and RV sites at Buttle Lake Campground, and one group-exclusive site; reservations accepted. Ralph River Campground has 75 tent and RV sites; first come, first served. Camping fee. There are also walk-in wilderness camping sites open year-round; limited services June–Sept; fee. Strathcona Park Lodge (250-286-3122; www.strathcona.bc.ca) has outdoor education and wilderness skills training and accommodations.

Strathcona Provincial Park, Box 1479, Parksville, BC V9P 2H4; 250-474-1336; www.env.gov.bc.ca/bcparks/explore/parkpgs/strath

STATE PARKS AGENCIES

Alabama–Division of Parks, 64 North Union St., Montgomery, AL 36130; (334) 242-3333; (800) ALA-PARK; www.alapark.com

Alaska–Division of Parks & Outdoor Rec., 550 West 7th Ave, Suite 1260, Anchorage, AK 99501-3557; (907) 269-8400; www.dnr.state.ak.us/parks

Arizona–Arizona State Parks Office, 1300 W. Washington, Suite 104, Phoenix, AZ 85007; (602) 542-4174; www.azstateparks.com

Arkansas–Arkansas Dept. of Parks & Tourism, 1 Capitol Mall, Little Rock, AR 72201; (800) 828-8974; www.arkansasstateparks.com

California–California State Park System, Department of Parks & Recreation, P.O. Box 942896, Sacramento, CA 94296-0001; (916) 653-6995; www.parks.ca.gov

Colorado–Colorado Parks & Outdoor Recreation, 1313 Sherman St., Suite 618, Denver, CO 80203; (303) 866-3437; www.parks.state.co.us

Connecticut–Connecticut State Parks Division, 79 Elm Street, Hartford, CT 06106; (860) 424-3200; www.ct.gov/dep

Delaware–Delaware Division of Parks & Recreation, 89 Kings Highway, Dover, DE 19901; (302) 739-9220; www.destateparks.com

Florida–Division of Recreation & Parks, 3900 Commonwealth Blvd., MS 535, Tallahassee, FL 32399-3000; (850)245-2157; www.floridastateparks.org

Georgia–Department of Natural Resources; 2 Martin Luther King Jr. Dr., Suite 1352E, Atlanta, GA 30334; (404) 656-2770; www.georgiastateparks.org

Hawaii–Division of State Parks, Room 131, 1151 Punchbowl St., Honolulu, HI 96813; (808) 587-0400; www.hawaii.gov/dlnr

Idaho–Idaho Department of Parks & Recreation, P.O. Box 83720, Boise, ID 83720-0065; (208) 334-4199; www.idahoparks.org

Illinois–Illinois Department of Natural Resources, 1 Natural Resources Way, Springfield, IL 62702; (217)782-6752; http://dnr.state.il.us

Indiana–Indiana Dept. of Natural Resources, 402 W. Washington St., Rm.160, Indianapolis, IN 46204; (317) 232-4124; www.in.gov/dnr

Iowa–Department of Natural Resources, Wallace Building, 502 East 9th St., Des Moines, IA 50319; (515) 281-5918; www.iowadnr.gov

Kansas–Kansas Dept. of Wildlife & Parks, 512 S.E. 25th Ave., Pratt, KS 67124; (620) 672-5911; www.kdwp.state.ks.us/news/state_parks

Kentucky–Kentucky Department of Parks, 500 Mero St., Suite 2200, Frankfort, KY 40601; (800) 255-7275; www.parks.ky.gov

Louisiana–Louisiana Office of State Parks, P.O. Box 44426, Baton Rouge, LA 70804; (888) 677-1400; (225) 342-8111; www.crt.state.la.us/parks

Maine–Bureau of Parks & Lands, 22 State House Station, 18 Elkins Lane, Augusta, ME 04333-0022; (207) 287-3821; www.maine.gov/doc/parks

Maryland–Maryland Dept. of Natural Resources, 580 Taylor Ave., Annapolis, MD 21401; (410) 260-8367; www.dnr.state.md.us

Massachusetts–Department of Conservation and Recreation, 251 Causeway St., Suite 600, Boston, MA 02114-2104; (617) 626-1250; www.state.ma.us/dem/forparks.htm

Michigan–Dept. of Parks & Recreation, P.O. Box 30257, Lansing, MI 48909; (517) 373-9900; www.michigan.com

Minnesota–Minnesota Dept. of Natural Resources Information Center, 500 Lafayette Rd., St. Paul, MN 55155-4040; (651) 296-6157; (888) 646-6367; www.dnr.state.mn.us/state_parks

Mississippi–Department of Wildlife, Fisheries & Parks, 1505 Eastover Drive, Jackson, MS 39211-6374; (601) 432-2400; http://home.mdwfp.com

Missouri–Missouri Dept. of Natural Resources Division of State Parks, P.O. Box 176, Jefferson City, MO 65102; (800) 334-6946; www.mostateparks.com

Montana–Montana Dept. of Fish, Wildlife & Parks, 1420 E. 6th Ave., P.O. Box 200701, Helena, MT 59620-0701; (406) 444-2535; http://fwp.mt.gov

Nebraska–Nebraska Game & Parks Commission; 2200 N. 33rd St., P.O. Box 30370, Lincoln, NE 68503-0370; (402) 471-0641; www.ngpc.state.ne.us

Nevada–Nevada Division of State Parks, 901 S. Stewart St., Suite 5005, Carson City, NV 89701-5248; (775) 684-2770; www.parks.nv.gov

New Hampshire–Division of Travel and Tourism, 172 Pembroke Rd., P.O. Box 1856, Concord, NH 03302-1856; (800) 258-3608; www.nhstateparks.org

New Jersey–Division of Parks & Forestry, State Park Service, P.O. Box 402, Trenton, NJ 08625-0402; (800) 843-6420; (609) 984-0370; www.njparksandforests.org

New Mexico–State Park & Recreation Div., 1220 S. St. Francis St., P.O. Box 1147, Santa Fe, NM 87505; (888) 667-2757; (505) 476-3355; www.emnrd.state.nm.us/prd

New York–New York State Office of Parks, Recreation, and Historic Preservation, Empire State Plaza, Agency Building # 1, Albany, NY 12238; (518) 474-0456; www.nysparks.com

North Carolina–North Carolina Division of Parks & Rec., 1615 Mail Service Center, Raleigh, NC 27699-1615; (919) 733-7275; (919) 733-4181; www.ncparks.gov/visit/main.php

North Dakota–North Dakota Parks & Recreation, 1600 E. Century Ave., Suite 3, Bismarck, ND 58503-0649; (701) 328-5357; www.ndparks.com

Ohio–Division of Parks & Rec. Dept. of Natural Resources, 2045 Morse Rd., Bldg. C3, Columbus, OH 43229-9849; (614) 265-6561; www.ohiostateparks.org

Oklahoma–Oklahoma State Parks, 120 N. Robinson, Ste. 600, Oklahoma City, OK 73102; (800) 652-6552; www.touroklahoma.com

Oregon–Oregon Dept. of Parks & Rec., 725 Summer St. NE, Suite C, Salem, OR 97301-1266; (503) 378-6305; (800) 551-6949; www.oregon.gov/oprd/parks

Pennsylvania–Pennsylvania Bureau of State Parks, P.O. Box 8767, Harrisburg, PA 17105-8551; (800) 637-2757 reservations; (717) 787-6640 fax; www.dcnr.state.pa.us/stateparks

Rhode Island–Division of Parks & Recreation, 2321 Hartford Ave., Johnston, RI 02919-1719; (401) 222-2632; www.riparks.com

South Carolina–Dept. of Parks, Rec. & Tourism, 1205 Pendleton St., Columbia, SC 29201; (803) 734-1700; www.scprt.com

South Dakota–South Dakota Game, Fish & Park

Dept., 523 E. Capitol Ave., Pierre, SD 57501; (605) 773-3391; http://gfp.sd.gov

Tennessee–Bureau of State Parks, L & C Tower, 401 Church Street, 7th Floor, Nashville, TN 37243-0435; (888) 867-2757; www.state.tn.us/environment/parks

Texas–Parks and Wildlife Department, 4200 Smith School Rd., Austin, TX 78744; (800) 792-1112; (512) 389-4800; www.tpwd.state.tx.us/spdest

Utah–Division of Parks & Rec., 1594 W. North Temple, Suite 116, Salt Lake City, UT 84116; (801) 538-7220; (877) 887-2757; www.stateparks.utah.gov

Vermont–Dept. of State Parks, 103 S. Main St., Building 10 South, Waterbury, VT 05671-0601; (802) 241-3655; www.vtstateparks.com

Virginia–Virginia State Parks, Dept. of Conserv. & Rec., 203 Governor St., Suite 306, Richmond, VA 23219-2094; (804) 786-1712 office; (800) 933-7275 reservations; www.dcr.virginia.gov/state_parks

Washington–State Parks and Recreation Commission, 7150 Cleanwater Dr. SW, P.O. Box 42650, Olympia, WA 98504-2650; (360) 902-8500; www.parks.wa.gov

West Virginia–State Parks and Forests, 324 4th Ave., South Charleston, WV 25303; (304) 558-2764; (800) 225-5982 all state offices and reservations; www.wvstateparks.com

Wisconsin–Dept. of Natural Resources, 101 S. Webster St., P.O.Box 7921, Madison, WI 53707; (608) 266-2181; www.dnr.state.wi.us/org/land/parks

Wyoming–Division of State Parks, Historical Sites & Trails, 2301 Central Ave., Barrett Bldg., 4th Floor, Cheyenne, WY 82002 (307) 777-6323; http://wyoparks.state.wy.us

CANADIAN PROVINCIAL PARKS

Alberta–Parks Division, Oxbridge Place, 9820 106th Street, 2nd Floor, Edmonton, Alberta T5K 2J6, Canada; (780) 427-3582; (866) 427-3582; http://www.albertaparks.ca/

British Columbia–Ministry of Environment, P.O. Box 9047 Stn. Prov. Govt., Victoria, BC V8W NE2, Canada; (250) 387-1187; http://www.env.gov.bc.ca/bcparks/

Manitoba–Parks and Natural Areas, 200 Saulteaux Crescent, Winnipeg, Manitoba, R3J 3W3, Canada; (800) 214-6497; http://www.gov.mb.ca/conservation/parks/index.html

New Brunswick–Tourism & Parks: Centennial Building, P.O. Box 6000, Fredericton, NB E3B 5H1, Canada; (506) 453-3009; http://www.gnb.ca/0397/index-e.asp

Newfoundland–Provincial Office of Environment & Conservation, West Block Confederation Building, P.O. Box 8700, St. John's, NL A1B 4J6, Canada; (709) 729-2664; (800) 563-6181; http://www.env.gov.nl.ca/env/parks/parks/index.html

Nova Scotia–Nova Scotia Department of Natural Resources, Halifax, Nova Scotia, B3J 2T9, Canada; (902) 424-5481; http://parks.gov.ns.ca/

Nunavut–Nunavut Parks & Special Places, Department of Environment, Station 1340, Iqaluit, Nunavut X0A 0H0, Canada; (867) 975-7700; http://www.nunavutparks.co

Ontario–Ontario Parks Reservation, 300 Water Street, Peterborough, Ontario, K9J 8M5, Canada; (888) 668-7275; http://www.ontarioparks.com/

Prince Edward Island–Department of Tourism & Culture, P.O. Box 2000, Charlottetown, PE C1A 7N8, Canada; (902) 368-4801; (800) 463-4734; http://www.tourismpei.com/index.php3

Quebec–Place de la Cité, Cominar Tower, 2640 Boulevard Laurier, Quebec, G1V 5C2, Canada; (800) 665-6527; http://www.sepaq.com

Saskatchewan–Ministry of Tourism, Parks, Culture, & Sport, 1919 Saskatchewan Drive, 4th Floor, Regina, SK S4P 4H2, Canada; (306) 787-5729; (800) 205-7070; http://www.tpcs.gov.sk.ca/parks

Yukon–Tourism & Culture Centre, 100 Hanson Street, Whitehorse, Yukon Y1A 2C6, Canada; (867) 667-5036; http://www.tc.gov.yk.ca/

U.S. STATE PARKS INDEX

CANADIAN PROVINCIAL PARKS INDEX

447

ILLUSTRATIONS CREDITS

Cover, VisionsofAmerica/Joe Sohm/ Getty Images; 1, Robert Essel NYC/ CORBIS; 2-3, Rich Reid/National GeographicStock.com; 4, Kindra Clineff; 5, George H.H. Huey; 7, Larry Cruikshank/BigStock.com; 8, George H.H. Huey; 10, José Azel; 12, Stephen G. Maka; 14, Phil Schermeister/COR-BIS; 17-20 (all), William H. Johnson; 23, David Muench; 25, William H. Johnson; 26, Jerry and Marcy Monkman/Danita Delimont Agency/drr .net; 28, PaulOBoisvert.com; 31 & 33, William H. Johnson; 34, Andre Jenny/Alamy; 35, Tom Till; 36, Jonathan Wallen; 38, Steve Dunwell; 40, Fort Adams Trust, Newport, Rhode Island; 43, William H. Johnson; 45,

Tom Till; 46, William H. Johnson; 49, A. Blake Gardner; 50, Pat & Chuck Blackley; 52 & 53, Wolfgang Kaehler; 54-55, Peter Gridley/Getty Images; 56, Jeff Gnass; 58, Hardie Truesdale; 59, Douglas Weldon; 60-67 (all), Jonathan Wallen; 68, Jeff Gnass; 70, Jonathan Wallen; 72 & 73, Scott Barrow; 74, Hardie Truesdale; 74-75, Steve St. John/NGS Image Collection; 77, David Muench; 79, Jonathan Wallen; 80-81, Robert W. Madden; 83 & 84, C.M. Glover/ OutToSee.com; 85, Bates Littlehales; 86, Gene Ahrens; 88, Richard A. Cooke III; 90 & 92, John Henley; 94, Steve Shaluta, Jr./West Virginia Division of Tourism; 97, David Muench/CORBIS; 99, John Henley; 101, James P. Blair; 102, Ed Cooper Photo; 104, Tom Till; 106, Kelly Culpepper/Transparencies, Inc.; 108,

Sam Bland/Hammocks Beach State Park; 109, Jonathan Wallen; 110, Tom Till; 113, William H. Johnson; 114, Zandria Muench Beraldo; 116, Tom Till; 118, William H. Johnson; 120, Fred Hirschmann; 121, J. Faircloth/ Transparencies, Inc.; 123 & 125, Tom Till; 126, John J. Lopinot/ Silver Image; 129, A. Blake Gardner; 132, Bruce Borich/Silver Image; 134, Michael Warren/Silver Image; 135, A. Blake Gardner; 136, David Muench; 139, Tom Till; 142 & 144, Raymond Gehman; 146, David Muench/CORBIS; 148 & 151, David Muench; 152, Robert Falls, Photography; 153, Leonard L. Rue III/www .bciusa.com; 155, David Muench; 156-157, Randi Hirschmann; 158, George Terrizzi; 161, Bates Littlehales; 162, Balthazar Korab Ltd.; 164, David Muench; 166, Thomas

R. Fletcher; 167, J. Miles Wolf; 169, Kent Dannen; 170, Declan Haun; 174, Fred Hirschmann; 178, Rob Torresen, Courtesy Michigan Department of Natural Resources; 180, Dan Dempster/DPA; 183, Balthazar Korab Ltd.; 187, Dan Dempster/DPA; 188 & 190, Willard Clay/ DPA; 191, Terry Donnelly/DPA; 192, Bates Littlehales; 195, Tom Bean; 196, Terry Donnelly/DPA; 198, Balthazar Korab Ltd.; 199, Clint Farlinger; 200, Greg Ryan/Sally Beyer; 203, MN DNR; 205, Tom Bean; 207, Greg Ryan/Sally Beyer; 208, Annie Griffiths Belt; 210-213 (all), Tom Bean; 215, Stephen G. Maka; 216, Tom Bean; 218, Clint Farlinger; 220, Tom Bean; 221 & 222, Annie Griffiths Belt; 225, Greg Ryan/Sally Beyer; 226, Tom Till; 228-229, Clint Farlinger; 230, Ken Formanek/Iowa Department of Natural Resources; 231, Wayne Frantzen; 232, Annie Griffiths Belt; 235, Tom Till; 237, Nick Decker/Missouri Department of Natural Resources; 238-239, Kent Dannen; 240, Tom Bean; 242, Bruce Dale; 244, David G. Fitzgerald; 246, Greg Ryan/Sally Beyer; 248, Tom Till; 249, Fred W. Marvel/Oklahoma Tourism; 250-253 (all), Greg Ryan/Sally Beyer; 255, A.C. Haralson/Arkansas Parks & Tourism; 257, A.C. Haralson/Arkansas Department of Parks & Tourism; 258, William H. Johnson; 259, Bates Littlehales; 261, C.C. Lockwood; 263, Fred Hirschmann; 264, Laurence Parent; 267, Fred Hirschmann; 269, Raymond Gehman; 271, David Muench; 272, Jeff Gnass; 274-278 (all), Tom Bean; 280, John Shaw/www.bciusa.com; 283, Erwin & Peggy Bauer/www.bciusa.com; 284, Tom Bean; 286, George H.H. Huey; 288, Tom Bean; 290, Courtesy Arizona State Parks; 293, Bill Weir/Arizona State Parks; 294, Tom Till; 297, James Randklev; 298, Fred Hirschmann; 300, Tom Bean; 301, Fred Hirschmann; 302, Nick Kelsh; 304 & 307, Annie Griffiths Belt; 308 & 311, Laurance Aiuppy; 312, Kent Dannen; 314, Nick Kelsh; 316, Mark E. Gibson; 318, Niki Humphries, Courtesy Idaho Department of Parks & Recreation; 320, Tom Brakefield/www.bciusa.com; 321, Adam Silver/iStockphoto; 323, Jeff Gnass; 325, David Muench; 326, Fred Hirschmann; 329, Natalia Bratslavsky/iStockphoto; 330, Peter Kunasz/Shutterstock; 332, Ed Cooper Photo; 334, Robert Rathe/Folio, Inc.; 337, Wolfgang Kaehler; 338, PlaceStockPhoto.com; 340-341, Ken Graham/Accent Alaska; 343, Malcolm Lockwood; 345 & 346, Fred Hirschmann; 348, Jeff Gnass; 351 & 352, Tom Bean; 354, Jeff Gnass; 355, Tom Bean; 356, David Muench; 358, Randi Hirschmann; 361, David Muench; 363, Index

Stock/Alamy; 365, Marc Muench; 367, David Muench; 368, J.C. Leacock; 369, Jeff Foott/www.bciusa.com; 370, Ed Cooper Photo; 373, Hardie Truesdale; 374, Tom Till; 377, Clint Farlinger; 378-379, Bob Wallace; 382, Parks and Natural Areas Division, Government of Newfoundland and Labrador; 384, Nova Scotia Provincial Parks; 386, Barrett & MacKay Photo; 389, Barrett & MacKay Photo; 392, Michael Broughton; 394, Michael Lewis; 395, Michael Lewis; 398, Michael Lewis; 400, Michael Lewis; 402, Gerry Racey, Ontario Ministry of Natural Resources; 404, Michael Lewis; 405,

Ontario Tourism; 407, Brock May, Outside Exposure Photography; 408, Raymond Gehman; 412, Raymond Gehman; 414, Travel Manitoba; 416, Raymond Gehman; 418, Raymond Gehman; 420, Yoga Das; 423, Raymond Gehman; 424, Raymond Gehman; 427, Raymond Gehman; 428, Diego Echeagaray/Bigstock.com; 429, Raymond Gehman; 431, Raymond Gehman; 433, Raymond Gehman; 436, Raymond Gehman; 439, Chris Cheadle/CORBIS; back cover: up left, Tom Bean; center right, Dan Dempster/DPA; center left, Richard A. Cooke III; low left, William H. Johnson.

Founded in 1888, the National Geographic Society is one of the largest nonprofit scientific and educational organizations in the world. It reaches more than 285 million people worldwide each month through its official journal, *National Geographic,* and its four other magazines; the National Geographic Channel; television documentaries; radio programs; films; books; videos and DVDs; maps; and interactive media. National Geographic has funded more than 8,000 scientific research projects and supports an education program combating geographic illiteracy.

For more information, please call 1-800-NGS LINE (647-5463) or write to the following address:

National Geographic Society
1145 17th Street N.W.
Washington, D.C. 20036-4688 U.S.A.

Visit us online at www.nationalgeographic.com/books

For information about special discounts for bulk purchases, please contact National Geographic Books Special Sales: ngspecsales@ngs.org

For rights or permissions inquiries, please contact National Geographic Books Subsidiary Rights: ngbookrights@ngs.org

National Geographic Guide to the State Parks of the United States, Fourth Edition (2011)
ISBN: 978-1-4351-3834-6
This 2011 edition printed for Barnes and Noble, Inc., by National Geographic.

The Library of Congress has cataloged the second edition as follows:

National Geographic guide to the state parks of the United States /
   prepared by the Book Division, National Geographic Society--2nd ed.
      p.   cm.
      Includes index.
      ISBN 0-7922-6628-5 (reg.).
      1. Parks—United States—Guidebooks. 2. United States-Guidebooks. I. Title: Guide to the state parks of the United States
   II. Title: National Geographic Society (U.S.). Book Division. III. Title:
   National Geographic's guide to the state parks of the United States

E160.N2442 2004   2003061515
   917.304'931—dc22   CIP

Printed in China
14/PPS/6